LAUGHTER IN THE NEXT ROOM

THE AUTHOR, 1919

LAUGHTER IN THE
NEXT ROOM

BEING THE FOURTH VOLUME OF
LEFT HAND, RIGHT HAND!

An Autobiography by

OSBERT SITWELL

THE REPRINT SOCIETY
LONDON

FIRST PUBLISHED 1949
THIS EDITION PUBLISHED BY THE REPRINT SOCIETY LTD.
BY ARRANGEMENT WITH MACMILLAN AND CO. LTD.
1950

PRINTED IN GREAT BRITAIN BY PURNELL AND SONS, LTD.
PAULTON (SOMERSET) AND LONDON

To

DAVID HORNER

ACKNOWLEDGEMENTS

I SHOULD like to offer here my very sincere thanks to those who have so generously assisted me in the preparation and production of this volume. Mr. A. Beverley Baxter, M.P., has allowed me to quote a passage from his *Strange Street*, and I am indebted to Mrs. Dorothy Cheston Bennett for permission to use several extracts from the *Journals of Arnold Bennett*. The letters by the late Dr. Greville MacDonald which form part of Appendix A are reprinted with the kind consent of his daughter and his Executors, and of the Editor of the *New Statesman and Nation*, whom I have also to thank for confirming the permission given me by my friend Mr. Clive Bell for the use of his notice of the exhibition of French art to which they refer. The Editor of the *Sunday Times* has permitted me to quote from an article by Mr. Ernest Newman, and Messrs. Constable & Co. have authorised the use of a passage from Colonel Repington's reminiscences. My text contains a letter by Dr. Edith Sitwell and some lines from her poems, as well as some letters by Mr. Sacheverell Sitwell, to both of whom my thanks are due for this and many other kindnesses. To my friend Mr. Evelyn Waugh I am indebted for the account of his meeting with my father given in Appendix B, and my friend Dr. William Walton, among other services, has enabled me to reproduce Mr. John Piper's design for the curtain for *Façade*. The material for Appendix C I owe to Signor Guido Masti, custodian of Montegufoni, and the photograph of 2 Carlyle Square is the work of Mr. E. J. Mason, and is included by permission of the Editor of *Country Life*. Sir Max Beerbohm has most kindly allowed me to reproduce his drawing of my brother and myself.

OSBERT SITWELL

CONTENTS

Book VII

THREE LIONS IN A GROVE

CONTENTS

LIST OF ILLUSTRATIONS

Book Seven

THREE LIONS IN A GROVE

CHAPTER ONE

Three Lions in a Grove

AFTER the Second World War, Winged Victory dangles from the sky like a gigantic draggled jackdaw that has been hanged as a warning to other marauders: but in 1918, though we who had fought were even more disillusioned than our successors of the next conflict about a struggle in which it was plain that no great military leaders had been found, we were yet illusioned about the peace. During the passage of more than four years, the worse the present had shown itself, the more golden the future, unreal as the conventional heaven, had become to our eyes: an outlook common, perhaps, to those of all ages of war and revolution. And today—the 11th of November 1918—that long present had suddenly become changed to past, clearly to be seen as such. Hence both the joy and the earnestness of dancers in street and square tonight: hence, too, the difficulty of finding a way in which to describe to the reader the movements that so precisely interpreted conflicting emotions: the long drawn-out misery and monastic stultification of the trenches, and then the joy of a victory that in the end had rushed on us with the speed and impact of a comet—for it *was* difficult, I realised that fully, as, with my companions, Diaghilew and Massine, I stopped to watch for a moment the shifting general pattern of the mass of people.

With something of the importance of a public monument attaching to his scale and build, the great impresario, bear-like in his fur-coat, gazed with an air of melancholy exhaustion at the crowds. I do not know what thoughts were passing through his head. The dancer, on the other hand, so practical an artist, and in spite of the weighty tradition of his art, so vital in the manner in which he seizes his material from the life round him, was watching intently the steps and gestures of the couples, no doubt to see if any gifts to Terpsichore could be wrung from them. It was, for example, his observation, a year or two previously, of the dancing in the popular festivals in Andalusia, that enabled him, in the course of the coming months, to create the inspired choreography of the ballet *Le Tricorne*. But, alas, moving as the scene was, and impressive, it did not afford the particular stimulus towards art that outbreaks of feeling in southern countries so often present— as well expect Goya to draw an egg-and-spoon race at a rectory garden-party with the same force as that with which he portrays a bull-fight! The egg-and-spoon race may be kinder, it is less tragic; but the Muses do not preside over it. . . . Yet it was, this release of feeling so unusual with the English, worth describing: for it possessed happiness, a kind of recognition by the crowd itself that steadfastness had been rewarded, an underlying sadness, too, together with something as near gaiety as ever you get in a northern people. As for myself, when I looked at the couples—and a few who were dancing by themselves!—I felt lonely, as always in a throng. My thoughts turned inwards, and to other occasions.

It was curious that now that the battle was over and the Captains and the Kings had become dead leaves overnight, rattling down from their trees, whirling head over heels in the air, my mind, which had so perpetually during the course of it avoided thoughts of war, and even when compelled thereto by professional necessity could never for more than a few seconds at a time fix itself on such matters as maps, or even instructions for an offensive (which I could understand no better than formerly I had comprehended the drill-manual), did not busy itself with the future, enticing as that seemed to all of us, but reverted ever to two scenes. First to the landscape of an early September morning, where the pale golden grasses held just the colour of a harvest moon, as they shone under the strong, misty sun of autumn in northern France; a wide flatness of gentle, tawny land, where dead bodies in khaki

and field-grey lay stiff and glittering in the heavy dew, among
the blue clouds of the chicory flowers, which reflected the sky
and, as it were, pinned it down. (Though khaki differed from
field-grey, and the helmets were dissimilar, the attitudes were
the same; so, too, were the greenish-grey skin and the in-
curious eyes.) These flowers that seemed cut rosettes of
azure paper I had always loved as a child at Renishaw: but
now they came to hold a terror for me, to be haunted by the
thought of dolls lying spangled with them; dolls whose knees
should move, but never did, whose eyes *should* shut. Though
tainted subtly by tear-gas and by the smell of earth freshly
flung up from the craters, and by the odours of decomposition,
it was a superb morning; such a morning, I would have
hazarded, as that on which men, crowned with the vast
hemicycles of their gold helmets, clashed swords at Mycenae,
or outside the towers of Troy, only to be carried from the field
to lie entombed in air and silence for millenniums under their
stiff masks of thin virgin gold: (how far had we descended,
crawling now, earth-coloured as grubs, among the broken
stumps of trees, and the barbed wire, until we were still,
among the maggoty confusion, and our faces took on the
tints of the autumn earth and the rusty discoloration of dry
blood!). Then the alternate scene switched before me: No-
Man's-Land, that narrow strip of territory peculiar to the
First World War; the very dominion of King Death; where
his palace was concealed, labyrinthine in its dark corridors,
mysterious in its distances, so that sometimes those who
sought him spent hours, whole days, a week even, in the ante-
chambers that led to his presence, and lay lost in the alleys and
mazes of barbed wire. Throughout the length of time that the
sun takes, you could hear their groans and sighs, and could
not reach them. . . . All that was over, for everyone. No
wonder that the world rejoiced at a cessation that seemed
more splendid than many a thing won!

So that night it was impossible to drive through Trafalgar
Square: because the crowd danced under lights turned up
for the first time for four years—danced so thickly that the
heads, the faces, were like a field of golden corn moving in a
dark wind. The last occasion I had seen the London crowd

was when it had cheered for its own death outside Bucking-
ham Palace on the evening of the 4th of August 1914; most of
the men who had composed it were now dead. Their heirs
were dancing because life had been given back to them. They
revolved and whirled their partners round with rapture,
almost with abandon, yet, too, with solemnity, with a kind of
religious fervour, as if it were a duty. It was that moment
which sometimes only occurs once in a hundred years, when
strangers become the oldest friends, and the dread God of
Herds takes charge. As a child I had first beheld his countenance, sweaty and alight with rage slaked and with pleasure, on
Mafeking Night:[1] but this evening he was in more benignant
mood, chastened and by no means vainglorious. A long nightmare was over: and there were many soldiers, sailors and airmen in the crowd which, sometimes joining up, linking hands,
dashed like the waves of the sea against the sides of the
Square, against the railings of the National Gallery, sweeping
up so far even as beyond the shallow stone steps of St. Martin-
in-the-Fields. The succeeding waves flowed back, gathered
impetus and broke again. The northern character of the
revellers—if they may be described as that—was plain in the
way they moved, in the manner, for example, in which the
knees were lifted, as in a *kermesse* painted by Breughel the
Elder, as well as in the flushed and intent faces. It was an
honest, happy crowd, good-natured, possessed of a kind of
wisdom or philosophy, as well as of a perseverance which few
races knew: but it had nothing of Latin grace. . . . The vision
which rose before the eyes of the soldiers was very different
from that which has lately opened for their sons: it was a
deliverance from mud—and mud as one of the great engulfing
terrors of mankind can easily be under-rated—from mud and
poison-gas, from night patrols and No-Man's-Land, and going
over the top, from tetanus, tanks and shell-fire, from frost and
snow and sudden death. To their dung-coloured world of
khaki in sodden trenches, it seemed until today as if the
politicians had clamped them for ever.

No-one, then, who had not been a soldier, alive on the
morning of the 11th of November 1918, can imagine the joy,

[1] See *Left Hand, Right Hand!* p. 240.

the unexpected, startling joy of it; for in 1945 victory came with deliberate step, in 1918 at a gallop. It had flung itself on us. The news had been—or at any rate had seemed—beyond what could be believed: the only way of persuading oneself of its truth was by doing something one had never done before, such as dancing in Trafalgar Square. It was with this feeling, I think, that the units composing the crowd danced. . . . When the news had first come with a ringing of bells and sounding of maroons, men and women who had never seen one another before, spoke, to ask if it were true. All day long the news pelted in, as the first of the two tidal waves that were to destroy Europe swept over it to the furthest end. Russia had already been submerged for a year: now the Kaiser was in flight, the routed German armies were returning home, as is their habit after laying a world waste, and were kicking their officers in front of them. In Bavaria, the Communists had seized power, and were torturing in a ten days' coven, and in Hungary, too, under their leader the infamous Bela Kun, persecution and death were rife, and anyone with a clean shirt had to hide. The Emperor Karl had been deposed in Austria, which was now little more than a derelict great city lost in the mountains. In remote turreted castles all over Germany and Austria, the princes cowered, had not even the heart to go hunting. The dark wind of destruction tore like a falling angel across the European sky. In short, the popular reign of piracy, exalted to a creed, had begun. Whole classes were eradicated so that the world should in time be made safe, on the one hand, for a beer-logged trades-unionism in the victorious countries, and, on the other, for Hitler and Bolshevism. Hitler belonged to the people: like Stalin, he was no gentleman—and when I say *gentleman*, I mean what I say, and say what I mean, without fear of ridicule, since the world still contains the truth of its evident meaning. Boasting, roaring, tears, dervish-like howling, fist-shaking, lying over never-ending toasts in vodka and champagne were, by general consent, substituted for the traditional decorous voices and considerate behaviour of the old diplomacy. That day, we entered a world of wolf-and-buffalo politics, where to howl over your prey is to be realistic, where to bellow is to prove strength, and to whine is to show grace: the world in which we still—but only just—survive: the world in which the sabre-toothed tiger and the ant are our paragons, and the butterfly is condemned for its wings, which are uneconomic.

In London, however, the capital of the burgess order, the citizens were dancing, oblivious of the creaking of the scaffolding under them. To them—and to me—it appeared that they danced not without reason. Only six weeks before, the Allies had been so plainly losing the war. Though eyes were tired, they saw open up before them long vistas of quiet, renewed activity, displacing the former almost universal prospect of a stretch of noise and misery, followed by death. Even furnaces and factories looked attractive to those coming back from mud and darkness. Slum or castle, town or a cottage in an isolated region, each seemed equally welcoming to those who returned. During four long years, furthermore, the sole internationalism—if it existed—had been that of deserters from all the warring nations, French, Italian, German, Austrian, Australian, English, Canadian. Outlawed, these men lived— at least, they *lived*!—in caves and grottoes under certain parts of the front line. Cowardly but desperate as the *lazzaroni* of the old Kingdom of Naples or the bands of beggars and coney-catchers of Tudor times, recognising no right, and no rules save of their own making, they would issue forth, it was said, from their secret lairs after each of the interminable checkmate battles, to rob the dying of their few possessions— treasures such as boots or iron-rations—and leave them dead. Were these bearded figures, shambling in rags and patched uniforms, and pale with a cellar dampness that at first put men off their guard, so that they were unprepared for their ferocity; were they a myth created by suffering among the wounded, as a result of pain, privation and exposure, or did they exist? . . . It is difficult to tell. At any rate, the story was widely believed among the troops; who maintained that the General Staff could find no way of dealing with these bandits until the war was over, and that in the end they had to be gassed.

Now, however, the barriers which war had created were down, and the singular conditions it had produced were finished. Life was thawing, would soon flow with an amazing rush and profusion, bringing friends, travel, experiences of every sort. We were on the verge. The world lay open again. The old instinct for travel of the British peoples, as much a part of their insular composition as is their poetry, revived. While the thought of some turned to farming, to square, lonely buildings of stone on small hills close under the fleecy sky, with a square garden of vegetables, planted in rows, all of it neat and set for eternity in its chequered landscape, to factories of brick caked in soot, to small, unwanted shops in village streets, to bow-windows full of jars of sweets, of boot-laces and pearl buttons, others saw again the lofty early mornings of the far Sudan, with the imprint of a lion's paw fresh upon the tawny sand, or the thousand grasses of the veldt and its clusters of rush huts, geometrically organised, or they gazed up once more at the wide skies of Canada—surely the widest in the world—, or smelt the yellow autumn-spring of Australia, when the grey-leafed trees bore a brief mane of sweet gold, or the incense, heavy with age and sleep, wafted from domed temples in the East, or they heard once more the carillons that the spice-wind rings on the storeys of the pagodas, diminishing upward into the heavens, or the lumbering creak and screech of the ice as it melts in spring in the furthest North. This, then, was the greatest renewal of life that had come for a century—so it seemed, and for this reason the crowd danced. Not only was it the places they had lived in before the war had wrenched them away, that now rose up before men's senses, but they saw once more a future, now again so much longer than the past. Those of my generation had hardly been given time before the war to discover in what direction they were going; now, at least, we knew what we wanted: though some, no doubt, wanted too much, and some too little. A kind of light revolutionary fervour inspired us. The bad old days had gone (they always have!). What I feared—and what happened (Left Hand!)—I said in a poem entitled *The Next War*, quoted later in the course of this chapter: what I wanted at that time (Right Hand!), I wrote in another poem, *How Shall We Rise to Greet the Dawn?* This appeared a week after Armistice Day in the *Nation*, then edited by H. W. Massingham, and the chief organ to publish

my satires. I here reproduce lines from it because of the
insight they afford into the mind of a young man of the epoch.

How Shall We Rise to Greet the Dawn ?

How shall we rise to greet the dawn,
Not timidly,
With a hand before our eyes?

    .   .   .   .   .

We must create and fashion a new God—
A God of power, of beauty, and of strength—
Created painfully, cruelly,
Labouring from the revulsion of men's minds.

It is not only that the money-changers
Ply their trade
Within the sacred places;
But that the old God
Has made the Stock Exchange his Temple.
We must drive him from it.
Why should we tinker with clay feet?
We will fashion
A perfect unity
Of precious metals.

Let us tear the paper moon
From its empty dome.
Let us see the world with young eyes.
Let us harness the waves to make power,
And in so doing,
Seek not to spoil their rolling freedom,
But to endow
The soiled and straining cities
With the same splendour of strength.
We will not be afraid,
Though the golden geese cackle in the Capitol,
In fear
Lest their eggs may be placed
In an incubator.

    .   .   .   .   .

Continually they cackle thus,
These venerable birds,
Crying, "Those whom the Gods love
Die young"
Or something of that sort.

But we will see that they live
And prosper.

Let us prune the tree of language
Of its dead fruit.
Let us melt up the clichés
Into molten metal,
Fashion weapons that will scald and flay;
Let us curb this eternal humour
And become witty.
Let us dig up the dragon's teeth
From this fertile soil
Swiftly,
Before they fructify;
Let us give them as medicine
To the writing monster itself.

.   .   .   .

We must create and fashion a new God—
A God of power, of beauty, and of strength;
Created painfully, cruelly,
Labouring from the revulsion of men's minds.
Cast down the idols of a thousand years,
Crush them to dust
Beneath the dancing rhythm of our feet.
Oh! let us dance upon the weak and cruel:
We must create and fashion a new God.

To some, wiser than I, the future appeared in other colours;
though these, too, proved delusive. Thus, on the night in
question, among the guests at Swan Walk, in addition to Miss
Ethel Sands and those I have mentioned, was my friend
Madame Vandervelde, the English wife of the Belgian statesman. A woman of striking intelligence and humour, Madame
Vandervelde was notably devoted to the arts, and her house
throughout the war had been the resort of modern painters
and writers, and of the more unconventionally minded of
politicians: for she hated fools with a passion that transcended
that of Mr. F.'s Aunt. Intrepid in mind, with a liking for all
new ideas, in music, literature or politics—indeed she tended,
perhaps, to like the new for its newness—, she was very well
informed about matters political, and she possessed an energy
which inevitably heightened the spirits of others in her company, while at the same time it left her with neither leisure

nor inclination to be depressed. Yet tonight the prospect
before us a little quelled her spirits. She foresaw an era of
political assassination (two German Governors had recently
been killed in western Russia, she remarked), and that the
whole of Europe would go Bolshevik. After that, it would only
be a question of how long the new doctrine would take to
cross the English Channel, which usually delays the arrival
of every idea, whether political or esthetic, for at least twenty
years. Albeit this picture appalled me, both my brother and
I admired the Bolsheviks for putting a stop so quickly to a war
that had become for the Russian troops, left without arms,
increasingly a shambles, and for defeating Germany in so
novel a manner, by first themselves pretending to be van-
quished, and then by inoculating the German armies with the
virus of defeat and revolution, which had, in fact, worked on
them so swiftly. The war had made us impatient of politicians
who relied on oratory rather than arms, and of generals who
had never a new idea, but insisted on their forces being sacrificed in the old, inefficient way. Besides, we were ignorant of
the sort of horror that was taking place in Russia even while
we talked. But I said little, for Diaghilew and Massine were
Russians, and were present. And Diaghilew, indeed, dwelt
on the low cunning of the Bolshevik leaders, and remarked
how strange it was to have been born and to have lived in a
great country, to think that you knew by sight, or at least by
name, every prominent leader of opinion, and then to wake up
suddenly one day and find your country ruled by men of whose
very names, both real and assumed, you and the large majority
of your fellow-countrymen were totally ignorant.

Yes, the barriers were down, there was no doubt about
that, and it was difficult to see the future, though most of us
regarded it with varying degrees of hope. Democratic Europe,
expressing itself through the League promised by President
Wilson, the noble-minded man of the coming era, would never
allow another war to break out, (or that was what we held with
our heads—because it was only common sense for every
nation to avoid war—as opposed to what we feared in our
hearts). War was to us the evil—and that was over. So we fell,
soon, to talking of other things. Diaghilew, I remember, told

us of Nijinsky's conduct since he had been released from the prison-camp in Austria[1] and of how, when last he had heard of him, a few weeks before, this genius, always so ungrudging in his praise of others, had no longer wanted the accustomed applause from crowded theatres, but only to be allowed to return to the soil and work it himself; thereby evincing the curious and persistent nostalgia so often to be found in members of a nomadic race, who pine for something neither they nor their ancestors have ever really known.

Though this dinner at Swan Walk had been arranged a week before, when no-one had been able to foresee so rapid an end to the destruction, it seemed to me most happy that Diaghilew and the new great dancer—for such Léonide Massine had become in the four years that had passed since his début in *La Légende de Joseph* at Drury Lane in 1914—, should dine at my house on the night of the Armistice: most fitting, for several reasons; chief among them—and with that I will deal in a moment—, that the return of the Russian Ballet to London had constituted a private and sole omen of peace. Then, too, I hold that the music that floats idly through the head to form a kind of personal climate to the mind, is of consequence to every artist, affording him background rhythms and colours and tones. It is for this very reason, as I have stressed in the third volume of this work, and perhaps, as well, because it enters into a kind of national or folk consciousness, that popular music is so vital an ingredient in the culture of peoples—possibly of more importance than education itself. How much, for example, one would give to know what airs Leonardo or Michelangelo sang to himself at various times while he worked, or Dr. Johnson, on another level, when alone in his room. So (without placing myself on these heights) throughout the early years of my adult life, I had been a devoted adherent of the Russian Ballet, and in consequence, during the two winters I had spent in the trenches, the music that had come to my rescue—apart from the current and most vigorous American dance tunes of the time before crooning had been invented—to support me for

[1] In which, it will be remembered by the reader of *Great Morning*, Madame Amboise had also been interned.

an hour or two under the bleak, intolerable burden of modern warfare, had all been gathered by my subconscious mind, as I had sat during the various weeks of 1912, 1913 and 1914, watching the ballets I grew to know so well. *Thamer, The Fire Bird, Schéhérazade, Le Rossignol, L'Après-Midi d'un Faune, Le Coq d'Or*: (how often had not the *Astrologer's Song,* from this last piece—both sung and danced—, with its strangeness of melody and its beautiful, baleful absurdity, helped temporarily to banish for me the caves of mud in which I was living and might die!). That one would ever see the Ballet again had then seemed a hope beyond ambition: nor afterwards, when I had come back to England, was there any sign that the Company would ever reappear in London. For years little news of it had reached England, and none of its most faithful followers could say where it was. Therefore its return in September 1918 possessed for my brother and myself all the force of a portent. The projected season was first announced in an advertisement in the press on 29th July of that year, but little more was heard of it until the very week, the very afternoon that, with a singular lack of the publicity which usually attended Diaghilew's ventures, the Ballet Company made its bow on the stage, and proved itself as remarkable as ever, though different now, re-created; as it continued to be re-created throughout the years until the great impresario's death. This time its productions manifested a new accent, a new emphasis, more modern and with a Spanish tang often occurring in them as a result of the long sojourn of the *Ballet Russe* in the Peninsula under the special patronage of the King of Spain, but for whom it would probably have had to be disbanded. (Indeed lovers of beauty owe a great deal to the late King Alfonso[1] for his support of it, and Diaghilew always

---

[1] King Alfonso was seldom gratefully used. In the 1914–18 war, in spite of his Austrian blood, he was practically the only friend the Allies possessed in Spain. He maintained a private organisation for procuring news of Allied officers who were prisoners of war. As many knew, it was most successful, but it cost him the equivalent of sixty thousand pounds a year. Yet the King never received, difficult as it is to believe, a single letter of thanks for his efforts! . . . Similarly when he came over to England to try and get into touch with Ramsay MacDonald, in his second term of office as Prime Minister, in order to discuss the question of a United States of Europe, he met with nothing but rudeness from the newspapers and neglect

in subsequent years showed his gratitude by staging a special gala for the King when he paid one of his frequent visits to London.) It was through the royal kindness that the Company had been able to be transported to England: but it was all the more of a marvel that Diaghilew had arrived with it, for he was a very bad sailor, and entertained, in addition, a great superstitious horror of the sea, since it had been foretold many years before that he would die on the water,[1] while on this occasion he had been obliged to face, not only the usual horrors of a rough passage on the Channel, but also the lurking, omnipresent menace of the U-boats. It must be remembered, moreover, that even in normal times, when urgent business should have taken him and, let us say, Stravinsky from London to Paris, he would often travel only so far as Dover, when, after having luncheon, and regarding disconsolately from the window the movement of the sea outside, he and his companion would return by the afternoon train to the safety of the Savoy Hotel. And it was said that once on board, if the sea proved to be stormy, and though he was a man without religious belief, he would order his faithful Tartar servant, Vassili, who had been in Diaghilew's service since he was nineteen years of age, to kneel down in the cabin and pray for his master's safety. (Certainly this had occurred on an Atlantic crossing.) It was, then, under these circumstances little less than miraculous that the Ballet had actually reached England.

Now, for two whole months it had again been delighting a London audience. The most popular of its productions—and in consequence that given most often—was a ballet based on Goldoni's comedy of the same name, *The Good-Humoured Ladies*, danced to music arranged by Vincente Tommasini from some of the five hundred sonatas of Domenico Scarlatti's, and given a simple Guardi-like setting by Léon Bakst. In

from the authorities. I interviewed the King at this time, and was much impressed by his vision and grasp of affairs. When I asked him if I might put him in touch with H. G. Wells—a writer who, being an ardent republican, had attacked him in the past—the King had replied, " Yes . . . and tell him I am in some ways a much more modern-minded man than he is. I have not stuck fast in 1900! "

[1] He died in Venice.

this work it was the grace, pathos, entrancing cleverness, the true comic genius and liveliness of a dancer new to this country, Lydia Lopokova, which made the chief impression and won for the Company in general fresh devotees in every part of the house. Her face, too, was appealing, inquisitive, bird-like, that of a mask of comedy, while, being an artist in everything, she comprehended exactly the span and the limits of her capacities: the personification of gaiety, of spontaneity, and of that particular pathos which is its complement, she had developed the movements of her hands and arms in a way that hitherto no dancer had attempted, thereby achieving a new step forward in technique. Her wit entered into every gesture, into everything she did. Moreover this great ballerina, fair, with the plump, greenish pallor of arctic flowers, formed the perfect foil to the dark, grotesque quality which Massine instilled into his masterpieces of satiric dancing and choreography. These two famous artistes led the Ballet into its second Golden Age, with such superb creations of grotesque genius as *La Boutique Fantasque* and *Le Tricorne*, though *Parade*, with Karsavina and Massine in the leading rôles, was, in essence, the most tragic and the most original of the newer spectacles. *Parade* had already been given in Paris, but not in England; while the two new productions were to be ready in the near future, and to be presented in London the following spring, when the Company was to provide a whole evening's entertainment at that beautiful theatre the Alhambra, to my mind always the best house in the capital in which to show ballet.

At present, the Company only filled a part of the bill at the Coliseum, with a single item from its repertory at the two performances. One result of this was that the true lover of ballet was now to be found sitting next to those who worshipped at the shrine of the Red-Nosed Comedian. Fortunately for myself, I was happy with both arts, though I cared more passionately for the first. Moreover, the amateur of the Ballet had himself at last changed, for now the leaders of the intellectuals, seven lean years too late, had given the signal O.K., and their followers flocked to it, replacing the old kid-glove-and-tiara audience of Covent Garden and Drury Lane.

Many of the newcomers seemed more mazed by the music-hall turns than would have been the wearers of the stiffest shirt-fronts and most scintillant diamonds from the Royal Opera House, while, for their part, the members of the general audience gazed in wonder and anger at the bearded, angular balletomaniacs, who talked with confidence of things of which they themselves had never heard, in voices clear or squeaky, but that could not be shaken off their tone. What made it worse was that these unusual persons, though they obviously saw so much, appeared only to see their friends, and to perceive no-one near them.

In the audience at this time was very frequently to be seen Lady Ottoline Morrell. With a mass of chestnut hair falling on each side of her face, with her emphatic features, and wearing a yellow gown with a very wide skirt, she resembled a rather over-life-size Infanta of Spain, and there was some-thing, too, in her appearance that recalled the portraits of her remarkable ancestress, Margaret, Duchess of Newcastle, the poet. I recall being amused when one night, oblivious, plainly, even of the name of the kind of theatre in which she now found herself, she gazed with an air of considerable disapprobation at one of the turns, and then sighed in her very individual voice, muffled but distinct for all that, "Rather Music-Hall, I'm afraid!" Though Lady Ottoline had been one of the earliest supporters of the Ballet, when first it came to London, her personal distinction, her individual style, her way of looking, talking, thinking, her magnificent manner of dressing, her brocades and silks, as natural to her as tweeds to the owner of a fox-terrier, made her seem as much out of place at Covent Garden as at the Coliseum. Notwithstanding, Diaghilew, one of whose failings was an inclination to find repose in the bosom of the fashionable world, which Lady Ottoline despised for its complacent stupidity, yet came to depend on her for advice. And she knew precisely how to manage him. With certain other geniuses—for it is by no means a fault confined to the foolish, and is perhaps in the present dustman-democracy age over-condemned—he shared often a snobbish attitude: (it may have been necessary to him in his profession). At any rate, on one occasion, when he had motored down to luncheon at Garsington, Lady Ottoline's country-house, and was plainly chafing at the company he found there—for on the day in question there were writers and painters of an unfashionable kind, but without the genius which would have rendered them supportable to him—, and remained glumly regarding the shaggy figures round him, Lady Ottoline roused him from his sullen lethargy by pointing at Miss Dorothy Brett, the painter (who had a studio in the house), and by insinuating into his ear the healing phrase, "That woman is sister to a Queen". It is true that the Queen in question was Queen of Sarawak, but the words nevertheless produced a tonic effect.

This, however, occurred later than the time of which I write, and when social life had already begun to blossom again a little. At present, almost the only entertainment London afforded for Diaghilew was tea at Garland's Hotel in Suffolk Street with Lady Ottoline. There, too, in her old-fashioned sitting-room, furnished with plush, and a marble clock on the chimney-piece, the ballerinas would be found after the first house, eating strawberry or raspberry jam in silver spoons, dipped previously, after the Russian mode, in tea without milk. . . . We talked, as many did in her lifetime, of Lady Ottoline as we sat in the drawing-room in Swan Walk, a room that glittered with colour like a parrot's tail. But soon we set out for Monty Shearman's rooms in the Adelphi, for he had invited us all some days before to come to a party he was giving.

It was not until we reached the far corner of the Mall that the full degree of the general rejoicing became evident. We had found a taxicab—by no means an easy feat at the end of the 1914–18 war—but we were obliged to crawl, so thick was the crowd, and so numerous were the revellers who clambered round, and rode on, the roof. Eventually we reached the Adelphi. The spacious Adam room, covered with decoration as fine as a cobweb, was hung inappropriately with a few large pictures by the Paris School—by Matisse, for example, —and by several of the Bloomsbury Group, its satellite and English Correspondent. There were a number of paintings, for instance, by Mark Gertler—at that moment an artist much patronised by the *cognoscenti*: (heavy designs of Mile-End-Road figures, very stiff but oily, of trees, fleshy in their aspect, under the solid shade of which trod ape-like beings, or still-lives, apples and pears of an incomparable rosy rotundity falling sideways off cardboard cloths—yet these possessed some kind of quality). Here, in these rooms, was gathered the élite of the intellectual and artistic world, the dark flower of Bloomsbury. And since this name has occurred twice already in this paragraph—as it surely must if one is to attempt to describe the achievements or environment of the early post-war generation—, a word or two is necessary to indicate what it stood for before its so rapid decline.

The great figures were Roger Fry, Virginia Woolf, Clive Bell, Vanessa Bell, Lytton Strachey and Duncan Grant. After them followed a sub-rout of high-mathematicians and low-psychologists, a tangle of lesser painters and writers. The outlook, natural in the grand exemplars, and acquired by their followers, was one of great tolerance: surprise was never shown at any human idiosyncrasy, though an amused wonder might be expressed at the ordinary activities of mankind. The chief, most usual phrases one heard were "ex-quisitely civilised", and "How *simply too* extraordinary!", the first applying to some unusual human concatenation, the second to some quite common incident of burgess life, such as a man going to a railway station to meet his wife returning after a long absence from home. But, no less than by the sentiments themselves, the true citizens of Bloomsbury could be re-cognised by the voice in which they were expressed. The tones would convey with supreme efficacy the requisite degree of paradoxical interest, surprise, incredulity: in actual sound, analysed, they were unemphatic, save when emphasis was not to be expected; then there would be a sudden sticky stress, high where you would have presumed low, and the whole spoken sentence would run, as it were, at different speeds and on different gears, and contain a deal of expert but apparently meaningless syncopation. Many sets of people in the past have developed their own manner of talking, al-most their own language: the Court of Caroline of Ansbach, composed of such persons as Molly Lepell and Lord Hervey, possessed their own cant, and so later did Georgiana Duchess of Devonshire and her Whig friends, and, almost in our time, Mrs. Hwfa Williams and her Edwardian circle. Most of these lingoes had their own voice, as well as phraseology and words, and arose, I believe, on a basis of clan. Thus the Bloomsbury voice, too—that characteristic regional way of speaking, as rare and ritualistic outside the bounds of West Central London as the state voice of the Emperor of China beyond his pleasances and palaces—originated, I believe, more in a family than in a flock. Experts maintain that it originated as an apanage of the Strachey family—of Lytton Strachey, that is to say, and of his brothers and sisters, in whom it was natural and delightful—, and that from them it spread and took captive many, acclimatising itself first in the *haute vie intellectuelle* of King's College, Cambridge: thence it had marched on London, prospering particularly in Gordon and Mecklenburgh Squares and in the neighbouring sooty piazzas, and possessing affiliations, too, in certain country districts—Firle in Sussex, for example, and Garsington in Oxfordshire. The adoption by an individual of the correct tones was equivalent, I apprehended, to an outward sign of conversion, a public declaration of faith, like giving the Hitler salute or wearing a green turban. Once, indeed, I was privileged to be present when one of the Lesser—but now Greater—Bloomsburys took the plunge. I had known him well before he joined up, and then, gently-spoken reader, he talked as you or I do—and so judge of my surprise when, in the middle of a dinner-party, I heard his tongue suddenly slide off sense, making for a few moments meaningless but emphatic sounds that somehow resembled words, and then, as quickly, creak into the Bloomsbury groove, like a tram proudly regaining its rails! . . . I wondered what initiation rites and tribal ceremonies had taken place in the local Berlitz School.

Tonight, at Monty Shearman's, the Bloomsbury Junta was in full session. In later years, towards the moment of its disintegration, Bloomsbury, under the genial viceroyalty of my friend Clive Bell, took a trend, hitherto unexpected, towards pleasure and fashionable life: but in these days it was still austere, with a degree of Quaker earnestness latent in it. (But then Roger Fry, its leading and most engaging esthetic apostle, came of Quaker stock.) The women were of a type different from that to be seen elsewhere. Something of the Victorian past clung to them still, though they were so much more advanced than their sisters, both in views and intelligence. Virginia Woolf, for instance, notably beautiful with a beauty of bone and form and line that belonged to the stars rather than the sun, manifested in her appearance, in spite of the modernity that was also clearly hers, a Victorian distinction. She made little effort to bring out the quality of her looks, but she could not destroy it. It has often occurred to me, when I have seen Roman patrician busts of the fourth century, how greatly she resembled them, with her high forehead, fine, aquiline nose and deep-set, sculptural eye-sockets. Her beauty was certainly impersonal, but it was in no way cold, and her talk was full of ineffable fun and lightness of play and warmth. I have never known anyone with a more sensitive perception of the smallest shadows cast in the air round her: nor could I ever understand why people were—but certainly they *were*—frightened of her; because, though there was, and I am sure she would have admitted it, a human amount of malice in her composition (and how greatly the dull-minded would have complained if there had not been!), there was very much more, and most unusual, gentleness. To the young, to poets and painters, but not to dons, she was invariably kind; kind, moreover, to the extent that, in spite of the burden of her own work and correspondence, she would take trouble for them. She would, I am aware—for I have been present—lay traps for the boastful and the blunted, and greatly she enjoyed the snaring of them (I once had great difficulty in rescuing alive a popular American novelist, whose name was at that time written as a sky-sign round the roofs of Cambridge Circus): but for the most part they deserved their fate. She possessed, too, a beautiful, clear, gentle speaking voice. Though sometimes, when many people were present, she could be seen swaying a little, preparing herself with nervous effort to say the words, to break through the reserve that lay over her, yet I have heard her dare to make a speech. It was at a dinner for the London Group of painters about a year later than the party. Roger Fry, who was president or chairman, had asked me to be present and to speak. When I arrived, I found to my great pleasure that I was sitting next to Virginia. But she was pitiably nervous that night because of the prospect of having to make a speech; her distress was obvious. I felt miserable on her behalf and tried, indeed, to comfort her: for after having just fought an election, oratory held temporarily few terrors for me. I concluded—and it may have been the case—that she was unused to the strain of these occasions, and had only consented to speak because Roger was one of her oldest friends. If so, what happened was the more astonishing. I spoke first, and adequately, I hope, in a matter-of-fact sort of way. The audience laughed at the jokes I made. Then I sat down, and the moment I had dreaded for Virginia arrived. She stood up. The next quarter of an hour was a superb display of art and, more remarkable, of feeling, reaching heights of fantasy and beauty in the description of the Marriage of Music to Poetry in the time of the Lutanists, and how, in the coming age, Painting must be similarly united to the other arts. It was a speech beautifully prepared, yet seemingly spontaneous, excellently delivered, and as natural in its flow of poetic eloquence as is a peacock spreading its tail and drumming. Somehow I had not foreseen this *bravura*; it was a performance that none present will ever forget, and, as she sat down, I almost regretted the sympathy I had wasted on her.

There were few women of a distinction equal to Virginia's in the room tonight: but all, pretty or *fade* or plain, wore their own clothes, either more fashionable than elsewhere, without fashion, or smacking of Roger's Omega Workshop, wholesome and home-made. Some of the men were in uniform, but a proportion—equally courageous in their way—had been conscientious objectors and so were able to appear in ordinary clothes—if *ordinary* is not, perhaps, a misnomer for so much shagginess (the suits, many of them, looked as if they had been woven from the manes of Shetland ponies and the fringes of Highland cattle in conjunction), and for such flaming ties as one saw. It was a singular dispensation—though welcome to me, because I admired their moral bravery, sympathised with the standard they upheld with a singular toughness, and liked them personally—that in the next few years several of the chief artistic and literary lions of the fashionable world, itself in every country then invariably chauvinistic, had been conscientious objectors: but the war, thank heaven, was over, and a moratorium on patriotism set in for about fifteen years. Those present tonight included several, I recall, who had worked at farming in the Arcadian colony presided over by Lady Ottoline Morrell. At Garsington during the war some of the best brains of the country were obliged to apply themselves to digging and dunging, to the potato patch or the pigsty. Lady Ottoline had thrown herself into the rôle of farmer only in order to help her friends—to her credit, ever to be found in the minority—in a time of affliction to them, when intellectuals discovered that mind was more than usually contemned by the majority of the nation. Among the ribald, however, it was rumoured that some employed by her came in the course of time to regard themselves as very able and competent farm-hands, shockingly underpaid, and that they were perpetually threatening to strike. Indeed it was alleged that some cantankerous if cultivated hinds had broken into the Manor House, shouting "Down with capitalist exploitation": (as justly might the silken shepherds of the Petit Trianon have roughly demanded a living wage from Queen Marie-Antoinette!). If this be true, it must have been disturbing for Lady Ottoline, as she sat, quietly eating bull's-eye peppermints out of a paper bag, in her room of small, sixteenth-century panelling, painted green like that of her ancestral Bolsover, discussing sympathetically and seldom with more than one person—it might be D. H. Lawrence, the present Lord Russell, Aldous Huxley or Mark Gertler—the sufferings and foibles of mankind, thus to be reminded, too, of their perversity and ingratitude.

Some of the donnish farm-labourers who were supposed to have invaded her sanctum with their harsh cries for "More" had gathered here tonight. All equally, soldiers, Bloomsbury beauties, and conscientious objectors—all except Diaghilew—danced. I remember the tall, flagging figure of my friend Lytton Strachey, with his rather narrow, angular beard, long, inquisitive nose, and air of someone pleasantly awaking from a trance, jigging about with an amiable debility. He was, I think, unused to dancing. Certainly he was both one of the most typical and one of the rarest persons in this assembly. His individual combination of kindness, selfishness, cleverness, shyness and sociability made him peculiarly unlike anyone else. As I watched him, I remember comparing him in my mind to a benevolent but rather irritable pelican. A man now of about forty, he had achieved no renown (though he had possessed a high reputation for wit, learning and personality among his own friends from Cambridge), nor had sought any until the publication of _Eminent Victorians_ raised him to the zenith of fame and popularity with a generation no longer tolerant of either the pretensions or the achievements of the Victorian great. Some chapters of this book I had, in the autumn of 1917, been given the pleasure of hearing him read aloud—rather faintly, for he was recovering from an attack of shingles, and sat in an armchair in front of a large fire, with a Shetland shawl draped round his shoulders. I remember that our hostess, a cousin of Lytton's, pressed her lively young daughter of seven to allow him to see her imitation of him. While the precocious mimic showed off, Lytton watched the child with a look of the utmost distaste, and when asked by the mother what he thought of the performance—one of real virtuosity—, remarked in a high, clear, decisive voice, "I expect it's amusing, but it isn't at all _like_!" . . . As I say, he was at this moment enjoying great celebrity: my father, however, as was his way, had never heard of his name (it could not, I suppose, penetrate the loopholes of an ivory tower of medieval construction). Thus one day, a few years later, when Lytton had come over to have luncheon with us at Montegufoni, and when the issuing of his _Queen Victoria_ had carried his work to an even wider public, his host demanded angrily, after the visitor had left, "Who is he?", and further initiated what remains a haunting mystery, by adding, "I do wish you'd ask some really interesting people here. I don't know why you never invite the great novelist."

"Who do you mean?"

"Mitchell, of course. You know quite well!"

Plate II

HENRY MOAT IN FANCY DRESS

Plate III

THE AUTHOR AND SACHEVERELL SITWELL, 1923
By Sir Max Beerbohm

But though my father, after this, often mentioned the Master, and held him up frequently to us as a pattern of style and content, neither Sacheverell nor I was ever able, though the problem fascinated us and we tried perseveringly to solve it, to gain any clue to his identity. Sometimes we thought that he was, perhaps, an idealised composite figure formed from the various celebrated novelists of the day, Hardy, Conrad, Wells, Bennett, including all their various excellencies in his books, and with this workmanlike name thrown in to give reality to a dummy. All that we could get from my father, when we pressed him for the name of one of Mitchell's master-pieces, was, "You know quite well. I saw you reading one of his books only the other day! He's much the finest of them —a real genius, they say!" . . . Certainly the elusive Mitchell was absent, again, tonight: but among those I recall as being there were, in addition to Diaghilew and Lytton Strachey, Clive Bell, Roger Fry, Mark Gertler, Lady Ottoline, D. H. Lawrence and his wife, Maynard Keynes, Duncan Grant, Lydia Lopokova and David Garnett.

To everyone here, as to those outside, the evening brought unbelievable solace. The soldiers could return home, the members of the rustic community at Garsington could come back to London, and to work that was their own and would make them famous: the writers could write the sort of book in which they were interested, the young men and women could see the people they wanted to see, without immediately being ordered to Baghdad or York. . . . No one, I am sure, was more happy than myself at the end of so long, so horrible, and so more than usually fatuous a war. When the party began to draw to a close, I left the Adelphi alone, on foot. In street and square the tumult born of joy still continued. Smilingly, the people danced; or intently, with a promise to the future— or to the past, which weighed down the scales with its dead. Strange things occurred. Late that night, a young man who had been at Monty Shearman's party almost succeeded in setting fire to the plinth of the Nelson column,[1] as if in inauguration of an epoch that was to dismiss the lessons of our history, and emphasise that henceforth one man, whether

---

[1] The damage still shows.

great hero or criminal, genius or cretin, was as good as another. The next afternoon the rejoicings were still in full swing. My brother—now also an officer in the Grenadiers—came up to London from Aldershot, and on his return that night, so he told me later, saw at Waterloo Station drunken women being rolled along the platform like milk-cans, and piled into the guard's van—but this was an aspect both of war and of the coming of peace that the public resolutely ignored. Only virtue and heroism exist to war-eyes.

Yes, the war had ended. The moment in which I had never been able to believe had come. The sight of the scenes in the streets left me in two moods, unhappy and furious at the waste of lives and years, and frantically glad, on the other hand, that the struggle was over: full of improbable hopes and equally of probable fears. The first found expression in the poem already quoted, the second in that which is appended below. This poem, published shortly afterwards, was dedicated to my brother and seemed to me, as I wrote it, to have a vein of prophecy in it: a sense which unfortunately the intervening years have justified. In addition, a singular story attaches to it. It was included in the first book of poems by my hand alone (I had already appeared jointly with my sister): but many months before the volume was published in England or America,[1] Witter Bynner was kind enough to send me some cuttings relating to this poem (he had later found out it was by myself) from Californian newspapers. It is a long time ago, but one such extract is before me now, and explains itself, though the title of the journal is lacking. It is dated Berkeley, Dec. 28th, and runs:

UNKNOWN POET SCORES WAR
STANZAS FOUND ON MENU
GOOD VERSE, SAYS BYNNER

A poem scribbled on a grease-spotted menu in a San Francisco café bears so obviously the marks of genius that prominent authors and critics are today looking for the author of the unsigned verses. The owner of the copy received it from a French waiter on the night

[1] *Argonaut and Juggernaut.* (Chatto & Windus, London. A. Knopf, New York, 1919.)

of the peace celebrations. . . . Bynner says that in the technique
and word selection, the unknown writer shows himself to be a master
of his art. The only mark of identification is the letter M. The title
is THE NEXT WAR.

The Next War

The long war had ended.
Its miseries had grown faded.
Deaf men became difficult to talk to,
Heroes became bores.
Those alchemists
Who had converted blood into gold
Had grown elderly.
But they held a meeting,
Saying,
    "We think perhaps we ought
    To put up tombs
    Or erect altars
    To those brave lads
    Who were so willingly burnt,
    Or blinded,
    Or maimed,
    Who lost all likeness to a living thing,
    Or were blown to bleeding patches of flesh
    For our sakes.
    It would look well.
    Or we might even educate the children."
But the richest of these wizards
Coughed gently;
And he said:
    "I have always been to the front
    —In private enterprise—
    I yield in public spirit
    To no man.
    I think yours is a very good idea
    —A capital idea—
    And not too costly . . .
    But it seems to me
    That the cause for which we fought
    Is again endangered.
    What more fitting memorial for the fallen
    Than that their children
    Should fall for the same cause?"
Rushing eagerly into the street,
The kindly old gentlemen cried
To the young:
    "Will you sacrifice

Through your lethargy
What your fathers died to gain?
The world must be made safe for the young!"

.   .   .   .   .

And the children
Went. . . .

The poem was correctly quoted. . . . As for the initial *M*. it may have been a shortening of *Miles*, under which name my satires were invariably printed in the *Nation*, during and after the war, until I was quit of the Army. . . . Even then, however, the odd destiny of this poem was not fully accomplished. Some twenty years later, when it had become plain that we were on the verge of the war its lines had predicted, it was published in the columns of the *Nation's* successor and descendant, the *New Statesman and Nation*.

Nevertheless, at the moment the Next War was still twenty years ahead in time and it seemed clear that men were not such fools as ever to let it occur again. The crowd had reason to be glad. For drunk and sober, for living and dead, for the bodies torn and twisted, and eked out with the flesh of others, the war was over, the first great democratic war, and we were entering the period for which we had fought. Now the years had arrived in which we could prove our worth. For me, as for many others, a period of the most intense activity set in: all the energy repressed for years, or let loose into unsuitable channels, was freed at last. I attempted to make up for the years of which I had been cheated. Within two years I had stood for Parliament, produced a long book of poems, become an editor of a quarterly devoted to modern art and literature, interviewed D'Annunzio at Fiume, contributed innumerable articles on many subjects to the newspapers, and in conjunction with my brother had organised the first large exhibition of modern French pictures held in London since 1914. We had also contrived to arrange—no mean feat of diplomacy where my father was concerned—for Severini to fresco a room at Montegufoni. I had formed, also with my brother's help and advice, a collection of modern pictures, defective in some respects though it was because of our lack of money; I had written art-criticism, and had become a regular contributor of *vers-libres* satires which appeared as leading articles (the only ones of their kind in any paper) to the *Daily Herald*, then edited by George Lansbury, with Siegfried Sassoon as the literary editor. From these I selected two satires, and adding to them a third which had appeared in the *Nation*, made of them a sixpenny book, entitled *The Winstonburg Line*, devoted for the most part to an attack on a great historic personage. This assault was directed against a policy that, by supporting ineffective armed resistance to the new regime in Russia, made of it an enemy, for ever suspicious, and at the same time sealed the fate of those poor weak creatures it had deposed, and who were now held in its clutches. This pamphlet was published by the late Mr. Henderson of "The Bomb Shop" in the Charing Cross Road, an elderly Scottish Socialist in a brown tweed suit, with a flaming red tie, spectacles, and a Trotskyite beard. He was very kind and genial, in spite of a certain cynicism of appearance, as well as enterprising, and under his auspices the volume sold at Albert Hall "Hands-off-Russia!" meetings and elsewhere in such great numbers—though without profit to myself, for I had neglected to ask for a contract—that for many years it remained my best-known work.

It will be seen from the foregoing passage with what fury I applied myself to life; equally it will appear from what follows that it did not impress everyone, any more than did the similar multiform energies unloosed by my brother. Thus there was a well-known remark made at this time by Miss Burton, Robert Ross's faithful housekeeper, who now let rooms in Half Moon Street. A rotund, warm-hearted, loyal and likeable comedy-character from Shakespeare, she had somehow strayed into the Victorian Age and dipped herself in its finery. Always elaborately dressed in silks and velvets, with fretwork insertions, her large contours hung about with keys, brooches, signet-rings and Wagnerian jewels (she had a great love of Wagner's operas), while to crown all there would be on great days, balanced on high brown-grey rolls of hair, a large-brimmed flat hat, spread with ostrich feathers, she suggested something of the jovial, indeed rollicking, good sense of a portrait by Frans Hals, and many of her dictums delivered in a voice that still retained a delightful Hampshire coo and burr were memorable, and gained a circulation among connoisseurs. Thus she confided to her tenant and my friend, Lord Berners, that "Them two Sitwells 'ave got into a grove." . . . On another occasion, again, I heard myself described as lazy. Arnold Bennett was present when this judgment was passed, and began to roar with his laughter, with which he was obliged to struggle as with his words, until his whole face grew red, rather as the body of an octopus changes colour, and the upstanding hair of his head, and his moustache, always so bristly, seemed to bristle still more. When he had mastered his attack, and could again get his breath, he remarked, "That's good! The trouble with Osbert is that he has seven professions, not one, and a life devoted to each."

Of some of the activities to which he referred, I shall have something to say in their place, or at any rate in that which, for the greater convenience of the writer, I assign to them: but I will refer now to the quarterly, because it was a matter which greatly occupied my mind in November 1918. Elsewhere I have written an account—though it will not be published until later—of how a first meeting with Arnold Bennett had led eventually to my becoming one of the three editors of *Art and Letters*. Arnold had most generously offered to finance my editorship of it: but this in the end had not proved necessary, for Frank Rutter,[1] the owner of the paper, wished to reconstitute it, and of his own accord offered to Herbert Read and myself the joint-editorship of the literary side, while allowing us, moreover, to influence him in the pictorial.[2] It

[1] Frank Rutter, *b.* 1876; *d.* 1937. A well-known art critic and author. He was sub-editor of the *Daily Mail* 1901. He founded the *Art News* and edited it until 1912, and was the art critic of the *Sunday Times* from 1903 until his death. He founded and was chairman from 1915 until 1922 of the Allied Artists Association and wrote numerous books on painters and painting.

[2] It is interesting to look back at the contributors to this quarterly. Our first number of *Art and Letters* (Winter 1918–19) included poems by Richard Aldington, Ford Madox Hueffer (later Ford Madox Ford), Aldous Huxley, Siegfried Sassoon, Edith Sitwell, Osbert Sitwell and Sacheverell Sitwell; prose by Ginner, Wyndham Lewis, Herbert Read and Frank Rutter; illustrations by Gaudier-Brzeska, Kramer, Wadsworth and Wyndham Lewis; by whose hand also was the cover design.

was in connection with the revival of *Art and Letters*, at the old Café Royal, with its smoky acres of painted goddesses and cupids and tarnished gilding, its golden caryatids and garlands, and its filtered, submarine illumination, composed of tobacco smoke, of the flames from chafing dishes and the fumes from food, of the London fog outside and the dim electric light within; through which haze one caught sight of such monumental figures as Jacob and Mrs. Epstein, immense in this artificial gloaming, and superb in their own way—the same way as his busts, conjured up, and transposed by magic from colour into form, out of the most intractable material, from the later and more lurid portraits of Rembrandt—, of Augustus John, like some kind of Rasputin-Jehovah, and of Ronald Firbank, seated askew, and laughing consumedly to himself or shuddering in the intervals between the glasses, and of a hundred bowler-hatted bookies and artistic publishers; it was here, then, in these surroundings, that the three prospective editors had luncheon. This was the first time I had met Herbert Read, at the time a very young officer, beginning his career as a poet. I had seldom known then anyone of a finer, more unselfish, personal quality, possessed of so little self-conceit, or with a more true and whole-hearted devotion to those paintings and writings which, though others may think sometimes wrongly, he esteems. Perhaps I liked him so greatly because of the difference in temperament between us; like a Roundhead, he is extravagant only in the lengths to which art-austerity carries him: whereas I am extravagant in all else. He bears a plain distrust towards the sumptuous and the easily pleasing; whether owing to the early struggles which he has so vividly, and often touchingly, described in his autobiography,[1] to his experiences in the war, which had earned him the D.S.O. and the Military Cross, or to his very nature itself, he had already developed a look of premature seriousness.

The second number (Spring 1919) published poetry by Wilfred Childe, Susan Miles, Herbert Read, Siegfried Sassoon and Osbert Sitwell; prose by T. S. Eliot, Ronald Firbank and Wyndham Lewis; a translation by Helen Rootham; music by Bernard Van Dieren; illustrations by Kapp, Rupert Lee, Matisse, John Nash, Paul Nash and Edward Wolfe.

[1] *The Innocent Eye* (Faber & Faber, 1933).

His rather rueful smile was not easy to command; but when it suddenly broke up the gravity of his face, it certainly lightened his whole appearance. Making an acquaintance, which grew into friendship, with him was a source of great pleasure to me at this time, and subsequently to my brother and sister.

Most of the contributors to *Art and Letters* were friends of mine already: and the majority of them were young, of my own age, though among them, too, were numbered men older than myself, such as Matisse (whom I have never met) or the veteran soldier and writer-painter, Percy Wyndham Lewis, who had returned lately to civilian—I nearly wrote civil—life. For many years now, he had been simultaneously at the centre and on the outskirts of the circus dirt-storm his presence invariably provoked. In fact, his geniality had long been proverbial. He had been the leader of the Vorticists, the editor of *Blast*, a celebrated publication of pre-war days; he had been, in earlier times, a student at the Slade School, though I do not know quite when. But it was in the days of which I write—in the summer of 1919, to be precise—that one night we were dining, he and my brother and sister and I, at Verrey's when he made a celebrated pronouncement. The restaurant was full; many of the diners sat by themselves at table, in order better to appreciate the excellence of the dishes (due to the fact that the elderly *patron*, with a pointed beard, walked slowly from table to table, in the French manner, to see that all was properly served and well cooked). Against a setting of dust-coloured brocade, and opposite my brother, sat Lewis. At the end of dinner, in the quietness, he first made a calculation with a pencil on an old match-box and then, with the usual yellowing cigarette-stub clamped to his upper lip while he spoke, its smoke drifting across his left eye, which, in accordance, he had partially to close, thus imparting to his face a more than customarily knowing look, said firmly, but in a carefully lowered voice,

"Remember! I'm thirty-seven till I pass the word round!" The seriousness with which he laid this injunction upon us so intimidated my sister that she has told me that, until many years later, if a doctor came to see her and, in the course of

examining her chest, commanded "Say 99!" she would instinctively and invariably reply instead "37!"

In those days whereof I write, a Norwegian fishing-cap
made apparently on a pudding-basin model, and I suppose of
some kind of cloth (though the material more suggested
brawn)—with a short, fat all-round rim, the front of which
just afforded shade to his eyes—had long ousted his black
sombrero, in the same way that a robust and rather jocose
Dutch convexity had replaced the former melancholy and lean
Spanish elegance of his appearance. A carefully produced
sense of mystery, a feeling of genuine suspiciousness, emanated
from him and pervaded all he did, hovered, even, over the
most meagre facts of his daily life in the large, rather empty
studio. (Caramba! how had the haddock arrived, sur-
reptitiously, after this fashion, and wrapped in a copy of last
Monday week's *Daily Mail*?—his mind reverted darkly to
Lady Rothermere, who had been lately to see his pictures:
had she any connection with the happening? Why had the
washing—he held it up: had it been *washed*?—returned on
a Tuesday instead of Friday, what were they up to? And
wherefore did the sly rat not emerge from its hole, instead of
waiting, waiting there, listening? Why?) But he was covered,
too, with bohemian bonhomie, worn like an ill-fitting suit, and
he could be, and often was, a diverting companion and a
brilliant talker.

Every Thursday evening when we were in London, my
brother and I would dine at a restaurant on the first floor
of a building in Piccadilly Circus, in company with certain
friends, who as a rule comprised T. S. Eliot, Herbert Read
and Ezra Pound as well as Lewis. Each of us sat, back to the
wall, at a separate table, and this distance helped to make
conversation self-conscious or desultory. Ezra Pound was
inclined to mumble into his red beard, a habit perhaps brought
on by his defensiveness, the result, in turn, of attacks delivered
on him during the years of his domicile in England. He was
particularly a type the English do not understand or appreciate. As a consequence of his attitude and conduct in the 1939
war, little good is heard of him today: and it is perhaps as well
to recall that among the considerable number of poems he has

written, some of which are apt to seem pretentious—for his scholarship is not sure and he often relies on it overmuch—, there are some very beautiful and original works. His kindness was very great to many young authors and artists, but he seldom allowed it to be suspected by its recipients. And I remember almost the last time I met Yeats, I mentioned that I had seen Pound in Italy, and he remarked, "Anyone *must* like Ezra, who has seen him feeding the stray cats at Rapallo". More important than all else, it must be remembered that he discovered Gaudier-Brzeska, and did much to make known the genius of T. S. Eliot; whose work was a source of so much pleasure and excitement to my sister, my brother and myself, both at the time of which I write and through all the years that have passed since. I had already enjoyed the privilege of counting Eliot as a friend for some twelve months. In the autumn of 1917, he and my brother and sister and I were among the poets chosen to read their verse for charity one afternoon at Mrs. Colefax's house. The night before, a dinner-party was given for the chairman, Sir Edmund Gosse, the organisers, Madame Vandervelde and Robert Ross, and for those reading. It was then that we saw Eliot for the first time: a most striking being, having peculiarly luminous, light yellow, more than tawny, eyes: the eyes, they might have been, of one of the greater cats, but tiger, puma, leopard, lynx, rather than those of a lion which, for some reason, display usually a more domesticated and placid expression. His face, too, possessed the width of bony structure of a tigrine face, albeit the nose was prominent, similar, I used to think, to that of a figure on an Aztec carving or bas-relief. Though he was reserved, and had armoured himself behind the fine manners, and the fastidiously courteous manner, that are so particularly his own; though, too, the range and tragic depths of his great poetry were to be read in the very lines of his face; and though, in addition, he must have been exhausted by long hours of uncongenial work, his air, to the contrary, was always lively, gay, even jaunty. His clothes, too,—in London he usually wore check or "sponge-bag" trousers, and a short black coat—were elegant, and he walked with a cheerful, easy movement. If it be or be not true that the technique of a poet is his etheric body, yet, in this instance, the comparison is particularly apt: for Eliot's muscular conformation and his carriage and the way he moved seem to explain the giant muscular control of rhythm he has acquired. . . . To return to the reading, the next day the poets met again on a platform in a drawing-room. Sir Edmund was in the chair, with four or five of us on either side of him. . . . When Eliot arrived a few minutes late, he was rebuked publicly by Sir Edmund (though in fact the young man had come straight from the bank in which he was then working). But the high-lights of the day were already gathered there: Robert Nichols—who seemed to have added to his own considerable rôle that of a benevolent vice-chairman—and Irene Rutherford McLeod. Their renderings of their poems deeply moved the fashionable audience. As for Eliot, he showed no trace of annoyance at being reproved: for one manifestation of the good manners I have cited was that he never allowed his companions to suspect the fatigue he must have been suffering: nor did he ever repine openly at the extraordinary fate which constrained such a poet to such a task, but endured it, if puzzled at times, with a jaunty patience—though doubtless with all a tiger's fiery core of impatience at the heart.

My work, no less than my inclination, had brought me, in the last two years before the end of the 1914 war, into touch with many of the creative intelligences then at work in England. The Poetry Bookshop constituted, under the most considerate and, indeed, inspired of hosts, Harold Monro, a great meeting-place: for not only was he a friend of all the poets of his own generation, but new work always attracted, though it may sometimes have irritated, him. He was indulgent to all poets. He liked new ideas even when they did not match his own, and in the large, comfortable, panelled rooms above the shop, he would often of an evening bring together whole schools of poets of the most diverse faith, opinions and temperament. Since his death there has been no-one to match him in this respect. Sometimes there would be battle, but always one heard the literary news and was told of small incidents which, though the world's foundations have been shaken since those days, continue even now to come back to the mind. Thus I recall meeting there one night a young Anglo-Italian writer. His name, we will say, was Giorgio di Dragoni. He proceeded to relate to me how he had entered into a correspondence with Amanda M'Kittrick Ros, whose innocently garish and ridiculous books were enjoying a great vogue with the literary *élite* who were short of a joke at the time. He had hoped to draw her out. But when he had written to her, telling her how much he liked her novels, instead of receiving the amiable reply he had expected, he found in its very first lines a memorable snub—

"Dear Mr. Giorgio di Dragoni," it began, "your name— if such it can be called—is unfamiliar to me."

Whatever outbreaks had taken place, one left Harold Monro's parties enlivened, and grateful to him: for he was an excellent host. But though I formed several friendships at the Poetry Bookshop, the chief were with my host and his beautiful wife Alida. When I felt worried I would often go in and interrupt the business of selling books, in order to consult them and gain the benefit of their valuable advice, or sometimes myself to amuse them by describing some ridiculous incident of literary life, until occasionally customers would grow resentful and Harold would be recalled with a jolt to enquiries and prices.

Harold Monro's establishment was, of course, in its scope and personnel, in the volumes of verse and the occasional or regular periodicals it published, as different from other bookshops as it was removed from them in space, for it occupied a medium-sized house of Rowlandsonian aspect—with a pediment bearing in its centre, within an elliptical frame, an appropriate date—in Devonshire Street: a narrow street, running out of Theobald's Road, rather dark, but given over to screaming children, lusty small boys armed with catapults, and to leaping flights of eighteenth-century cats. Nevertheless, albeit the Poetry Bookshop was so unlike in character to the ordinary run, yet there were others in their various ways no less distinctive, and this is perhaps the place to emphasise how large a part bookshops played in the lives of my brother and myself— as, no doubt, of all authors, who, even those most widely apart, share perhaps this one trait in common. Thus the broad length of the Charing Cross Road, sloping downwards from the Palace Theatre to the Hippodrome, especially constituted a favourite saunter in a free hour. Walking down the road, and zigzagging continually across it, you came first to Jaschke's, now Zwemmer's, the spot of all others in which to find new editions of foreign books and the latest quarterlies or monthly magazines devoted to modern art and literature from Paris, Rome, Berlin, Munich, Vienna and the other capitals of intellectual life. . . . A little further along, you reached "The Bomb Shop", which I have already mentioned, where the proprietor waited, standing near a table at the back, ready to discuss politics sympathetically with any of the eager Fabians, Socialists, Anarchists or Bolshevists who peered myopically through their thick lenses at the books stacked on shelves painted scarlet, or who read the newspaper-cuttings relative to capitalist atrocities that hung pinned up on the wall. He showed himself equally ready, too, to slang, in his sharp Scottish voice, any intruding Tory who ventured to make a remark of any sort. Books, the political theories and implication of which prevented their being in demand elsewhere, could always be obtained here, for this was the rather combustible political centre of the district. . . . Almost opposite, a little higher up, you could visit one of the esthetic centres of the quarter, as devoid of all political tendencies, except a love of personal freedom, as it was full of ideas: a shop presided over by C. W. Beaumont, now the eminent writer on choreography and dancers, the historian of the ballet in Western Europe and the leading English balletomane. Even in those early days, he was already a friend of my brother's and mine, for we had first met him in 1913.

The scene of so much action was small, consisting of a front room of no great size, a winding iron staircase at the back of it, that seemed to belong to one of Harrison Ainsworth's novels and certainly must descend to a dungeon (how often have I not started to climb down it to make sure, only to be halted once again by the vertigo inevitably induced by its mazy metallic convolutions!), and, behind the shop, the proprietor's diminutive sanctum, lined with books, lit always by electric light, and containing many relics of great dancers, past and present. On a shelf on one wall could be examined a speciality of the shop, a line of flat figures cut out of wood, and painted to represent dancers in such works as *Carnaval*, *Petrouchka*, *L'Oiseau de Feu*. Sitting by the door—and, as for that, so minute was this closet, by everything else, by wall and books and window—Cyril Beaumont, with his closely-cropped, suave, orange head of hair which revealed the shape of the cranium, was always to be found smoking a cigarette and occasionally glancing at the desk before him, a Babel's Tower of books and papers. He would be thinking out new schemes —such as the printing-press below, now celebrated, which he was already then planning—with so much intentness that the entry of a customer would often give him a start. Notwithstanding, once he had grown used to the idea, he was, plainly, pleased to see us, and would tell us of many things, of incidents, for example, that had occurred during the day, and of strange customers, for life in the Charing Cross Road is always full of surprises. Mrs. Beaumont would enter, too, to talk or sometimes give us tea. But all such conversation was misleading, for Cyril Beaumont's even and casual voice disguised a will of iron: the shop was pervaded by his personality and by that of his wife, and as full of energy as a dynamo. . . . So it was that often, in an idle moment, Sacheverell would say to me, "Let us go and see Beaumont".

I was a habitual, too, of bookshops in other parts of London. Mr. Shepherd and Mr. Gilbey of Hatchard's had been numbered among my friends from the time I was still a boy, for I had dealt there almost as a child, and certainly owed to it disgracefully large bills when I was fifteen or sixteen; but my family had bought caricatures and books from this famous institution ever since it acquired its present name, and if I am not mistaken, before that, in the latter years of the eighteenth century. . . . Other booksellers I grew to know well through other causes: because, when I was joint-editor of *Art and Letters*, I went round personally to canvass the bookshops for orders, and I have always remembered my pride when, after a talk with me, my friend Mr. J. G. Wilson, of the august house of Messrs. John and Edward Bumpus, doubled the dozen he had asked for; because already, though he was then a stranger

to me, and not the friend and guide he became, I knew him to
bear the reputation of being one of the shrewdest judges, no
less of literature than of the book-market, whom London—or
should I write Scotland?—possessed.

As will be seen from the foregoing pages, I had found then
very numerous friendships among an unusually large range, I
believe, of persons: but I acknowledged no claim except that
of the artist. I had shed, too, many inherited friendships, and
tried to free myself from the shackles of class: (but voluntarily
to unclass oneself is no easy matter!). With the same eagerness
with which I sought new intellectual contacts, so I fled from
my elderly relatives, near or distant. When I saw them, I
tried to elude them, for the war had drained my patience, and
they seemed to enclose me in the atmosphere in which I had
grown up. I loved to be with my brother and sister: I sought,
too, the society of various cousins of my own age: but the rest,
the Golden Horde, now stiff-jointed, and unable to hunt more
than four days a week, the Fun Brigade, its laughter stifled or
wheezy, the Bevy, all of these I endeavoured to shun. As the
years went by, I found myself inevitably drawn back to my
beginnings. It is impossible to escape. The lines of the left
hand are indelibly incised, more deep than those of the right,
which are subject to change. Certain people are given you in
life, as are the places in which to see them. You can add others,
newcomers: but the first group returns, is forced back on you
by circumstances! I cannot presume to pronounce how or
why—but that is my belief. Perhaps in the beginning the
illusion of freedom of choice is necessary. At any rate I
possessed it. . . . At the party in the Adelphi that night there
was no single person I had known before the war.

By the end of the following month, December 1918, I had
already fought and lost an election, and by the middle of April
had succeeded in leaving the Army—ever a difficult thing to
effect when troops are no longer wanted in great numbers.
After a long period—or at last it seemed long—in a Military
Hospital in London, I was given a medical board, and told I
could go on leave pending my release from the Service. . . .
I suppose I was in the ward for about a month or six weeks.
The hospitals everywhere were crowded with the victims of the

great plague, Spanish Influenza as it was called: (surely a death disease born of the holocaust and carrying the very sense of the dead and their sufferings into the bones). Placed on arrival in the Influenza Ward, I contracted the illness three times, and it affected my heart. But the nurses seemed impervious to mortal ills, chatting brightly through the groans of the dying under the naked electric-light bulbs swaying in an icy draught. Tea was the great uplifter of souls—Indian tea, of course. Even the corpses were called at four in the morning.

Into this artificial paradise created by germ and tea-leaf immersion, visitors were admitted on certain afternoons—it may have been on every afternoon—, and the silent elongated forms of Aldous Huxley and Lytton Strachey could occasionally be seen drooping round the end of my bed like the allegorical statues of Melancholy and of a rather satyr-like Father Time that mourn sometimes over a departed nobleman on an eighteenth-century tombstone. Lytton's debility prevented him from saying much, but what he did say he uttered in high, personal accents that floated to considerable distances, and the queer reasonableness, the unusual logic of what he said carried conviction. As an instance of his brevity, so off the point and on it, there is a remark of his that comes to my mind. When he was in Rome, Princess San Faustino entertained him to luncheon, and treated him and her other guests to a long explanation of a scheme she had recently thought of to aid the unemployed. It was all dependent on growing the soya bean. Factories, and synthetic chocolates and motorcars and building-material and bath-salts, all were to be made of this magic substance. She worked the whole idea up to an enthusiastic but boring climax, when she turned to the guest of honour, and appealed to him.

"Mr. Strachey, what do you think of my scheme?" He replied in his highest, most discouraging key,

"I'm afraid I don't *like beans*!"

As for Aldous, Nonchalance, perhaps, more than Melancholy, should have been the image we took him to represent. He was then very young, I think twenty-three. Though often silent for long periods, he would talk for an equal length of

time with the utmost fascination. Versed in every modern
theory of science, politics, painting, literature and psychology,
he was qualified by his disposition to deal in ideas and play
with them. Nor would gossip or any matter of the day be
beneath his notice: though even these lesser things would be
treated as by a philosopher, with detachment and an utter
want of prejudice. But he preferred to discourse of more
erudite and impersonal scandals, such as the incestuous mating
of melons, the elaborate love-making of lepidoptera, or the
curious amorous habits of cuttlefish. He would speak with
obvious enjoyment, in a voice of great charm, unhurried, clear
without being loud, and utterly indifferent to any sensation he
was making. Thus the most surprising statement would hover
languidly in air heavy with hospital disinfectants. "From his
usual conduct", I remember his announcing on one occasion,
"one must presume that Every Octopus has read Ovid on
Love." Unconscious of the public interest, Aldous would proceed on his conversational way in a genial effort to amuse me.
And to the invalids, as they lay there with nothing to do except
read an old, torn, tea-stained copy of the *Tatler* or *Punch*, a
whole new world was revealed. Many of them understood
for the first time what was being said round them, for they
were in that passive state where they were bound to listen, so
that truth could enter. How greatly I enjoyed this conversation! But soon Aldous would fall to silence again, drooping
into a trance-like state of meditation.

These and other distinguished visitors, then, created a stir
among the inmates of the ward, for they little resembled the
friends of other patients, either in appearance or in their conversation. It was plain that every one was enjoying himself:
and this suited nobody. So it was soon rumoured with confidence among nurses and doctors, I was told, that if I remained there much longer, such was the force of my subversive
example, "the whole ward would go Bolo"—then regimental
and hospital cant for Bolshevist. . . . In the course of time,
however, I got better—or at any rate well enough to be allowed
out for walks. My sojourn in the Military Hospital had in no
way helped me, and I still felt very ill. Indeed it must have
shown in my looks, because when I met Roger Fry one day in

the street, he was so much struck by my pallor and thinness that, with his invariable kindness, he said that, plainly, I needed feeding up, and must come and have luncheon with him the next day in his studio in Fitzroy Street. I arrived there accordingly, and found luncheon set out for two amid the confusion, the rags, paints, turpentine, pile of drawings, books, shoes, dead flowers, cracked looking-glasses and shaving-brushes and all the other litter of a painter's room. My generous host, who would certainly never have troubled to provide such delicacies for himself, had ordered oysters: but as I tasted the first, a horrible doubt assailed me. . . . Waveringly, I began:

"What *unusual* oysters these are, Roger! Where did you get them?"

"I'm glad you like them," he replied, with the spirit and intonation of the quarter. "They come from a charming, dirty little shop round the corner!"

After that, I somehow curbed my hunger, and hid the oysters under their shells. As he cleared away the plates, he took a tin out of some steaming water, and said,

"And now we will have some *Tripes à la Mode de Caen.*"

Setting my jaw, I ate on.

My illness continued for some weeks after I left hospital: but, all the same, life was returning, flowing into its old channels (that, the pre-knowledge of it, was precisely what the world had been celebrating on 11th November 1918). Old friendships were now able to be renewed. Already, before I had left London, Robins had returned from Germany. So much had happened to him and to me since I had last seen him on 2nd August 1914, that at first he seemed almost a stranger, and he did not talk much of his experiences at Wittenberg, the notorious prison-camp where typhus had been rife, and in which he had been incarcerated from December 1914 until December 1918. He told me of one incident, however, that occurred at the end of his captivity, and which I have always remembered. Of the Armistice he heard in the following fashion. For several days previously, the most brutal of his gaolers, Under-Officer Hildebrand, had been noticeably more amiable in his manner. Now, on the morning of the

11th November, this man rushed into Robins's room, looking distraught, and shouting:

"Our good old German God has deserted us!"

"Didn't you know that, Under-Officer?" Robins replied. "I did. Why, he's been a prisoner in England for these past three months!"

Henry Moat, too, had swum, whale-like, into our ken again. During the election in December, I had gone, as I have described in *Left Hand, Right Hand!*, to see Bill Moat, Henry's brother. Hearing that Henry had been, or was being, demobilised, and would shortly return to Whitby, I asked for his address, and my mother wrote to him and invited him to stay with us at Scarborough at Christmas. (My father would be away—and that was an advantage, for he and Henry still at that time strongly disapproved of each other.) He accepted. We found him very little changed, a trifle heavier, his face a shade redder, perhaps. Naturally he possessed in the town a great many friends of over twenty years' standing:—among whom, notably, was Mr. Follis[1]—and he had seen none of them since 1913. Though there were occasional rifts in their relationship, and I can just remember, when I was about three or four, Henry appearing at breakfast one morning with a black eye on a really large scale, and Mr. Follis coming in to curl my mother's hair an hour or two later, with his eyes hardly showing at all behind mountainous ridges of scarlet and black: for Mr. Follis, too, in spite of his finical, jackanapes airs of a *coiffeur*, his pointed shoes, his unusually grand vocabulary and stylised manner of speech (on being asked his politics, he always replied—and as children we were continually trying to prompt him into saying it—"I berlorng to the Cornstitootinal Clorb, and *that* Speaks Vorlumes!"), was full of bantam fire as his professional spirit-lamp, a real fighter, as was Henry. We pretended to notice nothing. It was known, however, that they had been to a dance together the previous evening—for they were fond of each other's company and of enjoying themselves. And the two of them must have made a momentous appearance at a fancy-dress ball in 1906, for Henry, who had gone in the livery and white wig he had worn

[1] *The Scarlet Tree*, pp. 232-3 of this edition.

some ten years before as footman to my father when High Sheriff of Derbyshire, was announced as Leonardo da Vinci, while Mr. Follis, in pasteboard armour, entered as Captain Cook! . . . So, on this Christmas Eve, Henry had been enjoying supper with Mr. Follis once more. . . . At about midnight, my sister and I were sitting talking to my mother in her bedroom, when suddenly we all three heard a heavy, unfamiliar footstep dragging along the passage. My mother was rather alarmed and called out "Who's that? *Who* is it?" . . . There came no answer, but after a moment's shuffling, a knock, and then the door opened, and Henry's huge form appeared, swaying in the doorway. He steadied himself and, with a perfect mock dignity and composure, pronounced the words,

"My lady, have mercy on an erring lamb!"

Then, first giving a deep bow, he left the room and shut the door behind him.

Henry brought with him the assurance of the past: but the future, too, was shaping itself, and soon, after a fortnight or so in Oxford, I went abroad for pleasure for the first time since 1914, to stay with Mrs. Ronald Greville, a close friend of mine and a personality of power and discernment. She had inherited great riches and, being herself a brilliant organiser and woman of business, had much increased them. But her outward life—for few persons can have guessed the attention she gave to her affairs and to charity—was spent at Polesden Lacey and 16 Charles Street. These two houses were the resort of foreign and imperial, no less than metropolitan, statesmen, and of foreign ambassadors, and they possessed a kind of unobtrusive luxury of life and background that I have never encountered elsewhere. The potency of her character enabled her to infuse her splendid entertainments with a sense of fun and enjoyment that rendered them more memorable even than did their magnificence, or the beauty of their setting. A word, a look, a glance would indicate a complete grasp of any situation which might arise, and a sure knowledge of how to handle it. She liked to fill her house with celebrated and beautiful people, but was equally happy dining with an obscure friend at some small restaurant in an unfrequented French or

Italian town. Her influence was remarkable, and she lived at the centre of things, knowing what was taking place, and judging it with accuracy. In addition, in the course of long journeys through Africa, Asia and America, her eye had been as observant as it was at home, and she could foretell who would be the coming figures in the countries she visited. As a result, her advice was most valuable, and she was consulted by many people of importance, and played thus a considerable part behind the scenes. In the best sense, worldly—that is to say, versed in the ways of the world, and supremely well qualified by nature and experience to manage people and situations, she retained a natural simplicity that on the other hand inspired her with a certain contempt for the fashionable life in which she nevertheless spent much of her time.

The only daughter of the Scottish millionaire and Liberal member of Parliament and Privy Councillor, William Mc-Ewan, she had been brought up very frugally, in spite of his great wealth and generosity. She always retained a slight Scottish intonation and use of phrase, exemplified, for instance, in the way she would say "Amn't I?", and she had inherited from her father the shrewdest powers of appraisal. She used often to say, "My dear, I know I'm not an educated woman", and she was certainly better versed in the hearts of men and women than in books—but she was a clever woman herself, though clever in the most feminine way. Her grasp of politics and business was masculine, it is true, but the way in which she went to work was essentially feminine. Politics, more than art, was what she loved and best understood (though her sense of personal quality often told her which were the good writers): and she could distinguish and sum up the virtues and the failings of politicians with an eye—and occasionally a tongue—as sharp as a needle. Since her mind weighed men and women so finely, with so much acumen, and since, in consequence, they were not able to take her in, she possessed, as well as many devoted friends—especially among the young, in whom she found the qualities upon which she set the greatest store, quickness, courage, directness, and freedom from affectation and pomposity—many enemies. This enchanted her, for she was a courageous and an accomplished warrior, and liked to be able to make use of her technique, acquired through many years. Pretensions enraged her, and we of a younger generation especially admired the almost Elizabethan gusto with which she set out to combat and vanquish those of her contemporaries who indulged in them. If the point had been reached where a bubble had to be pricked, no one could perform the operation with a more delicate skill and, indeed, virtuosity. Looking at the complacent and the assured, conventional and pompous, she would often start her campaign with the slogan, "I think I must have Gypsy blood". But, alas, she often found these women against whom she marched with banners flying—they were nearly always women, for she had few enemies among men—too timid to show their hostility to her to her face. On the contrary, they would try to ingratiate themselves, only to be rewarded for their trouble with snubs that, like Allingham's "Four Ducks on a Pond", they were "to remember for years, to remember with tears". Thus, when she entered an assembly, many a fashionable hostess quailed: but her manner, unless she was specially provoked, was unimpeachable, even to those she disliked, though it left them in no doubt of the feeling she entertained towards them. An all-too-comprehending word, a congratulation where an attack might have been expected, would lay her enemies low: but she never committed the error of under-rating them, and made full allowance to them, even for such imponderable assets as personal charm, manner or amusing talk.

To her friends she was as loyal, warm-hearted and generous as she showed herself implacable, in some instances, to others. She had been particularly devoted to her father, and when in 1908 she had been left a widow, she had gone to live in his house, to look after him. As a very old gentleman—so thin, my mother told me, as to look almost transparent—he still insisted, though he had been knocked down more than once in the traffic, on walking everywhere by himself. He enjoyed these rambles, and to have insisted on someone accompanying him would have meant a painful admission, a lowering of his dignity in his own eyes: so his daughter thought out an ingenious scheme. She engaged a private detective whose job it was for several years to see old Mr. McEwan, without his being aware of it, safely over the dangerous crossings. . . . As for myself, from the time of our first meeting in 1916, until her death in September 1942, she was a never-failing friend, and of the greatest help in giving me counsel in the innumerable positions of difficulty into which I contrived to get myself. Invariably her advice would prove correct, even when it concerned that most difficult of matters, the management of my parents. Nor was she ever afraid of telling one straight out in what direction one was following a wrong or delusive track.

I had not seen Monte Carlo since the visit I had paid it for the day when I was eleven,[1] and it was so long since I had been in a Mediterranean country—for four years at twenty is a long time—that I had forgotten, in those fifty months of darkness, the sumptuous plenitude of Italian light[2]—the spears and beams, and banners illuminated even on apparently sunless days, the golden-spangled afternoons, the glowing of hillside and mountain in the evening sun—which clothes it with eagle wings; still more, the marvel of its flawless days, when the great azure dome is only flecked occasionally with a golden ripple, or a huge, flat, white cloud sails like a swan across the calm immensity, and when there are minute beauties as well as majestic, and every small rock-cactus or tiny plant can be seen radiating light, drawing in the heat, basking like an emerald lizard; and then the beauty of the hackneyed sunset hour, when the sea has a pallor as though the moon were already shining on the blue transparency of its water, and the vast circular sun sinks into it, and as it goes, piles and rains rose petals on to the mountains before the acronychal grape-bloom of sky and sea enfolds them. I had forgotten the bombastic, contaminated beauty of this particular place, the cliffs of bright painted houses, row after row of cube and rectangle lying on the rock shelves, the lines and garlands of lights at night, the iron stations, light as Chinoiserie pavilions, throughout the year wreathed carelessly with clumps and clusters and bouquets of flowers in pastel shades, the flights of steps, steep

---

[1] See *The Scarlet Tree*, pp. 247–8 of this edition.
[2] The writer wishes to save his correspondents unnecessary trouble: he is aware that Monte Carlo is not in Italy.

or shallow, the bulbous, preposterous hotels, the citadel of the whole Principality, the Casino, contorted, heavy, over-rich, but the very Temple of Chance, situated in a sacred grove, the statue by the hand of Sarah Bernhardt that graces the side of the enormous building, the miniature quays down below, the tunnels, with their sudden blare of daylight, loud as a great sound, the small yachts and sailing vessels in the harbour, the bars and cafés, the Italian smell of coffee in the back streets, the shapes of octopus, sun-fish and mollusc in the Marine Museum, repeated in fleshy but more stilted green forms by the succulent vegetation outside.

Now, in March 1919, the little pleasure-city was balanced between two worlds, past and present. The Russian influence was already dead or dying: but its symptoms remained, the great villas, to be pulled down later or split up. People still talked of the luxury in which the Grand Dukes had lived here, of how, when they went back to Russia, they would send their linen from St. Petersburg right across Europe, to be washed at Charvet's, the famous shirt-maker in the Place Vendôme in Paris, and of how, when they could not come to Monte Carlo in the winter, special trains from the Principality and its neighbourhood would bring them carnations and roses for their Muscovite banquets. But today the members of the Imperial family who had frequented Monte Carlo were scattered, many of them in prison or murdered. Only the Grand Duchess Anastasia, whose behaviour had not long ago shaken whole countries—notably Germany, where her daughter had married the Crown Prince—was still to be seen, wearing a flaxen wig, sitting on a stool at the bar of the Hôtel de Paris or in the old Sporting Club. The Grand Duke Dmitri, on the other hand, subsequently for many years to be met in these surroundings, was still near to the horror of Rasputin's death, which he had helped to plot and carry out, and had not yet arrived here. Harry Melville, that stylised cosmopolitan, the singular product of the genteel 'eighties and epigrammatic 'nineties, was staying at the Hôtel de Paris, and in the intervals of telling those interminable stories that won him a certain social renown, was working excessively hard at introducing his many acquaintances to one another, especially,

I thought—he being perhaps actuated in this by the genuine spice of wit and grain of malice in his nature—those least equipped by disposition and circumstances to make friends. But, if this were so, the great conversationalist, as many had for long deemed him, defeated his own purpose, for, when present, he prevented all others from making their views heard, stifling them under the lightweight *longueurs* of his tortuous and trivial monologues:[1] nevertheless, he was by habit gay, and by conviction he wanted others to enjoy themselves. Among the persons to whom he ceremoniously presented me were the mistresses of several Grand Dukes now lost, captive or massacred in the country which for so long had cherished them. These placid Frenchwomen, of middle age, so well conducted, so quietly if fashionably dressed, who still liked to dance a little, had been pastured for almost a generation on meadows of malachite, where the field flowers to be plucked were composed of diamonds, rubies and sapphires: yet now they could hear nothing of the fate of their masters. One must make the best of things, they would sigh to themselves: they were not badly provided for, with enough to leave to their relatives, to give their nephews and nieces a start in life (they were full of family feeling and domestic virtues, and did not wish their young people to know the same privations they had been through). Their little musical laughs trilled out as coyly as ever, and their jewels shone under the winking electric light of the Principality.

Yet they noticed the change, they admitted: the sound of

---

[1] As a young man I once received a printed invitation from some friend " to hear Mr. Harry Melville talk ". I accepted and found about sixteen people gathered together after dinner, at about 9.30, in some beautiful rooms in the Temple. . . . Harry Melville began to tell us the story of a murder. About half-way through it, when the tale had lasted already for three-quarters of an hour, a sound of snoring, gentle snoring, made itself heard. The talker at first paid no attention, the host and hostess were too tactful to notice: but the guests counted and scanned each other. Gradually, but inexorably, the susurration swelled and mounted to an awful, wheezing climax. Impossible to ignore it longer. It quelled even the talker. But where did the sound come from? We said nothing, the talker smiled, and we stared at one another. Then the hostess remembered. " Bingo! " she cried, and a paw was stretched out from under a sofa. It was her dog, an Aberdeen, who had concealed himself. . . . But it was impossible for the story to continue.

the Russian accent had almost vanished from the Rooms. No longer did bearded boyars and Grand Dukes make even hardened gamblers hold their breath as they watched them play. That had gone on right up till the outbreak of the war. But the golden age of its reign had been in the years just before and just after 1900, and a story Mrs. Greville told me at this time illustrates the lively corruption of the earlier period. In 1892, a famous Russian lady went to live with the Grand Duke X: but while the Grand Duke was away, she was visited by his cousin, the Grand Duke Y. . . . In the early 1900's Mrs. Greville was staying at the Hôtel de Paris, so as to be near her father, who was very ill and under the care of the famous Swiss doctor who then practised at Monte Carlo. Going up in the lift one evening, she met the Grand Duke X, who greeted her with the remark:

"You're just the person I wanted to see. Your father, I hear, employs the Swiss doctor: is he really a good man? My little son is very ill with tuberculosis, and I thought he might be the right doctor for him."

Mrs. Greville was astonished, for this was the first she had heard of the Grand Duke's son. However, she showed no tremor of surprise, and gave the doctor the excellent character he deserved. Soon after this, she returned to England, but was obliged to come out to Monte Carlo again six months later. The very morning she arrived, the doctor sent a message to ask if he might call on her to obtain her advice on a difficult matter. She sent back word to say she would be delighted to see him whenever he liked to call. He came the same afternoon, and looked worried and nonplussed.

"I find myself in an awkward position," he began. "I know you will not betray my confidence. I have been treating a Russian, a young boy, for tuberculosis. When he left my clinic, the Grand Duke X wrote me a letter, in which he thanked me for curing his son, and enclosed a cheque for three thousand francs. . . . Now, the Grand Duke Y has written me a letter in identical terms, and sent me the same amount. What am I to do?"

"Accept both cheques," Mrs. Greville replied firmly. "Never impugn a woman's honour!"

Among the few persons to whom Harry Melville introduced me that I wanted to meet—though, even then, not fanatically, for I had never seen her dance, and knew little of her—was Isadora Duncan. She was dividing her time between Nice and the Hôtel de Paris at Monte Carlo. We spoke for a moment one evening. The next morning, early—early, that is to say, for Monte Carlo, about half-past nine (at which hour the porters have stopped washing the marble steps of the Casino, and the green-aproned gardeners have ceased sweeping up the few leaves that have fallen on to the precious circle of grass, so carefully tended, have removed a cobweb or two from dewy hedges of green, and have watered beds of carnations and begonias and nameless variegated leaves, writhing in blue and puce)—,I went out for a walk. Only the tops of the palm trees caught the light, which lay like feathers, soft and rosy, on roof and terrace. In the side-streets no one was yet stirring, except a few tradesmen, who still presented their ordinary appearance, without the oily-eyed smiles reserved for customers, smoked cigarettes while they pulled the shutters up with a roar of wooden slats, and fumbled rather clumsily as they placed in the windows the jewels intended to lure lucky gamblers. Piles of oranges and tangerines, baskets of flowers, were revealed in the florists' and fruiterers', and the girl in the chocolate shop was taking rows of chocolates from trays of paper and arranging them on silver dishes in a window. A strong, sweet, sticky smell issued from the door. Otherwise there was no sign of the life for which the flights of steps, the streets, the terraces and colonnades lay set. The glass roofs of winter-gardens flashed in the sun. . . . Suddenly, in front of me, down a steep street which seemed crushed between the grey, bulky backs of elephantine hotels, and yet, for all its featurelessness, to bear a resemblance to a complicated stage background, I saw a figure advancing with a peculiar grace of carriage and spring of step, in her hands a bunch of violets and narcissi. It was Isadora Duncan. The beauty of the apparition—she was no longer young—was entirely unpremeditated. Though she had known tragedies, there was an irresistible air of life in her approach, and as she advanced she appeared to bring with her some of the care-free sweetness and innocence of the antique world, of Greece and the heroes in their world of sea and sky and trees. So, she walked down this street, where, under the light, even the dull plaster façades seemed burgeoning with the spring, until she came to the young avenue of pepper trees, the plumy leaves of which made a trembling shadow on the pavement. Now, however, she recognised me, and we walked together. In the next few weeks, I saw a certain amount of her, and came greatly to like her. And I had reason, withal, to be grateful to her, for I had developed a rather severe infection of the eyes from the Riviera dust of those days, and the foreigners' doctor whom I had called in told me that it would be a long business and that he must come to see me twice a day (at a charge of two guineas a visit). But when Isadora Duncan heard this, she said, "Nonsense. I'll take you to an eye-doctor I know in Nice: only you mustn't mind having to wait for half an hour in a queue." She motored me over there in the afternoon, to a house in a back street. After I had waited in the queue, I was summoned into the dingy consulting-room, where a fat, bearded little figure peered up at my eyes. After a careful examination, he mixed me some drops, grunted, squeezed two drops into each eye, charged me ten francs, and sent me away. . . . By the next morning, to the other doctor's great consternation, I was cured! In later years, as indeed in earlier, stories reached me of Isadora's wild existence, culminating in her strange death. However, in a favourite phrase of Davis, my old nurse, "I must speak as I find", and I can only vouch for the dignity clearly to be seen in her, and for the delight with which she invested life when you were with her, and for her kindness, and for her intelligence, as keen, I presume, in her art as in matters of everyday life. And when her name is mentioned, or I see it written, I recall with pleasure that figure coming down the steep incline of street, against the immense background of the big hotels, and think of the humanity and warmth her coming imparted to the scene.

A few weeks later, I accompanied Mrs. Greville to Biarritz, and Sacheverell joined us there. He had been in Paris, and for the first time in his life had seen streets lined with galleries full of modern pictures, of an unmistakable style and audacity, full of a beauty that is the reward of adventurousness. I recall his excitement as he told me of the shop windows, showing paintings that could belong to no other age. He had been especially impressed by the work of Picasso and of Modigliani, and had made arrangements for an exhibition in London the following summer by the various modern masters of Paris. He had also purchased a fine drawing by Modigliani, and brought this with him, together with the remains of a very exquisite silver-point drawing of Modigliani and Jeanne Hébuterne in the nude by Herbin.[1]

It was at Biarritz that the news reached me that I was at last a free man, released by the military authorities. Immediately packing my uniform, my gold-braided hat and great grey coat with brass buttons, in a hamper, I launched it on the turbulent waters of the Bay of Biscay. At first the waves kept on bringing it back to me, as if to indicate that a new war was coming, but eventually I could see a speck floating away under the wheeling sea-gulls towards the Spanish coast, where doubtless it was washed up, and its contents taken to be connected with some spy mystery of international ramification —or is it still locked, perhaps, in the frozen Antarctic, or caught and mouldering in the Sargasso Sea? . . . My splendid peace-time scarlet tunic, the fitting for which I have described in *Great Morning*, had been lost—and never to this day has it been found, unless by moths, satiated with their favourite feasts of camphor, naphtha and D.D.T., and now winging their way, as if hunting, through forgotten lofts. The bearskin I still retained in London, and later gave to Mrs. Powell—my brother's and my own dear friend, cook and housekeeper from 1917 until her death in 1930—so that she could have it made into a muff.

Mrs. Powell had an ample, beautiful presence, like that of some Venetian with braided hair in a portrait by Titian or by Palma Vecchio, and she resembled, too, one of the mysterious women who sit, always in the background, in the shade cast by the fat-leafed trees in a picture by Dosso Dossi. Her skin was clear, her eyes were wide, grey-blue and generous, her hair was brown, full of wheat-coloured lights,

[1] See *Left Hand, Right Hand!* p. 226 of this edition.

her face of a heavy but classical mould. With her she brought
an air of happy, primitive abundance, so that she might, else,
have been a corn-goddess presiding at a harvest festival: and
all her stories of early childhood (she was the eldest of the
many, I think ten, children of a Herefordshire farmer)
reflected this quality and outlook: tales of pigs and geese and
poultry, of eggs and honey, of gathering mushrooms in
meadows, picking bilberries on mountain and moor, or
plucking apples in the gold and red livery of the sun from the
tops of old trees in walled orchards, or stories of cattle, or of
lambs lost on the mountainside, and of the escapades and
tumblings of her small brothers and sisters. Since she had
been given but little education save that which the spectacle
of nature afforded her, I often wondered at her generosity of
spirit, no less than at her usually fine taste in objects and
literature, and her true and subtle understanding of people.
In the course of time she became a leading authority on my
father's psychological foibles and cunning plans for my
improvement, as well as expert in foiling them on my behalf.
And she had many strange experiences with him: as, for
example, when he called at my house in London, having only
just found out—or, rather, come to suspect—that I possessed
it, though my brother and I had been installed in it for two
years. In order to make sure, he walked from the end of the
street, rang at the door, and asked who lived there. Mrs.
Powell had happened to answer the bell herself, and albeit
he would not give his name, and she had never seen him, she
immediately guessed who he was, and in reply to his enquiries
improvised brilliantly a hostess of her own name—a Mrs.
Powell, to whom the house belonged, and with whom Sacheverell and I were staying. Mrs. Powell was away for the day,
it appeared, and had left word that no one was to be let in.
. . . On this occasion my father retired, no wiser than he had
arrived: and she said to me about him, "He's the finest
gentleman I ever saw, but he has a thin voice: I don't like
thin voices". It was a long time before he found out that
the house was rented by my brother and me, and when, still
ignorant of this fact, he later succeeded in making good an
entry, he remarked to me wistfully, as he looked at the pictures

Families are wonderful.

hanging on the walls, "I had no idea what an interesting woman your hostess, Mrs. Powell, must be".

At thirteen years of age, she had been taken away from the school she attended and sent out from the remote farm to earn her living in service. In later years, though she was so uncensorious, this fact a little rankled; and I recall how after returning from a summer holiday she told me of this visit to her father. He still lived in the same ancient, square stone house, so remote from the life of towns, standing in a dark stretch of country among the peaty airs and bilberries native to the stony uplands bordering Wales. All day long she would be out, for she still loved all young animals and birds and plants: and in the evening she would sit in the kitchen, opposite her handsome old father in his high-backed chair.

"When I die," he used to observe to her in his lordly way— for he always talked, and unfortunately acted, in a spacious manner,—"I intend to be buried in the city of Hereford."

And Mrs. Powell would always reply, "Well, I'm sure *I* don't know who's going to pay for it. I'm not, this time: that's certain! I've had to pay often enough for you while you're alive!"

This repetitive, rather gloomy fragment of evening conversation was founded on her resentment at having been sold into slavery, and was out of key with her character: which was on a grand scale. But she had been still a child, and had suffered acutely from homesickness, crying herself to sleep every night in an attic at Castle Howard, above the painted cupids and allegorical figures, and under the beams of the great house in which she had been given her first situation. All her money had to be sent to her parents, and when she began to earn more, indeed, for most of her life, if anything was wanted at her home, Mrs. Powell was obliged to find the money for it. After she had left Castle Howard, at seventeen or eighteen, she had become stillroom-maid, under the authority of the redoubtable Mrs. Selby,[1] at Londesborough, in my grandmother's time. So she had known many members of my mother's family, and revered them, and she loved

[1] *The Scarlet Tree*, pp. 44–6 of this edition.

Londesborough and the country round it. In London, she liked to get out of the hot kitchen—a rather old-fashioned basement, hung with modern pictures—into the air as much as she could, and so sometimes, of a rich autumn evening, I would see her sitting at the open window, her face glowing, her dress assuming classical folds, both taking on part of the glory of the setting sun. Her expression on these occasions, as she gazed over the tree-tops at the sky, was one of puzzled but genial melancholy, if such a slight contradiction may be allowed, and her hands would rest on the warm, golden sill. She liked, too, to take the air in a doorway, as an animal does, and in it, or indeed in the window, she would remain framed by wooden rectangle or square as in a portrait, and there would be something monumental about her, calm, benign, good, beautiful.

In the morning, she would go out, for she liked to do her own shopping. Just as, herself an artist in her own profession, she had, as I have said, esthetic feelings, so that in later years she was the only person who warned me not to sell a magnificent picture by Modigliani which hung in my London house, and she could understand also the full scope of the masterpiece Arthur Waley had created in his great translation of Lady Murasaki's novel, *The Tale of Genji*, so, too, she found a pleasure, comparable to the gratification that can be provided by pictures or books, in the material of food, and when she came in would greet one with such words as, "I saw the loveliest piece of turbot in the King's Road: a really *lovely* thing", or "They've a *beautiful* saddle of lamb at Bowen's, sir, I wish you'd go and see it". And the phrases she used, after this style, were perfectly sincere, the meaning to be accepted literally. She loved her art and was expert at it. In illustration of this, it is no less indicative of Mrs. Powell's nature than of Mrs. Greville's special understanding of character, that towards the end of Mrs. Powell's life, when she had made a transient recovery from a severe illness and operation, and when Mrs. Greville wished, because of what my housekeeper had been through, to show her kindness of a sort that would really appeal to her, suddenly the inspiration came: would Mrs. Powell, she asked, care to spend the evening of the following day in the kitchen at 16 Charles Street, watching the celebrated French chef who was in charge there cook and dish up for a dinner party of some forty people? Mrs. Powell accepted the invitation with rapture, and it was my opinion that the enjoyment she derived from, and interest she took in, all she saw on that occasion benefited her health more than would have a whole month spent by the seaside. She returned at about midnight, in an entranced condition at the splendour of the batteries, the china, the service: though she told me, with the confidence that a perfect knowledge of her own great gifts inspired, that she knew she could have turned out a finer, better dinner herself, had she possessed a kitchen equally well equipped, and similar aids and accessories.

It is a singular instance of poetic injustice that the only direct mention of a dinner cooked by her, in the journal of a well-known writer, records a curious culinary solecism, which I remember, and of which it was always impossible to find any explanation. This entry occurs in Arnold Bennett's Journal for 15th June 1919,[1] and I reproduce it here, since it a little gives the impression of life at Swan Walk at that time.

Dined at Osbert Sitwell's. Good dinner. Fish before soup. Present W. H. Davies, Lytton Strachey, Woolf, Nichols, S. Sassoon, Aldous Huxley, Atkin (a very young caricaturist), W. J. Turner and Herbert Read (a very young poet). The faces of Woolf, Atkin and Read were particularly charming in their ingenuousness. Davies, I liked. He had walked all the way from Tottenham Court Road to Swan Walk. A house with much better pictures and bric-à-brac than furniture.[2] In fact there was scarcely any what I call furniture. But lots of very modern pictures of which I liked a number. Bright walls and bright cloths and bright glass everywhere. A fine Rowlandson drawing. Osbert is young. He is already a very good host. I enjoyed this evening. . . .

Though fish before soup was an unique aberration, sometimes Mrs. Powell's enthusiasm, no less than the inherent profusion so evident in all she did or said, carried with it consequences equally unusual, and always to herself unexpected.

[1] *The Journals of Arnold Bennett, 1911–21.* Edited by Newman Flower. (Cassell, 1932.)

[2] This is quite true, but may I modestly point out that the pictures and bric-à-brac were things I had bought? The furniture belonged to the owner of the house.

Thus when, for example, she purchased cranberries, in order to make a sauce to accompany a turkey, there might arrive— admittedly because calculation was not her strongest point, but also, no doubt, because this lavishness fitted in with her entire temperament—a whole scarlet mountain of these bitter berries. After the fashion of goats on the hills we would be obliged to feed on them for weeks on end, and even then many would ultimately have to be given away. But her esthetic perception seldom led her astray, she never bought any food that was not perfect in its own fashion, nor did she ever purchase an ugly object for use in the house. Once, however, it is true, I returned from abroad to find that in my absence she had made for me a cushion of black satin, and had embroidered upon it an ice-cream-pink rose, with a few leaves of an arsenical green, and had placed it in the drawing-room: but she quickly saw her mistake, and before I had been home two days, and though I had thanked her most gratefully for her present, and I believe had shown no signs of my real feelings, it was withdrawn. It just disappeared, and was never seen or mentioned again. But to pictures she brought an eye unafraid, observant, receptive, and unaffected by the current trends of respectability and condemnation. Almost the only time I saw traces of her having been annoyed was when a contemporary chat-spinner had contributed the following item to an evening journal: "The Sitwell brothers have achieved the impossible, and persuaded their cook to work in a kitchen hung with pictures of the modern school." I came in late the night that this had appeared, and found on the table a piece of paper addressed to myself. On it, scrawled in Mrs. Powell's straggling hand, was written:

SIR,
    Please tell the young gentleman who wrote about the kitchen that servants are individuals like other people, and not a separate race. I happen to like modern pictures.—Your obedient servant,
E. POWELL.

But she liked old masters too, and, shortly before her death, spent a holiday in Spain, with a friend, Mercedes, a niece of the Grand Penitentiary of Seville. She stayed for a happy day or two in Madrid, to see the El Grecos there, and at Toledo, and then moved to Seville for Holy Week. She appreciated and understood the people and the works of art and the dances and music, even Flamenco, and her power of enjoyment, her generosity, which a little resembled that of a Spanish woman, and the lovely amplitude of her flesh, won her many friends among the Spaniards. I like to think of her, in an embroidered shawl, and wearing a mantilla and high comb, sitting in the garden or the *patio*, full of orange blossom and of violets, so much finer and more scented at Seville than in any other region, taking the air, so delicately fragrant, full of light as a crystal, even in the shade, but when I write of her it is in London again that I see her, going out, finding a pleasure in the frosty morning (for frost seems to carry you back to the country and its life), having to be careful not to slip on the pavement, and so moving at a leisurely, stately pace, with the muff on her arm. At her side would accompany her my enormous tawny mastiff, Semiramis, lifting her paws and prancing with the joy of the morning, and having some of the same steadfast and beautiful attributes.

A most handsome muff, indeed, the bearskin had made, and its adaptation was less wasteful than the way in which I had disposed of the other portions of my uniform. But this casting of it upon the waters had been symbolic and necessary to me. By means of it, I vainly sought to be rid of my own past. Yet, though perhaps less diffident than formerly, I was still doubtful of my own capacities, dissatisfied with them as every young artist should be: (otherwise what causes would impel him towards new experiments?). In particular, therefore, I remember one long walk with Sacheverell by the lion-voiced waves of the Atlantic. Here, though the air was soft in spite of its strength, the ocean had the force of a winter's gale in Scarborough, thundering upon the rocks, beyond the dry, powdery sands into which the feet sank so that walking was difficult: but we went on and on, while Sacheverell rallied my spirits—for I was still ill, weak, and angry after the cruelty and folly of a long war, and distressed, too, by new and more grave difficulties with my father, many of them arising from my own fault, as well as harassed by the slowness with which I worked—and adumbrated a sketch of the future, telling me in what direction I should evolve, and what would be my standing in twenty-five years' time, if my writing developed as he hoped it would. Even then he already exercised the curious power—which, contrary to the usual process, has grown with the passing years—of being able to inspire other artists, whether older or younger than himself, with a new creative force. . . . But the diffidence I have mentioned was not, I believe, the attitude that I adopted in the world: it was a part, only, of my character, and not to be viewed by the public—least of all by that section which had read of, but had not read, my work. I possessed my share of vanity and conceit as well, a quick mind, a quick tongue—which often spoke before I was ready—and I hope a sharp pen. To many, therefore, who were led to adopt this view of me by angry critics, I seemed—for the great public of the newspapers has no sense of background or of category—an arrogant *arriviste*, who indulged in what could, at the most kindly, be considered as automatic writing; who had no sense of the past, no care for tradition or for the future. And in the course of the next ten years, many caricatures of me appeared, and showed me as an elderly dwarf, obviously of middle-eastern origin. This was of considerable help to me, for my unknown enemies were surprised and baffled when they saw me, large, fair and, I suppose, of a very English style.

In the space since the reader parted from me at the end of *Great Morning*, I had, by means of another of those transformations to which my biography has accustomed him, though still an officer in the Brigade of Guards—a Captain now—, become a writer; a poet, more precisely, for up to this point I had attempted nothing else but verse. (Indeed, it was only because a friend of mine, a respected contemporary novelist, stole my stories, and because I resented the manner in which he twisted and spoilt them, and because I felt I could write them better myself, that I took to prose.) It is difficult to assess how high or low I stood then in public estimation, for I have never been aware of it, any more than I have been class-conscious. Moreover, it is still more hard from this distance to appraise exactly the joint position at that time occupied by my brother, my sister and myself: but it is necessary to try and form some idea of the measure of them, in order to set the stage for this act, so that the eye of the reader can properly gauge the scale and perspective. I find it, however, no more easy to focus myself in the mirror of the past than I do now to recognise my likeness presented, and thus, as it were, guaranteed, by the numerous reflections in the looking-glasses that line a tailor's fitting-closet. There sometimes, left alone for a few minutes while the cutter goes to fetch more pins or find a new chalk, I try to turn myself into a stranger, examining intently my personal appearance, to see how I must look to others, and what could at first sight be deduced from my physiognomy, build and characteristics. But this effort to bisect myself, to split my consciousness in two, into looker and looked-at, induces after a few seconds the sensation that a great flood of time has passed by, accompanied by the same degree of physical nausea which afflicted me as a child when I tried to capture and define for myself the idea of eternity. And, moreover, how little knowledge is to be derived from it! Only, perhaps, the consciousness that the middle-aged stranger sitting opposite, facing you, must be related to your family, for his features and general air constitute a variation on a theme well known from earliest years. It is impossible to guess even his profession. In the past two decades I have been mistaken, several times in each of the capacities, for an actor—an actor by trade, I mean, and not for any particular star—and for a Russian Grand Duke. Thus, in instance of the first, I remember, when travelling up by train from Folkestone to London, a lady suddenly leant forward and earnestly asked, "Excuse me, but *oughtn't* I to *know* your face? . . . Are you on the boards?" As for the second, one incident was rather strange: I was sitting in a cubicle at Trumper's,[1] having my hair cut, when a stranger approached me, bowed, and began to talk very rapidly in Russian. When, having listened for a moment, I said, "I don't understand Russian, I'm afraid", he regarded me with a look of mingled anger and amusement, and after saying in broken English, "It may suit you at present, sir, to pretend that", bowed again and

[1] See *Great Morning*, pp. 200–5 of this edition.

walked away. Never once, I think, has my trade—in spite of a permanent stain of blue or purple ink on the left inner side of the middle finger of my right hand, surely an occupational symptom, if one were needed—been correctly divined. But then, as I have said, when even I regard my own image, I can see for myself how difficult must be the problem.

Similarly, it is hard to see oneself as one *was*, to see oneself from outside, looking back through the dust of a lifetime. Yet we must, my brother, sister and myself, although we were young, have been already well-known enough for people to turn round and look at us in the street. Indeed, it was hardly a year later, when I first met Ada Leverson, that she had looked up the entry devoted to my family in *Burke's Peerage*, and, upon reading at the end of it the technical description of the Sitwell coat of arms, "*Barry of eight, or and vert, three lions rampant . . . crest, a demi-lion rampant, erased . . .*", had been struck, she told me afterwards, by its prophetic nature, because, she averred, Edith, Sacheverell and myself were clearly the three lions rampant, and my father must be the demi-lion, erased. . . . And yet, if one is to conclude that we were already famous, one of the lions was a boy of only twenty-one at the time. Certainly he—Sacheverell—was the most precocious of us three, for the poems in his first book[1] were written when he was eighteen, and published when he was twenty. And *Southern Baroque Art*,[2] which revealed a whole new world in a new way, and is, in prose as in esthetic criticism, a work of the first order, appeared when he was twenty-five. Incidentally, it was written when he was twenty-two, and I may add, for the comfort of young writers, that I hawked about in person this magnificent and now celebrated book, and saw it refused by several eminent publishers, although when finally published it obtained an immediate and immense success, and set a whole generation chattering of the Baroque and the Rococo. My sister had already published two remarkable books of verse,[3] and a third volume in conjunction

[1] *The People's Palace.* (Blackwell, Oxford, 1918.)
[2] Grant Richards, 1924.
[3] *The Mother* (Blackwell, 1915), *Twentieth Century Harlequinade* (in conjunction with Osbert Sitwell. Blackwell, 1917) and *Clowns' Houses* (Blackwell).

with me. She was also editing an annual collection of modern verse, *Wheels*.[1] This yearly anthology, which ran for six years, attracted considerable attention from the critics. One notice, I recall, described the first series as "conceived in morbid eccentricity, and executed in fierce fictitious gloom"; a sentence I have always liked. The other day, I bought a copy of the first number of *Wheels* in a bookshop. It had been presented by Edith, Sacheverell and myself to Lady Colvin (see *Great Morning*, pp. 28-31), and contained a letter, undated, from her to an anonymous friend—just "Dearest" —to whom she had sent it. This letter throws some light on how we stood at the time. (S.P. is apparently a pet name for Sir Sidney Colvin.) "S.P. . . . says he knows nothing hardly of the Sitwells' work, and has a fine contempt for it as far as he does know. Of course they are relations of mine, by marriage. . . . She is a daughter of Sir George, the Bart., and the young school of poetry look upon her as their high priestess. . . . They are in Poetry what the Post-Impressionists and Cubists are in Painting—very hard to make head or tail of what they write—it is really to make the Bourgeoisie sit up, and with the Sitwells there is a vein of humour wanting to see how far they can gull the public. It is the latest and newest school, but nothing will come of it. S.P. can't stand it *at all*. I am posting you one of their '*Wheels*'. . . . They are quite nice and amusing young people if only they would not write poetry. We are so very sorry about the dear bird and do hope she is better."

As for myself, though, as will emerge, my father was determined to prevent it, as far as lay within his power, I was resolved to devote my future, my whole life, to writing: that was the urging of my left hand—and of my right: for the years stretching ahead now that the war was over seemed so infinite a time, albeit I always greatly worried in a neurasthenic way about my health—an unpleasant trait which in part I may have inherited—, that it seemed there would be time to accomplish everything one could wish. Besides, at that age, one felt oneself to possess enough energy to furnish the whole

[1] *Wheels*, 1916, Blackwell; 1917, Blackwell; 1918, Blackwell; 1919, Blackwell; 1920, Leonard Parsons; 1921, C. W. Daniel, Ltd.

of the seven careers that Arnold Bennett later declared were
mine. And so I allowed my left hand to encourage me to
attempt to effect a compromise with politics and with my
father: the claims of political careers in so many directions in
the past asserted themselves, and gave me enthusiasm: while,
in addition, the brutality and stupidity of a long war, and the
muzzle that, during its course, it always clamps on the mouth,
had left me and many of my contemporaries as eager now to
speak our minds as those older than ourselves were determined
not to heed us. In consequence, I fought an election at
Scarborough, where my father had contested seven elections
in the Conservative interest: but I stood in the service of the
most unpopular of political faiths at that time—and ever since:
as a Liberal, of the old kind, and without being furnished with
the approval of Mr. Lloyd George. At first I had obtained
the promise of Labour support, but later a strong Labour
candidate of local origin—a member of the influential Quaker
clan, the Rowntrees—came out against me. H. W. Massingham, with his usual courageous directness, urged him in a
telegram—through Rowntree was a member of the family
that owned the *Nation*—to stand down: for Rowntree was
then a man of about seventy, I suppose; I was twenty-five, and
Massingham considered that younger men were needed in
Parliament, and had a belief in my ability. Indeed, in his
telegram, he went so far as to say that he would regard my
return for the constituency as a guarantee of peace. The
Conservative candidate was Sir Gervase Beckett, the sitting
member for the division, and brother to my godfather.[1] The
old borough of Scarborough had now been merged in an
electoral district which included Whitby, Pickering and the
country between.

The Orderly Room, instructed by the War Office, allowed
me three weeks' leave in which to conduct my campaign: (but
it was difficult to avoid a feeling that Liberals were not popular
in high regimental circles; were, indeed, classed with dangerous revolutionaries). Accordingly, I went to live at Wood End,
taking with me Richmond Temple, a dynamic and resourceful
friend of most modern outlook who had just left the Air

[1] See *The Scarlet Tree*, p. 59n. of this edition.

Force, and who was capable of acting with great speed and decision, as well as being by nature endowed with the gift of infusing energy into those round him. Immensely I enjoyed being brought into personal contact with the remarkable variety of types to be met with in this area: solicitors and trawler-owners, Wesleyans and Methodists, Quakers and Catholics, tradesmen and fishermen, dry schoolmasters and sly insurance-agents. Some of the farmers, living in isolated communities on the moors, spoke so broad a tongue that only occasionally one recognised a word such as "bloody" (pronounced "bludy") and clung to it as a raft of sense in an unchartable sea of sounds. The ancient houses of Robin Hood's Bay, again, were manned by whole crews of sea-captains, retired. These old men, at the time, owing to the war-boom in shipping, each worth some twenty to fifty thousand pounds, were bulky, bearded, and still spent the day up ladders, which they dwarfed, painting their own houses and making them shipshape. In Scarborough, in the old town, there were the colonies of fishermen and their wives whom I already knew, and on the South Cliff a memorable population of curates. The life that opened for me, though it lasted in this intense form only for so few weeks, forced me to be adaptable; to be at home at high-tea with members of the Low Church and the Sects, at supper with the fishermen, or when reading a play by Bernard Shaw in the inappropriate setting of a circle organised in a drawing-room by a curate (I have always remembered the little cough he gave, when, while he was reading, he came suddenly in one scene upon the word "*damn*!" and substituted for it, in such a jolly voice, the more innocuous "*drat*!"). Accompanying me everywhere, on all occasions, was my mastiff, a huge animal, like a lioness of palest gold, and I have always thought that her appearance, steadfastness and devotion on the platform won me more votes than any speeches that were delivered: for if the English love—or loved—a lord, how much more do they love a dog! The meetings varied in interest; but there would always be present, at the back of the hall, wherever it might be, a thin old gentleman with a bald head, secured by a few thick strands of hair as though it were a runaway football or a melon caught in a fine net. Directly I had finished speaking, he would rise to ask whether I agreed with him in his view that the Pope had been solely and in person responsible for the outbreak of war in 1914, and of the Bolshevik Revolution in 1917. Then, also, there would be sitting in the third or fourth row a lady with white hair, and an expression of sickening kindness, who thought it was cruel to clip or cut trees, and wanted me to promise, if I were returned, to protest to the French Government concerning the gardens, with their pleached alleys, at Versailles, and the pollarded avenues that enclose many French roads. And at every meeting, wherever it might be, I was asked to make sure that the Kaiser was hanged.

During the progress of the campaign, indeed after only the first two days of it had gone, my father decided to come over from Renishaw and stay at Wood End, so as to give me the benefit of his experience and advice. It was the same with everything. If he saw a poem of mine, he would rewrite it, or, if he had found out that I was working on one, he would rush in to "help" me, always saying in explanation and in the most affable manner possible, "Two brains, dear boy, are better than one!" As for the election, if only I would listen to him! It was quite simple to get in, he said (though himself had been rejected five times out of seven), if only one knew the *right way* to set about it! When I was preparing a speech, he came continually spinning into my room like a tornado with a few new hints. Last time, he said, I had made a mistake, to his mind, a great mistake! I had been quite wrong to talk about what I believed in. Never on any account mention the War or the League of Nations. People weren't interested. The voters did *not want* to be troubled with problems: they liked facts. Give them tables of interesting figures, and a little comparison between costs of living in the reign of Edward III—or Edward the Confessor, only that might be rather too early for them; as a rule he'd found they weren't very much "up" in anything before the Conquest—and those of today. (He had been studying the matter, and it was most interesting: Wilhelmus de Killamarshe had paid a farthing for 2 sheep in 1386.) A few more figures after that, and then, just as they weren't expecting it, swing sonorously into a peroration, culminating in a passage, if possible, from Byron. For instance, that quatrain from his "Ode to Napoleon Bonaparte." It would apply to the Kaiser, and the audience would love it.

> 'Tis done—but yesterday a King!
> And arm'd with Kings to strive—
> And now thou art a nameless thing:
> So abject—yet alive!

Nobody, I could be sure, would vote for a candidate whose speech did not end with a quotation, and the longer the better. He was afraid the one he had given me was a bit short. Horace, however, was out of date. . . . My father would, too, waylay supporters, or possible supporters, and point out where I went wrong, and, worse, would instruct the agent in his business, and the Committee and Chairman in their duties. In short, it soon became impossible to get anything done at all while he was in the house. . . . My mother swept to my rescue. "Leave it to me, darling!" she said lightly, "I'll see to it." She watched the situation closely and when, about ten days before the election, he discovered—as he was often wont to do—a new pain, this time in his back, just at the waist, she allowed it to be seen that, although as a rule she declined to take his illnesses seriously, she regarded this as of the utmost gravity. She advised him to go to bed at once. He allowed himself without much difficulty to be persuaded, for he was frightened by her alarmed expression, and as soon as he was safely ensconced, she sent the footman out to buy a strong mustard plaster, and had it applied to the place. The plaster naturally produced a feeling of heat and a discoloration of the skin. My mother came in, just after, looked at it, and asked:

"Does it burn, George?"

When he admitted that it did, she said:

"Then it can only be shingles! It's a dangerous complaint. You ought to be very careful."

She told him, further, that it was very lucky for him that she had found it out and that it was better not to call in doctors, for they never understood that kind of thing; the only cure was prolonged rest and to keep warm, and never leave his room. It would be madness to get up. He seemed much flattered at her concern, and followed her advice. Thus though there was absolutely nothing the matter with him, he was kept in bed until the very day of the election, when she hired a bath-chair for him and sent him to the booth to vote for me. He had by now really begun to look pale and worn, and his air of pathos, together with his vehicle, and his obvious bravery in coming out, straight from his bed, to record a vote for his son, made a most favourable impression and must have gained many waverers to my cause. . . . However, I did not win. When the result of the poll was declared, Sir Gervase Beckett had obtained some twelve thousand votes to my eight thousand, while the Labour Candidate had won a few hundred and had forfeited his deposit.[1]

I nursed the constituency for two or three years afterwards. At first, I had not wanted to do so, because I longed to devote myself entirely to my proper work. Realising in what direction my inclinations lay, my father at once wrote to me in an opposite sense. (Never be good at *one* thing. Learn to make up your weak points.) On 17th July, 1919, he sent me a letter which included the sentence, "Whether you do or do not intend to take up political life, you should fight the next election". Four days later, he was writing more emphatically:

I think you ought to make good your position as a poet, and am all for your having leisure to bring out a volume. But I don't think your life should be sacrificed in this. You have mentioned to me[2] that an ordinary balance sheet is Greek to you, and it is obvious that at present you have no capacity for dealing with business matters. You would do well to try and fit yourself for that and for public-life.

On 5th September he repeated some of the various pieces of advice he had given me at the election. "As to politics, remember that at the moment people are not interested in them, and (if you are) avoid speaking on directly political subjects. Give them good facts. . . . Be careful of your

[1] The figures were:

Sir Gervase Beckett, C.U.	11,764
Capt. Osbert Sitwell, L.	7,994
Mr. J. W. Rowntree, Lab.	1,025

[2] I had never done so.

humour, which is dangerous." (The old, old trouble.[1])
When, however, it became clear that, fortune favouring me, I
might win the seat for the Liberals at the next election, he at
once became gravely concerned, and advised me to give up
politics and turn to farming. I had grown to like the life I
had been obliged to lead, and to love the district, and I re-
linquished my candidature with a sore heart, forced thereto by
an attack of poverty from which my father suddenly perceived
himself to be suffering. I had made one discovery, however,
which helped to ease the wrench: that though it might have
been possible for me to win the friendship and confidence
of the electors, and though they possessed their full share of
northern idealism, yet nobody else in the neighbourhood or
elsewhere was in the least curious about the particular new
world that I wanted to help build, and had thought to be a chief
and abiding interest for English people. In general, the voters
contented themselves with repeating either that no new war
would come, or else that the inclination to war was so firmly
planted in human nature that it would be wrong to try to up-
root it: though they were eager, too, that each child should
have a better start in life than his father, and thus, through
education, be able more easily to assimilate the moral and
ethical truths contained in those Sunday papers they
patronised. ("At his age, I couldn't read the News of the
World!" a father remarked proudly to me, as he pointed at
his son of thirteen.) For the rest, the Germans must pay; the
Kaiser must be hanged, and we mustn't be soft with the
French, or truckle to the Americans either. Get rid of the
Junkers, and you would lay the road open for real democrats,
people uneducated, and therefore qualified to govern—house-
painters, for example! Only those who were of my generation
understood the nature of the recent war, or what it meant. It
took me a full lustrum to recover from the state of spiritual
and mental fury, misery and despair into which experience
of the war in France and observation of the civilians in England
had thrown me. I was still thinking about the last war—and
the next, which would come inevitably within a generation
unless men made a real effort for earth-wide peace—, at a

[1] See *Left Hand, Right Hand!* pp. 168–9 of this edition.

time when most people had entirely forgotten it, except for a compulsory two minutes on recurrent November days.

As I had walked home to Swan Walk, however, on that night of 11th November 1918, though my life, as I then saw it, was to be divided between the creation of beauty and the giving shape to ideas, and an effort to improve conditions of life for the workers and to prevent the recurrence of slaughter which, though it temporarily raised the wages of the fathers, massacred half their sons, it was, nevertheless, and though the election was so imminent, not politics that occupied my mind, but writing; how one was to crystallise, refine, condense to the ultimate point, and yet retain nimbleness, wit, above all, energy. It was impossible, it seemed to me: for very often I doubted with a haunting, mingled rage and despair: though it never occurred to me, oddly, to doubt my political abilities. (That was my left hand, giving support, I presume, and dispelling incertitudes.) . . . Now I must trace my steps back further than the opening of this chapter, and try to explain the course of my personal life, the things that had happened to me and those round me—or, if not explain, at least record them: what had happened, and why, quite apart from the impact of the war, in itself violent as an earthquake, the world to which I was now returning as a civilian was so greatly altered; why the people reassembled round me, by the force of my left hand, were, though in some respects so much intensified in their character as previously outlined, in others so greatly changed; why those I collected about me, by the force of my right hand, were so different in kind, and how, too, in the space of four brief years, during which—quite apart again from family disasters that rent the fabric of private life, as the war of public—I had been obliged to surrender so much time to duties distasteful to me, the claims of my right hand had asserted themselves, and I had been able to substitute new friends, chosen by myself, for many inherited and tedious associations.

CHAPTER TWO

The Word

IN *Great Morning* I took leave of the reader at the palmist's, in November 1914. . . . Even when my father and I were on the worst of terms, he would favour me with his views on the war in talk or by letter. Though, if it were in conversation, the discourse must not be allowed to go on for too long, since he possessed in the highest degree the art of squeezing the life out of an hour and of making it drag its weary length along, nevertheless a short ten minutes on a subject impersonal, and not entirely confined to the errors of his children, was always a delight. The nonconformity of the opinions he aired was exhilarating, albeit, of course, he was so far carried away by the consciousness of frustration and futility that must haunt all individuals, as opposed to units, caught in an age of democratic wars, that often plainly he trespassed across the borders of common sense in an opposite direction. Moreover, he was a little prejudiced, by his love of German medieval art, and because the Kaiser, on account of his family pride, his similar interests, and perhaps because, too, he claimed to be an authority on nearly every subject, had always been a hero to him. Indeed, the two men bore some resemblance to each other, physically as well as in mind (they had been born on the same day of the same month, though a year divided them in age, the Kaiser having been born on the 27th of January 1859, my father on the 27th of January 1860), and as they grew older and adopted beards, this likeness emphasised itself: but I do not know if my father was aware of it. . . . Ever since the war broke out, then, he had pursued his own line about its origin and conduct, and had remained firm in his attitude until the end, often becoming the dupe, as he was wont to do, of his own propaganda: (a habit which finally made him liable to the propaganda of others, too; so that after the war he changed, and adopted a new bellicose, contemporary-newspaper attitude towards Germany). Thus, as early as the day after war was declared, he wrote, from Renishaw, to me in London:

I don't blame the Germans. I think the Czar's want of judgment has brought this upon Europe—unless, indeed, it was Russian state-craft to force Germany into war. . . . I fancy the Kaiser spoke truly when he said the sword was being forced into his hand. . . . However, this reading of the situation will be very unpopular at the present moment.

And, as late as 8th August 1918, before the sudden swelling of the Allied fortunes, he was writing:

. . . We are told we are fighting for the triumph of democracy, which has so managed the affair that we could hardly expect to get at this moment the *status quo ante* terms we could have obtained after the first battle of the Marne. But what we have really been fighting for, of course, during these last three years is the triumph of Bolshevik principles in England—bound to come if war continues much longer. Everyone of sound military judgment knew at the beginning of the war that we could not hope to break completely the military strength of Germany: we could, however, without ruining civilisation, as we have already done, have made Germany accept peace without spoils, which would have meant popular reforms in Germany, and have kept Russia alive as a counterpoise. Now we have got to the gambler's last stake, and must go on for a time on the chance that Germany may go Bolshevik first.

"Everyone of sound military judgement" meant, of course, himself, the former Adjutant of the Volunteer Regiment he had commanded, and the omniscient Major Viburne, who had been staying at Renishaw, the reader will remember, when the war broke out. At any rate, from the first moment my father had begun resolutely, and almost with unction, to prepare for the worst. He threw his gothic imagination into this, as formerly into the more decorative aspects of life, with real abandon: but his frame of mind varied. In some moods he would make notes on the various projects he had not yet had time to undertake—life, he noticed, was beginning to sweep him past at a great pace, though I doubt if he or any victim really could estimate fully the speed of his transit—and meant, directly the war was over, to embark upon: in other moods he would allow his forebodings equally full play. Personal, no less than national, ruin loomed: (that was true, but he did not comprehend the kind or direction). By the 10th of August 1914, not a week after war had broken out, he had already made certain plans for preserving his family and belongings; he wrote from Renishaw:

If the Germans come over, I think of sending your mother and Sachie to the Peak, and shall stay to dismantle Renishaw of tapestry, pictures and china. . . . If the Germans don't come over, we may let Wood End for several months, and go into lodgings at Scarborough.

The pattern, however, did not work out quite as he designed it. And the family—that is to say my father and mother, for family and household were both much dispersed—settled itself once more at Wood End in November 1914. Edith had now established herself in a small top-floor flat in Bayswater (in spite of its size, for many years it became a centre in London for painters, musicians, writers, and especially for young poets), Sacheverell was at Eton. Henry Moat had, the reader may recollect, left my father's service in April 1913, this constituting the longest of his absences. On leaving he had applied at the agencies for a job, stating, as one of his qualifications, that he spoke "five languages including Yorkshire". Eventually he had found a very well-paid situation, which he thought would suit him, as butler to a rich, retired fur-merchant in Hampstead. His employer, however, proved to have a temper of the most violent oriental kind, and in reply to furious verbal assaults, sprinkled with inopportune foreign turns of phrase, but all accusing him of breaches of the decorum of major-domodom, Henry would remain calm, and then with his immense butler's dignity, which he could assume like a robe of office, would observe:

"You must remember, sir, I'm accustomed to the gentry!"

He did not, in truth, ever grow used to the ways of the house, and in consequence, as soon as the war broke out, had joined the Army Service Corps. Poor Robins,[1] who had replaced him, had been recalled to his regiment early in August, and had gone abroad with the First Expeditionary Force. At the moment he was in France, under peculiar circumstances:

[1] See *Great Morning*, pp. 131-2 *et sqq.* of this edition.

for, having evaded capture for a month, he was living behind the German lines, with the other survivors of the same troop. Eventually, early in December, they were obliged to give themselves up, in order not to compromise those persons who had provided them with food and shelter, chief of whom was the heroic Princess de Croy. Next they were taken to Germany, court-martialled, and the majority of them, including Robins, were sentenced to be shot. It was only at the very last moment, when they were lined up for execution in the yard, that a reprieve came, suddenly and without reason.

In the house, then, Pare alone remained, of all my former friends; Pare to whom day and night were the same and brought nothing but work and sadness. He still was not allowed to visit his mad wife, whose condition had seemed to worsen every year. The servants who had replaced those who had left were foreign: a Swiss footman, a French maid. But Scarborough itself, the town and the people, were unchanged in most respects, though the town was full, and busy with a military activity new to it. I had a good many letters from my mother and father, Miss Lloyd and Major Viburne, and could, as a result, piece together what was happening there. Miss Lloyd, now growing into a very old lady, had taken upon herself—as might have been expected—innumerable labours on behalf of the local young men who had volunteered for service. In addition to these tasks occupying most of the day—cooking, knitting, sending parcels—, she had fallen a little under the spell of the then epidemic spy-mania, which always intoxicates and renders its victims happy by allowing them to exaggerate their own importance in the contemporary scene. And this, in turn, threw upon her more work, for it necessitated her remaining, for at least half an hour at a time, in the bow-window of her drawing-room, with the brass and shagreen telescope she had inherited from her uncle (to me, though never seen, a figure familiar from my earliest infancy, and legendary in scale albeit slightly misty; "Oncle," she said, a character who had been a friend of Charles Dickens, and a sea-captain, though sometimes, in the heat and excitement of conversation, which with her acted on a subject like a magnifying glass, raised to the dignity of owning a yacht)—with her telescope, then, clapped to her eye, searching the wide sea-scape for the periscopes of German submarines, and the convergence of streets below her house for disguised "Huns". And she would, indeed, make amazing discoveries, since half-coconuts and bits of fat were still suspended in the window-box for hungry beaks to peck at, and in consequence she would sometimes, with the aid of the lens, misinterpret the distance of the scurry of wings immediately below, and read instead of it a distant naval engagement, which would leave her in a temporary vain agony of disquiet. . . . What could they be? a new form of boat, of aircraft, perhaps; real devils, those Huns! But no, it was only the dear little blue-tits again! Nor did her duties terminate with the day, for often at two or three in the morning she would creep to the window to look for Germans (and one never knew now who were or were not Germans) signalling out to sea, giving their chiefs news of the latest Rectory Sale of Work or Scout Jamboree. (They were so methodical and devoted to detail that nothing, she held, was too trivial for them to notice.)

To Major Viburne, too, now well over eighty years of age, the war had brought new interests, new life. While it was true that he had, together with all the other old gentlemen in clubs, long foreseen the struggle coming, it was equally not to be denied that his own military experience had been limited. Long ago, I had been present in the pantry at Renishaw when a footman who had been startled during dinner by Major Viburne's tales of his own martial prowess had asked Henry:

"Excuse me, Mr. Moat, sir, but in what war did the Major see service?"

Henry had replied, to the young man's complete satisfaction:

"My lad, the old boy served right through the Canteen Campaign, from start to finish!"

And so it was that now ancient memories stirred in him, memories of other wars—of which he had read in other newspapers. It can be imagined how frequent and how free were the advice and exhortations he lavished upon the somnolent forms of fellow-elders in the Gentlemen's Club; sometimes, again, one of them would rouse himself and similarly address the Major, when he, too, was asleep in his armchair, dreaming of the days when he had been Captain Commandant of Scarborough Castle. When awake, or not talking, he was reading *Caesar's Commentaries* again, which somehow made the present war seem so much more vivid.

My mother's troubles appeared at this moment to have taken a turn for the better, even to have dispersed. First of all my cousin, Irene Denison, had on her own initiative and without the advice of her parents or mine made a most gallant effort, at a sacrifice of part of her own fortune, to save my mother before it should prove too late. Next, in November my mother went up to London for a few days, for a lawsuit that Messrs Lewis & Lewis were conducting on her behalf against Julian Field.[1] She won it, was triumphantly vindicated and the action exposed his dealings. Yet she was still unhappy and agitated—though perhaps agitated is not the correct word, for in the daytime she averted her mind from her troubles, which returned to haunt her only at night.

My father was immersed in his usual interests, and on 8th December wrote to me from Scarborough:

I don't think I told you I am turning the Ladies Room at the Renishaw Park Golf Club into a locker-room. It will be so much better for them to have as a sitting-room the cottage beyond—which will open into the passage. This will make a splendid room, two storeys of windows, a coved plaster roof and a south aspect. I think I shall put up in it the 16th century Italian marble chimney-piece, as it may as well be there till it is wanted elsewhere, as lying about. . . .
I have been busy getting copies of wills for the family history. Mary Revell, who was a Sitwell, in 1670, John Milward, who was Francis Sitwell's brother-in-law, in 1679, Hercules Clay, who was Ann Sitwell's grandfather, in 1685; and Mrs. Kent, who was her stepmother, in 1687. . . . Mrs. Revell had a table-carpet in her bedroom, but no floor-carpet. John Milward leaves his hawks and spaniels to one friend, except his setter-dog, Lusty, whom he leaves to another. . . .
I have been working, too, at old costume. The modern coat was only invented about 1670–5: before that it was doublet, waistcoat and breeches. In this way, I think I have been able to date the picture of old Derby. . . .

So things were going, until the morning of my last day in England before I left for the Front—the same morning that

---

[1] See *Great Morning*, pp. 160–5 *et sqq.* of this edition.

Germans came over the North Sea and chose to bombard Scarborough!

The noise of the great naval guns thumping and crashing through the mist, which magnified the sound, was enormous. It was about 8.15 A.M., my father was just dressing, and lost no time in finishing the process and getting downstairs. A piece of shell went through the front door, pierced a wooden pillar (part of the elaborate Edwardian decoration he had installed) and then buried itself in the smaller hall, while many fragments penetrated into the house. The Swiss footman went upstairs and watched the attack from the roof. My mother, who was in bed when the bombardment took place, refused to move: but half an hour later, after it had just stopped, she rose, dressed, and, in order to see me before I left England the next morning, caught a train, unusually crowded, to London. Her maid supervised the luggage, but my mother personally took charge of a rather heavy piece of shell, which she was anxious to give me as a mascot. She entered my sister's flat, where I was having tea, and pressed her offering into my hands, saying:

"Here you are, darling! I've brought it with me specially, for you to take to France. I'm sure it'll bring you luck!"

My father had taken refuge, with the rest of the household, except my mother and the footman, in the cellar; though, as will appear in a moment, he had found a more dignified name for it. In those days he still possessed no motor, and so when, as soon as the German ships had sheered back into the grey vapour that separated our two countries, he emerged into daylight again—but cautiously, since he feared that the retreat might be a ruse; the object of a new raid, if it occurred, being in his opinion the determination of the enemy fleet to secure himself as a hostage—, he sent immediately for his medical attendant of many years' standing. When the doctor entered the room, my father said to him, without preface:

"Dr. Mallard, if the Germans come back, I shall need your motor to drive me to York."

"But what will happen if Mrs. Mallard wants it, Sir George?" the poor man asked despairingly.

"I'm afraid I really can't help that!" my father snapped

at him, and allowed a look to show plainly his disgust at other people's selfishness.

Meanwhile his power of fantasy had set itself to work on another plan for the moment when the emergency he foresaw should arise: an alternative of which he often told me in later years in example of the heroic lengths to which he would have gone and could go. . . . A little way beneath the western, tall, brown-brick wall of our garden, in the depths of the Valley, as it was called, a wooded public pleasance, with a road running through it, lay a small but rather elongated shallow pool, carrying in its centre a diminutive island where elegiac trees drooped over the water. In the middle of this rose a rustic thatched hut of the 'sixties, fashioned of wood that still retained in places its bark as a shelter for earwigs, while the outside—and inside—of the cabin was much discoloured by bird-droppings: for it was the home and haunt of many water birds. Hither my father proposed to wade or swim, or, who knows, perhaps proceed by some private method of funambulation, should he be surprised in Scarborough by the returning Germans and unable to make a get-away in Dr. Mallard's motor. In this idyllic retreat, he had determined to hide during the Captivity, residing there, a Wild Man of the Weeping Willows, living among—and I suppose upon —the ducks and other decorative fowl to which in more peaceful times it was abandoned.

"I should have been quite happy, too," he would comment at the end of a disclosure of his plans in after years, "with a few books down from time to time from the London Library." And then he would add the familiar reproof, "*I* never *allow* myself to feel bored!"

Of this Red Indian's dream of his, he did not inform me at once by letter. (It might be dangerous to me as well; the Germans were sure to steam open his letters, and by that means would find out that I had gone abroad): but he told Sacheverell of it during the Christmas holidays. Nor did he allow his fears to prevent him from writing to me of other things: for when I reported to the Adjutant in the front-line trenches, only two days after the bombardment of Scarborough, I was at once handed a letter from my father! I read it later, by myself, and was startled out of the dull melancholy that had settled on me when I arrived—at the first sight of the flying fountains of dead earth, the broken trees and mud, and at the first sounds, growing ever more ominous as one drew nearer to the bumping and metallic roaring which resembled a clash of comets—by the sheer fun of its contents.

Wood End, Scarborough
16th December 1914.

My dearest Osbert,

As I fear a line sent to Chelsea Barracks may not reach you before you leave tomorrow, I write to you, care of your regiment, B.E.F. so that you may find a letter from me waiting for you when you arrive in the trenches. But I had wanted if possible to give you a word of advice before you left. Though you will not, of course, have to encounter anywhere abroad the same weight of gunfire that your mother and I had to face here—it has been my contention for many years that there were no guns in the world to compare for weight and range with the great German naval guns, and that our own do not come anywhere near them—yet my experience may be useful to you. Directly you hear the first shell, retire, as I did, to the Undercroft, and remain there quietly until all firing has ceased. Even then, a bombardment, especially as one grows older, is a strain upon the nervous system—but the best remedy for that, as always, is to keep warm and have plenty of plain, nourishing food at frequent but regular intervals. And, of course, plenty of rest. I find a nap in the afternoon most helpful, if not unduly prolonged, and I advise you to try it whenever possible.

—Ever your loving father, George R. Sitwell.

Undercroft was a word new to me, and it was some time before I discovered with what trisyllabic majesty the simple word cellar had clothed itself.

So bored was I with life in France and Flanders and, as I have before had reason to stress, so incompetent in many ways as an officer, that I seldom or never knew where I was, in relation, not to the precise locality, but to the whole map. One or two places, like Ypres, possessed their own fame and history whether in war or peace; the rest was "the Front", a monochromatic geographical entity of its own, floating, cloudlike, across a continent. I felt utterly lost in a world in which all my old friends, with whom I associated regimental life, were dead, and already remembered here by but few:

while my new friends, of a few months' standing, had not yet been passed out from Chelsea Barracks. The very excess of bleak boredom and grey discomfort—albeit that seems an inadequate description for so entire and black a universe of physical sensation, of wet and cold and stench and mud— afforded me a sort of careless courage. Yet it was ever with dismay that I would hear, as alas I often did, a brother-officer remark, no doubt with a kindred sentiment in his heart,

"The Boches won't get me now! I've been out here too long!"

Whether with them it was that many dangers survived had induced a feeling of false security, I do not know, or what the chief cause responsible for it may have been, yet always I noticed that the man who said it would be dead within the space of a few days, or more often of hours. . . . The chance, when one reasoned, of continued existence in this world after the war, seemed as remote as that of life after death to an unbeliever. (My father, however, wrote to me on this matter, and treated it on a basis of computation or assessment. It would be a serious matter, losing an elder son, even if he were not altogether the success he ought to be; and so, it appeared, he had been making enquiries. "*According to the Insurance Companies it is eleven to one against an officer being killed in a* YEAR'S *fighting with the Germans, so I hope we may get you back safe and sound.*"

Even in the depths of spirit, however, to which the monotony of the life reduced me, I did not hate the routine here as I had hated it in my private school. At least Bloodsworth had done that for me. I had known worse. At least there were no masters, matrons, or compulsory games. The discomfort was, at times, perhaps a little greater, the food, though tinned, perhaps a little more palatable. (Indeed, as the reader knows, I have been inclined to wonder whether the education of myself and my contemporaries at private and public schools had not been conducted with the idea in view of affording us the ability to make this comparison. . . . Through the long course of Samurai-like discipline to which they were, with few exceptions, obliged to submit in their most impressionable years, the children of the former British governing classes had

been taught to bear with composure a high degree of physical
hardship and spiritual misery, while enclosed in an atmosphere
of utmost frustration: might not this apparent abandoning of
children by their parents have been deliberate, in order to
prepare them to cut their way out of the catastrophic booby-
traps which at that very time the politicians were so steadily,
and with such elaboration, getting ready for us? But if this
were so—and certainly the young of this class could bear
bodily suffering and exhaustion, and a sense of the cruellest
isolation, with a stoical equanimity unknown among those
who came from good working-class homes and had been
brought up, right from their earliest years to manhood, in an
unaltering atmosphere of domestic affection—, would it not
have been wiser to have elucidated the position for us at the
time?) No, the Front was certainly preferable to "the happiest time of one's life". Though my friends were dead, and
the sadness of this lay over me—albeit the abruptness of it
still rendered it difficult to grasp—, yet, since I was young,
new relationships established themselves. And in the Regiment, I found that the old tolerance, which had always so
greatly surprised me, still flourished oddly in this harsh soil.
I must again emphasise—for it cannot be exaggerated—the
degree to which, voluntarily and involuntarily, I continually
showed myself to be of an unmilitary and even anti-militarist
disposition. Not only, as I have said, did I hardly know *where*,
precisely, I was, but so deeply bored was I at this period that,
although in some directions my memory is very retentive, an
inner censor—perhaps the same who censors nightmares after
waking—stepped in to delete certain facts from the record.
Thus I am now quite unable to recall with what battalions I
saw service in France and Flanders, though I can still, on the
other hand, quite well recall with what battalions I served
in England a year or two earlier. Again, at moments driven
desperate by the placid acceptances of conventional minds,
I quite often said, in my own way, what I thought. I remember, for example, one very wet day, when out for a route-
march during a week's break from the routine of trenches
and billets in farms, covering my uniform with copies of *The
Times*. These were soon turned by the weather into a very

sodden, dirty grey mess, and in consequence I arrived at the end of the day looking very disreputable. When the Commanding Officer enquired what it meant, I replied,

"You seem to forget, sir, that it's very wet and I've had a long walk."

This unmilitary reply would have infuriated many commanders, less sure of themselves and of the discipline of their officers and men: here it raised no flicker of rage. So that, in the sense of companionship, I was happy enough, and it was only when—this occurred once or twice the following year—all the officers of the Battalion or Battalions were gathered together for a dinner that I found myself ill at ease, disliking then, as now, and as always, the manner in which the coalescent group-soul released from a herd manifests itself. . . . At some of these occasions, I would see the very young, slight figure of the Prince of Wales, then an officer in the Grenadiers, with his extreme charm, his melancholy smile and angry eyes, trying like myself, I suspect, to pretend he was enjoying himself.

For the rest, in the trenches one day was sad, cold and hopeless as the next. Sleep was the greatest prop and happiness known to any of us, I believe. To me assuredly, whether dreamless or the reverse, it was, during this period, peculiarly happy. (Perhaps the sleep of condemned but innocent political prisoners, for example, resembles it in this respect.) Though often in ordinary life of a melancholy or terrifying nature, my dreams were now peaceful and even radiant in feeling, imbued with the happiest imagining, and this certainly affords an inner psychical strength. Sometimes I have thought my subconscious mind to be lazy in the background it presents. Seldom, indeed, does it carry me to interesting places, such as when once it transported me for the night to the immense halls and galleries of the palace of King Nebuchadnezzar, and allowed me to look at the flat domes and colonnades, and towers stepped like Aztec pyramids, to examine at my leisure the detail of the great bas-reliefs in porphyry and basalt which adorned its walls, so sheer and lofty, and to watch the procession of men with blue-black beards, hook noses, and yellow skins hurrying through corridors to attend their royal but graminivorous master. For that hour's entertainment, a whole system of architecture had been improvised, a lost civilisation revived. But this was very rare: as a rule I am rationed in this other life, and usually am merely given distorted variations of the scenes most familiar to me, three in number like the crows-foot alleys in perspective of the Renaissance and seventeenth-century stage: Renishaw awry in a vast, flawless summer day or night, with its enormous rooms in the wrong order, or on occasion a new wing, suddenly revealed to me by my father—something he had been keeping secret—, but always beautiful, though with an atmosphere of curious suspense; or the rolling winter seas of Scarborough, dashing gigantic wings to batter falling cliffs, under the pounce and glitter of bitter-beaked sea-gulls materialising out of a misty nothingness of white foam and yellow sky, while a voice cries slyly in the hollows under the lull, "*Rags and Bones! Rags and Bones!*"; or London, with a prim brown-brick street, very neat and orderly, with its shops and railings. . . . But now, in the trenches, I was granted compensatory dreams, being allowed in them to see the people I wanted to see, and with whom I wanted—or thought I wanted—to spend my life. The background was of no importance: and though one of the chief deprivations I felt in these years was my enforced absence from Renishaw—which I hardly saw during the years of war, never in the summer, and only for more than a day or two when ill or at a moment of very severe personal distress—I seldom dreamt of it, or of Italy, which again would have saddened me when I awoke by the comparison the present would have offered with the past. The dreams of which I tell left, on the contrary, no after-taste. They were, as I have said, concerned with people more than places, and the degree of psychological observation latent, I suppose, in every novelist, whether practising or still in chrysalis, gave a peculiar sharpness to their doings and sayings: they behaved in this sharp, swift world reflected from their own behaviour, in a fashion that was more essentially typical of themselves than themselves were in everyday life! . . . Or, very often, sleep was dreamless, came on with the force and suddenness of a knock-out, and in one instance, after a particularly long and trying period in the trenches, though by nature a reluctant and nervous sleeper, I slumbered for eighteen hours, only waking at six in the evening.

Next to sleep, but certainly inferior to it as a pleasure, came reading. . . . As a pessimist, and in an effort to make this existence seem more tolerable, in general I avoided works of a cheerful tendency, and once more abandoned myself to the genius of Dostoievsky. To have been Raskolnikov or Mitya Karamazov would constitute a worse destiny than to lead this life until you were killed—lead this life, so dull in spite of its risk, and with the prospect of the humiliation and sadness that threatened us at home continually under the mind. (It was only, as I have told in *Great Morning*, a few days before I left for the Front that my father had written to tell me that the crop of lawsuits, claims and counterclaims, arising out of my mother's financial entanglements as the result of Field's machinations, was beginning all over again, and now with a yet more sombre tinge to it.) In this way, heroic tragedy proved a comfort. When after reading *The Brothers Karamazov*, *Crime and Punishment* and *The Idiot*, *King Lear* or *Othello*, I needed a change of feeling, I turned to the novels of Dickens again: for they were connected with the life of a great city, and I felt a craving for metropolitan interests. For so long as I read, the white winter vapours of Flanders and of France—mists so dull and lifeless, except to our eyes when we were on duty, for then every shape stirred stealthily, and the whole static world assumed movement at a sound—were exchanged for the glorious golden fogs (or such they now seemed to me) of my native city, and I exulted accordingly in the creative force of this great novelist, so dear to me and so familiar from boyhood. With what certainty he would have comprehended and rendered a night of duty: rats and mud, and the particular horror they hold for human beings, he already understood (think of the opening of *Our Mutual Friend* on the waters of the Pool of London!), and he would at once have captured the feeling of these coffin-like ditches, where death brooded in the air after the same manner that some fatal disease, such as malaria, hangs suspended, but ever-present, over the deserted marshlands of Italy and Greece. I had always, in so far as I had considered the question, regarded myself as being of both an imaginative and an apprehensive turn of mind: but here the suddenness of death and its sadness, the sense, above all, of waste, transcended any preconceived idea.

The second night after my arrival, I was sent out on duty just behind the line, lightly held at this point, though the enemy was within a hundred yards. Before me in the white, misty evening, pervaded by vague moonlight, could be seen just across our trenches the narrow territory of No-Man's-Land; to which the futures of all of us were restricted. Among plantations of barbed wire—whole copses, waiting to be felled one day, to be twisted into crowns of thorns—lay mounds of rags, broken trees, rusty helmets and the skeletons of animals. This must be, I thought, under my mind, the promised land—promised by that figure with bearded face and battered top-hat from whose discoloured lips I had in earliest infancy learnt my first words, "Rags and Bones! Rags and Bones!", as he slunk along beneath the nursery window, jerkily trundling his barrow, and insinuating his hoarse cry, full of an ineffable, wheedling guile, upon the frozen air of the northern dawn, so that it was caught up and carried far and wide by the rage of the wind swooping down from skies torn at this hour into shreds of light and darkness, but which would soon shed an implacable light, dull as the wings of sea-gulls. The town had seemed alone under the sky, abandoned to this one grotesque figure and his chant, "Rags and Bones! Rags and Bones!" And as now, twenty years later, I gazed for the first time clearly, though by night, at No-Man's-Land, the cry sounded in my ears again. (Looking back, it seems to me as though sometimes I had been able to catch at a clue, passing before one could seize it, and had thus momentarily been introduced to life's rhythm: a glimpse so terrifying in the vast span of the design it discloses, that though it can be intuitively grasped for an instant on a few occasions in a lifetime, it can never, even then, be comprehended; so with an eye applied to a microscope, observing the movement of an ant upon a blade of grass, might we, for a fraction of a second, perceive revealed to us the Day of Judgement and the world-wide dead arising, with arms upstretched from the ground, like the branches of trees, to implore mercy, yet testifying to Heaven, from tombs of every aeon. . . . But then common sense envelops us again, and we behold the purposeful gesture of the ant within its emerald grove.) "Rags and Bones!" Here the land was white, too, but with a different, skeletonal whiteness: here everything was silent and still, and white but without light. Everything stirred, but was motionless. . . . Suddenly the fabric of the whole wide night was ripped by a shot, and I had time to see, before he fell, a black flower or star expand upon the temple of a boy of twenty, who was within touching distance of me. There was a gush of blood, black in the greyness, from his mouth; he groaned, stirred, shuddered, and was dead. I do not think I felt frightened, for the blow came from nowhere, an act of God, but I *was* sick with sorrow, with a sense of pathos: he had been in my platoon at Chelsea Barracks. I do not recall to what profession he had formerly belonged—by his appearance he might well have been a garden boy until lately: but I still recall his rustic grace, honest and young, and the burr in his voice when he spoke, like a young, gentle animal that has learned to express simple thoughts. (Who else living remembers him today, I wonder?) . . . It was upon this night that a hatred of moonlight took possession of my mind, and it required a whole subsequent decade of peaceful years to free me of it: for several thousands of nights, every tree or bush that showed in the whiteness concealed the shape of a sniper, of the death which was every man's future, all our future.

Even here, in Flanders, cut off though we were by distance and by war, and albeit I was leading an existence the precise opposite of any that a young man could wish and, as a result, my mind was occupied with my own worries and troubles, nevertheless I still could not fail to distinguish the continuance of the two main threads woven into the web of my life at home by the Fates. For those who lived there now the shadow had grown to such dimensions that it stretched across the whole day as well as night. It filled the horizon for all these months. And just as pathos and ominousness had now hardened into something deeper, and more actual, so the humour of the situations had cheapened day by day into less and less realistic farce. To give a little the atmosphere of my home at this time, I will quote a letter from my brother, written from Renishaw at the beginning of the war, when he was aged sixteen.

This letter may bore you, but remember I am writing from the wilds of Derbyshire, surrounded by lunatics and octogenarians. Mother is at present carrying on a quarrel with almost every one of her acquaintance. And Father has been telling me about his system of taking the soap out of the eyes when washing. "It really took me twenty years to discover it!" And it seemed like twenty to tell it! I have to pay for my own postage stamps, as he is too poor owing to the war. However, he is still going on with Barber's Garden, getting further plans from Mallows and altering the Golf Club. He now makes me walk about and carry a book on my head for twenty minutes a day. It's too infuriating, but exactly like him, isn't it? . . . That old ninny Aunt Florence has just been in to say how dreadful it is to curse one's parents. Even Turks and Mohammedans don't do that! . . .

Only one good thing for me, I believe, had come out of the interplaying forces at work in my home life: they had developed to the highest degree a sense of mutual confidence and interdependence among my brother, my sister and myself, from earliest years devoted to one another. We formed a closed corporation, whose other members wrote to me while I was at the war with the greatest regularity, so that I knew from them exactly what was happening, and how it was happening. I think no brother could have two more sensitive and percipient correspondents. My mother also wrote at frequent intervals: as did my father, and for the most part kindly. Yet though primogeniture luckily afforded me, as I have before indicated, my own *ex-officio* position in the universe, and though undoubtedly he worried about me, yet in a letter written to me at this time he announced that, finding himself compelled to reduce expenditure, and because, as he said, I was in the trenches and therefore could have no need for money, he had decided as a measure of economy to cut off my allowance. And this despite the fact that he was under the impression—created, I must confess, by myself—that I was receiving no Army pay: for, after he had told me that, when it reached me, he would deduct an equivalent sum from the amount he first gave me and then continually snatched from me, I decided to lie, knowing that no lie was too absurd for him to believe—indeed, it had to be ridiculous for him to be taken in by it. Accordingly I declared that no sums were ever paid to my account by the authorities, and maintained this deception stoutly to the end of my military career. When he from time to time asked about it, and if all my other brother-officers were in the same unfortunate predicament, I said, yes, that it was a current scandal, widely commented on. (I am not trying to justify my attitude or conduct, no doubt both to my discredit, but before passing to the result, which was so disconcerting that I must record it, let me urge on my own behalf that I had been given some provocation, and that to a certain degree a sense of fun inspired me.) I was, however, most acutely embarrassed when, while standing for Parliament in 1918, I learnt from my father that he had consulted a cousin, in strict confidence, on what should be done to remedy the shocking state of public affairs I had so innocently revealed, and that, on this man's advice, he had gone to a firm of private detectives, and employed them to set on sleuths to watch the Army Pay Department and to make enquiries in general of the clerks. The detectives, however, had obtained no satisfaction, and had been received, when in the end they had to become more direct in their questions, at first with bewilderment, and then with anger. . . . I thought it best now to admit the whole of my iniquity, *i.e.* that I had kept the money I had earned, and which, if I had admitted to receiving it, I had realised, would have been taken away from me. And not the least singular part of the story is that my father seemed in no way put out by my confession; if anything, on the contrary, rather pleased. . . . I felt some shame at what I had done, but at times, when I thought of those long months in 1918 during which detectives had been watching the Army Pay Department, laughter would sweep away all other sensations.

However, we are still only in 1914; I am at the Front, and though my father sent me there—as well as letters—hampers, wading boots and various necessities of life, yet he had been as good as his word, and had proceeded to retrench in his favourite and familiar style. I did not know where to turn for *take a position De would not expect > ad. invent a situation to support it*

money, but at the same time a certain ludicrous side to it, and perhaps a love of adventure, forbad me to take the matter too seriously—although I was resolved to give my father a fright and regain my allowance. Moreover, I had already learnt a lesson: always, in any disagreement with my father, to be inventive, to view the question in dispute from an altogether novel angle, and whenever possible to indulge in a high degree of fantasy. (This was a rule by which, more and more, in the coming years I guided my dealings with him, and it proved invaluable by its results.) Now a year or two before the war my father had started to farm in a small way, and had latterly expanded the scope of his operations, into which he had thrown himself with a kind of fury. Before long the area had amounted to no less than two thousand acres, and he had founded a company, of which, since some of the land it worked belonged to me, I had been made a director.[1] . . . He started, of course, with no knowledge of agriculture, but he was keen on fault-finding. I was away, and in the circumstances this new occupation afforded him the fullest outlet for it. He drove about, balanced on his British-Museum air-cushion in a pony cart—a tub, smartly painted in green and yellow, and drawn by a skewbald pony—, criticising to the top of his bent.[2] Fortunately, Maynard Hollingworth, who made the plans and carried them out, was an expert in farming; and on his advice my father had particularly specialised in pigs and potatoes. I have mentioned that recently, where certain ideas, not political or esthetic, were concerned, he had rather unexpectedly shown himself liable to be very easily influenced by the press. Thus, in the years immediately preceding 1914, he had become an enthusiastic advocate of Standard Bread and paper-bag cookery, when those two objects or ideals were written up in rival daily papers. It happened that lately a correspondence had been published in *The Times*, concerning the possible benefits to be derived from reviving the medieval habit of payment in kind. My father had thoroughly enjoyed, and pondered on,

---

[1] Hence the cryptic entry of my war-service to be found under my name in *Who's Who* for 1925. " Fought in Flanders and farmed with father."
[2] A fragment of an eclogue:—
    " Fine crop of wheat, Sir George."
    " Yes. Yes. Yes! . . . But too long in the tooth, I'm afraid."

D

these letters, and had determined that his approval of ancient ways should find a practical application. He had returned to Renishaw in January 1915, and late that month or early in February had sent a letter to my brother's housemaster at Eton, to intimate that, having been particularly hard hit by the war, he could not afford to pay the usual fees at the end of the term in money, but instead would deliver to their value pigs and potatoes. The housemaster was, it can be imagined, perturbed by the novelty of the suggestion and when the story transpired it created much interest. Sacheverell, whose life had been made by no whit easier as a result, appeared far from enthusiastic about the scheme when he wrote to tell me of it. His letter reached me at the Front, at about the same time as that from my father in which he had cut off my allowance, and from this conjunction an idea came to me. . . . I was shortly due to proceed on leave and, after all, I remembered, I was a director of the Sitwell Farming Company!

I wrote to my father in the following terms, and without showing any sign of resentment.

MY DEAREST FATHER,

Thank you for your letter. I well understand that your present position forces you to make economies, because I am obliged to do the same. I come home on leave in about a fortnight, and, as I have no allowance now, I have been able to arrange, I am glad to say, with the guard on the leave-train to accept potatoes instead of my fare.—Ever your loving son, OSBERT.

In his reply to me, my father did not even permit himself to allude to the subject of my letter, and for a while I feared it had fallen flat: but not many more days had passed before, without a word of explanation, my allowance was restored in full.

On my return I learned more, and that my ruse had been successful: for Maynard Hollingworth described to me the following scene.

"One day Sir George rushed up to the office, waving a letter in his hand and shouting, '*What does the boy mean? They're not* HIS *potatoes: they're* MY *potatoes!*'

"I said to him, '*If you'd let me see the letter, Sir George, perhaps I might be able to help*'. . . . He gave it me and after reading it, I said, '*It's nothing, Sir George; it's Mr. Osbert's chaff!*' But he tore it out of my hand, and dashed out of the room again, crying, '*Oh no, it's not.* HE *would do it!*'"

In the end it had only been by stressing the improbability of there being guards on trains near the fighting, and the difficulties I should undoubtedly encounter in securing the transport requisite for moving the crop from Renishaw to the Front, that Hollingworth had been able to allay, though not to dispel, my father's fears.

My leave was still some weeks—it seemed many weeks—ahead. . . . At last the date was fixed, for March: at last intervening space dwindled until I reached St. Omer, where I spent the night; at last Boulogne, and again England. But this period of a few days for which I had so greatly longed was destined to be one of profound misery. It was now that the shadow completed the process of taking substance to itself, and strode, a giant black figure, across our lives. I came back fresh to the situation, having had other things to think of: nor was I in any way prepared for what followed. Sacheverell being still at Eton, there was no-one in whom to confide, or with whom to discuss the likely outcome of the present lawsuit, a Crown Prosecution, and the climax of many other cases almost equally pitiful and degrading: no-one, that is to say, except my sister and Helen Rootham, both of them in the same predicament as I, for my father would never accept their advice, any more than he would take my own. Indeed, to be of help in any practical way was impossible. My mother's careless, impulsive nature, her total ignorance of even the most simple fact of arithmetic—perhaps no more due to the life of great riches in which she had been nurtured than to an almost physical defect, an atrophy (as though in the past too great a strain had been placed upon them) of the very faculties which had enabled Joseph Denison[1] and his son to build up so fabulous a fortune—, my father's habit of refusing to see, when the using of his eyes might be painful or annoying, and his obstinate pride, proved too strong in their combination. (This was the abyss into which his careful persistence in not allowing himself to notice the mountain-ash berries had led him.)

[1] See *Left Hand, Right Hand!* p. 58 of this edition.

The London house he had taken at this time seemed to Edith and me to be full of a highly coloured, evil levity of spirit, so strong as almost to have a presence and become a haunting. When I arrived from Flanders, I was put in a bedroom on the ground floor, but entirely cut off from the rest of the house. It was dark and inconvenient, and I slept badly in it. I asked if I could be moved. My father, however, had read in the papers that the troops in the trenches were infested with lice, and he now explained to me that he had selected a room far away on purpose, in case I was acting as host to a pack of these vermin, since the distance made it less likely that they would attack him—for if they did, it might, he pointed out, entail very serious consequences! When I became angry, for personal cleanliness has always been something of an obsession with me, and protested that if thus afflicted I should not go to stay in any house and that it was a slur on me to suggest it, he fluttered his hand at me condescendingly, and replied, "Not at all, my dear boy. It's no disgrace. Any primitive form of life is most interesting!" As I was not a naturalist, this did not calm me. . . . Though inwardly no doubt greatly perturbed by the turn affairs were taking, he behaved as though nothing untoward were afoot, and enlivened on several occasions luncheons and dinners of the most fearful family anguish by discoursing on *The History of The Fork*. That subject, which as the reader may remember he had long had "up his sleeve", always remained dear to his heart. (The two-pronged silver fork had been, apparently, the first to be introduced into Western Europe, having been brought to Venice by Byzantine Greeks, flying from the Turks.) . . . It was impossible to make him talk of anything else, though at times I thought I could see in his eyes a look of perplexity and distress: but he quickly hid it. Nor was there any old friend in the house with whom to discuss matters. Stephen Pare alone remained of the servants among whom I had grown up, and though I could have perfectly well confided in him, he would not have wished it. He was too old, though he was only fifty, too sad, too blind to read the newspapers, too much shaken by the facts, usually reaching him in a confused form from other people, to say anything except, gently, "Poor

Lady!", as he polished the silver. It was singular that the final, appalling outcome—so utterly unforeseen by everyone, it seemed, but my sister and myself, who had long entertained doubts about the result of the suits, so absolutely unexpected by the victim herself until the very night before, when I sat up with her, trying to afford her some comfort, until three in the morning—affected Mrs. Pare, who had been away from us nearly all my life (for I can only just remember her), more strongly than, outwardly, it influenced anyone else. The news of it somehow had filtered through to her poor mad brain the same night, and she contrived, because of her devotion to my mother and father, whose service she had entered when they had just been married, to break out of the asylum in which she had been for so long confined. From Lutterworth, she telegraphed at 9.41 the next morning to Turnbull, the agent and old family friend. The thirty-years-old form lies before me now, as I write. At the bottom is noted in pencil in Turnbull's hand, "This must be from poor Mrs. Pare. I did not reply, not knowing her address." The message runs:

Turnbull. Sandybrook Hall Ashbourne Derbyshire. Could I go instead it must be cruel I promised his mother to stay with them can you help me Pare.

It was no wonder that Turnbull did not know her address, for she had, by the time he received her telegram, begun to tramp to London, through the howling winds and the rains of March. At night she slept on the gravestones in village churchyards. Eventually she was captured in London and taken back to her institution. But to me, the only radiance shed on those dark days is to be found, firstly in the courage and dignity shown by my mother, and secondly in the thought of this mad old woman driven to such lengths by a heart stronger than the brain, by her feelings of compassion and her sense of duty.

I left London, after going to see my mother, and then joined my father and Edith at Renishaw. Never have I known such storms as those which now battered the old house, until it seemed alone on its tableland in a world of fury. The tree-tops bent under gale after gale that, sweeping and tumbling over the moors, seemed to bring air from the distant battering seas, and the very smell of the waves could be detected. The wind moaned round the corners, and rattled the windows. It carried with it voices from a mile away—sometimes, I thought, from further. It swirled up the Chesterfield Approach, under the sombre trees, clumps of holly, box and yew, and brought with it to me an almost forgotten voice of prophecy, spoken, too, in an evil wind, but on a hot and sullen afternoon.[1] In the daytime the gale seemed to dwarf the human figures, and thus bring relief. But almost I preferred the whistlings and scratchings to the sudden silences of the night, to its darkest, calmest caves, when your ears so nearly caught the sound of a sigh, or a footstep, or some commotion, faint now through centuries of repetition. But not only the distant past had its ghosts in these days and nights: the bones of many old pleasures came to life, the remembered laughter that surged up from the marble pavement in the garden, and floated in at my bedroom window when I was a child, and the strong smell of many flowers when the world was young. . . . Often when I woke in the cold, dark mornings I thought, too, that I heard a sound of another kind, and one that perhaps it was as well I had learnt so early: the hoarse cry I have often mentioned, the first words I had practised: "Rags and Bones! Rags and Bones!" . . . But no, that was far away, and it was a long time ago that I had heard it.

Of this, our private calamity, I will write no more, and but little further of the public catastrophe, the First German War. I wish to concern my reader with life, and not with death. The skeletons have jerked themselves for a moment out of their cupboards: let them never again *with my consent* be disturbed; let them now then return to darkness behind bolted doors, there to moulder until the ultimate trumpets call to universal judgement.

I did not return at once to the fighting, but was in London for some months—during which time, in May, my grandmother Londesborough died.

[1] See *The Scarlet Tree*, p. 178 of this edition.

The second period of my service at the Front was from July 1915 until April 1916. The battalion to which I was posted trained for some weeks in Picardy, and then was used as a reserve battalion for the Battle of Loos. Never shall I forget the day before the attack, which was launched on a Monday. In the morning we had to attend Morning Service, with a long, meandering sermon on the immortality of the soul; and, after luncheon, while an air of deathly imported English Sunday still darkened the air, were given an address by an enthusiastic General, who explained how secret was our plan ("The Germans haven't begun to get an idea of it!"), and how novel it would seem to the enemy. (Taken together, the talks of morning and afternoon were like lectures delivered, surely, in the wrong order, on effect and cause.) Later in the day I talked to my old friend from Eton days, Peter Lycett Green, who had joined the Grenadiers soon after the outbreak of war, had lately been sent to France and now bicycled over to see me. We sat on a stone wall under some poplar trees and discussed the prospect, as we had done so often in the past, and I told him how profoundly the two talks, lay and ecclesiastical, had discouraged me. . . . When next I saw my old friend, a month or two later, his leg had been amputated, for he had been wounded within a few hours of our conversation on that Sunday afternoon in September. But time was difficult to reckon, for each twenty-four hours seemed to contain a century. To my last moment, I shall consider the hours from sunrise to long past sunset that the battalion spent on the road, blocked and choked by other units, as affording the greatest sense of stultification I have ever known. Every half-hour or so, a staff-officer, in manner either over-languid or over-brisk, and talking in clipped, fox-terrier-like phrases, would ride past us, giving to those officers he knew information of a great mythical victory. The complete success of our action had come as a surprise even to our Staff, we were told. The Jerrys were in full retreat, the Boches were smashed, the Hun was on the run. . . . And then, next morning at the earliest hour, we reached the battlefield. For many weeks the Germans had, of course, observed our preparations to attack them. They had been ready. Now the bodies of friends and enemies lay, curious crumpled shapes, swollen and stiff in the long yellow grass under the chicory flowers. A dry, rather acrid smell of death, just tinctured with tear-gas (this was the first occasion on which any gas had been used by the British), hung over the brown Rubens-like landscape. . . . One scene I remember particularly well because of its irony. I saw it a week after the battle. We were quartered in the grounds of an immense château, almost entirely destroyed. The large park, situated among the cinder-heaps and primitive machinery of coal-mines, was full of the remains of temples, summerhouses, bridges, caves and grottoes; everything, in fact, had been pulverised—except a sham ruin, plainly erected a few months before a war which was to bestow upon the neighbourhood as many ruins as the most perfervid romantic could have craved.

Several of my friends had been killed during the five-day battle: more were to disappear into the desolate background of this region during the month that followed: this time, men even younger than my exact contemporaries (I was twenty-two). Among those I was never to see again was Ivo Charteris, who with his cousin, and my most intimate friend, Wyndham Tennant, had joined the Grenadiers at the beginning of the war, and had come out to France in August. These two friends I must mention in more detail.

Ivo was killed on 17th October 1915, shortly after his nineteenth birthday. Looking back across the years, it seems to me extraordinary that these young men, at so early an age, could offer such marked character. I can see Ivo now, as he was in London in the last year of his life. Although so recently from school, he was, without any appearance of precocity, detached and ironic, nonchalant, in spite of decided opinions, and manifested in everything about him, even in the way he wore his top-hat, innate style. In fact—albeit in these years this fact may prejudice certain readers against one who in the past gave his life for them—his breeding showed in his whole appearance. He came plainly of a family long used to influence, and to the governing of others, and for many generations interested in things of the mind, the heart, the senses, rather than in a necessary scramble for bread. He possessed a great love of books—though, of course, this never had been given time to develop and flower—and above all, that rarest of traits in so young a man, a point of view fully perfected, showing in everything he said, in everything at which he laughed, and in the way he regarded the greatest or the most trivial subjects. When those days rise before me again, I call to mind the long route-marches near Marlow, where we were in camp, three months before his death, and how, as we rested for a moment on a steep hill-side in the sun, or in the shade of some great beech-wood, he would tell me of Stanway, the Elizabethan mansion that was his family home in Gloucestershire, and which he loved so passionately but was destined to know for so brief a time. He would talk with such comprehension of its countryside, especially in the sun-baked September days, of the feeling no less than the look of it, of the exquisite shape of the hills and how he would spend whole days on them, that it would be difficult for me to think that his spirit does not still sometimes return there. But though he exhibited this deep and rather unexpected understanding of nature, yet in all other respects a kind of eighteenth-century reasonableness, or love of reason, governed his outlook and conduct—a characteristic, again, most surely inherited. He did not yield to impulse. Whereas, in this respect, as in almost every other, his first cousin, Wyndham Tennant,— Bimbo, as he was called—was his precise opposite; only indeed resembling him in his death at the same age of nineteen years.

Bimbo was compact of energy as a cracker. To be in his company was like having an electric battery in the room, invigorating without being in the least tiring. Literary expression was as easy to him as talk to other people. He had great verbal ingenuity, and jokes of endless variety, from those concerned with ideas down to puns, poured from him. (For example, when it was announced that there was to be a concert at the house of Lady Beit, the wife of the South African financier, it was he who remarked, "I hope her Bach is better than her Beit".) But this capacity for fun was equalled by his compassion. Consumed with a raging generosity, brave, spontaneous, quick in word and deed, with the heart of a Christian and with a spirit higher than any I have ever known,

he had a love of human beings that knew no division of class.
So English in type—though a Scot by origin—, so English by
thought, humour, wit, there was yet something almost Russian
about his exuberance and the quality of his generosity. I do
not mean to indicate a profuse spending of money—though
he was, it is true, generous in everything—but a munificence
of attitude. If he saw a poor woman of the streets, he would
at once feel sorry for her and want to ask her to dinner to meet
his girl friends, the "hell-kittens", as his mother termed them.
Indeed, in spite of expostulations, I have known him do it,
with a startling—though to me not unpredictable—lack of
success. Fellow-guests of each team were outraged. Yet
no-one left him ever with a feeling of resentment. In the end,
however, his conduct always delighted—though it may have
dismayed—his friends: for we belonged to the same epoch, that
strongest of all links: whereas the members of the circle—
rather precious, it may be, though many of them were truly
distinguished in mind—which surrounded his mother, Lady
Glenconner, belonged to an earlier age, were dyed in the wool
with pale pre-Raphaelitic colours.

As readers of *Left Hand, Right Hand!* will recall, Lady
Glenconner[1] and her sister, Lady Wemyss,—Ivo Charteris's
mother—had been two of *The Three Graces* whose portrait I
had seen and admired as a boy of seven in Sargent's studio.
Now, Lady Glenconner was to the outside world a mature
woman of unusual beauty, with an air a little vague and far
from things earthly, who liked to lead a simple life among the
water-meadows at Wilsford, reading aloud through the long
summer hours to her children in the Stone Parlour, free to the
breeze, the poems of Wordsworth and Keats, and the old
ballads. I have just suggested that her circle was precious—
and so to a certain degree it was: but her immediate and intimate friends comprised the most eminent Liberal politicians
of the day, men like Lord Haldane, of massive intellect and
ponderous step. (How well I can see him now, in my mind's
eye, with his head bent, tortoise-like, a little to one side, entering

---

[1] Lord Glenconner died in 1920, and in 1922 his widow married Viscount
Grey of Falloden, K.G. She and her sister, the wife of the 11th Earl of
Wemyss, were daughters of the Hon. Percy Wyndham.

the room with the air of a whole procession!) There were
also to be found in her house various relics of pre-Raphaeli-
tism, such as Sir Philip Burne-Jones, the son of Sir Edward,
a rather grey, excitable manikin with a nervous manner,
always in a flurry of horror at the more significant developments of modern art, and men who influenced the literary
opinion of contemporary drawing-rooms: among whom,
notably, was Sir Henry Newbolt. But Lady Glenconner
avoided the more conventional fashionable life of the day, and
was in truth devoted to the country and to nature, offering
in this a strong contrast to her sister-in-law, Mrs. Asquith,
as she then was, who would willingly sacrifice the generous
brilliance of her own conversation to her chosen delights,
political chatter and bridge: whereas Lady Glenconner liked
politicians, but not, I think, politics. Mrs. Asquith would
quickly have tired, however, of talk about birds; and it is
related that on one occasion when Lord and Lady Glenconner
and Sir Edward Grey were staying with Mr. and Mrs. Asquith
at The Wharf, and when, at an early hour in the morning,
Lady Glenconner and Sir Edward were walking in the garden,
hearing the bird-chorus, and watching and talking about the
small creatures and their ways, they were startled to hear a
feminine voice, unmistakably that of their hostess, observe
witheringly just behind them, "And I know a damned old
robin, too, when I see one!"

Certainly there existed this side of Lady Glenconner's
nature; a side calm and given to quiet pursuits: but there
was another. Her French blood—she had been named
Pamela after her great-grandmother, Lady Edward Fitzgerald,
the daughter of Madame de Genlis and, it was generally presumed, of Philip Égalité—showed no less in the delight and
surprises of her conversation with people she knew well, than
in the warmth of the life she made for the members of her
family. (She loved them, it seemed to me, in a French and not
an English way; she wished to be with her children throughout the day—the last thing, as a rule, that an English parent of
her kind would desire—and to regulate absolutely their lives.)
Yet in spite of the gentle tenor of existence at Wilsford, Queen
Anne's Gate and The Glen, she was in reality of a much more

fiery disposition, but she possessed great powers of self-control, and I recollect, as a proof of this, that she once showed me the marks on her wrist she had made where she had dug the nails of the other hand into it, in order to prevent herself from being rude to a visitor she disliked during an interview of a painful kind: and this must have been all the more difficult in that, if she had chosen to allow herself this indulgence, her words would have been so apt. As a person, she was endowed with beauty and dignity, and cleverness and a strong will, but she was also very shy, so that it was only those who knew her well, as I came to, through my friendship with Bimbo and his exquisitely pretty sister, Clare (so different from her mother, so much more like her father's family in nature and outlook), who could appreciate the subtlety, no less than the occasional delicate malice of her descriptions of people—to be fully savoured, often, later—, the depth of her feelings or the brilliance of her personal imitations. Her lovely manners and her reserve prevented her from showing these gifts to the world in general, or perhaps she thought they should be kept for her home: in any case it made her appear a different woman in public and in private. Moreover (and this was to me the most fascinating and attractive part of her character; for no-one who does not manifest inconsistencies reaches perfection as a person) she was—though she in no way realised it—far from being a rather remote, reasonable woman, under which guise she saw herself, presented herself, and was accepted, but, to the contrary, remained violently and enchantingly prejudiced in a thousand directions. Anyone she liked, or who liked her, could do no wrong, and she would find in the womanly warmth of her heart, and in her subtle armoury, many weapons of the utmost casuistry and illogicality with which to defend them. Their enemies were her enemies. And she hated as actively as she loved. In her sitting-room, therefore, stood always a collection of photographs of the most astonishing rakes and rips, in whom she still believed, and whose conduct she would unflaggingly, and with the greatest display of ingenuity, defend, or, where defence was plainly outside the capacity of any human being, ignore. All her black sheep, as it were, became swans.

To me, as a friend of her dearly loved eldest son, she was always extremely kind: and from August 1914 until Bimbo's death in action in September 1916—months that constituted for me a very dreadful and stricken period—, Wilsford and the Glenconners' fine London house, 34 Queen Anne's Gate, with its famous gallery of eighteenth-century and nineteenth-century English pictures, became second and more peaceful homes to me when I was in England. . . . Sir Oliver Lodge was an old friend and neighbour of Lady Glenconner, and after Bimbo's death, which shook her whole being, Lady Glenconner turned with a burning zeal to spiritualism, in an effort to keep in touch with the son she had lost. Old friends were now continually augmented and replaced by those of psychical inclination and enthusiasm, until, I apprehend, she became almost uncomfortable in the presence of those who did not share her absolute faith in the revealed doctrines and manifestations of orthodox spiritualism, or indulge in tales of clair-audience, clairvoyance and controls and ectoplasm. One rather strange incident I recall. . . . A year or two after Bimbo had been killed, his mother sent for me urgently one evening to attend a séance with a celebrated female medium who had, during her trance, declared that his spirit had asked for me to be present, and would give proof of his identity and survival. Under the circumstances, I felt it impossible to refuse to comply, though I placed little faith in the creed. I tried to go there, however, with an open mind, and one ready to catch any suggestion or follow any clue emanating from beyond the grave; but so far as the immediate results were concerned, they were disappointing: the medium in herself appeared unconvincing, and nothing was said or done that could relate to any incident connected with my dead friend or, indeed, to any personal memory of him. The chief impression I took away was of a most peculiar and very sharp rapping, executed apparently on some system, in a definite unmistakable pattern of longs and shorts like the Morse Code. I certainly had never in the whole of my life heard furniture behave in this particular manner before, and I was absolutely persuaded in my own mind that it must be contrived by the medium or her husband, though I wondered how it could have been arranged, because it was so loud, regular, and unlike anything I had heard. It was singular, too, that when she awoke, the medium had made no effort to decipher it or to claim a meaning for it. . . . However, curiosity about the psychic was swiftly banished from my mind by the actuality of physical distress, since the same evening, on returning to my flat, I developed a severe attack of influenza. After passing ten days or so in bed, I was allowed to go to the country to recuperate. There, in the comfortable house of a very un-psychic friend, I was woken up in my charming bedroom at two in the morning by precisely the same kind of loud rapping in the furniture that I had noticed at the séance. It was unmistakable, and I have heard it only on those two occasions. It continued for some ten minutes after I had turned on the electric light, and seemed to issue simultaneously from all the pieces of wooden furniture in the room.

Lady Wemyss, though she had lost two sons in the war, never, like her sister, became a spiritualist. Indeed they did not resemble one another very greatly except in their beauty: and the quality of this, too, differed. About Lady Wemyss there was no suggestion of the precious. The aseptic, astringent nature of the wit of those surrounding her—and not least, of the members of the Charteris family—would in itself have prevented this: but further, she showed little inclination for it. Though she had a devotion to the arts, and a special liking for the company of painters and writers, her life was essentially that of a great lady, and its obligations, as she saw them, occupied her. Her extreme beauty, of so classical a form, and with a sort of luminous pallor about it, had made her company sought by many; by politicians of a lighter but longer range of mind than those to be met at her sister's—minds, too, imbued with a healthy cynicism; statesmen like Lord Curzon, or Lord Balfour, whom I met many times at Lady Wemyss's house. (Who could imagine the lean, tall form of the late Lord Balfour, or his placid, enquiring eye, applied to the ways of small birds? No! Human beings, albeit in an impersonal manner, and ideas, these alone interested him!) Even men with a rankling dislike of the fashionable world, and a contempt for it, cherished often a special feeling in their hearts

for her. For example, I recollect H. G. Wells telling me of
his gratitude to her and affection for her. That night we had
both been dining with Lady Mary Strickland; her mother,
Lady Wemyss, had been there, and was now an old lady.
As we walked away from the house, under the dark, leafy
trees of a London summer night, we talked of how exactly
the daughter echoed the mother's beauty, and then H. G.
told me that he never, much as he disliked going out in Society,
refused an invitation if he heard Lady Wemyss was to be
present, because she had been the first person of her sort to be
kind to him as a young man. He went on to relate how she
used to ask him to stay, when he came almost fresh to this life
from servitude in a draper's shop, and with what gentle care
and tact as a hostess she had guided his steps, giving him hints,
for his own comfort, on what clothes to wear on what occasions,
and in general how to behave so as not to make himself unhappy by feeling that he had committed a solecism. . . . Lady
Wemyss was also most hospitable to me, and I often stayed
for long periods in her house in London: there I learnt, as at
her sister's, to listen quietly to the conversation of those older
and wiser than myself, and famous: but sometimes, as I
considered the talk of the politicians, I confess that with
native, and it may be naïve, intolerance, I reflected how little
wiser, for all their experience, they were!

With Bimbo and Ivo my friendship—of choice, this time,
and not of circumstance—lasted for a period of months rather
than years; but looking back it seems to cover a whole section
of my existence; the death of these two friends and constant
companions left a great void. . . . Bimbo was not killed until
nearly a year later than his cousin, in September 1916.
During the second period of my service abroad, he was for
a month or six weeks in my Company: (a day or two after the
Battle of Loos, I had been promoted to be a Company
Commander). In the winter, however, he was appointed to
the Staff, and alas, I saw little of him subsequently during
the brief months that remained to him. . . . When the Battle
of Loos eventually subsided, leaving the Germans in much
the same position as when our attack had opened, the weeks
again began to assume the monochromatic tones of trench

warfare, a life penned in, pinned down, created solely, it seemed, for the tribes of rats and generals, who alone could benefit by it. Accordingly, I have not much to say, even if I felt inclined to dwell on it. There were, of course, episodes such as that which occurred while I was away for a few days in hospital: when my soldier servant, a charming natural character, who had been a navvy until the war came and he volunteered, drew the entire rum ration for the Company, and, with a chosen friend, drank the whole of it, and was as a result unconscious for forty-eight hours. Alas, I never saw him again, for the authorities were far from taking the same lenient view as that with which I regarded his escapade. But the reader would quickly tire of such typical events of our coffined life, and I will therefore confine myself to relating one incident that belongs to this time, and then, after a divagation, describe a scene or two that remains in my memory.

It was one evening in December 1915 that I saw, and spoke to, a ghost. We had been marched up at an hour's notice into the front line, to replace a Scottish regiment which had been so badly and unexpectedly mauled that the Staff had been compelled to withdraw it. It must be borne in mind that as a result we had been deprived of the usual few days' rest between spells of duty. It was, of course, dusk when I took over my portion of the trench, and after I had ordered the posting of the men I entered my dug-out. When I left it, a few minutes later, the evening had become already much blacker. In the corner of the bay opposite, I saw a private soldier, with his hands in his pockets, and noticed that his rifle was by his side, although it had long been an order that all the men should stand to, with their rifles on the parapet, at dawn and at dusk. I could not see his face very distinctly owing to the growing darkness: but I swore at him for his carelessness, asking him what he meant by it. As I finished, with the words, "I'm tired of having to tell you . . .", he was, suddenly, no longer there in front of me, and I was talking to nothingness. . . . I took up the abandoned rifle, and carried it with me to the dugout. It belonged to the regiment we had just relieved.

In the late spring I returned to England, suffering from blood-poisoning. Being rather seriously ill for some weeks, I was obliged during this time, while I was at Renishaw, to have a nurse: a fact which awoke the strongest feeling of competition in my father, who, through the course of his several-years-long breakdown, had come greatly to dislike not being the chief and most seriously afflicted patient in the house. The atmosphere at home had changed in some respects, and in others was more typical, and a letter addressed to Turnbull by my father in the first month of the same year transmits the feeling of it:

We have got new housekeepers here since the death of Mrs. Westby: Justin and his wife and daughter. They are Belgians who have been in service in South America. The new arrangement costs two hundred a year: but Mrs. Justin cooks well, and her husband can act as butler, buys the food, and is generally economical and useful. I have given up my valet, have let Wood End, and we have only Pare besides the Justins. . . . I could manage the war taxes, but taxation for cinematographs, cheap jewellery, cheap pianos, extra drinks and Sunday motor drives leaves one without a penny. I consider the economic position is that half one's fortune has disappeared for ever, that the war is a deadlock, and that, while both sides are being ruined, there is no reason to believe that Germany will be ruined first. . . .

My father had persisted in his fanatic farming, and into it he now poured as many ideas as formerly into more decorative directions. I have said earlier that he knew nothing about his new interest, but this statement needs qualifying: he knew nothing about *modern* farming, but all too much—as one soon learnt in talking to him—about the methods of husbandry in medieval times and in the dark ages; and even this he approached from a literary and not a practical angle. He had by heart every form of land tenure and cultivation under Richard Cœur-de-Lion, but could never understand why sheep were now not folded every evening, as they had been in the days of Robin Hood, and used to grow quite angry about it. He was continually astonished, too, to find that wheat was drilled in the autumn, saying, "But surely the winter kills it!" To come to the more modern practices he advocated, he often interviewed Hollingworth about a new scheme he was evolving for letting the various farms he was not himself working: the tenants need pay no rent (they'd like *that*, he pointed out!), but use instead their own capital, and surrender to the landlord their whole profit: but, if they made none, then on no account was their payment to him to fall below the rent due under the old system. He had no objection, he added, to the tenant finding his food and subsistence from the farm. And it was to be Hollingworth's popular job to go round assessing the profit of each farmer—or rather, of my father. . . . Then a new idea came to him. Why not use the weed in the lake as manure! It should make an excellent one. Sea-weed did, he'd read lately in *The Times*, so why not fresh-water weed? It should prove an interesting little experiment. . . . At the same time, as was his wont, he distributed discouragement impartially and in ample measure. When Hollingworth came to report to him that he had sold the potato crop for the record sum of a hundred pounds an acre, twice the usual price for it, he at once replied, very impatiently,

"Yes. Yes. Yes! But you'd have done far better to sell them to a first-rate London restaurant!"

And, indeed, at one time, in a year when potatoes were very scarce, he did supply the Curzon Hotel with them.

When I was better, the authorities posted me once more to Chelsea Barracks. In the months that immediately followed, my leisure was for the most part spent with those whose company I had frequented before the war. I still knew no writers or painters of my own age or period, and had been given no opportunity of meeting them: on the other hand there had taken place the most significant event in my career, of which I shall tell at the close of this chapter. . . . It was the end of the first period: henceforth I should make my own life, and not have it made for me. My right hand was becoming predominant. . . . But in this lull before a change, it is difficult for me to see myself, in the same way that, as I have described, it is an almost impossible task to regard, and realise, your own reflection in a looking-glass, so greatly does the very process encourage a feeling of disassociation. A glimpse of me as I then was occurs, however, in an unexpected quarter; through the protruding, epochal, observant but unreckoning eyes of Colonel A' Court Repington, for so long military critic of the *Morning Post*. His diary,[1] which forms a sort of *Catalogue*

[1] *The First World War* (1914–1918). Personal Experiences of Lt.-Col. C. A'Court Repington. (Constable & Company, 1920.)

Raisonné or Doomsday Book for a Social Revolution, renders very accurately the feeling of a time when, amid the prevailing gloom and muddle, people of all kinds and ages sought by means of pleasure to forget the war. The reference to me in the index to the volume is still given under the formal initials which had followed me all through my life at school and in the Army—*F.O.S.S.*, "Captain F. O. S. Sitwell". It is plain, I think, from the second passage that, however conventional I may have been in the amusement I shared, the range of my conversation had rather taken the old soldier aback.

Saturday, Aug. 26.[1] . . . Went off in the afternoon to Mrs. George Keppel's house, Watlington Park, Oxon, with the Dutch Minister, Van Swinderen. His servant took my luggage with him, and lost his master's, which did not turn up until Sunday night. I wonder if our secret service were looking it over! Found a gay party consisting of George and Alice Keppel, the two daughters, Violet and Sonia, the Hwfa Williamses, Lord Ilchester, Lady Lilian Wemyss, Baroness Daisy de Brienen, Mr. and Mrs. Nicolson, and Sitwell and another young fellow in the Guards. A nice house standing well at the top of the Chilterns, and a beautiful glimpse of the distance through a wood. A nice park, grounds and gardens. The weather was bad but I managed to get a few sets of tennis on Saturday afternoon. We had a great game of hide-and-seek in the house during the wet morning. The girls hid Van Swinderen over a *calorifère*, and he was nearly roasted alive. We also had some music and dancing, and played a lot of Bridge.

Monday, Aug. 28. Returned to town early with the three young men, and instead of discussing soldiering, we talked of nothing but pictures, Palladio, and palaces. They were all three extraordinarily well informed[2] and knew Italy well. The war has brought a strange medley of capacities and incapacities into the Army.

Soon after the period of Colonel Repington's conversation-piece, my views on the war began to make me feel in general uncomfortable in the company of those who did not share them, and grow intolerant of the fashionable world and its complacency: the manner in which it accepted the wholesale slaughter as just one more war (which must be fought to a finish)—whereas it was something different called by the same name; a massacre, and the sooner it ended, the better, if the fabric of European civilisation was to survive. But, though

[1] 1916.
[2] Harold Nicolson, myself, and a third, whose identity escapes me.

the world held war still to be war in a medieval sense, it yet
desired the end to be different from the end of medieval con-
flicts, when moderation always prevailed: now our aim was
an uncontrolled, and uncontrollable, victory and the collapse
of the enemy. For Democracy at war, and going to war,
resembles a runaway bus: it cannot be stopped until it has
come to a smash at the bottom of the hill. It is difficult indeed
to estimate the difference to the happiness of the world had
peace been made before the Bolsheviks came to power, had
Russia become a progressive modern nation instead of a
revolutionary state, and had Germany, instead of being ruled by
Hitler—an inevitable development of its 1918, imposed democracy—developed into a constitutional monarchy. It is scarcely
likely that the Kaiser or his son,[1] after so narrow an escape
as they must, in those circumstances, have realised that they
had been granted, would again have risked war. . . . But such
speculations are without profit and merely sadden the survivors.

I had never been able to see beauty in war, which from
the first had appeared to me as an endless foulness mas-
querading under an honoured but obsolete name. But now
came a phase of active rebellion: though my feelings were
based more, I believe, on intellectual than sentimental reasons.
I could observe for myself that war called out every bad feeling
in man or woman,—while the good it was said equally to
evoke, I could not see as "good". Heroism has never been
my favourite virtue: and still less do I sing the praises of
"taking it", the favourite merit, passive and uninspiring, of
the Second World War. Who can help being fired at, bombed,
or otherwise obliterated; of what use to panic, at such a
moment, even if there were time? Is the pheasant brave,
because it flies across in front of the guns on 1st October, or
the oyster more than usually courageous when there is an "r"
in the month? To quote a fable:

[1] Let us remind theorists in general that the test of a good system of
government is by its results. Liberty, Fraternity and Equality decimated
the French people; the abolition of the monarchy in Spain, and the introduction of ideals as a governmental aim there, involved that country in
the bloodiest civil war in history: whereas dynastic marriages, such as those
that originally united the four kingdoms of Spain or England and Scotland,
made prosperous and peaceful communities for several centuries.

Oh, the morale of the Oyster
On the first day of September,
Makes my eye grow moister, moister,
And my heart glow like an ember.
Please remember that the oyster
Never leaves its pearly cloister,
Never hurries,
Never worries,
Till the knife falls to dismember.

But while it can, I think, be denied that physical courage is a virtue, the fact remains that physical cowardice is so odious and unbecoming, if natural, a vice, that it ever makes us unthinkingly exalt courage un-allied to intelligence. Some people are brave in spite of themselves: it is a way of behaving, occasionally forced on us by the fact that there is nothing else to do, or no way of doing anything: or again as the result of a code or of inheritance. Thus in me there were currents of blood which ran against my reason, filling me with hatred of the Germans, with their clumsy cruelty, their forget-me-nots, their stupid cunning and their fondness for children and for home, and made me oblivious at times of my real tenets: that war, and not the conduct of those maddened by it, is the crime; that all wars and every war were inexcused and inexcusable, and that the politicians of any country who precipitated a war, or failed to end it at the first moment, were the true criminals. During the progress of the war, it became, further, clear to me that the only true heroism was to think for yourself, and then to act on your opinions; and, finally, that many conscientious objectors, though daily nagged at, and held up to ridicule and for hatred as cowards, in the contemporary daily papers, were, though often wrong-headed, as deserving of respect on this score as the greatest of military paladins. As for the voluntary stretcher-bearers and ambulance-drivers, their profession during war constituted a very high form, and needed a very high degree, of courage. To find the truth, and to state it unequivocally amid the general hysteria engendered by modern war, was, similarly, to perform a greater service to humanity and to your country than to hide it from yourself and stampede in one direction after another, like a sheep. Thus Shaw—almost the only famous writer who at this time did not betray truth, reason and his contemporaries and juniors in order to march with the band—, H. W. Nevinson and H. W. Massingham, with their calm protests concerning the war, and the conduct of it, became the men I chiefly admired at home.

Of Shaw and his work I had, indeed, long been a devotee. And I shall never forget the Sunday evening in the autumn of 1917 when I first met him at a dinner given for that purpose by Massingham and Nevinson. Nevinson's acquaintance I had made a little while before. Indeed I had become friends with the whole family. Mrs. Nevinson most nobly came to support me at the election in 1918—she was an accomplished and convincing speaker: and Richard[1] and his charming wife Kathleen were already old friends of mine. Richard, with his dark, pugnacious, handsome, rather melancholy face, was a striking figure, then at the height of his fame as a painter of war. He had found in the painting idiom of the day a fitting manner in which to record its physical struggle; the endless, rhythmic repetition of trench life, of the roads that so fittingly led to it, and to the beginning, born in mud, of mechanised man. I had met Massingham through Robert Ross, that benefactor of many young poets, who had been responsible for submitting to him, as Editor of the *Nation*, the first of my series of satires, signed *Miles*, which subsequently appeared in his columns. I was twenty-four now, and still unused to meeting men of Shaw's genius. It seemed to me the culmination of all for which one could hope. The rest of us waited in the hall at Romano's until the famous playwright made his appearance, a few minutes late. He entered, a tall figure, broad-shouldered, with the easy, loose-limbed gait that marks him, and in his usual warm, rough suit, while, in addition, and rather unexpectedly, a white bandage encircled the crown of his head. I had never seen Shaw previously, though of course I knew him well through photographs, paintings and busts: but I had been unprepared for his genial presence, his fine manners, his great stature, and his typical Irish voice, generous and compelling. In spite of this last attribute, which should call out a responding fire in others, when we had gone upstairs and sat down at our table in the gallery, I remained for long

[1] C. R. W. Nevinson (1889–1946).

mute, bound fast with wonder—with wonder, but not with awe: for Shaw's natural courtesy would have put anyone younger and less celebrated than himself at his ease. Merely, I wanted to listen, not to talk. He spoke much that evening of the great Duke of Wellington, a fellow-countryman in whose exploits and conversation he had always been greatly interested: he told us the story of how, on one occasion, when the Duke was asked by an admirer, "How did you really manage to beat Napoleon?", he replied simply: "Well, I'll tell you. Bonaparte's plans were made in wire, mine were made in string": a very good simile to convey strategic flexibility to a lay mind. When there came a silence, I had mustered sufficient confidence to say something. My eyes reverted to the bandage: it worried my curiosity.

"I'm sorry, Mr. Shaw," I observed, "to see you've hurt yourself: I hope not badly?"

"Well, you see," Shaw replied, "I'm a teetotaller, and my wife got in a new kind of non-alcoholic drink for me to try. As soon as I'd had the first glass, I became intoxicated, and in going downstairs fell and cut my head open!"

What a feeling of relief it afforded, to find people in whose presence any idea, whether original or conventional, whether accepted or rejected by the world, whether condemned and derided or praised, could be discussed on its own merits, without anger. This, though an atmosphere entirely new to me, after my upbringing, and in the environment I had so far known, was one, withal, in which I felt immediately at home. . . . Thus I was freed, and enabled to take my own line. Thus I spoke without fear. And, in the later war years, by which time I had formed my own opinion, I never hid my views. I was in a regiment of great traditions, I understood them and accepted the point of view of those in authority: it was only necessary to do one's duty. But the war was an evil, and should be brought to an end. And when Lord Lansdowne,[1] later in the same month that I met Shaw, published

[1] Henry Charles Keith Petty-Fitzmaurice, 5th Marquess of Lansdowne, K.G. (1845-1927), Governor-General of Canada, 1883-88, Viceroy of India, 1888-94, Secretary of State for War, 1895-1900, Minister for Foreign Affairs, 1900-1905.

his letter—first refused by *The Times*—in the *Daily Telegraph*[1]
and a storm of abuse, violent but innocent of thought, was
launched against him, I went at once to the Guards Club and,
from that military citadel, wrote—though I had never had
the pleasure of meeting Lord Lansdowne—to congratulate
him on his courage and sapience. . . . And again, when
Bertrand Russell came out of prison, to which he had been for
expressing unusual opinions about the war in an article in the
Cambridge Review, I organised a party for him the same
evening, when Lady Ottoline Morrell took him to hear Violet
Gordon Woodhouse play in her own unrivalled manner on the
harpsichord the great compositions of Bach and Mozart.
. . . I do not believe that I have ever seen Lord Russell since
that night. Another, but of my own generation, for whose
courage I then was able to feel an admiration, was Siegfried
Sassoon.

Apart from the abstract beauty of truth-telling, such as that
of Bernard Shaw and the others whom I admired, there was
no beauty, no virtue in war, as I saw it, but for the few scenes
I mentioned earlier. Thus it cannot be denied, I apprehend,
that Ypres, caught in its whirlwind of iron and fire, was
beautiful. For a week or more, the officers of my Company
were billeted and messed in the cellars of the Convent of the
Irish nuns there. These stone chambers, safe, under the ruins,
belonged to the late sixteenth century, had gracefully vaulted
ceilings, and still contained some rare objects, one supposes
brought hither from the houses round for safety at the beginning of the war. There were many books, seventeenth and
eighteenth-century, long, low chests of walnut or oak, richly
carved, old chairs, with leather stretched across for seats, and
gilded, floreated tops to the two stays that composed the frame
of their backs, and many jars and bowls of delft or of some
kind of Flemish majolica, lumpy but serene in colour, blue and
green. Outside, by day and by night, the heads of the gothic
stone angels, with their hair curling upward at the ends, with
narrow, smiling contemplative eyes which saw so much, and
subtle, inward-looking smiles, were falling from great heights,
from belfries and lofty, broken walls. One sculptured head I

---

[1] For this incident see *Those Were the Days*, p. 397 *et sqq.*

saw as I passed by, knocked off a figure high up on the Cloth
Hall. Picking it up and carrying it in my arms to the cellar, I
had it packed in a wooden box, and took it home when next I
went on leave. (It still survives, over a door in the garden of
my London house, having outlived the bombs of another war,
its state only a little further damaged by its having been, at
one time, while I was absent abroad, painted with white paint,
to bring out its beauty, by a servant who had been a sailor
and believed in keeping things shipshape.) The lofty stone
buildings seemed to gain in height by their devastation; they
towered up into the faint, misty, winter blue, where shrapnel
burst with puffs of whiteness like a plaster cupid's cloud. So
the broken and deserted city, the very capital of No-Man's-
Land, extended its smashed streets and avenues of trees, black,
angular shapes, sharp and ruthless, such as the contemporary
gangs of Futurists would have wished to create had they been
able to kidnap the God of Nature. (And indeed the whole
view, structures and landscape, presented a mirror to the
future of Europe; this was to be the pattern of a hundred, a
thousand, cities in thirty years' time.) The ruins possessed a
special, a spectral quality, such as is to be noticed in the green,
almost lunar towns, seeming to have been painted with
verjuice and verdigris, that are sometimes to be found in the
backgrounds of pictures by the great Venetian masters. At
night, by the moon, the long, icy silences, and bursts of
metallic chatter, were possessed of their own terror; to think
that this city which had exhibited not long before—so much
could be deduced from the objects still lying among the debris
on the ground—a warm, earthy beauty, imbued with typical
Flemish vigour and robustness, should have wasted to this
skeleton, coeval with bones long buried!

Another scene I recall with the stamp of physical memory.
After a particularly long and hard period in the trenches, it
became known that the Battalion was to proceed to Calais for
rest and recreation. In the minds of officers and men, Calais
became the Ville Lumière of the dunes, gay and warm and
generous, a resort famous for laughter and pleasure, and so
near England that almost one could hear her voice across the
sea. No wonder that King Henry VIII had chosen a site

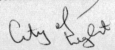
City of Light

near by, "'Twixt Guynes and Arde", as the meeting-ground known as the Field of the Cloth of Gold. . . . I thought of the gold tents in the background of the two pictures at Hampton Court. . . . Eventually the great day came that was to take us back to civilisation. And we too found ourselves quartered under canvas—but located, it seemed, within the bitter wind itself, on a high cliff above the February sea. Suddenly, an hour after we had arrived, the camp was caught, first in a whirling drift, then in a frenzy of snow which never for an instant ceased until an hour before our departure. For that interval, England, though so near, was curtained from us by leagues of frozen water falling through frozen air. The surf of the waves, or was it the waves themselves, could hardly be perceived through the eye-freezing, perpetual dance of the flakes. We were situated nowhere now, in a nothingness that put the poles to shame. Occasionally, about once every forty-eight hours, the cotton-wool screen lifted enough for us to be able just to make out the blurred white outlines of the hideously top-heavy and out-of-scale tower of the Hôtel-de-Ville,[1] but usually snow hid everything, lying on roofs and heads and hearts. Snow fell from the sky, from your hat, from your uniform, from tent-flaps, from trees, from beds. It dripped through your gloves, and jumped off your boots. England, of green English winters and warm rains, must be, one felt, ten thousand miles away, across Arctic seas. . . . Sometimes I think I have never felt warm again since that week.

It was about this time, during my second period in the trenches, that a development had occurred, so important to me that, though I remained for another three years in the Army, it altered the whole course of my life: it was during one of the brief spaces of rest, in a billet not far from Ypres, that I wrote my first poem. . . . First, I say: certainly it was the first published, albeit in the same manner as a great many other schoolboys I had, of course, at the age of fifteen begun to write immense tragedies intended to be in blank verse—one such, especially, I recall: it concerned Jezebel and Ahab, and was a rather lurid oriental fantasy, influenced by Wilde's

[1] Still standing, amid the wreckage of all else in the town, in 1946.

Salome, which I had recently read and immensely admired. (I recollect one line of the play still, I suppose because of my former pride in it: when the soldiers approached the Palace, to kill Jezebel, she rather provocatively leant out, and shouted,

"*Is Jezebel the woman to be wronged?*")

My sister listened with patience to the reams of blank verse—blanker than the author knew—, praised it with moderation, and after discreetly allowing a certain time to pass, for poet's pride to cool in, tactfully pointed out a fault or two, and finally, after a month had elapsed, hinted that I might like to burn it, and attempt a new poem on the same subject later with a fresh mind. All this she accomplished gently and with so much grace that, unlike most youthful writers subjected to criticism, I bore her no ill will for her counsel, and quietly carried out what she suggested—or at any rate the first part of it.

I had written little or nothing since that time. My life in the Brigade of Guards before the First World War may, looked back upon, seem to have been idle. It had been both too busy and too fragmentary to allow me to read with any intensity, still less to write. . . . But now some instinct, and a combination of feelings not hitherto experienced, united to drive me to paper, this time to compose a poem: and never has anything astonished me more than to find how entirely I lost myself in the process, and yet was able to concentrate. Next ambition swelled up in me. . . . It is, moreover, true that in one respect this first poem qualified me as an unusual poet: for through the good agencies of our friend Richard Jennings—who, the reader will remember, had similarly sponsored the first poem of my sister's—these verses of mine were shown to the Editor of *The Times*, and shortly afterwards appeared under the title *Babel*, and signed with my name, in the columns of that great journal. This début, in the issue of the 11th of May 1916, must constitute, I opine, the sole instance of a first effort by a young author being printed in an organ of such national and international celebrity, so that, in so far as writing was concerned, it can be said that

Absorption

my muse was born with a silver pen in her mouth. Therefore
I reproduce the poem in question here, so that the reader, with
all indulgence, may judge of it for himself.

Babel

And still we stood and stared far down
Into that ember-glowing town,
Which every shaft and shock of fate
Had shorn unto its base.   Too late
   Came carelessly Serenity.

Now torn and broken houses gaze
On to the rat-infested maze
That once sent up rose-silver haze
   To mingle through eternity.

The outlines once so strongly wrought,
Of city walls, are now a thought
Or jest unto the dead who fought . . .
   Foundation for futurity.

The shimmering sands where once there played
Children with painted pail and spade,
Are drearly desolate—afraid
   To meet night's dark humanity,

Whose silver cool remakes the dead,
And lays no blame on any head
For all the havoc, fire, and lead,
   That fell upon us suddenly,

When all we came to know as good
Gave way to Evil's fiery flood,
And monstrous myths of iron and blood
   Seem to obscure God's clarity.

Deep sunk in sin, this tragic star
Sinks deeper still, and wages war
Against itself; strewn all the seas
With victims of a world disease
—And we are left to drink the lees
Of Babel's direful prophecy.

From the moment of my beginning to write, my life, even
in the middle of war, found a purpose. Within the bounds of
a few years, the new power revealed to me had sharpened my

haracter, late, like that of all the members of my family in
he past, in developing. To me hitherto work had always been
 bugbear, something wan and listless, like a ghost, to be
.voided, haunting the end of every spell of freedom and
)leasure. I had acquired through my education no ability to
:oncentrate. My mind rambled dully if I sat behind a desk.
n short, I loathed work with all my heart, whether at school
)r later, and whenever possible evaded it. . . . But now I
liscovered my greatest pleasure—yet pleasure is not the
:orrect term—, my greatest concern, an immersion and a
ransport, in this labour that had been revealed to me for
ny own. And the story of the next few years is necessarily one
)f increasing self-application, until within the span of a
lecade I was able to reach that point where the idea of a book
ay so near me as to abide with me by day and night, returning
o me at first waking, and permeating the hours with its
)articular scent and shape, until, indeed, I was able immedi-
ttely to supply a lost page of my first novel, _Before the Bom-_
ardment, because I knew the whole book by heart. But this
)itch could only in time be attained to, and through being able
o live quietly abroad with my brother for a large part of the
^ear, during which periods I gave myself up entirely to my
vork, living for it; for in London I had only to appear, to find
nyself the centre of a whirlwind, a battle, and of many dust-
.torms raised by scrubby feet, as well as constantly being
;oaded by parents and becoming the victim of a thousand
esser worries. Moreover—and I believe it is a confession of
veakness—, I am an artist whose ideas seldom come to him
·xcept when a pen is in his hand.

Already, even at the start, I realised the sacredness of my
ask: because, long before I had detected any capacity in
nyself, the artist had appeared to me as priest, prophet and
aw-giver, as well as interpreter: the being who enabled men
o see and feel and pointed out to them the way. That I
.hould myself prove to belong to this order at first constituted
oo great a happiness to credit—still greater, and rare, indeed,
o find two such artists as my brother and sister, one on each
.ide of me. Yet fortunate as I was in this respect, fortunate
ibove all others in my generation, there was always hereafter

a lurking duality: the excitement and interest to be derived from the lives we led, intellectual and devoted to art, and underneath, the knowledge of the powerful enmity of many (not least among them, of that new type, the carrion-fed or shrike-artist, who seeks to devour or impale his own kind, not only in order to magnify his own importance and that of his pseudo-strong work, which resembles the straining of a professional strong man at a fair, but also in order to have no rivals), the bitter loathing of the Philistine, and its continual symptoms in the press. For I was never under any illusions as to the hostility of the great book-hating public: a large and powerful body. All this I believe I understood instinctively as well as from the results of experience, and better than most of my calling. I realised that everything I said or wrote would be misunderstood by a great many—and my heredity, coming as I do on all sides of stock that for centuries have had their own way, and have not been enured to suffer insolence passively, made it hard for me, and for my brother and sister not to fight back: (so it was, I am inclined sometimes to think as I survey the past three decades, that we gave as good as we got!). We knew, in addition, all three of us, that henceforth the sillier, more spiteful acquaintances of my father's and friends of my mother's, who never tired of mischief-making would misrepresent every line we wrote and every opinion attributed to us, and that this would be reflected in our parents' conduct to us. (Already my father had invented his slogan "Edith's poems make *me* look ridiculous!") Continually they were working to kidnap us, and put a stop to our independent lives. . . . Yet through all this, other more abstract things were more important, and the professional preoccupation of my mind, concerned with words, was my continual ecstasy as well as torment. . . . And who can wonder at such an attitude? For in the beginning was the word, we have been told, and, albeit to the divine or to the usual layman this may seem merely an inaccurate translation, to the born writer— and I claim to be a writer born as well as self-made—it stands as the truth, the whole truth, and true in more senses than that in which it was meant to be interpreted.

In the beginning was the word. The word itself, of which

our works of art are fashioned, is the first art-form, older than the roughest shaping of clay or stone. A word is the carving and colouring of a thought, and gives to it permanence. We do not yet know, if ever we are able to trace, how language first began, though we may deduce that words to express love were those first used, since love is the emotion, just as speech is the instrument, that in even its lowest, most primitive form clearly distinguishes human beings from their humble cousins of the animal world. Love, or sometimes its complement and opposite, hatred, is for the most part the source of literature, as words are its material. Not seldom the author may repine, crying aloud in his desert of intolerable anguish, in the wakeful darkness of word-haunted nights, when settling once more to his toil in the morning, or in one of those periods of nervous exploitation and subsequent exhaustion which are bound to be his lot, that he wishes he were a carpenter, a watchmaker, a farrier. And during the moment it takes to express the sentiment, it may be true—yet is he all three, for the very word *artist* in Greek enshrines that original meaning of "joiner", then by the productions of each period you may read the whole clock of civilisation, and tell how far you have gone, when it was dawn, and how distant is the dusk, while as for the farrier's trade, have I not struck a thousand times more sparks under the gold hooves of Pegasus than any hammering smith? But again to review an artist's just complaints, often in this country he may wish himself, rather than an English lord of the English word, a French master of the French: for French writers are spared even at the outset of a career, when hardest to support, the impertinences, the questions, the mockery that have ever been the lot—except in the Elizabethan Age—of the English writer of individual trend, especially of a poet: moreover wit among the French is accorded a ready place, whereas in our land it renders its owner an object of suspicion. Yet are all these small matters, for what language can compare with in richness, or excel in tradition, that which the English author is privileged by his birth to use?—a language, withal, that has tamed and taken captive whole continents and offers them to him for his field of exercise. No! let the writer be content with his birthright (though the laws of current democracy, the pursuit of the Lowest Common Denominator, should induce him to barter it for a mess of Esperanto, or to confine his ideas with the rationed Basic English), even if he may be forgiven because, from time to time, he sighs and vows aloud that, instead of an author, he wishes he were a painter, a sculptor, a composer: since it is true that the art of letters (note the name I have chosen for it) offers apparently a less easy approach for the audience than do the other arts. No lover of sculpture or painting need *learn* to look at a picture or a statue—at least he will not know he has to; the lover of music will find something to satisfy his ear at every age, and when he has reached maturity can never have enough music during the whole of a day, though an hour of it can suffice to reveal to him the entire glory of humanity or tragedy of man, so that for the instant he catches sight of the machinery of the universe. The book-lover, on the other hand, must as a child have passed through the arduous process of learning to read and write. (How well I remember those mornings, when I sat in a small room, facing the sea, the golden, enticing expanse of sea on a June morning, and could hear, or thought I could hear, the sounds of the summer's chattering, the notes of a barrel-organ, the cries of pierrots and acrobats, from down below on the sands, out of sight, and all the while I was obliged to sit with a pencil clamped in my left hand—it was always being snatched, and firmly placed in my right—, the pencil's point continually catching, as it were, in the contours of a letter, losing itself in angles and curves of unknown meaning that confronted me, empty O's, and S's shaped like swans. The semi-amateur governess, with blue lips and a nose I used to think like a bunch of Parma violets—a flower my mother wore sometimes and of which I was very fond—, who taught me with a sort of frost-bitten and wrinkled kindness like the sweetness of the crystallised cherries that I on occasion snatched from the kitchen table, would willingly, poor, gentle, downtrodden lady reserved by Providence for this particular task of letters, would so willingly have let me go, had it been permitted!) After, in the course of years, the infant, now grown a man, has acquired the whole difficult matter, knowing how to read freely and what he likes, his eye may nevertheless be tired out

Plate IV

THE AUTHOR
Photographed in a niche at the Escorial by William Walton

Plate V

THE AUTHOR IN HIS STUDY AT RENISHAW
From the photograph by Bill Brandt by courtesy of " Harper's Magazine "

before the day's occupation is finished: while—and this is by
far the most serious disadvantage under which he labours—,
whereas the lover of painting, architecture or music can
approach without hindrance the pictures, buildings and compositions of any country, even the most distant, equally at
liberty to understand them, the national language a writer is
compelled to use fixes a boundary of frontiers to his influence
—or at any rate to the exertion of its full extent—, and inter-
poses a barrier between him and many who would enjoy his
books. Notwithstanding, the writer possesses one proud
distinction in chief, at the same time that it is a difficulty. He
is concerned with a living medium. He must use the quick,
and not the dead: (the reader can notice for himself how the
word *quick* has grown and altered out of the recognition of this
particular sense, since it was employed for this antithesis when
the Bible was translated: we can think, too, of quicksilver,
and how it must have seemed to the medieval alchemists
different from all other metals, a swift, living thing). The
word grows, even as the author writes it, grows slowly every
time a word is written, a fresh feeling conveyed, and the
boundaries of sense—or even nonsense—extended. As an art,
no other, unless it be some way, of which as yet we have
hardly dreamed, of disposing and remodelling a landscape,
can attempt to match it in this respect. More limited than
painting, more material than music, less spatial than architecture, at least it deals with the living word, and can, if directed
towards that purpose, in spells, or to incite whole populations,
overthrow the greatest tyrant or the most powerful state. It
can lull or drive to fury. Reverting to it as art, considered
purely as that, and not as a means of prophecy, a disguise for
evil politics, a method of expressing religious sentiment, for
the instilling of ideas, the instigation of revolts, or for their
quelling and a call to order, each monosyllable, then, each
polysyllable, can boast a millennium-old history, and carries
with it a whole corpus of suggestion, a whole orchestra of
echoes. Thus, though trivial work may die an easy and merci-
ful death, a book, if it be great, continues to live for centuries
after the death of the writer, to prosper, to deepen in beauty, in
the same way that a garden, possessed of its own architectural

E

system, will develop along the lines laid down for it. The trees will grow more lofty, more majestic, more striking in the green and living contrast they offer to the stone-work of wall and buttress; the shadows will oppose a deeper and more sweeping blackness to the light, and the vast pleasances will come to glow with a patine derived from hundreds of years of exposure to sun, rain, snow and the free air of the immense and almost infinite skies. Similarly, for example, the Bible—in the authorised version, and regarded as a book and nothing more—has, by the growth and mellowing, the ever-altering values of its words, become more impressive than when first translated, more imbued with poetry. Now it is part of the consciousness of every literate Englishman. The writers of each succeeding generation owe to it a debt, which they repay throughout their lives: (and how much beauty, too, has been derived from the dry and formal Collects, learnt at school, a kind of Euclid of language!). Yet in the end is almost every book doomed to die with the language that gave it birth: whereas the fruit of the sculptor's and mosaicist's career can, with good fortune, endure until the vault of the temple of the firmament cracks and time itself perishes in the universal and consuming fire. But, albeit this is so, and though the painter can give a more visible shape and colour to his creations, and the composer be able to translate more completely an hour of his audience's time into, as he wishes, a minute or a day of his own, yet none, I proclaim, can induce in the mind those overtones and echoes, those matchless rhythms and transcendental glimpses, that are insinuated there by the great poet or prose-writer. Under everything that a sentient man with a soul fully awakened perceives and comprehends, the word persists: the word, spoken or unspoken, frames every feeling and, like the trumpet of a herald set on a tower, sounds to announce every new discovery, every conquest of fresh territory, and every new thought wrenched or reclaimed from the universal matrix, chaos.

Book Eight

LE GALOP FINAL

CHAPTER ONE

The First Stone in the Sling

THOUGH the practice of his art may afford a writer his chief pleasure, no less than his principal and constant source of worry, though, too, a sudden inspiration may constitute his greatest luxury, yet a minute account of this, his real existence, would be—could only be—of but slight interest to the reader. How is it possible to picture for him the quotidian miseries and splendours of a life attached to the inkpot, the many months spent at a table, the hours when every disturbance is furiously resented, the other, more occasional moments when every interruption is welcome, the evenings when an author looks on his work and finds it good, or those frequent nights when it seems to him to have fallen unbelievably short of what he had intended, the inflations of self-conceit and the agonies of self-reproach, the days when everything grows to giant proportions because it has meaning, the afternoons when all dwindles to pygmy and shows none? What of the racked and sleepless hours before the dawn? Who would wish for a book composed of these? Further, though authorship is, in a sense, a peripatetic profession, since the Muses commune with an author often on long walks through woods, or on the top of mountains, and he is able after this fashion to conquer obdurate details, and albeit he can pack his fountain-pen and write anywhere so long as the place pleases him for writing, yet also it is the most static of careers, entailing for the majority of its practitioners a nearly monastic seclusion and regularity of life during a greater part of the year. Because, even if the particular poem or story on which he is engaged, or proposes to start, does not in reality occupy many weeks, nevertheless to have the energy and leisure in which to give the process of creation and growth its chance of fullest development, the author should be allowed to dwell within a nobly proportioned edifice of days and hours, which offers vistas of space on every side so that he does not have to hurry or cramp his productions. He cannot press out the final flicker of fire or obtain the last spark of energy, if he knows he must soon begin preparations to leave his work in a fortnight's time, in order to deliver a lecture or, it may be, see his mother. He must be granted, if he is to achieve his best, as many days as are necessary for him not to be obliged to count them, a period peaceful and unharassed. Adventures, troubles, joys, the irruption even of a dearest friend into the quiet and regular rhythm of life that a writer has to establish, can break up a whole book. Moreover, if employed upon a poem or something which requires an equivalent trance-like intensity, the writer will remain for some days, or it may be weeks, in so nervous and supersensitive a state, or feel so dull and numb to the outer world, that any slight shock, a pointless altercation or a mere change in his mode of existence, may destroy the life in what he is at work creating. Remember, too, when next you turn the pages of the book you have by your chair, that, if it be a serious attempt, it can scarcely have been completed in under eighteen months and may have taken much longer, and thus you touch the very essence of an author's time, as well as a solid block of it. This does not mean, of course, that he has been slave to the pen-wiper and the blotting-pad day and night for that whole period; but in the volume, notwithstanding, will be, I should hazard, twelve hundred hours of actual composing, writing and revising; that is to say, if it were concentrated, fifty days of twenty-four hours, without time off to eat or sleep. And in addition the book will have consumed countless weeks of indirect labour, and will have cost him the endless troubles provoked by forgetting to answer letters and keep appointments; because he has had something better to do, gentle reader.

If, for these among many reasons, it is useless to try very exactly to portray the life of a working author, nevertheless a consideration of one or two joys or sorrows peculiar to his calling may interest persons unacquainted with them. They resemble, I believe, those of no other profession. As a writer's fame increases, he is, for example, occasionally, though seldom enough, granted the singular sensation—almost I had written pleasure, but that is not an exact enough description to apply to the mixture of nervous apprehension, curiosity and gratification roused in him—of noticing, first that he seems unusually conversant with the book which the fellow-guest in the hotel, or fellow-passenger in an omnibus, is reading, and then, with a shock I have tried to define, of realising why: that it is one of his own books.

Then, again, as an author grows older, he can read a book of his own, when it has become stone cold. This, I think, is one of the most extraordinary experiences he can professionally undergo, more unusual and stimulating than the first sight of a copy of his own first printed book. Before, he has seemed to be part of the volume, or has only read it with a view to correction and revision, while the body of it was still warm with his blood, and he could recall the particular difficulties he had encountered in one paragraph, or the unexpected ease with which the next had been completed. But now he can approach it, as he takes up other books, with the same wish to derive pleasure or an extension of experience from it, with the same casual eye for merits and faults, and with no memory of the processes of making it—though doubtless at the end of it he cannot help trying to reckon the loss and gain accrued in the intervening years. Thus last year I celebrated a private jubilee by reading *Before the Bombardment* twenty years after it had come out, and must confess to having greatly enjoyed it. It was most strange to be presented, after this fashion, between the lines, with the likeness of myself as a young author. There seemed to be no tie between us, yet plainly we were the same person.

Less rare, but none the less a pleasure, is the settling down in a new place for a long stretch of work, the happiness of unpacking, probably in a hotel bedroom, and of the technical preparations, the finding of a table that is steady, of a chair of the right shape, the purchase and spreading of the blotting-paper, the filling of pens. The room in which an author writes is of infinite importance to him, his whole world for those fifty periods of twenty-four hours. Light, heat and absence of noise are the first and most essential requisites: but the feeling of the room, the view from it, the way the light falls in it, are also of great concern to him. To speak less generally and more of myself, I love large apartments, richly furnished, but to rest in, and not for work. A great deal of my writing has been done—in the course of a page or two I will explain why—in the barest of hotel bedrooms. *Before the Bombardment*, which I recognise as the corner-stone of the house I have tried to build, was begun and finished in two consecutive winters in South Italy, in the whitewashed cell of a hotel which had formerly been a monastery, with a fire of logs of orange-tree wood glowing on the hearth with its own peculiar green and yellow flame, or hissing and perfuming the dry air of the bitter mountain cold (which in winter descends to sea-level), and with a window placed so that from where I sat—often, as I thought, just looking out of it when I should have been concentrating (though that, too, had I known it, was an indirect part of the novel),—a view of sea, plumed like a peacock, and of distant ranges beyond, presented itself to me, and seemed to stretch for ever into the innumerable and diverse beauties of air and sky at that season. *Escape With Me!*—at least, the second half of it—was written in a disused kitchen, domed and shaped like a Moorish marabout, opening on a terrace, in the ancient ruined city of Antigua, Guatemala. There, in tropical heat, the great prospect girdled by volcanoes and the blue blossom of jacaranda-trees, I sat picturing Peking, the while a sentry-vulture, posted at a small window, no doubt by the order of his organisation in case I should die during writing, would, at intervals of about an hour, flutter a hideous blue-bottle-dark, serrated wing in at the aperture or, more perturbing still, poke his bald, carrion-coloured neck through it, to see if I were yet ready for him and his band; when, with an accuracy of aim of which I should never have dreamed myself capable, I would hurl my copy of the *Concise Oxford Dictionary* at him through the narrow opening, and he would give a squawk, which said all too plainly, "As you know, duty is duty, and it's only a question of time if you stay here long enough", and then flap hungrily away, only to return a minute after I had gone out on to the terrace to retrieve my invaluable missile: wherefore in time the lexicon lost its cover, and on my return—for it is difficult to carry about the world a book in this condition—I gave it away to the Estate Office at Renishaw; but I could see that when I said to Maynard Hollingworth, "It is only in this state owing to my having been obliged to throw it regularly at a vulture", the excuse sounded, and he thought it, far-fetched. . . . To take another instance, most of the poems in *England Reclaimed* were composed in the bedroom of a hotel outside Syracuse, as was, a few years later, *Winters of Content*, in spite of the many troubles, and the perpetual letters that in consequence would assail me and had to be answered, relating to a previous book over which a libel action was threatened. (The injured lady, I recollect, gave an interview to a newspaper in which she said, "Sitwell compares me to Madame Bovary. I do not know who she is, but my friends tell me she is a French classic!") The volumes of *Left Hand, Right Hand!*, so far as they have progressed, have been written at Renishaw, in my small study enclosed within the thick walls of the oldest part of the house, and hung with the originals of the illustrations to this work by John Piper. Here, among towers of books and accumulated papers, are to be found, too, many objects familiar to me since my earliest childhood, for the room formerly served my father as his chief writing-place.

By now, I conclude that the truth of the statement made at the beginning of this chapter has been established for the reader: that the story of an author's pursuit of his profession can hold little of concern to the outside world. The facts exampled above, slight and dull though they may be, are the chief I can muster. On the other hand, his, as it were, extra-mural activities (and the way he, as a writer, looks at them) can entertain and even, who knows, instruct the reader. Fortunately, my exterior adventures in the time of which I write were numerous and varied, and soon I return to one in particular. But first I must ask him to hold in the background of his mind for the remainder of this book, during most of

Was author homosexual, latent or otherwise? Are these his lovers?

which I talk of other things, the many long, often arduous but contented months devoted each year to writing; those vistas of days, for the most part unexciting and of a regular rhythm, spent usually abroad and in company with my brother Sacheverell, William Walton or Adrian Stokes, and other practitioners of the arts.

Possessed of many interests and, I am thankful and proud to write, of many friends, I found it needful, if I was to become a writer, to escape from them for long periods. The world was both too much with me and against me. And in this connection I recall that when, after the publication of a book which had enjoyed a great success, my sister received an invitation to luncheon from a woman we had known for many years, but who never remembered our existence until reviews in the newspapers reminded her of it, Edith sent her the following logical reply.

DEAR MRS. ALMER,

After five years, you have again been kind enough to ask me to luncheon. The reason for this is that I have just published a successful book: the reason I have had a successful book is that I do not go out and waste my time and energy, but work hard, morning and afternoon. If I accept your kind invitation, I shall have to leave off earlier in the morning, and shall be too tired to work in the afternoon. Then my next book will not be such a success, and you will not ask me to luncheon; or, at the best, less often. So that, under these circumstances, I am sure you will agree it is wiser for me not to accept your present kind invitation.—Yours sincerely, EDITH SITWELL.

PTSD

On the whole, then, so bitter had the long war made me, so full was I still of rage and despair, and of contempt for those who would not see, that I did not, in the years immediately following 1918, make new friends with the ease of the days before the war. But to this there was one glittering exception. Certain friends helped greatly, moreover, instead of hindering, and chief of these was my new friend, Mrs. Henry McLaren, or Lady Aberconway as she is now. Indeed, any account of my daily life between the end of the First World War and the present day would be incomplete without the mention of her. I had been first taken to her house in 1916 or '17, and in 1926 I dedicated to her *Before the Bombardment*: so that it must have been somewhere between those dates, I think in 1920, that a mere acquaintanceship first sloughed its dull and torpid chrysalis, and soared as friendship: yet as sometimes happens in things important to me, I cannot be sure of the precise moment. I am, indeed, grateful to her, no less for her wisdom than for a rarer and opposite quality which transcends it; that is to say that she never hesitates to fly in the face of common sense should the most loyal and scrupulous principles of friendship she upholds demand the adoption of such tactics. Many of the most delightful hours of my life have been passed in her company and, if it were only for that reason, I must try to describe her remarkable personality, albeit to attempt to seize on either her appearance or character and endeavour to add permanence to their other attributes is far from easy: for both are volatile, not in the sense of being gay or lively— though as a companion she can often be that—, but because every quality about her is so much relative to other qualities, and so finely constituted; her looks, for example, her bearing, the words she speaks depend to such an extent on her colouring and expression, more particularly on the aquamarine glow of her eyes which dominate her whole face, as well as on a singular style, an individual elegance and general crystalline sparkle, that they are difficult to isolate and fix in dull ink on paper. With the immediate impression she produces on entering a room, of delicacy of texture and sensitiveness of feeling, goes, too, at first sight and most misleadingly, what appears to be an unusual formality, this being produced by a natural precision of demeanour and speech, which, as one grows to know her better, adds an element of surprise to the effect of the discovery of her most unconventional wit and wits, in the same way that one finds out, too, before long, how her discretion covers an unusual and warm understanding of human beings.

The daughter of Sir Melville Macnaghten, a former famous head of Scotland Yard, and of Lady Macnaghten— whom the late Lady Oxford once told me she considered the most beautiful woman she had ever seen—, it must be from her father that Christabel has inherited so many of the qualities that go to make a great detective. Just as she is one of the two or three people to whom I should apply in a case of human suffering, so, if I wanted to know what had happened to someone or something, and why, she undoubtedly would be the first person to whom I should turn for information, sure that if she were not already in possession of it, she would soon obtain it. For, in addition to being inexhaustibly resourceful, she permits herself the utmost bias on behalf of her friends, and there would therefore, I think, be no lengths to which she would not go to help them. Further, the elegant fragility of her appearance masks a formidable will-power. All this, then, helps to explain the unusual kind of compliment I once heard my brother pay her.

"Christabel!", he observed, "I've suddenly realised that you would be the ideal companion for a shipwreck!"

"Why?"

"Because one could depend on you to push someone else off the raft to make room for a friend!"

Yet this tribute, though it sums up a little of what I want to signify, altogether leaves out of account the pleasure and fun of her company, and the sort of surprise that it offers you, while it also entirely omits the beauty she can create in her surroundings. The raft would, after it had been made safe for her friends, have very soon become, I think, a most desirable, habitable, comfortable and even beautiful retreat. Her extraordinary gift of tact, and her effacement of her own wishes—though never of her captivating personality—in every friendship upon which she enters, make her singularly unlike the general run of people in her every response.

There were others, however, who made up for her unselfishness. There were many who wished to waste their own time, and many who wished merely to waste yours. Quite apart, then, from attempts at forcible feeding, from requests to write prefaces or epilogues, or a few favourable words to be quoted on covers, to read manuscripts and send criticisms gratis, open—or shut—exhibitions, give interviews on any subject, autograph books, attend conferences, join clubs, sign letters of protest and manifestos, take part in symposiums, speak on the B.B.C. for infant fees, support every sort of society for the prevention of one, and encouragement of another—or sometimes the same—thing, write articles, celebrate centenaries, deliver lectures, and all those perpetual and ingenious schemes to make you catch colds and agues in a thousand different ways, and so prevent you from working for a time—or better still for ever; quite apart, then, from all this (which is the lot of every well-known English-speaking writer), my parents by themselves would have been sufficient to render impossible any serious and consecutive effort. To their children they constituted a profession in themselves, and one which wore out health and exhausted patience. You never knew what they might not do next. When, a few years later, I was at last, as will be seen, successful in persuading my father that he would be happier if he resided abroad, the paths of his children became a little easier: but until that moment it was out of the question to work untroubled and with ease at home in England. The letters from my father which rained in by every post, on subjects ranging from the composition of the atom to the best empirical methods of cutting your toe-nails, but, so far as I was concerned, for the most part relating to business and complaining of my lack or misuse of ability, concluded often with a *catalogue raisonné* of my faults of character and conduct, and were enough to oblige one to use up every scrap of energy in reply. My sister faced the storms in her own flat—even though, by coincidence, she was curiously liable to be away when my family came to London. My father's views on woman's place in the world—which were that she should be out of it—allowed her a little more freedom from his letters (on the other hand, my mother demanded her presence the whole time), whereas it was his duty as father, ancestor and descendant in one, to torment my brother, and still more myself in my character of eldest son, on every conceivable occasion. He liked to make plans, to inflate and deflate them at will, in the manner of a child playing with a toy balloon, and would plague an idea as a dog worries a bone. In addition, he must know exactly what we were doing or proposing to do. "It is dangerous for you", he used to point out, "to lose touch with me for a single day. You never know when you may not need the benefit of my experience and advice."

To combat this, first to obtain half of one's own life, and subsequently a still greater proportion, I was obliged to invent a technique. In this direction, success crowned my efforts—to such an extent that at one moment I had thoughts of opening a *Bureau for Advising Sons with Difficult Fathers*. The position nevertheless held continual possibilities of further trouble, for nerves became exacerbated and if somehow we tricked our parents into allowing us the time in which to write a book, the reviewers of the period would be sure to fall on it in the particularly insolent and vituperative manner then reserved for us. Hardly any other writers of the epoch incurred the same degree of obloquy. The works of the Georgian poets, for example, were received with acclamation. Thus—for the reader may doubt the truth of this, dismissing it as a symptom of that occupational disease of the artist, persecution mania—when *Before the Bombardment* appeared, one popular critic of a Sunday paper said that in it I spat on the whole of the Victorian Age and that the book should have been called *Great Expectorations*! "It is not", this same sensitive being pronounced, "so much a matter of taste or good breeding, as a matter of sportsmanship. . . . I shudder at the vulgarities." . . . The *Outlook* pronounced that I was "fussy" about the war, and through the general storm and roar of rage, the still small voices of the then Mayor of Scarborough and of the then Rector were heard to say respectively, through the medium of an interview, "I have not read the book . . . it is in thoroughly bad taste", and "It is a vulgar caricature. The best thing is to treat it with silent contempt." Alas, the critics did not adopt the last, singularly original remedy recommended to them. Let me add in gratitude that almost the only understanding review I received of this novel, as, a year or two earlier, of *Out of the Flame*, was from the benevolent pen of Mary Webb. In a review in the *Bookman* she wrote, "His [the author's] considered judgement is very terrible. We must remember when we shiver under this savage irony, that the author and others like him are recently come from Calvary, and that the vinegar they proffer there is surely this vision of life as a bleak irony—a cruel and obscene jest. . . . The book is packed with wit, humour, subtlety, and, though liking some of the author's poems extremely, I had not realised his reserves of intensity until I read his prose."[1] But "Merely caddish", said the *Yorkshire Post*, the paper chiefly read by my mother's friends, who would, when they were in London, go round to see my parents, giggle in an embarrassed but jolly way about us, and confirm my father and mother in their view that as writers we possessed no talent and no future. ("You ought to stop it. It isn't fair on you two dear things!") It would be almost sure, as our old Nurse Davis used to say, to "set them off" again. By then, the writer of the book would also find himself often in quite a bad temper.

Therefore, to avoid altercations, and because the unhappiness my parents caused, and the contemplation of their own unhappiness responsible for it, might have attained to the quality of tragedy, the technique to be applied was bound to be farcical, for farce lowers the temperature and reduces proportions. . . . First, I will take the most gross example of the kind of incident that resulted.

In January 1922 my father was in London and asked me to come and see him. Wise from experience, I knew that the interview he proposed could only lead to further trouble between us, for he was in a most intransigent mood. But I could hardly refuse to meet him. In consequence, I made the excuse that I was ill. (This seemed serviceable, because it was

[1] I only met Mary Webb twice, but on each occasion was struck by the quiet and pleasant friendliness of her demeanour. This appeared surprising to me because she was about twelve years older than myself, plainly very shy, one could tell by her over-prominent eyes and general look that she was suffering from her health, her interests were of another range, and, lastly, because what she had set herself to do was of so completely a different order from what I was attempting. I would have expected, in fact, to encounter a certain hostility: but she was fair-minded, generous and understanding. The first time we met, I sat next her at a dinner organised by the Tomorrow Club—of which I was a guest—, I had not at once realised the identity of my neighbour. The second occasion was more curious. Some months later, I had gone up to Hampstead to see the work of a painter who lived there, but by a stupid sleight of memory had gone to the wrong address. When I arrived on the heights and rang the bell of what I thought was the house, the door was opened after a moment or two by Mary Webb. . . . I then realised what had happened, and was somewhat taken aback, for it is always a nuisance to a writer to be disturbed: but she was so welcoming and kind, rather as if she had been expecting me to call, that I suffered no sense of intrusion, and though I refused to go in, we stopped for about a quarter of an hour or so in the doorway and talked.

most improbable that we should meet by chance, and if we did, it was, I knew, still more unlikely that he would recognise me.) He replied, on Monday of the week in question, that he would call on me at 5 P.M. on Saturday. . . . In the days which followed I forgot both my alleged illness and my father's proposed visit, and on the afternoon he had selected, I had gone, quite unperturbed, to tea with Jean de Bosschère, at the other end of London. He lived in Bayswater, in one of those streets that are peculiar to our great city: long streets where identical yellow-brown houses, each with an identical projecting pillared portico, of a magnificence unrelated to its surroundings, face one another in an eternity of yellow fog. Standing under the canopy supported by Doric columns, you saw, if you looked opposite, what might be a dim reflection in a fly-blown mirror, while if you glanced sideways, between the pillar and the house, an even more astounding vista of apparently reflected space, thus divided, greeted you. That way lay infinity, as well as eternity. However, I rang the bell, someone answered, and soon I was inside. My host, wearing as usual the lace jabot, brown velvet coat, knee-breeches, silk stockings and buckled shoes that, in the years of the First World War, made him so vivid if singular a phantom as he bicycled through the London streets, was entertaining various friends—among them Aldous—and I soon forgot the cheerless, formalised depression outside. Alas, before many minutes had passed, I remembered something. All at once, at 4.30, as though a bell had struck in my mind, I recollected the immediate menace of my father's visit. Dashing out into the growing January dusk that seeped from sky and ground, and squeezed between the pillars and the houses, I found the street empty of human life as an early canvas by Chirico, nothing but pillar after pillar, railing after railing, and a few distant, decapitated bodies walking under the wet circular extinguishers of their own umbrellas.

In those days I walked very fast, and since it was obviously hopeless to wait for a passing vehicle, I set out at once to cross London on foot, and reached Carlyle Square with only five minutes to spare, for my father was always punctual. I tore off my mackintosh and raced upstairs. . . . Alas, the doorbell rang before I had been given time to undress. Hastily removing my wet shoes, and ruffling my hair, I threw myself, still panting from the exertions of the past half-hour, into my bed, arriving in it just as my father opened the door. No doubt I appeared to be very feverish. Fortunately, Mrs. Powell never lost her nerve. Showing my father upstairs, she had remarked,

"Sir George, the doctors do not wish anyone to remain with the patient for more than five minutes. I will notify you when your time is up."

My father entered, seated himself in a chair, and regarded me, as I lay there, clutching my bed-clothes up to my chin, as in a French farce (for if I let go of them, he would see I was fully dressed), and wearing upon my face, no doubt, a wild expression.

"I'm afraid I hadn't realised, dear boy, how ill you were!" he remarked, "but I hope it's only nerves." Here he extended a finger towards my neck, to feel the heat of my skin; but I clutched the bed-clothes all the tighter, and had an inspiration.

"The doctors can't make out what is the matter with me," I said. "They've had several cases like it. Apparently it's infectious!"

My father pushed his chair back and got up with a jump. He uttered hastily the words,

"Well, I'm afraid I must be getting back now—so much to do!", and left the room, long before Mrs. Powell could return to usher him out. Indeed, almost before I had finished saying good-bye, I had heard the front door slam behind him.

In order to prevent this kind of occurrence, and other constant interruptions and interferences, it appeared absolutely necessary for Sacheverell and myself to absent ourselves from London for fully half the year, and to leave no address behind us. With this object in view, we ordered a supply of special writing-paper, of which for many years we made frequent use. Engraved on it at the right-hand corner was the name of an imaginary yacht, *S. Y. Rover*, and opposite this it carried a burgee, showing a skull and crossbones in white, on a black ground. By this means we could always reach my father by post, if so we wished, for we could write to him from where we were staying for the autumn and winter months, explaining

Privileged Life

that our friend Jonah's yacht had "just put in" at Ostend or Naples or Athens, or wherever it might be—and that we had "come on here for a few days' rest, while the craft is being overhauled". We would add, "In the meantime, dearest father, do not trouble to answer until we can give you an address. Our next stopping place is uncertain, and the letter will only be lost." The singular contradiction about this particular adapting of items from the classical repertory of farce was that two young men had to employ subterfuge against their stern father, not in order to shirk daily toil or to spend money lavishly, or to disguise the fact that they were living with the most shrill and gilded of mistresses, but merely in order to exist more quietly and cheaply that they would have been able to do at home, and to work hard at their profession! . . . This paradox imparted to the whole machinery a curious twist.

Occasionally, of course, plans miscarried. Amalfi[1] constituted our first-chosen and much-loved refuge, and we would stay there for many months in the Cappuccini. . . . Thus one morning, the day before we were due to start for Naples, en route there, but had given out that we were embarking on the *Rover* for a tour of the Polynesian Islands, we were in the Piccadilly offices of Messrs. Thomas Cook & Son, obtaining our tickets to Naples and places in the Wagons-Lits. . . . Suddenly I saw my father enter the office. Though it is true that, if he met us casually out, he never, or very seldom, recognised us, we could not take the risk. And, I apprehend, I rather startled even our tolerant friend who was attending to us, used as he was to the strange ways of customers, when I whispered to him hurriedly, "Excuse me! we must get under the counter for a bit!" and seizing Sacheverell hurried him through the opening, to the shelter of the hollow mahogany barrier, where we both hid, in a rather cramped and uncomfortable position, until our friend the clerk,—who knew my father and therefore soon sized up the position—signalled the "All Clear". In the end, we reached Amalfi safely. The hotel, which until a century before had been a monastery, belonged

---

[1] The reader will find a fuller account of Amalfi and the Hotel Cappuccini in *Discursions on Travel, Art and Life*. (Grant Richards, 1925.)

to the same proprietor who owned at Cava de' Tirreni, some thirty miles away, the hotel in which all English travellers of the late eighteenth and early nineteenth century stopped a night, on their way from Pompeii to visit the then newly identified temples at Paestum, or on their return thence to Naples. Don Alfredo Vozzi, the great-grandson of the first owner of the two hotels, was accustomed, therefore, by heredity to the ways of English travellers—he understood them. The employment of members of the same family in one profession over a long period seems naturally to produce physically an aristocratic type, and with his pointed beard, deep-set, sunken eyes with hooded upper lids, his aquiline nose, and his air of melancholy and distinction, he was no exception to this rule. He lived in the hotel, and occupied as his sitting-room a cell in the precise middle of the building. Its walls could not be seen for the number of pictures hanging on them: small paintings of the Neapolitan neighbourhood, executed in the romantic yet factual idiom of the so-called *Scuola di Posillipo*, which had flourished in Naples from 1820 to 1850. Here, with a large brass bowl of red-hot ashes standing on the cement floor, to give warmth to the place, Don Alfredo would pass the winter days, seldom going out—and never if there was a wind, for it afflicted his nerves, he said. So, though still wearing round his shoulders a large, thick, knitted, dark green shawl, folded like a rug, instead of pacing the terraces as he did in the summer, he would sit now by the door of his room on a small, rather elegant wooden settee or sofa, which just fitted the wall space, and would smoke endlessly very rank Toscana cigars, or occasionally indulge in the vague, quasi-philosophical, quasi-poetic but sonorous generalisations so dear to the cultivated Italian mind,

"L' uomo è vittima del Destino", or
"La volontà delle donne è come la volontà dei fiori".

But, in spite of his gentleness, an air of authority penetrated to every corner of the hotel from this, its nerve centre. Even as he talked of man and his fate, one ear was listening, one eye was watching with inherited skill. Suddenly—for the glass door was always open—he would call or just clap his hands, and the passage would all at once be full of hurrying house-maids and swarthy porters and valets. There was something about him, in fact, of both the patriarch and the *grand seigneur*, and he thoroughly comprehended the character of his own hotel, and refused, until circumstances compelled him, to modernise it.

At that time, no lift had been installed, and since the hotel hung high up on the cliff-side, a visitor could only reach it by climbing three hundred steps, or by allowing himself to be carried by two men in a chair. This remoteness from the world, and the absence of central heating, helped to keep it comparatively empty in the winter, when it became to my mind an ideal place for writers. The simple lines of the old white building, fitting into this fantastic landscape of mountain and sea, of painted villages poised on crags, of broken towers and castles of stone, of huge limestone cliffs, with natural caves and grottoes, and, here and there, the likeness of a window in the rock, of flying buttresses and turrets and sheer walls, as neatly as a snail does into a crevice; the belvedere, on a long gently curving terrace high placed on glittering, impregnable rocks, scattered over, from November till March, with jonquils; above all, the view, the unrivalled view of sea and distant mountains, and over these at all hours, in heat or cold, the light of Neapolitan skies, bursts of light from behind clouds, or torrents of light from a crystal-clear dome, light reflected from rocks and sea, and never playing twice the same variations on its themes of vertical and horizontal, of mass and plane, the dazzling celestial cities built of a stormy morning, when through the *sirocco*—a leaden day lined with gold, but with all its interest concentrated in the heavens and not on the earth, where roll scents of orange and myrtle—, there, on the horizon, a water-spout could be seen whirling, like a witch on a broomstick, at a pace the eye could not credit, across the waves toward the town, and, as you watched, the light again created new cities on the mountains, and above them great castles, metropolises of giants, whose tread now you began to hear, striding across from hill to hill, peaks beyond the reach of man, yet inhabited, and many fragments and repetitions of the Tower of Babel reared themselves up, gleaming, until the flashing of a gold lance broke them, and they dissolved into sound and water, water falling everywhere, on sea, on cliff, on terrace, on the world—all these features and effects made Amalfi to me a place of excitement and of inspiration.

I must emphasise, moreover, that the landscape affected me in a way in which no other has except my own. It made some deep personal appeal, sought to enforce some claim. Directly I had seen it, when I first stayed there as a boy of nineteen in 1912, I had at once felt with the landscape, and with its people too, this curious sympathy: (the same lure, perhaps, had called hither from their frozen seas and tangled mists the Norman invaders of nearly a thousand years before). During this first visit a glimpse of the future had asserted, or insinuated, itself, as it sometimes does, and though I had then entertained no suspicion that I should ever become an author, the knowledge had filled me that one day I should return here to spend much time engaged in a task that afforded me a sense of completeness—and, in fact, much of my earlier work was written here. No doubt the monastic air still retained by the Cappuccini, the atmosphere of peace emanating from its ancient, rustic cloister of Saracenic arches, painted a flashing white which gathered to itself all colours, would have helped any artist in his work.

I was aware that my father also liked Amalfi, but now when he came to Italy, his plans for the restoration of Montegufoni, no less than his fears of putting a strain upon his heart by having to climb so many steps—for he resented having to pay five lire to be carried—rendered a visit to it unlikely from him. In time the phantom *Rover* had begun to wear a little thin, and in 1922 Sacheverell and I abandoned it temporarily, and for the sake of variety, in favour of a mythical invitation to explore Asia Minor with a party of excavators. (Even this antiquarian plan did not recommend itself to my father.) Posts would be uncertain, we had explained: better to write no letters. We had then gone straight to Amalfi and begun work. . . . We were, respectively, progressing with it fairly well when one evening a feeling of suspense began to darken the air. What could it be? William Walton was staying with us. He spent most of the time by himself in a room containing a typical South Italian piano—similar to those upon which, as you pass beneath in the street of a southern Catholic city, you hear young girls practising, high up, from iron-barred convent windows. Here he would sit composing and copying out at a large table facing a window on the cloister, the whiteness of which in the sun filled the smoky air with a redoubled and spectral light; he would hardly move except to go to the window-ledge from time to time, where he would cut a Toscana cigar in two with a safety-razor blade he kept for that purpose. He smoked these half-cigars almost always as he wrote. Even William, then, who had not seen us for many hours, admitted in the evening that he also had felt some influence. It soon explained itself. At dinner, the German manageress came up to us and said,

"The herr-director at La Cava, he has joos telephone to say a big English Barone arrive here tomorrow mit servant, and we are to kill first thing in the morgen fourteen chicken."

To us the meaning of this esoteric message was clear. The news of the immolation—for so to a stranger it must have sounded, a sacrifice such as that ordained by Cetewayo or some other paramount Zulu chieftain—gave to those initiated the clue. In the French phrase, it signalled my father's approach. Especially in Southern Italy, where meat is always of an incomparable hardness of flesh, the killing and eating of chickens had become part of the System. They had to be slain as early as possible, otherwise they, too, would be tough, in which case my father, with a sigh, would push the plate away, saying in a voice of tragedy, "Troppo fresco per me!" . . . The stories on which I was engaged, *Triple Fugue*, and Sacheverell's *All Summer in a Day*, had to be thrown aside and hidden while we held a council. Fully interpreted or decoded, the words of the manageress had told us, then, that my father was sleeping the night at La Cava an hour away by motor, and was coming here some time the following day, accompanied by Robins, for a visit of at least a week; each chicken being the token of a luncheon or a dinner. . . . It would be of no avail to try to escape: it was too late, he would be sure to find out, and it would only look discourteous. The sole line of action open to us was to pretend to be expecting him, to have come here on purpose, and give him a touchingly warm welcome. In support, the spectral *Rover*, only just dismantled, would have to be brought out of dock again. The owner had changed his mind, we decided, and had persuaded us to board her at Naples, preparatory to a cruise in the Pacific. And hearing that my father might spend a week at Amalfi, we had come here on the chance of seeing him, and to rest for a few days beforehand. (He never objected to the idea of rest: but if you had mentioned that you were at work on a book, a look of intense concern would immediately be seen to fix itself on his face, and he would issue, in a tone suggesting that you were proposing something rash beyond hardihood, such as trying to swim the Atlantic for a wager, one of his customary and familiar warnings: "Oh, I *shouldn't* do *that* if I were you! You'd better drop the idea at once. My cousin Stephen Arthington had a friend who utterly ruined his health by writing a novel!")

No one knew at what time he was to be expected: but we were aware that he liked early hours, so it was better to be on the watch almost from sunrise. It proved a tiring day. All the morning we hung out of the loggias of our rooms, ready to wave enthusiastic greetings, our eyes straining at the immense and classic view; albeit on this occasion not for its beauty, though it was a perfect and typical October day of the South, strayed from the fold of summer, and far away, beyond the multi-coloured sea, mosaicked by the tides and little shiftings of the sand, by the clearness, too, of the water, that showed just the same degree of transparency in blue and green and purple and gold that is to be observed in the great mosaics of Cefalù and Monreale and other churches of the old kingdom of which this had been part, lay the thin girdle of gold and silver —of sand and foam—which divides the sea there from the land, culminating in the range of mountains, Mont' Alburno towering over them, its rocky bulk, owing to its bareness, catching again all the colours of sea, sky and air, and, as it were, presenting a kind of summary of them. No, our gaze was reserved for the road, which, here and there, could be seen ribboning its way precariously above precipices. When luncheon came, one of us had to remain on duty—but indeed we had little appetite, a single tortuous strand of macaroni and an unripe tangerine sufficed us. Then back again we went to our vigil for the entire afternoon. About five o'clock, when the sun rolled on the edge of the sea once more, facing our cliff, so that every weed in the rock, itself sparkling, every large pink lily springing from it, and every orange among its cluster of glossy leaves on the trees bordering the terrace, showed, vivid and unreal as the fruit and blossoms in pre-Raphaelite paintings, and the very road seemed magnified by the rays, and near enough for us to touch it, at last, then, a motor—or to be more precise visually, a high column of dust, could be seen whirling on the road in and out above the coast, towards the hotel. At the gate far below, it became stationary and began to subside, and out of it stepped a well-known figure in a grey suit, crowned with a grey wide-awake hat, and carrying a grey umbrella lined with green against the sun's rays, which made his red beard all the redder. Snatching from Robins, who followed him, the celebrated lifebuoy air-cushion, which was one of his properties, in case he should be tired during the climb and be in consequence obliged to sit awhile on the rock, he looked up at the hotel and saw us wildly waving our handkerchiefs. He pointed and said something to Robins. It was too far for us to distinguish very clearly the conflicting emotions passing over his countenance, but Robins told us afterwards what his words had been. Feeling his pulse, he had said, "Do you see them, Robins? . . . They might have given *me* a heart-attack!" . . . The visit, of a week's duration as we had foreseen, passed off quite satisfactorily. He seemed pleased to hear of the *Rover* again, and opined that its owner must be a most interesting man. My father then explained that he could not spend less than a week here—very likely it would take him longer—since he was obliged to motor forty miles every day, in order to examine the foundations of a villa in which Petrarch had been asked to stay (before going to Montegufoni), but had declined, probably owing, it was suspected, to a feeling that he would not be able to write while stopping there—a sensation with which we were able to sympathise.

(It seemed to us a pity that Petrarch had lived at too early a period to have been able to avail himself of the services of the *Rover*!) It was necessary to my father's work, apparently, for him to measure the foundations; so, during the seven days, he was away a good deal. But even thus we could get no writing done, and one more week was added to the countless others wasted in more or less identical fashion.

A later episode, connected with the same place and arising out of like circumstances, can be classified in a different, more frightening category: for a moment farce assumed a more imposing mantle. . . . One autumn my brother and I were just again leaving England for a long secret session of work at Amalfi, when, the very evening before our departure, my father remarked casually:

"Your mother and I thought of running over to Amalfi for the winter, and staying at the Hotel Cappuccini. She would be quite happy all day on the terrace."

(In parenthesis, just as no-one of my father's generation ever died, but "passed away", so he never took a train, but always "ran over" or "ran down". . . . "I ran down to London last week.") In this emergency the good ship *Rover* could be of little use. As so often before, I was obliged to improvise. Since, as I have pointed out, the essence of our opposing systems of strategy was that my father planned every move for months, or even years, ahead, it was impossible to defeat him along those lines: instead I must depend on the element of surprise, backed by inspiration, power of fantasy, élan and the feeling of the moment. Now, therefore, I summoned a landslide to my aid—and it responded!

"Oh, haven't you heard?" I asked. "There's been a very bad landslide at Amalfi; and several parts of the terrace have been carried away. It was in the *Daily Mail* only a few days ago. . . . I thought you would be sure to see it."

This news checked my father's plans. It rendered Amalfi, he said, quite impossible for a stay for him and my mother, as they must be able to take a walk on the level, without the necessity of always having to climb the steps to and from the town. But Sacheverell and I were not so sure they might not change their minds again, and decided it would be wiser to alter our own arrangements, and go elsewhere. And when, in a week's time, we reached our new refuge, in Sicily, the first local newspaper we saw informed its readers, in terms of magniloquent sorrow, that a grave landslide had just occurred at Amalfi, and that two portions of the famous terrace of the Hotel Cappuccini had been destroyed. . . . Henceforth I avoided making an excuse of that sort.

When in London—and the periods we spent there were now not so long, for, in addition to being obliged to seek sanctuary abroad while working, I was still prospective Liberal candidate for Scarborough, and had often to live there for a month or two—we liked to abandon ourselves entirely to its life. Though the years before August 1914 seemed now infinitely distant; though the whole inner consciousness of each of us who possessed a soul had been laid waste and tormented by the horrors which had taken place, the stories of torture, which might not be true, the mountains of dead, whom we had seen for ourselves, and the weight of whose sacrifice oppressed us still; though, too, the general hysteria engendered by democratic wars had envenomed our tempers, no less than the sight of suffering had embittered and saddened us; notwithstanding, we retained, as all of our age at the time must have done, a certain zest for life and an interest in it. The inner wounds would take many years to heal, but meanwhile the world was open to us, we could travel, make up for lost years, and observe what was going on round us. Part, at least, of the brilliant promise to be divined in the English world of art and literature in 1914, though all appeared to have withered at the breath of war, was now to be made good. The decade soon to open was one of the most brilliant in recent literary history, as a glance at the names of those writing will prove. There could be felt in the air of the great city much energy and a lively and pleasurable effervescence very different from the grey blight which lies over it after the Second World War: that kind of greasy, lethargic, puritan sloth which, I think, cannot have manifested itself again until now since the decade ending in 1660.

There were all kinds of amusements to be found or to be

made, both large and small. One of them—but I forget
whether in this year, or in one of the years immediately
following—occurred with the return of Tetrazzini to Covent
Garden. Sacheverell—already an ardent lover of Italian
opera and singing—asked our friend Richmond Temple, who
was a director of the Savoy, where the famous prima donna
was staying, whether she would receive us, so that we could
present to her a wreath of bay and myrtle as a tribute from the
young writers of England. Madame Tetrazzini indicated her
willingness, and it was arranged. The seven or eight persons
who formed the deputation included Aldous Huxley, my
sister, my brother and me. The night before, Aldous and
Maria Huxley very hospitably entertained us to dinner, and
afterwards, while Aldous was composing the speech for us, with
Sacheverell—who it had been decided was to deliver it—at
his side, Julian Huxley, I remember, walked up and down the
room in a state of enchantment at the idea of the ceremony,
offering to help his brother.

"Oh, why can't I be a young writer for the afternoon, to
take part in it? What shall we say now, Aldous? 'From the
young to the old?' 'From the future great to the past great?'"

"Do shut up, Julian."

"Oh, *why*, *why*? Or just 'From the *Future* to the *Past*'?
'From the *Young* Poets of England to the *Old* Singers of
Italy'?"

"Do be quiet. . . . *How* can we get on with it?"

Eventually the speech was finished, and the next day, after
luncheon, we assembled at the Savoy, and were conducted
to the Tetrazzini's private suite. Her sitting-room into which
we were shown had been converted for the occasion into a
bower of white lilac: several journalists and a camera-man,
with a towering camera and a flash-light assistant, were in
attendance. All was ready for her to make her appearance.
The bedroom door was now flung open, and the famous prima
donna entered. Short, fat, ageing, wearing an over-elaborate
brown *crêpe* dress, with much lace attached to it, she nevertheless had a captivating air of kindness and good-nature,
and walked as one used to receiving acclamation. She advanced slowly, making a conventional theatrical gesture of

greeting and pleasure, with her right hand to the poets, drawn up in line, and with her left hand to the camera-man, up his ladder ready to pull the trigger, and to the journalists, their pencils poised. The tall figure of Sacheverell, very young, —just over twenty—stood heading our number, with Aldous, over-topping him, just behind. Slowly, very slowly, she continued to move towards us. The camera-man was just giving the signal, when suddenly the great singer caught her foot in a rug and fell flat! . . . There are those, I know, who hold that no fall, whatever the circumstances of it, can ever be funny. All I can say is that I disagree with them. . . . Fortunately, she had come to no hurt, and still more oddly, seemed singularly undiscomfited by her misadventure. She was helped up, and straightened her dress: the poets straightened their faces: the camera-man again got ready: Sacheverell was just going to read our message, when, this time impelled I suppose by curiosity, Tetrazzini snatched the paper from him. Sacheverell, who dislikes speaking in public, was nevertheless determined to go through with it, so he snatched it back, saying at the same time in his deep voice, "Prego, Divinissima", and began to read. The camera clicked —and so there a delightful occasion remains, enshrined in the dusty office files of newspapers.

Our chief extra-mural activity in 1919—for my part-editing of *Art and Letters* counts as a professional—was the organising of the Exhibition of Modern French Art at the Mansard Gallery at Heal's: of which Roger Fry, sponsor of the two great exhibitions of Post-Impressionist pictures in 1910 and 1912, wrote that it was "the most representative show of modern French art seen in London for many years". Associated with my brother and myself in collecting the pictures was a Parisian-Polish dealer, who subsequently became celebrated, Zborowski. With flat, Slavonic features, brown almond-shaped eyes, and a beard which might have been shaped out of beaver's fur, ostensibly, he was a kind, soft business-man, and a poet as well. He had an air of melancholy, augmented by the fact that he spoke no English, and could not find his way about London (to which city this was his first visit). . . . The days before the opening of the Exhibition are memorable to me because of the interest of seeing the pictures unpacked, and of hanging them. During the war it had been for so long out of the question to see modern French pictures at all, except for a single specimen at some gallery, that considerable excitement now evinced itself. The July evenings were very hot, and after dinner, at about nine o'clock every evening, while my brother, Zborowski and I supervised the hanging, friends would come in from the Eiffel Tower Restaurant and from Fitzroy Street near-by, to watch. Among those present at these unveilings would be our hierophant, Roger Fry, who walked round from his studio. The Exhibition, though by no means enormous, included pictures by—among others—Othon Friesz, Vlaminck, Derain, Matisse, Picasso, Modigliani, Survage, Soutine, Suzanne Valadon, Kisling, Halicka, Marcoussis, Léger, Gabriel-Fournier, Ortiz, André Lhote, Utrillo, and Dufy, and sculptures by Archipenko and Zadkine. Derain and Picasso had both made their personal appearance in London that summer, when Diaghilew had produced the two finest ballets of his second period, *La Boutique Fantasque*, and *The Three-Cornered Hat*. I had been present at the first night of both performances, and shall never forget the excitement of first seeing truly modern works of scenic art upon the stage. Both ballets were exactly calculated to show the supreme qualities of satiric dash and comic audacity possessed by such great dancers as Massine and Lopokova, now at their zenith. Moreover Derain's dropscene for *La Boutique* and Picasso's for *The Three-Cornered Hat* were probably the most inspired and original that had been painted for over a century. Picasso had, of course, long been the favourite of the *cognoscenti* of modern art, but Derain was a comparatively new star, and had much impressed them. And I remember one evening at the Mansard Gallery, as a glazed and framed canvas by this artist was being unpacked, and Roger Fry was admiring it, a friend drew attention to the fact that a currant had become wedged between the paint and the glass. A philistine was just going to remove it, when Roger boomed out,

"Better leave it alone. He probably placed it there intentionally. It makes rather a swagger contour!"

Indeed, so much esteemed that year was the French painter by those who knew, that it was said that all the cows on the home-farm at Garsington had caught the fever from Lady Ottoline and her friends, and, when they lowed in their green, daisy-sprinkled Oxfordshire pastures, could be heard now, instead of making their former pointless, vacuous sounds, to moo at each other, with the correct Bloomsbury accentuation, a purposeful *Doë-rain, Doë-rain*!

Sacheverell and I were very eager for the Exhibition to be a success, as much for our own advantage as for the good name of the English public of art-lovers. Sacheverell was most anxious to leave Oxford (to which, as in the next chapter we shall see, he had gone): but my father would not hear of his doing so, if he intended to devote his life to writing. To be a dealer was different. However, in the end, the idea of our starting a gallery broke down, for an enterprise of that kind needed capital, and we could find none: so, as matters turned out, it proved our sole joint venture in this field— though one, I believe, of which we can be proud. Rather than the great established names, and familiar masters, it was the newcomers, such artists as Modigliani and Utrillo, who made the sensation in this show. And my brother and I can claim the honour of having been the first to introduce Modigliani's pictures to the English public. It had been possible before to understand the beauty of his drawings: but the paintings offered a new and a greater revelation. The nudes, especially the reclining figure derived from Giorgione and Titian, manifested an astonishing feeling for the quality of oil paint: a technical mastery and exploitation strange in itself, because the artist had always wanted to be a sculptor, and only the cost of the materials prevented it. I was not in a position to buy as many of these canvases as I should have wished, but at least my brother and I were able to acquire a magnificent example—for the Parisian dealers who owned the majority of Modigliani's work in the Exhibition suggested, knowing our great admiration of this artist, that, as a reward for our services, we might like to select a single picture and pay them what it had cost them. Accordingly, we chose his superb *Peasant Girl*, for which we paid four pounds, the average gallery price for a painting by him being then between thirty and a hundred pounds.

Of recent decades it has, I know, been held that poetic and psychological understanding entering into a picture should not be allowed to prejudice the connoisseur in its favour: for esthetic value it must rest on pictorial qualities alone. And it must be admitted that even without such adventitious aids this would have remained a great work of art. Nevertheless, considered from the point of view of a poet, it was something more, just as were the canvases of Utrillo. After Modigliani it may be that Utrillo, who lacks the monumental sense present in the Italian painter's work, seems at first sight dull, with his apparently plain statements in paint of the most banal *banlieues* of Paris. With no man, no woman, no child in sight among those white peeling walls and dented, ribbed roofs, the lamp-posts showing diminutive in the clearing between sheer walls, where a building has been torn down and not yet replaced, or, on the contrary, rivalling in height the small, two-storey houses, with doors, windows, shutters surely too plain to diffuse any sense of emotion, these studies of the suburbs nevertheless exhale the most poignant miasmas of mind and spirit. Nothing moves, no leaf stirs. A finger lifted outside these stucco walls would alter, not only the surface of them, but the illumination of street and sky. The flat ceiling of clouds, the grey, clear light would themselves begin to flake and fall in powder. These canvases, full of exquisite morbidity, demonstrate that no tenements, no fag-ends of brick and plaster are too mean to be captured by art, and that man's habitations are porous, permeable by the human spirit. The sensibility and restraint of the painter, his indifference to all but his art, is here carried, like that of a Chinese landscapist, to its ultimate pitch. He is recording: he is not pronouncing judgement—yet that is in effect what he *is* pronouncing, for these streets, waiting, empty, quiet, with a silence unbroken except for the barking of a pet dog, testify and cry aloud.

The opening day of the Exhibition, the first of August, proved that crowds could be attracted to a gallery even during the holiday season, then still rigidly adherent to a particular month. In order to prevent the public—who, it must be remembered, had seen no modern European painting for four years—from stampeding, we had persuaded Arnold Bennett, a friend of ours and a lover of pictures, to write the preface of the catalogue.[1] We had hoped that his acknowledged common sense, his plain respect for competency and success in any branch of life, together with his high contemporary reputation as a novelist, would to a certain extent shield the pictures from the ugly display of abuse and bad temper which here greets every manifestation of art new to the country: but in vain! For the truth is, I apprehend, that each of the two great popular massacres (let us, so as to shorten the matter in the fashion of our period, give them initials, rather than write their names in full; we will refer to the 1914–18 conflict as T.W.T.M.T.W.S.F.D.—*The War To Make The World Safe For Democracy*,—and to the 1939–45 outbreak as T.S.W.T. M.T.W.S.F.T.S.T.—*The Second War To Make The World Safe For The Same Thing*,)—had become increasingly in the course of it, and absolutely towards its end, A War Against Art. So long as art exists, and continues to live, the thugs cannot get humanity down, therefore the thugs hate it, for it speaks to them of other ideas. And war makes thugs of us all. T.S.W.T.M.T.W.S.F.T.S.T. may at first appear to have been more specifically a war against art, or at any rate against art of the past, than T.W.T.M.T.W.S.F.D., for on its banner it proudly bears the names inscribed of Rotterdam, City of London, Canterbury, Lübeck, Florence, Tivoli, Vienna, Caen, and hundreds of others, but both T.S.W.T.M.T.W.S.F. T.S.T. and T.W.T.M.T.W.S.F.D. tore up painters and writers by the roots, taught them that their profession was considered of less value to the community than that of a plumber or acetylene-welder, and dislocated every joint in the bodies of the Muses. Always after one of these great mass-slaughters is over it is clear that the public—or to be fair, those who represent it in the Press—hope that art is over too: that we have at last shaken off the beastly thing, and can confine it to tomb-like museums. Naturally, therefore, the first proofs that it still breathes and grows (and to the honour of mankind,

[1] Of this and other acts of imaginative kindness on his part, I have more to say in the pages devoted to him in the final volume of this work.

I believe you cannot kill it unless some gigantic disaster wipes out humanity: the artist is a freak, as sure to recur as is some rare physical type) evoke howls and screams all the louder because, at the end of each war, Britain is a nation of <u>Philistines</u> in Arms. It is therefore in no way surprising to find a satirical poem, summing up this point of view, which I wrote, and which was published a few months before the Exhibition in August 1919, equally applicable to the outbursts of rage caused twenty-five years later by the Picasso Exhibition at the Victoria and Albert Museum—I instance Picasso alone, since Matisse, who exhibited with him, had so manifestly become by then a French old master, comparable to Greuze or Boucher, a colourist whose grace and sweetness not even the most perverse of art-lovers could deny. The satire to which I have alluded, and which follows, was, in fact, re-printed as being recurrently topical in the *New Statesman and Nation* of the 29th December 1945.

An Old-Fashioned Sportsman

We thank Thee, O Lord,
That the War is over.
We can now
Turn our attention again
To money-making.
Railway Shares must go up;
Wages must come down;
Smoke shall come out
Of the chimneys of the North,
And we will manufacture battleships.
    We thank Thee, O Lord,
    But we must refuse
    To consider
    Music, Painting, or Poetry.

Our sons and brothers
Went forth to fight,
To kill certain things,
Cubism, Futurism and Vers-libre.
    "All this Poetry-and-Rubbish,"
We said,
    "Will not stand the test of war."
We will not read a book
—Unless it is a best seller.

There has been enough art
In the past.
Life is concerned
With killing and maiming.
If they cannot kill men
Why can't they kill animals?

But as the Pharisees
Approached the tomb
They saw the boulder
Rolled back,
And that the tomb was empty.
—They said,
"It's very disconcerting.
I am not at all
Narrow-minded.
I know a tune
When I hear one,
And I know
What I like:
I did not so much mind
That He blasphemed
Saying that He was the Son of God,
But He was never
What I call
A Sportsman;
He went out into the desert
For forty days
—And never shot anything,
And when we hoped He would drown
He walked on the water."

We were fortunate enough to sell a good many pictures on the opening day. Arnold Bennett bought on my advice a splendid nude by Modigliani, and to someone else who consulted me I recommended another fine picture by the same master, and an Utrillo. For these two he paid a sum of about seventy pounds: within five years he could have sold them for at least two thousand six hundred pounds. . . . The catalogue, with its preface by Arnold, was widely bought; unfortunately the beginning of the list of pictures in it carried the notice, "*This collection has been brought together by Osbert and Sacheverell Sitwell*"; which served to focus public rage on our two heads: though a considerable amount, on such occasions, was always reserved for my sister, even when, as

Plate VI

THE DINING ROOM AT CARLYLE SQUARE

From the photograph by E. J. Mason by permission of " Country Life "

Plate VII

WILLIAM WALTON
From the war-damaged drawing by Rex Whistler

in this instance, she was in no wise implicated. My brother and I acted in the Gallery as shopmen in turn with our friend Herbert Read, selling catalogues, answering enquiries, and often quieting, or trying to quiet, protests—about the pictures. The table at which sat the one of us who had taken on the duty, had been placed in the middle of the Gallery, and below, by its side, stood an enormous wicker basket full of sheaves of Modigliani drawings, from which the visitor could choose a specimen for a shilling. . . . I may add that my brief experience as salesman taught me much in a short time as to the manners adopted by people who ought to know better towards shopmen. Several times I was treated with gross rudeness by men and women, unaware of my identity, and in after days when I met and recognised them—though they seldom recognised me—I found it difficult to be persuaded to like them.

Every day the public tantrums, whether inside the Mansard Gallery or outside it, in the columns of the newspapers, increased. For the most part the critics showed themselves impressed, at the lowest were civil: it was in the news and correspondence columns that riots and mutinies broke out. A notably irate series of letters, arising out of a favourable account of the pictures by Clive Bell, appeared in the *Nation*, and continued for six weeks, a fortnight after the Exhibition had closed![1] Throughout, the attackers maintained a strong moral note, and one of them declared that at one moment he had felt the whole collection of pictures to be "a glorying in prostitution"!

The fury of the Philistine was reflected in unexpected quarters. . . . London had been suffocatingly hot during the last part of July, and since Mrs. Ronald Greville had most kindly asked my brother and me to stay with her at Polesden Lacey, we went there for the first part of August. Always we greatly enjoyed our visits to her, and the house was near enough to London for us to be able to go up every day to our Exhibition, and return in time for dinner. The immense

[1] I reproduce it *in toto* as Appendix A at the end of this volume, so that the reader can compare the art-tantrums after T.W.T.M.T.W.S.F.D. with those which came after T.S.W.T.M.T.W.S.F.T.S.T.

F

party at Polesden in the early days of August 1919 possessed
its own very distinctive features. . . . My brother and I
arrived about five o'clock on one of the last sweltering days of
July, at Bookham Station. Bank Holiday, due before very
long, had plainly produced in advance a sweaty yet listless
and confused bustle. Nobody, one could see at a first glance,
knew where anything was, and we found no motor waiting
for us outside. As we waited there under a projecting glass
roof, our feet burning on cinder-coloured, incised tiles, and
gazed before us into a vacancy of asphalt above which the
heat danced a fandango barely visible, we turned to notice,
standing by us, an old gentleman, plainly another prospective
guest at Polesden. We did not know who he was, but presently
a porter came lumbering along with his suit-case, and on the
label hanging limply from it I read *W. H. Mallock.*

This author already belonged to a remote and romantic
past. His book *The New Republic*, which had made him
famous, had appeared over forty years before, and the title of
none of his numerous subsequent works had become so
familiar in the ears of the public. I had never seen a copy of
The New Republic, far less read one, but I had constantly heard
it referred to, and with respect, by those members of the older
generation whose judgment in reading I trusted. Moreover,
I was prepared in my mind to like its author, since our friend
Robert Ross had greatly admired him and had, indeed, been
one of the advisers who had recommended and secured for
him a Civil List Pension, when the former beloved star, young
and brilliant, of literary drawing-rooms now fallen to dust
had come on bad times. My pity had been stirred by what
I heard, so that on realising the identity of the old Chinoiserie
tottering about in the heat in a state of despair, searching,
not too energetically but fussily, for the missing Rolls, and
ever and anon taking off his bowler-hat to mop his forehead—
as he did so disclosing a single damp strand of hair, long and
undulating by nature as the Monster of Loch Ness, but now
wound and flattened round his crown like a turban—on
realising, as I say, his identity, I went up to him, introduced
myself, offered to guide him the one and a half miles to
Polesden, and, what was more, volunteered to carry his

luggage for him, though nothing irks me so much as having to convey my own. So we started off on the long, long trek, he with a slight spinning motion from a giddiness of sorts that seized him, while Sacheverell and I staggered under our loads. We tried, though out of breath, to talk to him, to show we did not mind our burdens; but he was in some manner suspicious, perhaps especially of men younger than himself. Very far from him, we comprehended, were those days of amber when he had looked with the all too clear eyes of youth on the great of his time, on Matthew Arnold and Walter Pater and Jowett, and many famous men now forgotten and unlamented, had heard them talk, and had, in a novel, made their converse still better, so that he was their master, though so young, and they his puppets. In the years that had passed since his triumph —for the reception of his first book cannot be called less—, his rather cynical temper of mind had become accentuated, until he had grown to distrust all intelligence and artistic perception, and had been turned by the hardening of his arteries into a pillar of prejudice. Only a love of the classics remained to him out of all the gifts with which he had started —or so I thought.

When we arrived, the sight of ambassadors and ambassadresses, of statesmen and grandees, and the fleshy phantoms of former beauties, famous in his day, seemed to restore him. He almost unbent when our hostess greeted us. "I am so sorry you all three had to walk. And you carried Mallock's luggage! It was most kind of you." "Poor old Mallock!" she confided in me later. "I've hardly seen him since he used to come to Charles Street in my father's time, when I was a girl. I met him the other day, and asked him here for the sake of old times—but I'm afraid he's grown very old—too old for either work or pleasure. I only hope he'll enjoy himself here!" . . . I think he did.

Every day, accounts of our Exhibition, photographs of the pictures, and attacks on them caught his eye and inflamed his spirit against us: for he had allowed the fact that I had dragged his luggage through the heat in a temperature of 90° in the shade by no whit to mollify his feelings towards either my brother or me. And it soon became evident that in certain directions the passage of the years had not in the least impaired his powers, but had merely changed the course of them. What had been an ability to create—or at any rate interpret—imaginatively, had now become executant. He proved to be an ingenious and assiduous organiser. Each evening, when Sacheverell and I returned to Polesden, no less tired out by the heat of the days than rendered uneasy by profitless argument in the Gallery, and by the ferocious attacks delivered on us in the evening papers, which we had just read, unsuspecting, in the train, we would find the bulk of the guests assembled to meet us, grouped either just outside the front door or on the stone steps of the loggia. They were fresh as if they had just issued from a rest-cure, yet fiery in spirit as only bridge and golf can make people. It was plain that they had been marshalled here by an invisible intelligence for his own purposes, arranged in order of height and eminence, almost as if a photograph of the house-party was to be taken. This chorus of ambassadors, political peers, retired Speakers, ministers and their wives, were ready for us: the figure-heads had been supplied, if not with arguments, at least with sentiments of an unimpeachable respectability, by one more wily, though generally speaking less well preserved, who had contrived by a little judicious muddling to make them associate in their minds a political regime they disliked with certain works of art.

"I think Bolshevism should be put down!"

"I have no sympathy with Bolsheviks in politics or art!"

"I don't hold with Bolshevism!"

"Cézanne wanted shooting!"

"I should think Sargent was good enough for anyone."

Such were the *fade* but locally unexceptionable sentiments chanted impersonally into the air, as if spoken to spectres, at our approach.

It had to be admitted, then, that this nightly counter-revolution had been prepared with extreme skill and executed with audacity. Moreover it must have required a deal of patient planning and lobbying, all the more remarkable when you consider that, owing to physical disabilities connected

with his age, Mallock at that time could never find the answer
to any question put to him until it had been repeated to him
again twice, once by the interrogator and once by himself.
What was more, the whole of this work he carried out every
day in secret, without a word of it or of the nightly demon-
stration reaching our hostess or our several friends among the
guests, such as Mr. and Mrs. Maguire, or Lord Blanesburgh,
who would have championed us.[1] . . . I think it was the
photographs of the Modigliani portraits, appearing now nearly
every day in the press, which furnished Mallock with his
chief weapons: just as the pictures themselves exacerbated
the public. Especially the artist's manner of rendering necks
annoyed—but that is altogether too mild a word—those
unused to it. In the Gallery it was the same. "Why does he
paint people with necks like swans?" I used to hear asked,
with passionate, venomous derision. And out of this rage
I believe that it would have been possible at last to extract
a mathematical formula, the heat of the anger seeming to be
based on the number of times the neck of the given Modigliani
could be multiplied to make the neck of the person protesting.
Certainly, the thicker the neck, the greater the transports of
its owner, and the thicker still would it become, swelling from
fury.

Modigliani was nearing the end of his doomed life.
Zborowski had undoubtedly been of great help to him for some
years: but I cannot think him, kind and nice as he was, to
have been the pure philanthropist-poet that he is represented
to have been in a book published in 1941, and largely devoted

---

[1] It would seem that Thomas Carlyle put paid to our debt to Mallock in
advance for us. In *Talking of Dick Whittington* by Hesketh Pearson and
Hugh Kingsmill (Eyre & Spottiswoode, 1947), the authors tell us that
Kingsmill had recently passed on to Pearson a story he had heard from
E. S. P. Haynes. . . . Joseph Chamberlain, at the height of his fame as a
Radical politician, visited Carlyle one day with W. H. Mallock, who had
just come down from Oxford with the reputation of a brilliant youth with
a great career before him. Mallock, apparently, had been too brilliant
during the visit, for, as he and Chamberlain were putting their coats on,
Carlyle, who had gone up the first flight of stairs, leant over the balustrade,
and called out, "Can ye hear me, Mr. Mallock?" Mallock having expec-
tantly signified that he could, and no doubt thrown himself into a cordially
receptive posture, Carlyle continued, "I didna enjoy your veesit, and I
dinna want to see ye again."

to the story of Modigliani's life in Paris.[1] Nor should it be regarded as a picture-dealer's business to be a philanthropist. Zborowski became a very successful dealer. It is in that guise that he must be regarded, as a man with a flair, and in that same capacity he would no doubt wish to be remembered. I recall how, during the period of the Exhibition, when Modigliani, recovering from a serious crisis of his disease, suffered a grave relapse, a telegram came for Zborowski from his Parisian colleagues to inform him; the message ended with a suggestion that he should hold up all sales until the outcome of the painter's illness was known. My brother, who was inexpressibly shocked at this example of business-men's callousness, showed me the cable, and Zborowski asked us personally to refuse to sell, if a possible purchaser should appear. As it happened, Modigliani did not immediately comply with the programme drawn up for him. He appeared to have regained strength, and did not die before the following year. Within a short time of the great artist's death, however, the change in Zborowski's condition startled us. I shall never forget the richness of the fur coat, very Russian or Polish in style, with an enormous sweep of fur collar, in which he came to meet us in Paris after the turn in his fortunes, nor, I must add, his good-nature and the childish and evident pleasure he took in the style in which he was now able to live. There was, of course, no reason why he should not have made money by his judgement and taste, any more than that we should have abandoned the proposed deal, of which I am about to tell, had we succeeded in clinching it: but dealings of this sort remain matters of business and not philanthropy; bargains, and not acts of generosity to the artist.[2]

During the course of the following autumn, the terms on which we found ourselves with my father became less strained, and we determined to try to persuade him either to advance us the money to buy, or himself to purchase as an investment, a hundred or more pictures by Modigliani for which we were

---

[1] *Artist Quarter*, by Charles Douglas. (Faber & Faber, 1941.)

[2] Zborowski died, after a year's illness, in Paris, in the Rue Joseph Bara, on the 24th of March 1932. By that time the Slump had dissipated the great profits he had made.

in treaty. Some of them were already in England, and the whole collection could have been acquired for between seven hundred and a thousand pounds. Though I had almost refrained from making such a suggestion for fear of the reception it would most certainly incur, yet when at last I ventured to broach the subject, and even after he had seen some of the pictures, which surely did not match his taste, my father showed himself inclined to agree to some arrangement— it was but another of the fascinating contradictions in his character: ("They may think I shall, but I shan't!"). Still further to ease relations, and a little, perhaps, in order to pursue the point, my brother and I invited him to dine with us on the night of his sixtieth birthday, 27th January 1920, at our London house, 2 Carlyle Square.

We had migrated thither from Swan Walk in the previous November. Most of the possessions we took with us consisted of pictures, glass and books—for, as Arnold Bennett had noted in his diary,[1] the rooms at Swan Walk had contained little furniture. The little there was belonged to the owner. As often in my existence, I had just the bare luxuries of life and not the necessities. We owned neither beds, tables, nor chairs. This only made our glass and books more precious to us, and it was plainly safer to convey them to their new destination, personally, by taxi, than to trust them to carriers or furniture removers. In consequence, I had been forced to take a number of terrifying prismatic journeys in cabs, and I remember the winter sunshine suddenly streaming in as we turned a corner, and the dazing difficulty I experienced, like that a conjurer so often and so triumphantly poses to himself with billiard-balls, in keeping the fragile bubble-like cases, full of crystal ships or flashing-winged humming-birds, and the vases and bowls of coruscating coloured glass, simultaneously in their place. On the return passage I would rest in the cab exhausted, only immediately to set out again, this time with cubes and towers of books, shimmering in their own dust, tottering, hitting, knocking, falling at each jolt: then back once more, bruised by the violence of inanimate tomes, to start forth anew with a scintillating load of glass

[1] See p. 55, *ante*.

and crystal. When all these objects had arrived, there existed, of course, no tables on which to stand them. In the height of the furniture-boom of 1919, when small chests-of-drawers made of deal were selling for fifty pounds each, it proved no easy matter, with little money, many old debts and the expense of a new residence, to find the necessary furniture, and we were compelled for a year to camp out, rather than live, in the house. I contrived, however, to buy from the former owner half a dozen beds, and some arm-chairs. The dining-room table, painted in every colour, as if it were a palette, the surface then being ground down and polished to represent marble, had been a kitchen table, and was adapted for me to its new purpose by Roger Fry, who had also chosen the colours for the drawing-room and himself helped to paint the ceiling. A piece of furniture of rock-like strength, and with a real personality, it has served me at Renishaw in the last eight years for the writing of the several volumes of this long book. I sit at it at this moment, before my task, a large adjustable, 1840 gout-stool ready for swell-foot straddling across one central bar supporting it. Its top is now covered with sheets of blotting-paper of various colours, on which stand many fountain-pens, clustered together like reed-pipes, while round them surges a litter of note-books, piles of papers, ink-erasers, pots of ink, spectacles, spectacle-cases, india-rubbers, pencils, boxes of cigarettes, manuscripts, all in what must appear to strangers to be inextricable confusion. In a sense it exhales life, testifying to the daily struggles and long hours of an author's day: but, as between the sheets of blotting-paper I catch sight for a moment of a chink of the marbled surface underneath, it saddens me with other thoughts, by reminding me of many delightful hours that are past, and conjuring up many ghosts, not least among them the painter of the table himself: ghosts famous or obscure, who at one time or another sat round this table, and whose manner, whose voices, whose laughter, it now evokes, to reach me once more across the unfathomable gulf into which all must fall.

Certainly this table brings back more occasions pleasant than the reverse; but that of which I speak—one of the first evenings at which we sat at it—turned out to be one of the least fortunate. The dinner-party for my father's sixtieth birthday was a risk which, perhaps, should not have been taken. To begin with, the decoration of the rooms, being neither Italian, nor William Morris, nor a conceit of Lutyens', was sure to annoy him. If he liked any of our possessions, all he would remark was—(and how often has he not said it to me, in the grieved voice of altruism he reserved for such disguised strictures)—"I notice that you and Sachie seem to have much more pocket-money to spend than your Mother and I. . . . *We* can spend nothing on *ourselves*!" While if he did not like them, he would equally repine. In the same fashion, if Mrs. Powell provided us with a remarkably good dinner, we were extravagant: and if, on the other hand, in order to please him, we could persuade her to send up a bad and skimpy meal (which was a far greater effort for her), it showed how we mismanaged our affairs. To strike the happy mean was impossible. The worst mistake we made on this occasion, and one we were bitterly to regret before the evening was over and for many years subsequently, was to ask my father's only friend, Mr. MacTotter, the Silver Bore,[1] to meet him. . . . At first all went well; until the Silver Bore, who was as good-natured and, indeed, sentimentally friendly as obtuse (his continued friendship with my father must have been due solely to his never being conscious when he and his friendship were not wanted), brought out of his pocket a small package containing a birthday offering. After fifty years, the most elementary sense of psychology should have prevented him from falling into this error—for error it was, if he intended to please my father, to whom any present on an anniversary constituted an affront. When the paper was undone, the parcel proved to contain a gilded snuff-box, big enough to hold cigarettes, and though, of course, in the best of taste, unquestionably a pretty and elegant object. When my father saw what it was—for he refused to touch it with his hands, as though he thought it might communicate some fever, and allowed the Silver Bore to rattle about among the tissue paper for him—he sank into a slow, sulky, smouldering

---

[1] See *Great Morning*, p. 116–17 of this edition.

passion, of ill omen to his sons' plans. The entire mask of
bonhomie which he had prepared for the evening crumbled.
He drew me aside at once, and remarked, "A shocking waste
of money, much better spent in other ways. Most selfish!
I can't afford that sort of thing!" (In reality, he feared he
might later have to give a return birthday present to the
Silver Bore, and though not ungenerous with gifts, he liked
to choose his own time for them, and on these grounds disapproved of festivals such as a birthday or Christmas. At
hotels abroad, he would always try to wish the head-waiter
"A Happy Christmas!" first, before that smart and important
recipient of presents could get it in, and if Robins, on Christmas morning, offered him his greetings, my father would snap
out, in a tone of intense fretfulness, "Yes, Yes, Yes, I *know!*")
It took minutes that seemed like hours to restore any sem-
blance of good-humour to him, but eventually we succeeded
in coaxing him into a state of icy geniality, if such a contradiction in terms may be permitted. The dining-room itself
aroused no particularly unpleasant comment, and he ate the
meal with apparent enjoyment. Nor did he complain overmuch at having to climb upstairs to the drawing-room after
dinner.

Arrived there, I took my father into the back part of the
room, to show him our Modigliani, hanging over the fireplace. . . . Being at the lowest a man of imagination and
esthetic perception and, in some branches, of a liking for new
ideas, he treated the picture seriously, and listened to all I
had to say, until it seemed clear that he would at last fall in
with one of our plans, and that in consequence it would
reach fruition. Alas! at this very moment the Silver Bore,
who entertained a neurasthenic dread of being "out of
things", and whose eyes always roved fitfully—and when I
write *fitfully*, I mean it—away from the person to whom he
was talking, in search of suspected hidden diversions, broke
loose from the other room, where he had been prating and
gibbering to my brother of tea-spoons and porringers, and
stampeded up to my father and me. Noticing that we were
looking at a picture, the newcomer turned his gaze in the
same direction, and as he grimaced and quavered at it, a

new tempo of indignation began to govern his trembling, which grew quicker and more convulsive. As Modigliani's peasant girl, monumental, posed for ever in her misty blue world, peered steadily out of her frame, through her thin, goose-like eyes, at the quivering, agitated, but well-tailored mass of the elderly gentleman opposite her, the struggle between them became—if only it had not been too poignant, because I already recognised that my fortunes and my brother's were deeply implicated in it—an interesting duel to watch. Inspired as MacTotter was by Good Taste, which inevitably blindfolds its victims, since it arms them for their battle against art with a system, if not of esthetic values, at any rate of academical respectability and decorum that can ostensibly be used on behalf of beauty, rather than, as in reality, against it, something in the painting before him clashed, I suggest, with the ideals upheld by the Queen Anne Coffee Pot: wherefore this was not and could not be Art. Personal prejudice, moreover, no less than principle, entered in. The quality of her immense and static dignity not only outraged the burgessdom of England, of which he was an incarnation, but offended more particularly against his own involuntary vivacity, bestowed on him by St. Vitus. The peasant girl, he considered, had no expression, no movement. So intense was his emotion that at first it seemed as if he could not, for very anger, use his voice. But in the end all this agitation and waste of energy found their equivalent in sound, a high, defensive whinnying, long sustained. The peasant girl, immobile, held her ground. Not so, alas, my father. He would not look at the picture again: he was frightened out of it, by the force of conventional opinion as thus expressed.

A kind of sequel occurred some five or six years later. My brother and I returned to London after a prolonged absence abroad, spent in working at Amalfi. The evening after our arrival, a friend, himself a painter and a collector of modern pictures, came to dine with us. When later we were sitting in the drawing-room, he said, "I've been wondering, by the way, whether you'd like to sell me your Modigliani. I'll give you a handsome price, eighty pounds!" He was aware that I had paid four pounds for it, and when I could not make up my mind what to do, for I both needed money and hated to part with the painting, he added, "You won't be doing badly: you'll have made a profit of nearly two thousand per cent!" After reflection, and in spite of Mrs. Powell's protests, I accepted his offer—only to learn a week later that the purchaser had resold it for two thousand pounds, while two or three months subsequently it was to be seen in the window of a famous Parisian dealer for the equivalent in francs of four thousand pounds.

The great rise in the value of Modigliani's pictures had taken place during the months we had been abroad, and out of touch with the world of galleries. It was evident now that when my father had permitted the Silver Bore to giggle and jiggle him out of his almost formulated intention to buy the collection of Modigliani's paintings, he had been laughed out of a fortune. Since money values constituted a standard that the Silver Bore admitted and understood, I decided to write to him and point out what he had accomplished. This I gave myself the satisfaction of doing; for he was only a few years over sixty and, unless warned, might still have time to perform a similar offence, should he by chance again see a beautiful modern work of art.

I do not know where *The Peasant Girl* hangs now: but there, caught in the artist's net, is the cautious wry-necked peasant girl of Northern France, with her fair hair, sharp, slanting nose, and narrow eyes, who for so long as paint lasts will typify the thriftiness, shading down into avarice, the suspiciousness and obstinate endurance of the peasants of a flat and sandy country, where willows and animals, rather than hills, which scarcely exist, constitute the landmarks. Very near are these people, of whom this young girl is a representative, to the world of trees, animals and birds— especially, perhaps, of birds. She is related by blood to Breughel's peasants and to Teniers' boors, has the same powerful grip on life, but is less jolly and jocose (she would never take to drink or play a practical joke). Her smiles are rare, and there is about her a wooden melancholy that accompanies the quality of her strength. You can see her driving home a flock of geese, wearing on her head a kind of flat, black hat (otherwise she always dresses as she is shown in this picture), and guiding her charges sometimes with the aid of a long rod. A few early December flakes of snow begin to fall so that soon her cheerful-coloured face shines feebly, and then is lost in a whirling universe of goose feathers. Her walk, as she waddles along with a pertinacity which surely even death cannot subdue—it is her physique rather than her soul which seems eternal—, belongs less to the animals than to the web-footed families of birds. But her stubborn vigour is human, and in the light of it you can read her future. You can see her on a hot summer evening, kicking her foot listlessly against a stone, while the smallest birds jump and fly and sing in the branches of the willow or osier over her head. You can see her dutiful courtship, and the dowry, perhaps a necklace of pebbles, the linen and simple furniture she would bring her husband, and her life as a mother, a Frenchwoman of simple faith and belief in hard work, in scrubbed boards, polished brass and copper that gleams. You can see her sitting in church, listening intently and under-standing nothing, for the sounds of the farmyard mean more to her than the words of the good or learned. (To her think-ing, it is the capacity for hard work, I believe, rather than the immortal soul which differentiates human beings from beasts.) You can see her in the earliest morning, with perhaps the only flash of poetry that lifts the common sense of her spirit, resting for an instant against a wooden post in the yard, in the young light of a summer morning which has in it already all the buds of June's tender perfection of leafiness, stillness and expectation of a Golden Age never to come, while her ear yet remains attentive to the sounds of the animal world: the grunting of pigs, those earth-bound and translated creatures from a fairy story, the voices of the cows, calm and logical, with their occasional complaints of the supply of adrenalin re-duced, and nature tamed in consequence, and to the hissing of the geese, issuing now in formation from the door, across the roughly cobbled yard, littered with straw and dung. This flock is still her favourite, and through some process of un-conscious approximation her eyes and nose have grown still more to resemble those of the birds you saw her driving through the vanished flakes of fifty years or more ago. Now her voice, too, has a toothless hiss in it. But with all this she still remains the wry-necked girl, with the lank hair of the forsaken, with hands clasped, resting stoutly on a wooden chair in a transparency of vaporous blue.

CHAPTER TWO

"Façade"

THE DEATH of Robert Ross had taken place in October 1918 and made a great difference to myself and to other young writers. Pacific and genial by nature, he had provided a climate for us in which friendships throve: but now that his influence was removed, the usual quarrelling, ever rife among those who dedicate their lives to the peaceful pursuit of the Muses, began to manifest its accustomed ferocity with a more than accustomed lack of reason. Old friendships did not so much lapse as become riven apart, or were dissolved, almost before entered into, in loud, contentious thunder, while others, again, trailed into nothingness. Among those contemporaries of mine of whom I now saw less with each passing year—though I had never numbered him, it is true, among my most intimate friends—was Robert Graves. Him I had first known as a very young poet, a friend and brother officer of Sassoon's in the Royal Welch Fusiliers. I remained, however, on ostensibly good terms with Robert until the publication of his autobiography some ten years later.[1] In this he gave my sister, as well as my brother and me, public dismissal as a friend. My sister tells me she was sorry for it, since she had felt a genuine regard for both Robert Graves and his wife, and until the volume appeared and she read quotations from it in the press, had entertained no idea that their friendship had altered in any way, far less that it had ended. Sacheverell, I think, received his notice to quit the magic circle in the same spirit that I did, not minding it in the least, save for taking exception to the insolent manner in which it was phrased. I suffered no sense of personal loss, for I had always found Graves's character to be exactly divided, half and half, between schoolboy and schoolmaster—to me, as the reader of a former volume will have gathered, no very attractive combination.

[1] *Goodbye to All That.* (Jonathan Cape, 1929.)

Some of his poems I admired, however, and I still read
books of his poetry when they appear, knowing that I am
sure to find something in them to like. On the other hand, with
his long prose works, devoted to the divesting of a great legend
or story of its greatness, and reducing the supernatural to the
stature of the commonplace, I have never been able, if I may
use the phrase in this connection, to get beyond nodding
terms. . . . But, albeit old friendships were dying, new were
being born.

I must hark back to the short period I spent in hospital in
the early months of 1919: for during those and the following
weeks were planted many seeds which later were to germinate
and flourish. In January of that year my brother and comrade
Sacheverell had gone up to Balliol. It was a particularly listless
moment in Oxford, as yet by no means recovered from a state
of decayed emptiness, for war had hollowed it out. Sacheverell, though only twenty-one years of age, was already
accustomed to something more lively, to London and the
society of poets and painters which we there enjoyed. One
day, when he came up to visit me, he mentioned, I remember,
the sole redeeming point of Oxford for him: that he had met in
a—as it seemed to him—leaden city, the only English musical
genius it had ever been his lot so far to encounter, a boy of
sixteen, called W. T. Walton—and that was the first time I
heard the name. I did not pay much attention, since we already
possessed among our friends an undoubted and more mature
musical genius, Bernard van Dieren. Sacheverell, however,
pursuing the topic, told me, I recall, that Walton's talent had
first been discovered by the organist of Christ Church, Dr.
Henry Ley, and the late Sir Hugh Allen, and then fostered by
Dr. Strong, Dean of Christ Church for many years, and
subsequently Bishop of Ripon and, later, of Oxford. Dr.
Strong had been so greatly impressed by the evident musical
talent of this young boy from Oldham, who was in the Cathedral Choir School, that he had obtained a modification in his
favour of the rules governing the qualifying age, so that
Walton should be able to enter Christ Church as an under-
graduate at an early age. Walton was said, no doubt errone-
ously, to be in consequence the youngest member of the

University since the reign of Henry VIII. (In passing, we may note that in all probability it was his long training in the Cathedral Choir which developed his natural talent for choral music, such as *Belshazzar's Feast*, and for the setting of words, as so brilliantly evinced in *Façade*.) We must, Sacheverell continued, find some way of being of use to him, and of advancing his chances and genius. . . . But what could we do?

In the end, perhaps, all that we were able to accomplish directly for him was to have prevented his being sent to one of the English musical academies and to have lent him, as a musician, what prestige we ourselves possessed in the world of art and writing at a time when he lacked supporters, and when, in consequence of our attitude, we incurred a certain amount of odium, both from those who did not believe in him and from those who did. Especially were we blamed by these last—and rightly—for being responsible for his not attending in London one of the two or three colleges officially provided for an academic training in music. These people worked in different ways but united in tormenting about it Walton's father, a well-known teacher of singing in Lancashire, and fortunately a man of character. On one occasion, they so well succeeded in their efforts that Mr. Walton, very busy though he always was, came up to London especially to investigate, and failing to find my brother or myself, instead called on my aged Aunt Blanche, then rising eighty, who was speedily able to reassure him. The relationship between William and his father and mother, both of whom were fine musicians, was unusually happy, and it was said that almost the last words of his father were, "Let William have his own way: he knows what he is doing. . . ." Instead, then, of sending William to Kensington or Bloomsbury, we were able to keep him in touch with the vital works of the age, with the music, for example, of Stravinsky, and to obtain for him, through the kindness of our old family friend E. J. Dent, an introduction to Busoni, a modern master of counterpoint, who looked at some of William's compositions and wrote him a kindly polite letter about them. He also at times had the benefit of consulting Ernest Ansermet on various problems of composition. Moreover by travelling in our company in Italy, Spain and Germany, he soon acquired a knowledge of the arts, both past and present, belonging to those countries. It was noticeable from the first that he manifested an innate feeling for the masterpieces of painting and architecture, no less than of music: and inevitably the people, landscapes, festas and customs he observed increased the store of experience on which he could draw for the enriching of his work. . . . But this was all in the future. I had not yet met him.

On leaving hospital towards the end of February 1919 I had gone to Oxford, to be with my brother, and to see Siegfried Sassoon, who was living in rooms there. (In his company, I met during that visit Gabriel Atkin, a great-nephew of Leigh Hunt's. With his easy and natural talents in drawing, music and decoration, and his keen sensibility, he was for many years an enlivening and always welcome friend.) It was a very cold early spring, with long periods of frost that bit like iron into the flesh, and with the inevitable coal shortage that seems to be one of the jewels of the austere crown wherewith Victory likes to adorn herself in this country. Whenever, in these weeks, I saw Sacheverell, his hands, I recollect, were blue with cold, his fingers being too numb even to strike a match for the fire, ready laid and boasting a few precious pieces of inferior coal. He was very grateful, therefore, to Raymond Mortimer, who had come down to stay at Oxford, and who, although in those days we knew him comparatively little, would, with the genius of the Good Samaritan that he is, wordlessly materialise in the room, grasp the situation immediately, and, without being asked, at once rush towards the fireplace to set light to the sticks for him. . . . Siegfried Sassoon was the first of our friends to have met Walton, through Frank Prewitt, the Canadian poet, who had lately left the Forces to go up to Oxford. Sassoon had taken my brother to see the youthful composer, and he now invited all four of us to tea.

We arrived at Christ Church in the early afternoon. The room was rather dark, blue-papered, with a piano opposite the window, and in the middle a table laid for tea, with, in the centre of it, thrown in for the sake of the almost ostentatious sense of luxury it would inevitably evoke, an enormous plate of bananas. Our host, not quite seventeen years of age, we found to be a rather tall, slight figure, of typically northern colouring, with pale skin, straight fair hair, like that of a young Dane or Norwegian. The refinement of his rather long, narrow, delicately shaped head, and of his bird-like profile showing so plainly above the brow the so-called bar or mound of Michelangelo that phrenologists claim to be the distinguishing mark of the artist—and especially of the musician—, even his prominent, well-cut nose, scarcely gave a true impression either of his robust mental qualities or of the strength of his physique. Sensitiveness rather than tough-ness was the quality at first most apparent in him. He appeared to be excessively shy, and on this occasion spoke but little, for I think he was rather in awe of us, as being his elders. Talk was desultory, though there were sudden determined bursts of amiably-intentioned conversation from his guests. The atmosphere was not, however, easy; music showed a way out of the constraint, and after tea we pressed him to play some of his compositions to us. Accordingly, he got up from the table and then sat down at the piano, the few steps between clearly indicating the burden of his hospitality, a feeling of strain, almost of hopelessness, combined with that of a need for intense concentration. As he began to play, he revealed a lack of mastery of the instrument that was altogether unusual, and as a result it was more difficult than ever to form an opinion of the music at a first hearing. He played the slow movement from his *Piano Quartet*, later published by the Carnegie Trust, and other compositions which have no doubt disappeared. . . . It was, indeed, as impossible that afternoon to estimate his character or talents as it was to foresee that for the next seventeen years he would constitute an inseparable companion and friend, and an adopted, or elected, brother to Edith, Sacheverell and myself.

Sacheverell and I went for the Easter vacation—he had joined me at Biarritz—to Spain, where I fell ill. On our delayed return to England, he went back to Oxford, and I to Scarborough; where I found waiting for me a welcoming letter from my father. It began:

You show a lack of judgement—you allowed the Military Authorities
to put you, when run down, into the influenza ward: then, though
warned of the necessity of keeping quiet, you rushed about Spain
till you got jaundice.

At Scarborough it was my duty and pleasure, as Liberal
candidate for the division, to entertain among others Mr. and
Mrs. Asquith[1] and Violet Bonham Carter for a Liberal Conference and, in especial, for a great meeting of Liberal
delegates on the second evening. I remember the occasion
vividly: for this was the first time I found myself as a speaker
and had really won the audience. I recollect how, when the
first great roar of laughter went up at a joke I had made, I
was so unused to it—for, like my father before me, I could
only be at my best with a very large audience—, so greatly
astounded and taken aback, that I wondered nervously what
was amiss, and whether I had used the wrong words or committed some solecism, being convinced that the laughter must
be against rather than with me. After the meeting was over
my guests and a few local worthies, members of the Liberal
Committee or of the Borough Corporation, returned to have
supper at Wood End. For this party I had organised a one-
woman cabaret. It was a turn protean and unlike any other.
Only in the past few months had I discovered the talents of
Mrs. Haynesworth, a charwoman, who acted at times as
caretaker, and who was a member of the Salvation Army. . . .
Perhaps it would be more correct for me to write that she had
thrust her talents upon me than that I had discovered them
for though in her seventy-ninth year, she never tired of entering
my room dancing or singing, and she excelled at telling fortunes. Certainly she possessed gifts, in addition to a special
capacity for attracting bats and letting them into one's bedroom at night (in which respect I have never known her
equal). As soon as the bat had gone with the daylight, and I
was enjoying a few minutes' sleep, Mrs. Haynesworth would
burst in. It had seemed very peaceful, no sound in the house
until, throwing wide the door, and with a bang abandoning
the handle of the carpet-sweeper she was rolling behind her
as if it were the modern equivalent of the broomstick which

[1] Afterwards Lord and Lady Oxford and Asquith.

would in earlier times have conveyed her hither, she would roar out one of her raucous songs, banal except for their long-dead allusions to forgotten personalities, or in some cases for their almost rancid piety. She would thrust her head forward from her bent body as a tortoise does from its shell, her whole face taking on a look of cunning determination, as well as of that kind of summary of a concentrated act of memory one sees reflected on the face of a young child learning to read. She had for many months made it clear to me that her chief ambition was to perform before the ex-Prime Minister and his wife, and I was resolved, for my part, that her longing should be gratified.

Mrs. Haynesworth was small, grey-haired, with a hook-nose and a very clear, unlined, childish complexion, of a rather high colour, and resembled, if it were not a contradiction in terms, an innocent but crafty and slightly crazed witch. For this great occasion, which she had so often implored me to procure for her, she sported a parma-violet-coloured dress of antique plush and pattern, with a large feathered hat in the same shade. This, she confided to me, had been the costume she had worn for her wedding some sixty years before. . . . I must admit to having felt, as her impresario, a certain embarrassment just before she entered the room, and to having wondered how the turn would go: but directly the door opened, I knew it would be all right! She wore an impalpable panache, exhaled an indescribable air of triumph. She proceeded to march round and round the table at a rapid pace, with swinging arms and a long stride, singing a brisk Salvation hymn. There was on her face the kind of rapt expression I knew so well, and at first she looked at no one, being wholly intent on her own performance. Next, she favoured us with a ballad, rendered in a street-singer's acrid voice, and then gave us several comic songs. These possessed, in addition to their own quality, an antiquarian interest. My favourite—though I forget its title—began with the verse:

> Last night I sooped on lobster
> And a terrible dream I 'ud
> Of 'ow the great big H'Albert 'All
> Had been turned into a poob.

The second verse featured *'Enery, Prince of Battenberg*: so that one might hazard that it had originated in the year of Princess Beatrice's marriage. This, as I say, was the song I liked best, but others, in the more serious or sentimental vein, and comprising, too, a kind of prolonged, cat-like wailing, were also worthy to be remembered. . . . After the last song was finished—and we had been treated to many—the artiste, slowly at first, and then more and more swiftly, revolved round the table, until she went so fast that she seemed to circle us at an angle, and one could only just distinguish the violet flash of her figure as she spun like a teetotum past us and out of the door. . . . From the first it had been evident that no-one, except Mrs. Haynesworth herself, was enjoying the performance more than Mr. Asquith. He had throughout followed with round-eyed rapture her every gyration, missing no gesture, no single inflection of her voice. It was, I think, one of the few occasions on which the great Liberal leader found difficulty in maintaining unperturbed his antique Roman mask of statesmanship. His daughter Violet had liked the performance scarcely less, and Mrs. Asquith, with her sense of lively fun, was enthusiastic, as indeed were all the other members of the house-party. But the pillars of the Borough, the municipal grandees, were not amused: it was too near the grain. Their sense of dignity had been injured, a dream of pomp and decorum had been shattered, and I have since wondered whether the memory of it would have helped me in the minds of these local supporters at the next election, had I persevered as candidate. . . . But Mrs. Haynesworth, when she re-entered to take her bow, had proceeded to tell fortunes. Nearly everyone in the room, man and woman, was going to be Prime Minister. . . .

Later in the summer, I returned to Swan Walk, where Sacheverell joined me at the end of June; for the first time accompanied by William Walton. The young composer seemed still more shy and silent. Most of the summer days he appeared to spend in his room at the top of the house, where he sat by the window for long periods, eating black-heart cherries from a paper bag, and throwing the stones out of the window, down on to the smooth brown-tiled pavement outside the door. Swan Walk was so quiet that there was only to be heard a distant booming of traffic, and nearer, this dry, staccato rattle of cherry stones.

Soon a piano was hired for him, and in consequence he remained in his room for longer periods even than before, at intervals being peered at cautiously through the door by Mrs. Powell, "to see he was all right"; for she had quickly become attached to him, and possessed great faith in his talent. For the next twelve years, until her death, she looked after him also with much imaginative tact and consideration. The piano, though he attacked it so often, was seldom, through some process of personal magic, heard downstairs. If it were, I would sometimes advise him to have a dumb-piano to practise upon, when he would grow very indignant. He had, it may be noted, always to be near a piano, though his playing of it, I apprehend, never very much improved. And this was curious, for one of the first things a stranger would have observed about him was his manual dexterity: he could do almost anything with his hands, and by his ingenuity, so that often, for example, I would, when a key was lost, ask him to pick a lock for me. The instrument, however, continued to exert a powerful fascination over him and, in example of this, I recall his despair when, on his arriving one August some years later to stay with my brother, it was found that the ancient, rather rickety wooden staircase leading to his room was too narrow to allow of a piano being carried up it. Six men from the warehouse attempted it in the morning but failed: it was a plainly impossible task. Meanwhile it was arranged that the piano should be left on the first-floor landing at the foot of the stairs, until some two days later, when the men would come back with a trolley and crane and hoist it into the composer's room through the window. In the afternoon my sister and brother and I went for a motor drive: William—still grieving for his piano and the forty-eight hours that must be lost—asked to stay at home. . . . When we returned, the enormous instrument was safely in his bedroom. Often in the days which followed we implored him to reveal how, single-handed, he had accomplished this tremendous feat of skill and strength: but he could only explain, "I did it with a bit of string." Indeed we were never able to elucidate the mystery in any way, or find out more about the no doubt most intricate mechanism that his daemon, in conjunction with his own extreme inventiveness and acting through his considerable muscular strength, had devised.

Since William spent so great a part of his first weeks at Swan Walk in his room, it was not easy at first to grasp his very definite character. Scarcely until he travelled with us in Sicily and Italy, in the spring of 1920, did I begin properly to understand and know him, and rejoice in the incidents that his youth and inexperience, in conjunction with his temperament, provided. Of this kind of occurrence, I will single out an example. On one occasion, when he was staying with me at Scarborough in 1920 or '21, he was suddenly taken seriously ill and had to be removed to a nursing-home. There, a constituent in the division and, it might be, a future supporter of my candidature, a tirelessly kind, middle-aged matron, of prim outlook and near-church pursuits, who without ever reading or thinking was nevertheless almost professionally cultivated within Church-Bazaar limits, offered to sit with him and read aloud. But she came only once. William's taste in all things was naturally good, and often unexpected, and the book he handed her, open at one of its most rollicking passages, was Urquhart's translation of Rabelais! William saw no harm in it, and took pleasure in its exuberance: the reader had never heard of the author. She began in her clear voice, the same she used in her visits to hospital wards, but scarcely had she read a few words before she blushed, becoming facially more tattered every moment as she plunged through the sentence headlong to a full stop. William, I think, noticed nothing unusual: at any rate, said nothing: for music, not words, was his natural form of expression. And in this connection I may add that his mother told me he could sing bits from the *Messiah* before he could talk.

It would be, perhaps, accurate to say of him that he was wordless rather than, as I have written, shy, but the difficulty he appeared to find when he was a very young man in communicating easily with his fellows no doubt militated against his making friends rapidly at that time. Nevertheless, at Oxford he possessed several; notably Roy Campbell, then eighteen or nineteen years of age, and only lately arrived from South Africa. In this respect resembling William, he exhibited in his appearance a curious mixture of strength and delicacy. He also was inclined to be rather silent at first, but the unusual intensity of his appearance, his pallor, the clearness of his eyes and gaze, and their suggestion of tautness and of interior life, as well as his evident passion for poetry, set him apart as a strong personality. I remember, too, how we would always try to persuade him, when he came to see us, to say a few words in Zulu, for the clicking sounds were fascinating and required a true virtuosity to render them.

Later William came to make friends with greater facility: but at first he chose them principally among musicians. My brother, my sister and I already counted Van Dieren and Berners among our friends, and a year or two later we added to them Constant Lambert, at the age of seventeen a prodigy of intelligence and learning, and gifted with that particularly individual outlook and sense of humour which, surely, were born in him and are impossible to acquire. William had soon adopted these friends and been adopted by them, but in addition he possessed others among composers who were solely his own. Such was Philip Heseltine, an acquaintance of mine of whom I have given an account elsewhere,[1] and whose assumption of cloak-and-dagger elegance, combined with an excessive love of limericks and an airy promulgation of esthetic judgements and worldly opinions indifferently based on fact, I found antipathetic: but William entertained a high regard for him and greatly enjoyed his conversation, and, together with Constant, would go down to spend convivial evenings with him in Kent, where Heseltine was living: whence the two young composers would return very late, with footsteps faltering through the now uncertain immensity of night. . . . In these years, too, William became friends with George Gershwin, the Jazz Phoenix. Though Gershwin was not an intimate friend of mine, I knew him and liked him, and he would usually come to have luncheon with us when

[1] See *The Scarlet Tree*, p. 279 of this edition.

he visited London. He possessed a fine racial appearance: nobody could have mistaken him for anyone but a Jew. He was tall and vigorous, and his clearly cut face with its handsome ram's head, the features prominent, but as it were stream-lined, indicated will-power, character and talent. I have always understood that he was the son of immigrants from Russia, and was brought up in the poorest quarter of New York: but his manners were notably excellent, his voice was pleasant, and though the force of his personality was plain in his whole air, he was modest in bearing, and I never noticed in him a trace of the arrogance with which he has been credited. Many of his contemporaries, it may be, attributed an exaggerated value to his celebrated *Rhapsody in Blue*, but at least the hundreds of songs and dances he wrote were altogether typical in their audacity of the age that gave them birth; the 'twenties lived and expired to his ingenious tunes, so expert of their kind, and no chronicle of the epoch could fail to mention them and their pervasive influence; since they were as symptomatic of the triple capitals of the Insouciant Decade as Johann Strauss was of early Franz-Josef Vienna, or Offenbach of the 'sixties. . . . I must retrace my steps.

The first work of William Walton's I heard given in public was a piece of chamber-music which had been chosen as the only English contribution to the International Festival of Modern Music in 1923, held that year at Salzburg. To be present at it, the composer, Sacheverell and I travelled to the Austrian city. The quartet was an incursion into atonal music, and was not too successful, though the second movement showed considerable mastery.

Of Salzburg, that summer, I recall nothing that is not pleasant—Austria was a world unknown to me, and, esthetically speaking, the first great conquest made by the Italian Baroque. In the buildings, here of stone instead of plaster, I recognised a more clumsy but still beautiful reflection of the Italian cities I loved. In these surroundings, mountainous, humid and umbrageous, the expensive follies of a hippophile Bishop of the eighteenth century, who must almost in his passion have rivalled Caligula, attained an unwonted solidity: but the sobriety of their material and

lover of horses?

execution made them all the more fantastic. The gardens—Mirabell and the rest—exhibited, moreover, an admirable leafiness and earthiness and an obvious usefulness, unknown in the great pleasances of Italy. The very roads were bordered with the lichened trunks of tall old apple trees, and high above, as you drove, the younger peasants would be swarming in the trees, picking the fruit, standing with one foot on a lower branch, the other, with knee uplifted, on a higher, in an attitude typical of the figures portrayed in the paintings of Breughel the Elder. Within the walls of stone or red-brick, peach, apricot and cherry, rather than cypress, framed the view, and the purple aubergines and other vegetables scattered round the winged horses of copper, and among the struttings of the stone dwarfs, seemed to add to the flights of imagination, in the same way in which, in old-fashioned pantomimes, the homeliness of the harlequinade brought out the strangeness of the transformation-scene that had preceded it. . . .

At Salzburg that year we saw much of our friend Berners, with his keen understanding and appreciation of everything that is fine, and his particular gift of reconciling the irreconcilable, both in people and circumstances, so that you are conscious, when in his company, that anything may occur—anything that is unusual, but the usual only when it is so unexpected as to be new. Melancholy I believe by nature, and with a number of talents of uncommon degree most evenly distributed among the arts, when not at work he is addicted to wit or humour, as less gifted individuals are victims to drink or drugs. It is difficult to drag him away from a joke, and he would willingly return to it, but, rarest of attributes in a conversationalist, he listens as well as he talks. In the years between the wars, he did more to civilise the wealthy than anyone in England. Through London's darkest drawing-rooms, as well as through the lightest, he moved, dedicated to their conversion, a sort of missionary of the arts, bringing a touch of unwanted fun into many a dreary life—fun perhaps all the more funny for its being unwanted. At Faringdon, in his own spacious, arcaded villa in the Palladian taste, its dove-grey outer walls covered in August with magnolias the size of soup-plates, he pursued his coincident tasks in music, writing and painting, unruffled by the passing flights of fan-tailed pigeons dyed in light tones of green, pink and blue and in scarlet. Sometimes in the drawing-room a horse would sit to him for its portrait, and once, when I was staying there, and the luggage of a guest who had been staying the night stood ready in the hall to be taken to the station, a large portmanteau with a glass top was seen to contain an immense boa-constrictor, neatly coiled for its journey, but showing that it was alive by an occasional glistening shudder of its scaly skin. But this did not worry him in the least, though it a little distressed his mother, for it seemed to her dreadfully inhospitable to allow even a reptile to leave the house without having partaken of a single meal under her roof. . . . But she remained, for a sensitive but conventional old lady, singularly unruffled under every circumstance. The hunting field and country pursuits claimed her interest, but her son's friends from London could not surprise her. From one evening I remember a scrap of dialogue—she was engaged in solving a cross-word puzzle.

"What do you do," she asked me suddenly, "when you are dealing the cards at bridge?"

"Put the ace up my sleeve."

"Quite a wit, Mr. Sitwell," she replied.

Almost alone of the other musicians I met at Salzburg, I recall Alban Berg,[1] the future composer of *Wozzeck*; the only man I have ever seen who bore an unmistakable resemblance to Ronald Firbank. His colour was not so high, for he was pale, and plainly more ascetic, but he had the same profile, waving in and out with something of the line of a sea-coast, and the same physique, the same thin, rather long, neck, the same nerve-racked movements of the head, the turning away suddenly, as if to speak over his shoulder, and even the identical air of listless languor which had caused an American sitting at a neighbouring table in the Café Royal one night to lean forward and bray heartily to Firbank,

---

[1] Alban Berg, born Vienna 9th February 1885, died there 24th December 1935. He wrote numerous compositions. *Wozzeck* and *Lulu*, his two operas, are perhaps his best-known works. He was still engaged on *Lulu* at the time of his death, and even in his last delirium it occupied his mind.

"If you were to come to New York, they'd give you an injection of vitality!" But from Berg's personal appearance there was to be sensed, too, a certain morbidity, a sadness, or more accurately, a despair, that is certainly reflected in his music. . . . Berg greeted Walton as the leader of English atonal music, and took him, with Berners, to see Schönberg, living near one of the neighbouring lakes. They found the austere master composing at a piano, but were quickly hurried out of the room, and when they returned all signs of work had been hidden. . . . Walton had scarcely as yet, I believe, emerged with his own style. I had recognised at once his lyric and elegiac gifts, but it was not until the rehearsals of *Façade* that I fully realised his genius.

In the past twenty-five years, *Façade* has been given many times—and again on three occasions since I began to write this chapter, at the Lyric Theatre, Hammersmith. At its first public performance, on the details of which I propose to expatiate a page or two further on, it created a scandal and involved all connected with it in a shower of abuse and insult. But it was actually first given on the night of 24th January 1922 in the drawing-room of Sacheverell's and my London house, 2 Carlyle Square—which William was sharing with us—, and the rehearsals for it also took place there. It is not easy to describe *Façade*, nor to explain the kind of entertainment it provides: but its history is not without fascination, and that I can give you, together with an account of the details of which it was built up. First, however, I must emphasise that its primary objects were to exalt the speaking voice to the level of the instruments supporting it, to obtain an absolute balance between the volume of the music and the volume of the sound of the words—neither music nor words were to be treated or taken as a separate entity—, and thus to be able to reach for once that unattainable land which, in the finest songs, always lies looming mysteriously beyond, a land full of meanings and of nuances, analogies and images, hitherto only fragmentarily glimpsed, and wherein parallel sound and sense, which here never meet, can be seen, even from this distance, to merge and run into one broad line on the horizon. Another chief, equally difficult, aim to achieve was the elimination of the personality of the reciter, and also—though this is of lesser consequence—of the musicians, and the abolition, as a result, of the constricting self-consciousness engendered by it and sufficient to prevent any traveller from reaching the lunar landscapes I have sought to indicate above. Towards our purpose, the instrumentalists were secreted behind a painted curtain.

Façade has, in the course of its strange career, had three curtains designed for it: the first by Frank Dobson, used for the private and public performances of 1922 and 1923, and also in 1926 at the several performances at the Chenil Gallery; the second, for the International Music Festival at Siena in 1928,[1] by Gino Severini; the third by John Piper, for the Aeolian Hall in 1941, and in use at the moment of writing. Because of its function, an enormous mask occupied the centre of each of the three of them, but in the first and second the round, open mouth was filled by the receding hollow cone of a trumpet, whereas in the third this has been replaced by a microphone. The trumpet-shaped instrument to which I refer was a megaphone of a kind invented some years before by a former singer in Grand Opera, and an authority on voice production, who had in the first place devised it to help his own performance in the rôle of Fafner.[2] In time, however, the

---

[1] See below, pp. 286, 289.

[2] The story of this invention is not without a pathetic and ironical interest. Senger, who was Swiss, and said to be a Jew, sang for several seasons with the Metropolitan Company of New York, but as a rule he performed in Germany and Switzerland. There he alternated, night by night, in the part of Fafner, with a large German singer who was a natural prototype of the later Nazi bullies. This man persecuted Senger, the culmination of one campaign being that after his own performance was finished one night, he broke up the megaphone used by both Fafners on the stage, so that the next evening, when it was Senger's turn to employ it, he found to his chagrin that it no longer existed. Consequently his voice was inaudible, and the newspapers the following morning drew the most wounding comparisons between his singing and that of his rival.

Senger now set out to retrieve his position. This he did by inventing the fibre trumpet, which he subsequently patented in England as the Senger-phone. He kept his discoveries a secret, until a given night when he was able, by the use of his new instrument, to produce a booming so true, memorable and superb, that it resounded throughout the opera house. As he left, he knew that his talent was vindicated, his fortune made—but what he did *not* know was that by an error the management had substituted his rival's name for his own in the evening's programme. The following day, the papers vied

Admiralty took it up, and it was widely employed during both wars, and during storms at sea when the captain had to shout orders from the bridge through a bellowing wind. The Sengerphone—the inventor, Senger, had named it after himself—triumphantly preserved the purity of the tonal quality it magnified. Its success was due in part to the material of which it was made—a fibre derived, I believe, from compressed grasses which altogether removed the metallic timbre once associated with the word megaphone—and in part to the fact that the orifice of the amplifier covered, not only the mouth, but also the lips and nostrils of the speaker, thereby retaining, and increasing the volume of, the resonance caused by the nasal cavities; matters of importance to us in an entertainment in which, by its very nature and object, the speaker is obliged to be incisive in diction and to preserve with severity the rhythms. Thus the audience saw no-one speaking. The painted curtain was provided instead for it to look at, and it heard the human voice speaking, not singing—but speaking at last on an equality with the music. We had, in short, discovered an abstract method of presenting poetry to an audience.

The idea of *Façade* first entered our minds as the result of certain technical experiments at which my sister had recently been working: experiments in obtaining through the medium of words the rhythm of dance measures such as waltzes, polkas, foxtrots. These exercises were often experimental enquiries into the effect on rhythm, on speed, and on colour of the use of rhymes, assonances, dissonances, placed outwardly, at different places in the line, in most elaborate patterns. Some of the resulting poems were sad and serious:

> Said King Pompey, the Emperor's ape,
> Shuddering black in his temporal cape
> Of dust: " The dust is everything—,
> The heart to love and the voice to sing,

---

with each other in protesting how wonderful the false Fafner had been, and how right they had been on a previous occasion in castigating the wretched Senger! . . . Disgusted by this treatment, Senger emigrated to England, where he founded his firm, and became very friendly with Steinway and with Sir Henry Wood.

Senger died in 1936: but his firm, The Sengerphone Company, continues its work.

> Indianapolis,
> And the Acropolis,
> Also the hairy sky that we
> Take for a coverlet comfortably. . . ."

Others were mocking and gay:

> When
> Sir
> Beelzebub called for his syllabub in the hotel in Hell
>   Where Proserpine first fell,
> Blue as the gendarmerie were the waves of the sea . . .

All possessed a quite extraordinary and haunting fascination.

Otherwise, apart from this general origin in the words, it is difficult to say which of us thought of the various parts of the production, for we were all four continually in one another's company, and as soon as the initial idea had somehow or other entered the air, it had filled us with enthusiasm. The title itself, *Façade*, was taken from the remark—it had been repeated to us—of a bad artist, a painter, with the side-whiskers of the period but with a name which, as it proved, has not attached itself to the epoch. He had passed judgement on my sister in the words, "Very clever, no doubt—but what is she but a Façade!" This had greatly delighted us, since what can any poet hope for better than to constitute a façade for his poetry? It seemed an admirable summing-up, and the very title for the sort of entertainment we wanted to present. William was of course to compose the music. I remember very well the rather long sessions, lasting for two or three hours, which my sister and the composer used to have, when together they read the words, she going over them again and again, while he marked and accented them for his own guidance, to show where the precise stress and emphasis fell, the exact inflection or deflection. . . . For the rest, I had thought of the manner of presenting *Façade*, of the curtain and the use of a mask, Sacheverell had found the Sengerphone, and he and William went up to Hampstead by bus to interview Mr. Senger. I never saw him myself: but I have always understood that he was enthusiastic to the point of fanaticism in all matters concerning his profession. On one occasion when he attended a rehearsal of *Façade*, and my sister was engaged in

practising the most difficult of the poems through the megaphone, her eyes at that minute intent on the conductor, Mr.
Senger suddenly hurled himself at her throat, exclaiming, "You
are using your voice the wrong way", and gave her glottis
so powerful a twist that he nearly strangled her in the process!

At the same period, while the minds of the four of us were
much engaged with the idea of the poems and music, I was
sitting nearly every day for three months to Frank Dobson
near-by in Manresa Road. These sittings, I may note, were
interrupted on several occasions by the singularly inaudible
incursions of Colonel T. E. Lawrence, who would seem suddenly to materialise in the studio without one being able to detect
how he had arrived; just to be there, and to have as suddenly
departed. Dobson was at work modelling a head of me in clay,
and Lawrence maintained that it was the finest portrait bust
of modern times, and liked, accordingly, to view its progress.
(When finished, three copies were cast in brass; one of which
was presented by Lawrence to the Tate Gallery.[1]) I never
grew to know Lawrence well, though I often met him,
especially in these years: but, for all his parade of ordinariness,
for all his vanity, which led him to believe that he possessed
such powers as would make the world safe only if he were not
in a position to exert them, for all the perky banality of the
mask he wore, it would have been impossible not to like him,
or not to realise, even though you did not understand, his
remarkable qualities. But most I liked him some ten years
later, at luncheon in Whitehall Court with G.B.S. and Mrs.
Bernard Shaw. Perhaps he was always at his best in their
company, for they loved and comprehended him; and there
was, I noticed, a sort of audacity of mischief about his attitude
and conversation when they were present that was enchanting.
The appearances he made in Dobson's studio were welcome,
for the mornings were long. He would just enter, look at the
head, talk a few moments, and then—be gone. To while away
the cold, stiff hours spent on the platform in the studio, it

---

[1] Some two years later, visiting the Gallery, I was startled when the
custodian at the turnstile gave me a smart salute as I entered. Noticing that
I was surprised, he genially remarked, " Bless my soul, sir, we're old friends.
Scrubs your head every Wednesday, I do! "

G

seemed natural enough to tell Dobson and Delia—his Cornish
wife, and a woman of intense character and temperament, the
warmest-hearted of friends—of what we were planning.
Dobson, who quickly seized the idea, offered to design the
curtain; and I remember how impressive was the sketch he
made for it: in the centre an immense formalised mask with
fair hair, and high, angular colouring.

The rehearsals for the first performance dwell with an
ineradicable vividness in my memory, and there prosper with
their own warmth, kindling even the bleak prospect outside.
The drawing-room is of the usual L-shaped London type.
Three windows look out on the square, and one, at the back,
on to a tall sycamore, the branches of which in this peculiarly
bitter February weather looked black as night, except where
hoar-frost lay on them, so that the whole tree took on the
glitter and flash of a tree in a Hoxton tinsel-print. The
instruments formed a sextet: flute, clarinet, saxophone,
trumpet, 'cello and percussion. The players sat at the wide
end of the room, near the three windows. Through these
poured the implacable whiteness derived from the snow-
covered ground outside, from which beat up a pure and alpine
vibration under a green-white sky. Inside, the room, with
its tones of pink and blue and white and violet, seemed filled
with polar lights from windows and tropic lights from fires:
for all the glass objects, of which there were so many, and the
doors lined with mirror, glittered with redoubled vehemence.
As the strange new sounds shaped themselves under the
hands of the rather angry players, the evening outside began
to envelop the world in a grape-bloom blue, the lights had to
be turned on, and the pictures glowed from the white walls.
. . . I say the players were rather angry, and so at first they
were: irate with the young conductor who seemed to know
his way about in this new and difficult world he had evolved.
He stood there, holding his baton, with something of the air
of an elegant and handsome snipe—for in the last three
years his appearance had grown more stylised—, or, if there
was a hitch in the music and a pause had to ensue, he came,
as I often told him, to resemble a famous animal music-hall
star of the period, the Boxing Kangaroo. But William pos-

sessed persistence as well as genius, and led his players safely through. Soon they became interested, if puzzled, then amused and pleased. I remember the clarinet player enquiring, during a pause, of the composer, who was conducting:

"Excuse me, Mr. Walton, has a clarinet player ever done you an injury?"

In spite of the two piled-up, blazing fires of Derbyshire coal—it had been cut deep under the park at Renishaw—the room remained at freezing-point; but soon Mrs. Powell appeared from downstairs, carrying a tray on which stood glasses and two gigantic straw-covered Chianti flasks full of sloe-gin which she had made in the autumn, bringing back the berries from her native Herefordshire uplands, and as, like Ceres in a late-Italian picture, she dispensed it in generous measure, the instrumentalists warmed to their work, and the long afternoon itself began to glow, to possess its own perfumes, its own atmosphere, unique, never to be recovered. I had, of course, always comprehended the genius of the words, but as I heard the music I understood, too, its genius, the incomparable manner in which the composer, who was not yet twenty years of age, had played with every idea, and matched, underlined and exhibited the words. This music was full of the feeling of the growth of animals and green things, of crude bird song, of breaths of a world of felicity forfeited, of a tender melancholy, and in some numbers, of the jauntiest, most inexplicable gaiety.

The performance took place the following evening at 9.30. The programme,[1] typewritten, bears no date, and the cover carries the words:

> ## " FAÇADE "
> *Miss Edith Sitwell*
> *on her*
> *Sengerphone*
>
> with accompaniments,
> overture and interlude
> by
> *W. T. Walton.*

[1] I am enabled to give the contents of the programme by the kindness of Mrs. Edwin Evans and Mrs. Donald: so far as I know, the copy they gave me is the sole example extant.

Then follow the titles, and the poems, in this order:

(1) Overture.
(2) Madame Mouse Trots.
(3) The Octogenarian.
(4) *Aubade*.
(5) The Wind's Bastinado.
(6) Said King Pompey.
(7) Interlude.
(8) Jumbo's Lullaby.
(9) Small Talk (1)
         (2)
(10) Rose Castles.
(11) Introduction and Hornpipe.
(12) Long Steel Grass.
(13) When Sir Beelzebub.
(14) Switchback.
(15) Bank Holiday (1)
         (2)
(16) Springing Jack.
(17) En Famille.
(18) Mariner Men (Presto.)

After the final poem comes the notice:

" FAÇADE "

All these poems, and some additional ones, will appear in a book called " Façade " which Miss Edith Sitwell is publishing privately in a limited edition with a special frontispiece in colour by Gino Severini—at the Favil Press, Kensington.

The front part of the room was so densely packed with thin gold chairs, it was scarcely possible to move. Across the narrow opening where had been the conventional double doors, now stretched the Dobson curtain. . . . The music began. . . Painters, musicians and poets, of whom a large proportion of the audience consisted, were naturally enthusiastic in their reception of *Façade*, for it was essentially an entertainment for artists and people of imagination. The late Mrs. Robert Mathias, the patron of the Russian Ballet, found herself, for example, so pleased and stimulated by it that, in spite of the no doubt numerous remonstrances of her less enterprising friends and relations, she asked me to arrange another pro duction of *Façade* at her house in Montagu Square.[1] But it must be admitted that in the comparatively small drawing-room of Carlyle Square, the sheer volume of sound was overwhelming and that many of the more orthodox friends whom we had invited to be present were so perturbed by a performance unlike any other they had seen or heard, and for which they could not pick out from the repertory of party-experience the correct label, "Charming", "My dear, we *loved* every moment of it!" or "It reminds me of old days at Covent Garden!", that they did not know what to say, or where to look. We had fortunately arranged for an ample supply downstairs of hot rum punch, an unusual but efficacious restorative. It had been brewed after an old recipe supplied by our friend Barclay Squire, the learned archivist and historian of music, and included among its ingredients, as well as rum, I remember, green tea, sherry, China tea and the juice of a fresh pineapple. This served to revive quickly those who had lost their bearings on a voyage of discovery, and had arrived back feeling somewhat confused, concussed and self-conscious.

Fifteen months later, we gave *Façade* at the Aeolian Hall, at 3 o'clock in the afternoon of 12th June 1923. During the space of time that had elapsed, we had striven to smooth out the imperfections of the entertainment. I have not been able to obtain a copy of the programme, but I remember the wording ran:

Osbert Sitwell presents Miss Edith Sitwell in "Façade".

The press—or rather that section of it now defunct, the gossip-crew, which cherished a deadly parasitic hatred and fear of all work, manual or intellectual, but more especially artistic—had been engaged for days past in trying to whip up the public to pretend to feel rage and resort to insult. Many hours before the curtain rose—or, more precisely in this case, was lowered—the air had grown so tense that I recollect how it rendered my brother and me ill at ease to the extent of being unable to eat any luncheon. From 1 o'clock, therefore, we sat silently within the Burlington Fine Arts Club's demure precincts—at that hour deserted, for they included no dining-

[1] This took place on the night of 7th February, 1922.

room—until it was time to walk the short hundred yards or so to the Aeolian Hall. A large audience had already assembled when we arrived to join my sister in the Artists' Room. I proceeded on to the platform first, walking in front of the curtain to make a speech describing the novel elements in the performance, and attempting to explain its aims. After acknowledging the applause, I went behind the curtain to announce the various items of the entertainment through the mouth of the mask, smaller than the principal head in the middle. Then the fanfare which heralds *Façade* sounded, and the fun began.

On this occasion the entertainment took full effect, though not in the manner we had expected, or at least had hoped for: without apparent reason now infuriating a house that, twenty years later, was to wax to the same degree enthusiastic. The front rows, especially, manifested their contempt and rage, and, albeit a good deal of applause countered the hissing and indicated interest and enthusiasm in certain quarters, nevertheless the atmosphere was so greatly and so evidently hostile that at the end of the performance several members of the audience came behind the curtain to warn my sister not to leave the platform until the crowd had dispersed. For several weeks subsequently, we were obliged to go about London feeling as if we had committed a murder. When we entered a room, there would fall a sudden unpleasing hush. Even friends avoided catching one's eye, and if the very word *Façade* was breathed, there ensued a stampede for other subjects and for safety. In fact, we had created a first-class scandal in literature and music.

The morning following the entertainment, 13th June, brought indeed a black, bleak dawn for us in the press. The fun, the wit, the tunefulness, the beauty, to which qualities, when three years later the performance was repeated at the Chenil Gallery, Mr. Ernest Newman was to draw attention in the columns of the *Sunday Times*—he was not present at the first performance in the Aeolian Hall—, on this occasion completely escaped the critics. All the papers except the *Daily Mail* combined in attack. The mask on the curtain was characterised as a "meaningless, crudely-painted moonface", the music as "collected from the works of the most eccentric of the ultra-moderns", while the words were dismissed as "drivel". Experiments with words, or the idea that a poem is composed of words, always seem to infuriate the English critic and layman alike. Especially do they distrust verbal wit and the play of ideas which wing their way lightly. Every poem, they think in their hearts, should consist either of sentiments and nature-notes commingled, or of leaden political pronouncements. Thus many years ago—I paraphrase from memory—I remember an old lady writing a very angry letter to the Editor of the *Spectator*, after she had read some of my sister's earlier poems. "I have long been familiar," she insisted, "with the best poetry. Shelley and Wordsworth were on my father's shelf from our earliest infancy—though somehow Keats did not find his way on to it until later. I am thus qualified to give my opinion—and of what do Miss Sitwell's poems consist but *words, words, words*!" And I may ask, of what else could they consist, dead larks, or fragments of a stage elephant? . . . Similarly, now, because my sister had plainly enjoyed herself as a virtuoso, and was indulging in enchanting exhibitions of professional skill, it was at once generally recognised that the future author of *Street Songs* and *Song of the Cold* was devoid of all heart and human feeling. They had hoped for another *Charge of the Light Brigade*, and instead they received mocking echoes, the sense of which they could not pin down. "Like Balaclava, the lava came down." The anger of the gossip-spinners was so vehement that all sorts of ingenious ways of discrediting *Façade* were thought out. Thus, though I know that the vigorous prose of "Mr. London"—then expressing himself diurnally in a paper which I will not name here—may break up the texture of this book, nevertheless a sole specimen of it must be produced as an epitome of the feeling, taste and civility of the gossip-writers of the 'twenties.

DRIVEL THEY PAID TO HEAR

If Beerbohm wanted to do a really funny drawing of the Sitwells, instead of the stupid one of them now on view at the Leicester Galleries, he should have gone to the ridiculous recital at the Aeolian Hall which I am surprised to see was taken seriously by some newspapers.

FIREMAN TELLS THE TRUTH

Edwin Evans sat through a series of meaningless, rhythmless, childish words called " Ass-Face ": but Noel Coward was strong enough to walk out, while the fireman, asked his opinion at the end, said that never in twenty years' experience of recitals at that hall, had he known anything like it.

Surely it is time this sort of thing were stopped.

While the entire passage above manifests a singular prevision of standards to become accepted in this country twenty years later, when effort and criticism in the arts, and even the materials for them, such as pens, paper, paint-brushes and canvas, seemed to be confined to, and reserved for, the members of the National Fire Service, yet the last line appears equally to have summed up the Fascist and Nazi approach to the modern developments of music, painting and literature —and before the March on Rome had even taken place. The consequences of *Façade* were several: one was that the notion, difficult to dislodge, now entered the Philistine public's head that Edith, Sacheverell and I were continually declaiming our poems through megaphones in order to call attention to ourselves: whereas the whole point of the procedure we had adopted was, as I have explained—and even explained on the day of the performance, precisely opposite in its intention, which was to conceal the reciter and abolish his personality. The idea, however, still persists or recurs from time to time in the more dusty sections of the press, and in little technical treatises on poetry written apparently by plumbers for their mates. I have, I may say, met people who even have convinced themselves that they have been present in the flesh at such gatherings, that they have heard and seen us read through megaphones—have watched us, with trumpets clamped to our lips, spouting. But faith is not all. So, marshalling my facts and my patience, I repeat once more: my sister has never at any time appeared anywhere with a megaphone, but has only recited poems through one, when herself concealed entirely from view, and when the poems had been written with the purpose of abstract recitation to music: similarly, the only occasion when I have ever approached

it he is right & the mole does exist —
& 3 siblings are striving to live individuals,
but are very "FAÇADE" eccentric. It is an aut... 191

a Sengerphone was when, hidden behind the curtain in the same manner, I announced or explained the items or, once or twice, at the request of the composer of the music, pronounced the single line *Black as a bison*, in order to obtain a variation of vocal texture. The same is true of my brother.

William also suffered: some very stupid and disagreeable remarks about him and his brilliantly lively music, original as it was allusive, appeared in the chat-columns. Yet I hold that musicians are in England better treated as a rule than poets: whom, it seems, age does not stale the pleasures of insulting, whereas elderly composers are praised and fêted. In pursuance of this theory, and before I leave the subject of William Walton and *Façade*, let me then dip again into the future—into, to be more precise, a rainy Sunday, 26th June 1927—and give an account of another musical afternoon on which I had the good fortune to be in his company. On the day in question it so happened that I, to whom, in spite of its genius, the music of Elgar is so obnoxious, so full of English humour and the spirit of compulsory games, was present at one of the last occasions on which the famous English composer and his circle of intimate friends and fervent admirers were given a private performance of his work. Frank Schuster, who had been so greatly devoted to the Elgar cause, and who, at the beginning of the composer's career, had accomplished so much in the way of making his work well known, not only to the social and musical worlds in England, but, through visiting musicians, to circles of amateurs abroad, had determined on a final fling, as it were: a concert to be given in the music-room of his house, the Long White Cloud, at Bray, in Elgar's honour. Schuster, whom we had originally met through our friend Madame Vandervelde, had been kind enough to invite my brother and William Walton and myself to this memorable winding-up of a career.

We motored down from London. The Long White Cloud had a garden on the river, facing Monkey Island, and as we were early, we went first, with Siegfried Sassoon—who I remember, though rather gloomy, was full of horse-play that afternoon—to look at the rooms painted with *singeries* in the

hotel, and to explore the eighteenth-century pavilion[1] in its
garden. Coming out of this structure, a single large room
delicately poised on pillars, I seem to recall that we saw
from the edge of the river, on a smooth green lawn opposite,
above an embankment, and through an hallucinatory mist
born of the rain that had now ceased, the plump wraith of
Sir Edward Elgar, who with his grey moustache, grey hair,
grey top hat and frock-coat looked every inch a personification
of Colonel Bogey, walking with Frank Schuster. Was it, can
it have been, a delusion? Am I imagining it?

At any rate, later we crossed the river, and formed part
of a gathering which, apart from Arnold Bennett and Dorothy
Cheston Bennett, and few others, was chiefly made up of
people who were strangers to me. The rain, as I say, had
stopped, and the music-room was so crowded that, with
Arnold Bennett, we sat just outside the doors in the open air.
In England, only a composer, an elderly composer, could have
drawn on this solid core of enthusiasm. The programme,
entitled *Homage to Elgar*, consisted of several works, for
example the Violin Sonata, played by Albert Sammons and
William Murdoch, and the String Quartet now given for the
second time,[2] and the Piano Quintet. . . . From where I sat I
could watch Elgar, enthroned at the side, near the front. And
I noticed, too, several figures well known in the world of
English music, but in the main the audience was drawn from the
famous composer's passionately devout but to me anonymous
partisans here gathered for the last time. It is true that these
surviving early adherents of Elgar's genius seemed to be endowed with an unusual longevity, but even allowing for this,
it was plain, looking round, that in the ordinary course of
nature their lives must be drawing to an end. One could
almost hear, through the music, the whirr of the wings of the
Angel of Death: he hovered very surely in the air that day,
among the floccose herds of good-time Edwardian ghosts, with
trousers thus beautifully pressed and suits of the best material,
carrying panama hats or glossy bowlers, or decked and loaded

---

[1] Built for the third Duke of Marlborough.
[2] It had been given its first try-out at Felix Salmond's house. Those who
played it at the Long White Cloud were: Albert Sammons, 1st Violin;
W. H. Reed, 2nd Violin; Lionel Tertis, Viola; Felix Salmond, 'Cello.

with fur and feather. And though the principal lived on until 1934,[1] most of them knew, I apprehend, as they listened so intently to the prosperous music of the Master, and looked forward to tea and hot buttered scones (for it was rather cold, as well as being damp), and to all kinds of little sandwiches and cakes, that this would prove their last outing of this sort. The glossy motors waited outside to carry them home, like the vans drawn up to take the fine beasts away from an agricultural show. Some of the motors were large and glassy as a hearse.

A future such as the present that Elgar was at that moment enjoying is never out of reach of a British composer: the wildest of English musicians can soon come to be regarded as a pillar of the Artistic Constitution. Even with *Façade* the scandal gradually ebbed: the balance shifted, for the writer no less than the composer. Far from "this sort of thing being stopped", as "Mr. London" had urged and hoped so fervently, the entertainment has been given many times at home and abroad since 1923. In Paris, The Hague, London and Siena, Constant Lambert, possessed of so many rare gifts, has proved himself to have yet one more: to be the perfect instrument of this performance, a speaker *sans pareil* of the verse, clear, rapid, incisive, tireless, and commanding vocally an extraordinary range of inflection, from menace and the threat of doom to the most debonair and jaunty inconsequence. *Façade*, however, existing in its own special dimension, still retains its old explosive force: time after time it has brought trouble in its trail: yet it would be impossible to overrate the amount of sheer fun, beauty, and gaiety, no less than the burden of annoyance and stupidity, that *Façade* has brought into the lives of all those, from author and composer to stage-hands, connected with it. Even the fireman at the Aeolian Hall seemed to have reconsidered his original esthetic estimate of the entertainment, when last I saw him officiating at a performance there of *Façade* in 1941. And I may add that he also attended the Poets' Reading, organised by my sister and myself at the same hall in 1942, and in both instances showed a personal enthusiasm.

[1] Sir Edward Elgar died on 23rd February 1934.

So, perhaps, after all, the fireman and his brothers under the skin were not the best judges on that afternoon on the 12th June, 1923. . . . But that which was hidden from them and from "Mr. London" was revealed to an Italian Cavalry officer. One hot afternoon of South Italian spring, my brother and William Walton and I were returning by train from an expedition to the Palace of Caserta. Normally, it took an hour, but we had been obliged in the end to catch a slow train. Since it had not seemed worth while to bring books with us for so short a journey, we were obliged to sit there restlessly, suffocating in the dust of the red plush carriage. Fortunately the view was superb: we stared out of the window over the plain of vines, their thick, sun-drenched branches stretched between high posts, and beginning to show coils of green and gold springing from them, towards where, in the distance, Capri rode like a dolphin her blue tides. Tiring even of this, we started in low voices to chant various numbers from *Façade*: the *Waltz*, *Rose Castles*, the *Foxtrot*, and *Trio for Two Cats and a Trombone*. There was nobody in the carriage but ourselves and a dignified figure in one corner, in black gaiters, sky-blue breeches, tunic and shako. He understood no English, we had found out in a trial conversation, and appeared to possess something of the Cavalry officer's international moroseness. As, however, we recited, his face began to glow with interest and then with pleasure, and half way through *Two Cats and a Trombone* he leant forward and, with an air of discovery and delight, enunciated in his beautiful, clear Italian voice his verdict,

"Ecco la vera poesia!"

CHAPTER THREE

The General Strike

THE SHORT chapter I now contribute to the history of the
General Strike is not concerned with the causes of it—
although I shall later have to recall briefly one or two facts
—but with certain negotiations which helped to end the
dispute. It may be that these few pages, forming in their
essence a hitherto undisclosed political history, stand a little
apart, beyond the proper scope of my book. Nevertheless,
though in August 1947 (in which month I write these words),
some twenty-one years later, when from the tops of our broken
towers and from the depths of our hopes irremediably shattered we can already descry the looming outline of a termination so different from the conventional happy ending with
which the Victorians held that the Gods, or their anthropoid,
self-helping prototypes or proxies, concluded every phase of
human existence—a termination the shape of which I have
tried to set down in the *Envoy* of which the last chapter of
this volume consists—, though, then, viewed from this distance, the General Strike of 1926 may seem to have been unim-
portant, yet at the time it was so great a matter, and I was so
much connected with those negotiations, and moreover,
they were in themselves so typical of the period, and of the
nonchalant way in which Englishmen conduct business and
reach decisions, that I could not omit an account of them, and
of the days in May they occupied, from any description of my
life, even though I am obliged on occasion, in order to present
a summary of what happened, to report things I have not seen
or heard myself, and to rely instead on the observation of
others. To these conferences, which played a part in the
secret history of our time, the only references, so far as I am
aware, occur in two books which I shall cite at the appropriate
moment: but these casual mentions, languid and desultory in

one instance, and over-excited and strained in the other, attracted little attention. Nor in the course of Mr. J. H. Thomas's book[1] (two chapters of which are devoted to this period of his career) do the Wimborne House negotiations, whereto I allude, figure even once: because, as he told me, he was only concerned in its pages with official negotiations. Notwithstanding, and though they were by no means the sole channels of communication between the Government and the strike-leaders—there was, for example, the all-important instrumentality of Sir Herbert Samuel,[2] to which Mr. Thomas so generously pays tribute—, they served, withal, a most valuable purpose.

To revert to my personal narrative, on 27th April 1926 took place the second public performance in London of *Façade*. We have just seen how it fared when first given, but in the three intervening years the wind had first veered and then gathered strength again, so that now an enthusiastic audience tried to encore every number. Yet in the main the programme was identical, except that the words were chiefly spoken by that accomplished actor, Mr. Neil Porter, my sister having decided only to recite a few of the slower poems. Of this occasion, Arnold Bennett noted in his Journals:[3]

Tuesday, April 27th. I drove to the Sitwell Concert, "Façade". Crowds of people, snobs, high-brows, low-brows, critics and artists and decent folk. I enjoyed this show greatly. The verses are

[1] *My Story*, by the Right Hon. J. H. Thomas. (Hutchinson & Co., 1937.) Mr. Thomas started work at nine years of age in 1883, as an errand-boy. He rose to be respectively engine-cleaner, fireman and engine-driver (G.W.R.), General Secretary of the National Union of Railwaymen, Member of Parliament 1910–31, '31–36, Secretary of State for the Colonies 1924, '31 and '36, Lord Privy Seal 1929–30, and Secretary of State for the Dominions 1930–35. . . . This long and successful struggle in no way impaired the vigour of his language, or abated its character, and he remained an entertaining and warm-hearted companion, a very amusing after-dinner speaker, and was a figure particularly dear to the cartoonists of the 'twenties and 'thirties.

[2] Now Viscount Samuel of Mount Carmel, G.C.B., G.B.E. This statesman, after a long career in the House of Commons, became Liberal Leader in the House of Lords. He has held many posts of the greatest importance, and has written a number of well-known books.

[3] *The Journals of Arnold Bennett*, 1921–28. Edited by Newman Flower. (Cassell & Company, 1933.)

distinguished; the music (Walton) equally so. The "scene" (flat) by Frank Dobson was admirable.

And Mr. Ernest Newman ended the long review to which I have alluded in the last chapter, and which appeared in the *Sunday Times*,[1] with the following two paragraphs:

Here is obviously a humorous musical talent of the first order; nothing so good in the mock serious line of music has been heard for a long time as the *Valse*, the *Polka*, the *Jodelling Song*, and *I Do Like to Be Beside The Seaside*; the deft workmanship, especially in the orchestration, made the heart of the listening musician glad.

The curious thing was the happiness of the correspondence between all the factors of the affair; the music, the words, the megaphone, and the piquant phrasing of the lines by the reciter were as much bone of each other's bone and flesh of each other's flesh as the words and the music are of each other in *Tristan*, or *Pelléas*. At its best, *Façade* was the jolliest entertainment of the season.

This sudden but avowed reversal of public judgement left us all three feeling nervously exhausted, yet rather flat. During the whole of the preceding fortnight or more, our minds had been exclusively occupied with the production of *Façade*. An entertainment of so novel a kind, dependent on a subtle combination of spoken words and music, required the utmost care: the rehearsals needed to be scrupulous in the extreme, with every detail clearly thought out and defined. To the outside world, therefore, I had hardly given a glance during these weeks—least of all to public affairs. Scarcely, however, had the plaudits of the audience died down —for we had been obliged to give one or two repeat performances, as well as some more ordinary recitals of poetry— when we perceived, as we looked for the first time for many days beyond the vistas of central gangways and the dusty routine of theatre or concert-hall which alone had existed for us, that the national prospect had darkened beyond recognition. Within the space of a few days, the entire state was in upheaval, the whole daily routine of life for every class of the people wrenched out of shape. Our last performance at the Chenil Gallery had taken place towards the end of the

[1] For Sunday, 2nd May 1926.

week beginning on the 25th of April—either Thursday, I think, or Friday—and the General Strike started on the night of Monday 3rd May.

Concerning the causes of the grave situation which emerged to view, I need only remind my readers that coal—as always in England during the last three decades, though before that it had for a century been regarded, if not by the miners, by the rest of the world, both here and abroad, as the great national blessing—was the root of the trouble. Mr. Baldwin's[1] Government had decided to discontinue the Coal Subsidy, and, for their part, the miners had rejected the findings of the Coal Commission, embodied in a report known as the Samuel Report.[2] The long neglect of the mines by all political parties had made those who worked in them stubbornly bitter. Now the Trades Unions, led by Mr. J. H. Thomas, were threatening to support the miners in their attitude of intransigence; an attitude born of despair, of the constant threat of unemployment or lower pay, and of the feeling, however unreasonable this might appear to others, that no one gave a thought to their welfare. But the final precipitant of the situation was the refusal of the printers to print the *Daily Mail* because it carried in its editorial some remarks which they considered to be strictures on the action the Unions proposed to take. Late on the night of Monday 3rd May, news of this development reached the Cabinet in session at Downing Street, and that body decided to break off negotiations with the Trades Union leaders. The Strike then opened.

I had spent Saturday and Sunday in the Thames Valley, staying with some friends, and owing, I suppose, to the fatigue and exertions of the past week, until I returned to London on Monday morning I had scarcely realised the position. Now that I did so, it touched me the more nearly, since coal-smoke, from chimneys slim as obelisks and slag-heaps angular as pyramids, is my native air (I begin to feel at home as soon as I breathe its harshness under the sweetness of hill and valley, near Nottingham, on the road from London

---

[1] Later Earl Baldwin of Bewdley, K.G.

[2] Because it had been drafted and signed by the Chairman, Sir Herbert Samuel.

wonder of D. H Lawrence (not Laurence of Arabia) would agree with this general view

to Renishaw), and I have always been friendly with many who were colliers, or have worked in the mines at some time. I was in this fashion aware, both of the hard conditions of their lives, and of their individuality as men; to whom a cramping and airless profession afforded a particular zest for open-air life, for walks accompanied by whippets or for time spent in gardening or fishing, just as the impossibility during working-hours of preventing their clothes and their faces from being clogged with coal-dust rendered them—even when they did not show in their style, as often they did, a natural dandy-ism—very careful to be clean and spruce. . . . Thus I was, as I say, greatly moved by my sudden comprehension of what was happening. And further, I was obliged to make one of those swift alterations of outlook, perhaps only possible to people who possess several strongly-marked veins of inheritance. For though a pursuit of the arts was incised in my left hand, and a life dedicated to them in my right, yet, as the reader has seen, politics were also deeply engraved in the left palm. (And I may observe here, in parenthesis, that if the few days which followed, and which I am about to describe, constituted in some ways the most exciting period of my life, since they allowed full scope to the repressed political side of my character, and if I was able to be of use, yet that this could be so was due to two predisposing factors: the first and chief, a new friendship, the second, a new motor-car—though not mine.) My traditions had been mainly political, as a glance at the beginning of *Left Hand, Right Hand!* will remind the reader. Notwithstanding, these, I believe, are the only pages in which I directly describe political events or undercurrents, and when I began, as is my habit in the matter of composition, to transcribe, correct and alter the cadences, examining the paragraphs I had written, I could not but notice with what singular persistence, as I approached the subject, the clichés clustered round and clotted the nib of my pen. . . . Is it because modern politics are inseparable in their essence from platitudinous expression? I do not know, but I can vouch for how frequently such phrases as "exploring the avenues", "leaving no stone unturned", and even such ancient sobriety-tests as "the British Constitution" rang in my head, and leapt in and out of my ink-pot while I wrote. . . . Not only, as I was saying, had my inheritance been mainly political, but my early memories reinforced the claim. Among my earliest had been that of a general election, in the course of which, at the age of two or three, I had been obliged to drive proudly with my father through the various wards of the borough of Scarborough. This, no doubt, had influenced me, in addition to the long strain of addiction to politics in my blood. Indeed, as a boy I had always expected to follow my father in his choice of career. I had, therefore, almost from infancy taken a continual interest in public affairs: nearly the sole exception being the period of a fortnight or so that had just passed.

The effect, then, on me of my sudden comprehension of the immediate outlook proved astounding, even to myself. I was appalled. Never have I been more disturbed, save by the two declarations of World War. . . . Twenty years ago, vanity much possessed me, and I still arrogantly maintained an attitude I had adopted in 1914, that one or two highly intelligent—that is to say, politically intelligent—men could, by cutting across the laws of the petrified diplomacy that prevailed, have prevented the 1914–18 war. Because no-one wanted it. No-one at all. And in this connection let me asseverate, for my country's good, that fishermen—freshwater fishermen—are not the best persons to be in charge of national or foreign policy in times when wars are near. *Cave piscatorem!* They have learned to follow too obediently the rules governing an ancient sport: they acquire, like caterpillars, a leafy philosophy, but not a zest for energetic action. I doubt whether Lord Palmerston was a fisherman; I am certain, if he were, he was never in that respect the equal of Sir Edward Grey. But he would, I think, have realised earlier that it was no use tickling the Germans. Be that as it may, here was a position, similar, it looked to me, in its capacity for disaster, to that which had existed in the first days of August 1914, and once again nothing apparently could be done to prevent it or to curb its powers of evil development.

As day by day the situation grew worse, I found myself utterly out of sympathy with the self-congratulatory, "Aren't

we all splendid!" attitude of the exasperated and now embattled bourgeoisie. To be a porter for a time, or a lorry-
driver, would be easy, I considered: for a *time*, but not for a
lifetime. Only as a holiday romp did it afford the contrast
that might make it seem pleasant.

The nation, it was clear, had drifted into peril, before that
danger had been realised fully by those in charge of the
Government, or by those who led the Trades Unions. Nobody
—or hardly anybody except one or two Cabinet Ministers,
dramatically-minded and fond of indulging in bloated, elephantine phrases, and who were said to advocate blood-letting
as a panacea—, had wished for such a calamity to fall on us.
Now, not only had trade ceased to flow, bringing with it
incalculable loss—a loss which would be felt not only at the
present moment, but in the future as well—, far worse, and
more serious, our long-settled civil peace, the greatest asset
of the British race, stood in jeopardy. Surely to force the
strikers, or prospective strikers, and perhaps the whole of the
Labour Party, by offering them no opportunity of saving their
faces and of returning to democratic paths, into supporting and
adhering to extremist threats, and then drive them into trans-
lating these menaces into practice, was foolish in the extreme.
For centuries there had been no internecine war in England;
at worst, a riot or two. There had occurred none of the re-
actionary or revolutionary massacres which had taken place
elsewhere: there existed as yet none of the hatred between
industrial North and residential South so evident in the United
States, none of the inter-class hatreds which flourished on the
blood-soaked continent of Europe. Even the English Civil
Wars of three hundred years before had been conducted with
a certain sense of decorum and lack of cruelty. . . . But now,
because of the blundering of both sides, the country was facing
a period of unknown duration, in the course of which, in spite
of British restraint, the most trifling incident might precipitate
fighting. Who wanted such a struggle? . . . Some pickets
were in militant mood: not less bellicose was the thug-militia
of St. James's Street, the bands of young, steel-helmeted
clubmen. Yet it was evident that no-one, not even these
strikers or strike-crashers, desired this particular outbreak.

(They would enjoy a battle, after the manner of the pugnaciou
everywhere, but they wanted still more to talk about it after
wards, and any fight would satisfy them.) It was merely tha
each side—and very rightly—resented the threats of the othe
and its assumption of infallibility. It stood to reason that th
Trades Union leaders must, if they were intelligent me
(which, deducing from my former slight acquaintance wit
Frank Hodges, and with Robert Williams of the Transpor
Union, both of whom I had met on the English Committee o
Clarté, I presumed them to be), very greatly desire to trac
their way back to the more normal conditions in which s
notable an advance had already been achieved for the workers
and in which so much more would, it was obvious, be secure
within the bounds of their lifetime and without civil disturb
ance. Now events were rushing along at too swift a rate. Soo
the leaders might find themselves beyond the law.

During the first days of the Strike, I hardly went out of m
house, so distressed was I at the position and its implications
At night, however, in order to obtain the latest news, I woul
go down to the offices of the *Daily Express*—being on one o
two occasions allowed to enter the door after the most carefu
scrutiny and examination by pickets—to see Beverley Baxte
who was then Managing Editor of Lord Beaverbrook's pape
But during the day I sat, the very picture of a drone, in a
armchair, with my back to the window, wondering what coul
be done. I did not wish to help my country by playing a
being an engine-driver. (Even as a child I had never har
boured that ambition, which now in so many adults foun
a sudden release and realisation.) Moreover, had I done so
neither I nor many of my passengers would have survived t
rue it. No, I wanted to aid my native land in a differen
perhaps more potent, fashion; helping it by contributing
through some means or other, to end the conflict, and so t
prevent the growth of that bitterness which must follow o
any even accidental clash between authority and the strikers
I certainly longed with my whole being to be one of those t
shut the gates once more against disaster: but the situatio
seemed to me to be slipping every day nearer the precipice
soon it would be beyond repair. . . . Still I waited, for, allie

to a conceited belief that I could perhaps exert some influence
on even such a great affair as this, I cherished a secret belief
in fortune and the moment. My approach—no doubt ridi-
culously youthful for my thirty-three years—was by nature,
and towards political problems no less than towards those of
art and literature, from an esthetic direction, and I remember
recalling to myself, though with a certain detached amusement
at what seemed to be a tendency in myself to paranoia, the
several heroes of D'Annunzio novels, who within their
monumental palaces of travertine stone awaited the signal.
Similarly, within my residence of glass and plaster, I awaited
the opportunity, whatever it might be, whatever it might
bring. . . . It was rather late in coming.

There I sat, for the most part alone; for my brother no
longer lived in the house. The year before, he had married,
and his wife, Georgia, was slight, exquisite, young, and warmly
and brightly coloured as a flower. She had soon come to be
not only my sister-in-law but one of my most intimate friends.
It cannot have been easy for someone gifted with so strong a
personality of her own to take up her place in a family united
as we were, but she had sailed effortlessly—or apparently
effortlessly—into our family life, and with her brought her
own transatlantic openness to new ideas, her own transatlantic
—she was Canadian—qualities of impatience and of reverence,
and her own witty but practical appreciation of the world
and understanding of character. While she thought things
out for herself, she came often to the same conclusions as we
did. Thus she viewed with comprehension and sympathy
the nervous battles continually in progress between the
younger and older generation, and came to be, from hard
experience, scarcely less of an authority on our parents than
we were ourselves, but always with tact and with sympathy,
though sometimes with amusement in her large and beautiful
golden eyes. . . . Thus, though, as I have said, I sat alone, it
was of choice, and not continuously, and the phrase is somewhat technical, for my brother and sister-in-law, since we
were such friends, had taken the house next door to me for the
summer, and whenever I wished I could go and talk to them,
or when they felt like it they could come and see me. Moreover,

William Walton sat upstairs, in undisturbed communion with his piano. My other visitors were few. Chief, there was Edith, of course. And Siegfried Sassoon, too, often came to see me, for, as always in these great crises, we found ourselves able to share the same feelings. In such times the warmth of his political sentiments, into which he puts his heart, made him a valued companion. Others I scarcely saw—except a very dear friend of mine, whom I had known for some few years, David Horner; who was my main link during these ten days with the more useful members of society; for he had volunteered as a lorry-driver, and he would now come to see me, between his spells of duty, with a cut over one eye which he had earned for his patriotic effort, and would describe to me the people he met on his journeys and the feeling that was in the air.

At present, then, I was staying resolutely in my home; I just sat there, in a room full of complicated and brittle decoration, hearing the roar of the amateur-driven lorries as they hurtled down King's Road. I was able to give my entire time to the process, and to thinking in general, for my father was abroad, and the Strike to my relief prevented his letters from arriving in great quantity. I waited. But nothing much seemed to happen. . . . Above all, however, the late 'twenties was the Age of Slogans, of bestial appeals to the appetites: *Eat More Bread! Drink More Milk! Guinness is Good for You! Join the Mustard Club!* A friend of mine, whose strike work it was to think out slogans for the Government, telephoned to me, I remember, to ask if I could suggest a cry suitable for the hoardings in this emergency; for, he insisted, he knew I was "good with words". I said yes, I could. What was it, he asked? I answered,

THINK LESS AND EAT MORE!

With his reply he seemed delighted, and rang off. The following day, however, the telephone bell summoned me, I lifted the receiver and heard his voice again. Somehow the words, he said, though they *sounded* just the thing, when you came to examine them . . . , well, he wasn't so sure. My slogan had been on the very verge of being struck off the machine, when the blackleg printer had come to him, and said, "Cut it out, Guv'ner! It won't work!", and had read it over to him. Was it, my friend asked, what I had really meant (and here he read it to me over the telephone); was I sure? I admitted my error at once. What I had intended to say, I explained, was,

EAT LESS AND THINK MORE!

This seemed as a new idea profoundly to excite him: (he was fond of new ideas). "Splendid!", he cried enthusiastically, "splendid!", and rang off. . . . I never heard any more of my slogan, however, though for all I know it may have appeared and have remained fluttering its draggled length from hoardings for many years in remote parts of the country.

Meanwhile, the days went by, each with its fresh burden of worrying little indications of evil. The attitude of both sides was hardening, and each half of the nation was growing tired and angry. . . . It was during these days—to be exact on Thursday, 6th May—that a Liberal leader, Sir John Simon,[1] openly threw in his weight with the Government against the strikers. Perhaps the most eminent authority on law in the kingdom, he came forward at this juncture to pronounce the General Strike to be illegal: a declaration which profoundly influenced both public opinion in the country and the course of events. Yet it is, I believe, to be doubted how far the great lawyer's statement concerning the matter was deeply considered, and whether it was not almost an impromptu, for he is said to have confided to a friend in the House of Commons, on his way downstairs to make the speech, that he had resolved, of a sudden, to give the matter this interpretation. Whatever may have been the history of it, and whether or no it was based on a serious study of the law, yet once such a pronouncement had come from the mouth of one of the greatest lawyers of the age, the whole issue presented itself henceforward in an entirely new and simplified light. This speech when it reached

[1] Now Viscount Simon.

them completed the discomfiture of the strike leaders, especially of Mr. J. H. Thomas, who resented it in an almost personal manner, since for several years he had been on particularly friendly terms with his fellow-countryman, Sir John Simon. (To not the least singular aspect of the General Strike, the degree to which those who played a prominent part in it from beginning to end, and either in the open or in secret, were of Welsh origin, I shall refer on a later page.) From this moment on, the strike leaders, in their blue serge suits, with their moustaches and bowler-hats, found that they had come perilously to resemble rebels, and must have felt from time to time on the verge of being proclaimed. It was difficult at the moment to foresee the effects of the speech, and others fell into the same mistake in their estimate of the national psychology as I did. Of what use was it, I asked myself, to inform politely an encroaching and overwhelming flood that it had transcended the bounds? But how wrong was I! Everywhere Sir John's declaration produced in the people of this country, tolerant and law-abiding by nature, an immediate response. "Good gracious!", they exclaimed primly, "what I'm doing isn't respectable!", and many of them longed in consequence to return quietly to work.

In those early days of May 1926, however, this reaction was one not easy to imagine, for the future, viewed in terms of days rather than of weeks, looked remote and fraught with possibilities of evil. To begin with, it was impossible to tell with any sense of confidence what was going on. From the first morning, a few newspapers published a single sheet with practically no news in it: *The Times* appeared as a typescript-printed page. The newsprint, if not the news, was mostly reserved for a Government bulletin of four pages, entitled *The British Gazette*. This unpleasant and ephemeral journal was issued from the offices of the *Morning Post*, and was edited by Mr. Winston Churchill; whose real genius, coupled with an adolescent instinct for striking an attitude, makes him what he is, a great man, but at times—and this was to my mind one of them—a great danger. To him might be applied the dictum of the late Lord Keynes, concerning a famous banker.

"Is he really a genius?", I asked.

"Oh yes," he replied, "he's a big man; a very big man indeed—the only man big enough to get us out of the mistakes he makes." . . . And, in the case of Mr. Churchill, it must be added, in fairness, out of the mistakes that others, less great, make as well.

News, then, remained scarce. Strikers and bourgeoisie both, as it proved, acted with restraint: but often rumours of the wildest and wickedest kind circulated, and certainly many contradictory influences were at work. A muddled outlook prevailed. Arnold Bennett, as usual, reflects very clearly and accurately the mood of the moment, and in the pages of his Journals[1] you can see how singular and conflicting were the currents which mingled. On Tuesday, 4th May, he tells us he sees "*a noticeably increasing gravity in the general demeanour*". The next day he had luncheon at the Reform, an edifice standing four-square for constitutionalism, its very embodiment in stone, and reports the "*General opinion that the fight would be short but violent. Bloodshed anticipated next week. Plenty of wireless messages, futile. . . .*" And he relates the trouble he had the following evening in obtaining any dinner at his Club because he was not wearing evening clothes. "*Imagine enforced evening dress in the middle of a General Strike!*", he comments.

The days dragged on. Already the outbreak of the Strike three nights before seemed removed from us by a whole lifetime. On Thursday afternoon, I received a letter brought by hand. It was from Lady Wimborne,[2] asking me if I could have luncheon with her the next day. She had only the week before returned from a visit to Paris, and since I had spent the winter in working at Amalfi—where I had been finishing *Before the Bombardment*—, we had not yet met in 1926. I

---

[1] 1921–28, p. 132.

[2] The Hon. Alice Grosvenor, daughter of the 2nd Lord Ebury. She married the Hon. Ivor Guest, who sat in the House of Commons from 1900 to 1910, when he was raised to the Upper House as Lord Ashby St. Ledgers. He succeeded his father as second Lord Wimborne in 1914. Created a Viscount in 1918. Paymaster-General, 1910–12. Lord Lieutenant of Ireland, 1915–18. Lord Wimborne died in 1939; Alice, Lady Wimborne, on 17th April 1948.

accepted with alacrity her invitation. Hers was the friendship to which I have alluded. I had first made her acquaintance— though I had met her vaguely several times before—as the result of her liking my first book of short stories, *Triple Fugue*, when it had appeared two years previously. Our friendship had prospered and to me had proved one of the most pleasant features of that period—and we found, too, that we were distantly related, for both of us shared Wellesley blood, being descended from Lord and Lady Mornington, the parents of the Duke of Wellington. And since Lady Wimborne's influence in the negotiations I go on to describe was all-pervasive, her winning grace and tact making things easy for everyone, just as her absolute discretion helped to render the proceedings secret, this is undoubtedly the place to mention her and to celebrate her gifts and personality.

For such a part as that which she was now about to play, she possessed superb qualifications. Her great beauty, subtle and full of glamour though it was, and the fact that she was the wife of one of the richest men in England, were apt to blind people equally to her political intelligence, interest and experience. The attitude she presented to the world of a fashionable beauty who dressed with daring and loved admiration, the guise of an accomplished woman of the world, which was hers naturally, by birth, tradition and upbringing, hid from the crowd the clever woman who inhabited this exquisite shell. But she was by no means the ordinary clever woman, for, in this unlike a type more familiar, she never imitated at second hand a man's way of thinking but approached every problem from an intensely feminine angle. Nor, it must be admitted, was there any necessity for her to ape masculine brains, for she could divine a situation with a rapidity of mind and an X-ray-like precision which were truly remarkable. Just as her more obvious gifts concealed her cleverness, so the wealth of her husband masked from people his talents and wide democratic sympathies. The world was ignorant of the fact—albeit it was well known in South Wales—that, alone of great Welsh landlords, he had tried in a practical manner to soften the effect of the leasehold system to the working-man. Similarly, what must to some people have seemed in its result to be his failure as Viceroy of Ireland, blinded them to the extreme narrowness of the margin by which he had missed achieving a settlement. Only perhaps those few politicians who had been responsible for defeating his hopes had realised how nearly they had culminated in success. But the office of Viceroy was in its very nature a difficult position for a man of character to fill. Though at the head of Irish affairs, with unlimited powers on paper, in practice he was obliged to bow to the decisions, however faulty he might consider them, of the Secretary for Ireland and the English Cabinet, and yet, most unfairly, was involved in the consequences of their policy. Nevertheless, during Lord Wimborne's term of office, Viceregal Lodge had become the true and obvious meeting-place of North and South. When the first insurrection—the product equally of long historical processes and of the then Government's immediate policy—broke out, it may well be the actions and conduct of the Viceroy which saved, if only temporarily, the English regime. Subsequently, in any case, Lord Wimborne was totally exonerated by the findings of the Royal Commission on the Irish Government, and at Mr. Asquith's request, to which were joined the entreaties of many Irish people of different creeds and kinds, he returned for a second term as Viceroy. Differences, however, soon occurred between the Viceroy and Mr. Lloyd George, who had succeeded Asquith as Prime Minister. Lord Wimborne returned to England. And since his relations with Mr. Lloyd George never improved and since he was, and remained, a Liberal by conviction, henceforth his great political ambitions were frustrated, his career was finished, and he became a disappointed man at a loose end.

It must be remembered, further, that in him political tendencies were innate. His mother, Cornelia, Lady Wimborne—who was still alive at this time—had been by birth a Churchill, daughter to the 7th Duke of Marlborough, and sister to Lord Randolph. Lord Wimborne was, therefore, a first cousin of Mr. Winston Churchill's, and a member of the same intimate and clannish circle. Cornelia, Lady Wimborne, as was natural in a member of her family, continued, even as an old lady, to find public affairs of the greatest interest, and though she had been a Conservative at the time her son, as a young man, had adopted the Liberal cause, she took always a progressive view, and during the General Strike and before it, wrote continual letters to her son, urging him to offer to mediate between the miners and the Trades Unions on one hand, and the authorities on the other. No doubt she recalled how the old gang of Tories had wrecked the career of her brother Lord Randolph, and distrusted the same lack of ability, the same absence of generosity which she thought she could detect again in their successors.

Here I must pause, to describe Lord Wimborne. Physically of imposing stature, there was similarly nothing small about him in mind or character; there was much right and much wrong about him, but nothing small. One of the first details to be noticed in his appearance was his unusually finely shaped hands, which gave a clue to his personality, to his love of beautiful objects and of sumptuousness. Under the crushing of his ambitions, his brain, penetrating, exploratory by nature and independent in its view, had been a little tamed. Moreover, as time went on, he began to suffer from that curious failing of many able Englishmen: he grew unwilling to exert his mental faculties, though no physical strain was too severe for him to undertake. At polo or hunting he would regard it as natural to exhaust himself. But he enjoyed, too, the planning and creation of beauty, and himself had largely contrived the Capuan vistas of Wimborne House, which he had remodelled. When I first knew him, though his ambitions had been disappointed, he was still capable of vigorous effort, and he contrived always to dominate the splendour in which he lived and to remain a person, a human being of great character. Finally it must be stressed that, throughout the crisis of which I write, he maintained a consistently generous and liberal attitude; which was, as it proved, of inestimable help to the country he served without claim or reward. In reading the account of what follows of the negotiations, all these factors must constantly be borne in mind.

Lady Wimborne—Alice—had continued the tradition of

entertaining all kinds of men and women which she had inaugurated in Ireland. Wimborne House itself remained a social institution, and in its hospitable rooms could be met many sorts of people, the heads of foreign states, many members of the cosmopolitan world of fashion, and the most prominent men of the three political parties in England, writers, editors and Trades Union leaders. In addition, this mansion, in the middle of the old aristocratic quarter of London, possessed its own older political traditions, to help the conducting of negotiations: for its roots lay in the heart of one of the greatest and of the earliest of British industrial centres. In South Wales, the great Guest Steel Works had for well over a century been ruled absolutely in succession by the head of the family. Each week the wages had been found by him personally, and he had supplied rails—the best in the world—to Great Britain, the U.S.A., Germany, Australia, South America and Canada. In consequence the name Guest was familiar to every working-man in South Wales—as it was, too, to every antiquary and Welsh patriot: because Lord Wimborne's grandmother, the wife of Sir Josiah Guest, was the celebrated Lady Charlotte Guest,[1] translator and collector of *Mabinogion*.

All these claims on Welsh esteem centred in Wimborne House, and made it a very fitting place for Welsh negotiations to be conducted: and to such, in fact, they almost amounted. The origin of the dispute was largely in the South Wales coalfields, and many of those who played a prominent part, acknowledged or unacknowledged, in the struggle of these few days were of Welsh origin: the Right Hon. J. H. Thomas, for instance, no less than Sir John Simon: and, in capacities less recognised, Mr. Tom Jones,[2] the Deputy-Secretary to the Cabinet—in other words, Private Secretary and Confidential Adviser to the Prime Minister of the day—, and

---

[1] Lady Charlotte Elizabeth Bertie, daughter of the 9th Earl of Lindsey. After the death of her husband, Sir Josiah Guest, in 1852, she managed the Iron Works at Dowlais. In 1855 she married again: her second husband was Charles Schreiber, M.D.

[2] Thomas Jones, C.H., LL.D., Secretary of the Pilgrim Trust, 1930–45. A Trustee since 1940. Late Deputy-Secretary to the Cabinet and Secretary to the Economic Advisory Council, and the author of several books.

Mr. Selwyn Davies, Lord Wimborne's secretary. And these two gentlemen, though little or no public attention was focused upon them, had much to do with the outcome of the affair. Mr. Tom Jones, whose name was not a household word (as well it might have been), was yet in several directions one, not only of the most able and experienced, but also of the most powerful servants of the state; a man of the utmost integrity, and of a mind naturally generous and well-disposed towards his fellows. Mr. Selwyn Davies, who had been with Lord Wimborne in Ireland, and had there, under his chief, learnt a great deal about the arts of negotiation, played an important part as intermediary. A devoted man, of intensity of character and of sound judgment, he never ceased from working in the most selfless and discreet manner to bring together the strands. During the ten days of the General Strike he was tireless in his efforts. Moreover, being continually in touch with Mr. Tom Jones, he was nearer the centre of events than many who filled more prominent positions. As we shall see, it was to him in the end that the actual announcement of the calling-off of the General Strike was made. Above all, where the negotiations of those who were not principals in the matter are concerned, the reader, to comprehend them, must never lose sight of the fact that the chapel system of the Welsh people, who worship in a language the English cannot understand, constitutes in its essence the surviving form of the historically persecuted creed of a formerly subjugated race. The emotion it engenders in the hearts of its flocks is admitted and well known and can no doubt in part be ascribed to this derivation. And the individual relationship of its members, one to another, is somewhat similar to that which prevailed in the Conventicles, or in the Synagogues of the European Middle Ages, and continues to afford to its adherents a particular and tenacious cohesion, even when their chapel days are past and abandoned, and they no longer dwell among their native hills. In fact, it might be said without much exaggeration that those of Welsh Nonconformist upbringing who reside in London resemble in their spiritual freemasonry, and in the solidarity they display, the Jews when in captivity in Babylon.

On the morning of Friday 7th May, on which day I was to have luncheon with Lady Wimborne, the taxicabs came out on strike, to manifest their support of the other forms of transport. This fact was obvious: for nobody could find a cab. But otherwise it was still difficult for anyone yet quite to know what was happening. The bulletins, now dry but effective, displayed naturally a governmental bias, while the continued absence of all but the most elementary forms of newspapers afforded growing opportunities for myth-making to public imagination, and to its dull and greasy dreams. . . . I have already stated that the acquisition of a new motor much aided me in my anti-strike activities. This machine had been bought by my brother and sister-in-law, and since neither of them could as yet drive it, they were temporarily employing a chauffeur. This arrangement exactly suited me, because always, from childhood on, I swiftly fall asleep if I move fast through fresh air, and therefore I had thought it wiser not to learn to drive a motor, but now they allowed me to borrow theirs whenever I liked, and I had only to go next door and ask for it. . . . On this occasion, however, something had gone wrong with plans, I could not have the machine. Wrapped in a mackintosh against the pouring rain, I was instead obliged to walk right across London to Wimborne House. Never shall I forget the frustration of that long wet search for a means of locomotion, that footsore, heartsore, forced ramble through deserted streets and squares. The sopping lilac heads—for the bushes at this moment were in full flower—dripped soddenly over the edges of railings, and at times there was so little traffic that one could hear the monotonous patter and drip of the rain, making sudden alterations in the rhythm and speed of the tune it played at every gust of wind. The residential quarters of the town—apart from such great thoroughfares as Piccadilly—seemed dead; more dead, even, than during the bombing of recent years, because they were still smart and respectable. Such vehicles as passed still showed an amateurish eagerness to draw attention to themselves, hooting and blaring through the interminable rain. I arrived at my destination very wet, and in no very good temper.

interesting

Wimborne House, the scene of the negotiations I am about to describe, stands in Arlington Street, a low, wide house with a two-pedimented front, set back behind railings, and overshadowed to the north by the flat plane of the sheer cliff-like back of the Ritz Hotel—and just opposite, incidentally, the small house, now pulled down, in which I was born. Thus my first memory had been[1] of this corner; and other links, too, connected Wimborne House with my left hand: for this enormous mansion embodied two residences, one of them, that nearest to the Green Park, having been the former Beaufort House, in which my grandmother Londesborough had been born. Though Ivor Wimborne had re-created Wimborne House, and, with his natural feeling for sumptuousness, had planned it as a background for entertainments—to a greater degree, I believe, than any other London house—, yet his good taste had saved from destruction the best of the old rooms, which survived more or less in their original state. Nevertheless, the general atmosphere of luxury and beauty belonged to an international eighteenth century, of which France was the heart, and its air seemed also to carry a little the heavy, forgotten aroma of the Second Empire. The rooms, after the fashion of such London palaces, were disposed almost entirely on the ground floor: room led out of room, hall out of hall. . . . I rang and the door was opened by a porter in livery, and as I entered I heard the squawk of the irascible macaw of the house, a more decorative watch-dog chained to a perch instead of to a kennel. In his uniform of blue and gold feathers, he screamed raspingly at all newcomers, and clanged the metal round him with his beak, testing it apparently, as a man with a hammer tests railway wheels. . . . I found Lady Wimborne waiting for me in her sitting-room, and she told me we were to have luncheon out, alone, at the Embassy Club, and to drive there in her Rolls.

Tired and angry as I was, yet having once drunk a dry Martini—for I felt so cold from my long, wet walk that I thought it would warm me—, that, and my company, caused the gift of eloquence to descend on me. I suppose if I had

[1] See *Left Hand, Right Hand!* p. 84 of this edition.

arrived by taxi, and kept dry, this would never have happened: yet I am not sure, for Alice by her sympathy could draw any man out of himself, and make him feel he was the sole person to whom she ever wanted to listen. In this instance, all her reward, I am afraid, was that I addressed her as if she were a public meeting. I was still angry, but now enjoying myself as well. My furious voice echoed, and came out from corners, like that of a ventriloquist. "Why", I demanded, "does no-one do anything to stop it?" . . . There were a good many people in the restaurant, but I could not control my emotion. I spoke on. "Why does no-one even *try* to stop the Strike?" . . . Lady Wimborne, always surprising in her response, did what few other women would have done: she listened patiently. I continued to explain, as best I could, the terrible position into which I thought we were drifting, the peril of a real split in the nation, and the evils of adopting towards the working-classes a semi-Fascist attitude, so alien to English tradition and ways of thought. The supreme national asset we possessed was, I added, that there had never been war between the classes: that, at all costs, must be avoided. At the end of my oration, Lady Wimborne asked me quietly:

"Well, what can be done? . . . What could we do?"

"You know every sort of politician, and ask them all to luncheon in ordinary times. Make use of the habit now."

"Yes: but how?"

"It is obvious that the Trades Union leaders have drifted into a false position, and into one they must hate in their hearts. Try to get them to meet the coal-owners privately—and ask Lord Reading. He's just returned from India and would be an ideal intermediary."

Instead of making difficulties, or pointing them out, as so many people would have done, she replied:

"Can you come and see Ivor about it, after luncheon?"

And she proceeded to tell me that her husband had already taken various steps and, at an earlier stage, had offered to the leaders of the miners his services as link between them and the coal-owners, and that, sequent to a meeting at Wimborne House with Mr. Abblett, the miners' leader from South Wales, the previous afternoon, he had begun to cherish

H

hopes that a settlement could be effected. . . . I felt, however, that it was better for me not to worry him at this juncture, and so Lady Wimborne went back alone to Wimborne House to see what she could achieve.

I returned—this time by motor—to Carlyle Square and my self-imposed solitude. But all the same, from this afternoon onwards till the end of the General Strike, the rhythm of life was changed for me—no less than for Alice Wimborne, who worked so indefatigably, and for Lord Wimborne, who now keyed himself up to still greater efforts. The hour had struck. . . . When I look back, it seems impossible that, viewed from the angle of that particular afternoon of Friday 7th May, the struggle should have been over by the morning of Wednesday the 12th. The few days, but many hours, of unending activity which followed immediately, seem in the memory—a more sure guide to inner truth than any clock or calendar—to have lasted for many months: while, contemporaneously, in that present, they constituted a whole lifetime. My own personal task, as I saw it, was to introduce a true vision into various minds of what might happen if things went wrong. I decided to appoint myself unofficial Jeremiah to those who united complacency to positions of power. Further, I resolved to do everything within my capacity—and out of it—to bring people into touch with one another who might be of use in helping to end the Strike, and above all I determined to be there, to supply a dynamo and the drive requisite, and to give Lord Wimborne confidence in what he had done and was doing, so that, in one of the moods of gigantic ennui to which he was liable, he should not just retire from the fray, thinking in his heart—and with truth—that men are fools and all further effort was hopeless in view of their folly, and saying, with geniality and no rancour, and with a large, endearing gesture, "I throw my hand in!"

During that afternoon my spirits had risen. It had seemed to me that some way out did, indeed, exist, albeit I had doubted it before, and that, though I was so private a person, unknown to politics, and in my more public capacity as a writer still regarded by the public as an incomprehensible poet whose name was only good for a conventional laugh on any music-hall stage in Great Britain, it might yet perhaps be reserved for me to exercise an indirect or vicarious influence on this dispute, in which I so passionately felt the need for moderation. I could, it might be, afford a certain buoyancy, resourcefulness and strength of purpose to those who, just because they were more experienced in public affairs, were the less hopeful. . . . But, once more back at home, surrounded by the familiar, glittering objects, I began to feel dejected again and to become a prey to common sense (that delusion of the unsuccessful, to be avoided at any cost by writers, painters, all those who are gifted in any artistic direction, and equally by gamblers and politicians, if they wish to achieve the rare things they have set before themselves to accomplish—for how, regarded in that dun light, can a million-to-one chance succeed, when the chances are acknowledged thus to be a million to one against?). I was obliged, in this mood, to recognise how hopelessly far away I was from having either the opportunity or the ability to help curb the storm. It seemed as if Lady Wimborne and I had been talking emptily in the air, supported in our ambitions by hopes only, and not by facts. . . . And then, about seven o'clock that evening—at a moment when, if truth is to be told, I had expected to hear no more of our rather vague plans or, at best, for the course of events to outstrip them—I received from her a letter, delivered by hand. In it she told me that, by a stroke of almost miraculous good fortune, all those she had asked to luncheon the next day had accepted, and she ordered me, whatever plans I might have made, to cancel them and be present. The other guests would be Lord Londonderry and Lord Gainford,[1] both great coal-owners, one Conservative, one Liberal—the second being President of the Coal-Owners Association—, the Right Hon. J. H. Thomas (Chairman of the Trades Union Council), J. A. Spender, for long Editor of

[1] Joseph Albert Pease (1860–1943), 1st Baron Gainford, cr. 1917, second son of Sir Joseph Whitwell Pease, Bt. For many years a Liberal Member of Parliament, he held various posts in the Campbell-Bannerman and Asquith Ministries. He was President of the English Coal-Owners Association, and became President of the Federation of British Industries, 1927–28, and Chairman of the British Broadcasting Company, 1922–26.

the great Liberal evening paper, the *Westminster Gazette*, Philip Snowden and Lord Reading.[1]

When, the following day, I arrived at Wimborne House, in spite of my almost excessive punctuality—a constitutional trait—I found several of the other guests already assembled, in a certain atmosphere of expectancy. Mrs. Snowden[2] was there—the only person I had not expected to see, but her husband had been taken ill, and she had come to fill his place. . . . We went in to luncheon to the minute, passing through a vista of fine rooms on our way to the dining-room. Almost directly we had sat down, the conversation took the turn we had so ardently wished it might, and, guided by Lady Wimborne's superb tact—for she never in any way interposed herself between the talkers or aired her own views, but adroitly, and with the utmost sympathy, drew everyone out—, maintained it until the end. So important in its matter, so vehement in its manner, so frank was the talk, that the footmen, I recall, had to be told almost at once to leave the dining-room, and only to return when summoned.

But first to describe the manner: even as Mr. Thomas, the last to arrive, had hurried into the room, it had been obvious from his flustered appearance that he was worried and tired almost beyond bearing. The long meetings of the Council before the outbreak of the Strike, and the joint conferences of three members of the Cabinet and three (of whom he had been one) of the Trades Union Council had worn him out. Often, for several weeks, he had been at work from eight or nine in the morning until two o'clock of the following day. These hours, and the extreme and deepening seriousness of the situation, which threatened to end either in the breakdown of parliamentary government or in the smashing of the Trades Unions, or possibly to culminate in a drawn-out and smouldering condition of semi-civil war, had most plainly told

---

[1] Rufus Daniel Isaacs (1860–1935), 1st Marquess of Reading. He was said as a boy to have sailed before the mast to India, and later to have been hammered on the Stock Exchange. He became Solicitor-General, 1910, Lord Chief Justice in 1913, H.M.'s High Commissioner, Ambassador Extraordinary and Plenipotentiary on Special Mission to the United States of America in 1913–19. As culmination he was Viceroy of India from 1921 until 1926.

[2] Now Viscountess Snowden.

even on his store of vitality and humour, and had sharpened his nerves: though, no doubt, he derived an inward strength from his consciousness that, until the sudden precipitation of the General Strike by the refusal of the printers to print the *Daily Mail*, he had done everything in his power to prevent such a catastrophe from occurring. Certainly what he had endured recently had in no way abated his vigorous methods of expression or taken the edge off his native turns of speech. . . . Everyone else seemed completely unchanged: Lord Wimborne, kind, amusing, quick to be amused, with no trace of the boredom he sometimes showed; Lord Londonderry with his accustomed air of Irish grandee and sportsman who has strayed into politics, with a certain nonchalance, combined with geniality, but also with, under the façade, a natural and special shrewdness that it would be easy to misinterpret and underrate; Mrs. Snowden, calm and comtemplative; Lord Gainford, restrained, tight-mouthed, orthodox in the Liberal parliamentarian fashion, a typical ennobled master of industry; J. A. Spender, clever, earnest, public-spirited, but with, enwrapping him, a spiritual aura of soft white wool that matched his hair. And finally there was Lord Reading. The element in him of Dick Whittington or Sindbad the Sailor, so largely stressed in contemporary accounts of his extraordinary career, had by now completely vanished, or at any rate was absent from his aura. Though he certainly brought with him a feeling of ambitions gratified and of marked worldly success, to me he resembled the phantom of a great man, but a spectre heavy in spite of his phantomhood and of his light weight physically. One seemed to see him, like an apparition at a séance, through curtains; an affable Caesar, ponderous, though thinly cast in bronze, laurel-wreathed, finely-featured, quick-witted (that could be deduced from his eyes), but slightly damaged by life and rendered complacent by the progress of the years. He had occupied so many exalted posts that above all men he knew the value of discretion, and in consequence he preferred in his talk to deal in golf values in a proconsular manner or relate some small story about Asquith or Lord Balfour (always referred to as "A. J. B."), rather than discuss high politics. After Disraeli the most eminent politician of his race to have made a career in England, he showed none of the exuberance or conversational excitement of the earlier statesman: but like him he had aged a little early, for the English climate is hard. . . . It must be added that he was dearly loved by his friends, and his advice on any subject was immensely prized by those who knew him. . . . Few scraps of conversation come back to me, but I remember someone remarking to Lord Reading,

"Whatever we do, we must not allow *you* to take any action at present. We must keep you in reserve as our queen-bee."

In reply to which sentiment, I produced, in a passing silence, and with a voice as though echoing from a tomb, the question,

"Even if the hive is being burned down?"

Out of the long session, which lasted until nearly four o'clock, a few facts of prime significance emerged. Quite early in the course of the meal, within a few minutes of our sitting down, it transpired that a final message despatched from the Trades Union Council to the Prime Minister had never reached him. What occurred to prevent his receiving it, remains to this day a mystery, though no doubt those concerned have formed their own opinions on the question. . . . From Mr. J. H. Thomas's point of view, two things that were of help to him in reaching his eventual decision came out of meeting these people round the luncheon table: the first, that Lord Reading offered to get into touch with Sir Herbert Samuel,[1] who was in Italy, and to ask him to return to London. According to Mr. Thomas,[2] Sir Herbert had telegraphed from Italy to Mr. Baldwin on the outbreak of the Strike, "Can I be of any assistance?", and had received in reply a laconic "No!". Mr. Thomas, however, felt that Sir Herbert, as the man who had drawn up the Report of the Coal Commission, could be of real service. In addition, Mr. Thomas was more than ever grateful to Lord Reading, an old friend of his, for offering help just at the moment when another old friend and most eminent lawyer had made a speech, which had only appeared that very morning (for though Sir John Simon had

[1] See p. 196, note 2.   [2] See p. 196, note 1.

delivered it in the House of Commons on Thursday, it had not been published in *The Times*, owing to the difficulties of space and printing, until Saturday): a speech, moreover, which still rankled in his mind. Evidently—so Mr. Thomas, I think, may have comforted himself—that most celebrated servant of the Crown, Lord Reading, though he was quite as much of a high legal authority as Sir John Simon, did not regard him as rebel or outlaw, or he would hardly have offered his services in this fashion as an intermediary. . . . The second, but scarcely less important, new factor was his consciousness of the personal kindness and anxiety to be of help of Lord and Lady Wimborne. This made the Trades Union leader feel that, after all, there were people of fortune and position who understood the difficulties which confronted the leaders, condemned equally with himself what seemed to them the ruthless Tory policy, and who were, further, to a degree sympathetic to the miners in their claims, and in their distress, which had been responsible in the first place for the General Strike. The attitude of our host and hostess did much, in short, to lessen the bitterness both of Mr. J. H. Thomas and of the various leaders of the miners who visited Wimborne House at different times during these days, and those immediately preceding and subsequent.

As for the outcome of the Wimborne House luncheon, the greatest concrete advance we achieved that afternoon towards peace was when Mr. Thomas finally committed himself to the admission that the miners were now in the mood to accept, with all its implications, the Report of the Coal Commission. This constituted a notable improvement on the position he had taken up the previous Monday, when negotiations had collapsed. Indeed, it seemed to Lord Reading so important that he composed and wrote down a formula, after which he and Lord Wimborne left immediately for the House of Commons, the first to see Lord Birkenhead, the second to see his cousin, Mr. Winston Churchill: but both those interviewed maintained that mere acceptance would not now be enough; we must engage in that blustering and platitudinous redundancy "A fight to a finish". . . . When later I heard this, I recalled from a quarter of a century before that pugnacious but generous countenance, at every age from two to twenty, as infant, child, boy, adult, as it had gazed at me in innumerable photographs from the walls of my schoolroom improvised within the mauve tents of Mrs. Moreton Frewen's house in Chesham Place.[1] The photographs, if they still existed, would be brown, yellow, and faded: but the face, though older, still retained its original quality and the characteristics remained unimpeached by time.

I had gone home to try to communicate with Siegfried Sassoon, inform him of what had taken place, and consult him about what we could do. Every moment of the next few crucial days was filled, and we spent a considerable time in interviewing those who might be of aid in our endeavour to organise support for a compromise. Sassoon, when formerly for a time literary editor of the *Daily Herald*, had met many people of different worlds, and I, too, through the considerable amount of journalism that my extravagance had compelled me to undertake, had entered into many connections with the newspaper world. We now exerted and exhausted every possible legitimate effort and influence on behalf of peace. But most people were in no mood for peace-making. One brief but angry chapter of the Class War had opened: and both sides were enraged. Hence the sense of frustration, danger and ennui in the air. It was an atmosphere in which any light relief was welcome, and I shall always therefore recall with pleasure a fragment of conversation with my brother's chauffeur on the way home from Wimborne House. He was an unconcerned young man, the flame of whose life played only round spanners, tyres, gaskets and the other thousand, but to me nameless, technical mysteries of his craft.

"You don't look very well, Peckover, today," I remarked to him. "Do you feel all right?"

"It's because I couldn't get my proper breakfast, sir, owing to the Strike."

"What do you usually have, then, Peckover?"

"A slice of Fuller's Chocolate Cake. My mother gets it for me."

[1] See *Left Hand, Right Hand!* p. 227 of this edition.

"Hardly the stuff on which to raise a breed of heroes, Peckover."

"I know—but it's kinda got an 'old on me."

That night Mr. Baldwin made his broadcast and affirmed that the General Strike had only to be called off for negotiations to be begun again, together with the long and laborious task of trying to rebuild on sound foundations the prosperity of the Coal Trade. Though the immediate result it produced among those eager for an early settlement of the dispute was a sense of discouragement, yet in reality this statement was most useful in helping to achieve peace, uncompromising as, at the time, it sounded. To our group, the speech seemed like a signal fired from headquarters in answer to the discussions of the day. And indeed later it became known to us that one of those present at luncheon had, unofficially and of his own accord, reported to Mr. Tom Jones, before the Prime Minister had prepared his speech, the trend of the conversation. While the Government, it was plain, could and would make no concession, yet this refusal in a sense rendered such negotiations as those at Wimborne House all the more important. In consequence, each of us redoubled his efforts. . . . On the other hand we were troubled by the growing conviction that a most influential and brilliant section of the Government now wished to avoid a settlement, and to "see the thing through". It advocated, in fact, a policy of Unconditional Surrender (one of the silliest and most deleterious of political catchwords, for all *surrender* must of necessity be unconditional) as the only terms which the Government could contemplate. It seemed, therefore, unlikely that any peaceful voice could lift itself above the bluster, din and brag, or that it would be in any way possible to build the hastily improvised bridge required to bring together the contending parties.

On Sunday Lord Reading went to luncheon again at Wimborne House. He still thought the only true path out of the present most serious position was for the miners to agree to abide by the recommendations of the Samuel Report: which, he added, Lord Gainford had told him that the Coal-Owners Association had just decided to accept. In any case, he said, the Government had already unofficially intimated that it would grant a loan to the Coal Industry during the period of reconstruction, and would guarantee a minimum wage directly the General Strike had been called off. This seemed to those who had spoken to them an improvement on the attitude adopted by Lord Birkenhead and Mr. Churchill.

Lady Wimborne, deducing from the Prime Minister's broadcast that the Government had decided to make no direct overtures, and grasping how much more important, in consequence, unofficial talks could be, requested his secretary, Mr. Selwyn Davies, to visit Mr. J. H. Thomas at Dulwich, and to try to persuade him to come up at once and talk with her husband. As it happened, Mr. Davies had already been in touch with Mr. Tom Jones, who in the course of conversation had suggested that it would be helpful if Lord Wimborne would resume negotiations with some of those whom he had entertained at luncheon the previous day, and that, were he to do so, he should particularly draw their attention to the significance of the broadcast delivered by the Prime Minister the night before. Accordingly Mr. Davies drove down to Dulwich to see the Trades Union leader, and at about 7.30 returned in Mr. Thomas's company to Arlington Street. Lady Wimborne, who was dining out with some friends, was summoned home in the middle of the meal, to find her husband and Mr. Thomas closeted together in the library. A talk of considerable interest, and destined to bear important results in the practical sphere, was in progress. At an early stage, while every development of the situation was being discussed, it became evident that Mr. Baldwin's broadcast in fact constituted an invitation to the Trades Union Council to examine once more its policy. Mr. Thomas seemed very anxious to reciprocate the spirit of the message he thought he detected in this speech. Lord Wimborne, as a result of the talk, decided to go round immediately to Downing Street, to see the Prime Minister, but then suddenly changed his mind, and said he felt the moment was not ripe—or else his occasional but recurrent lack of confidence in himself, which helped to undermine his great abilities, had asserted itself again.

In the meantime, every one of our group of peacemakers

had been busy. I was continually at Wimborne House, to give or receive news, and to see if I could afford support to those who were making so strenuous and worthy an effort, but one which taxed energy to the full, while it demanded, too, considerable delicacy of approach. . . . The afternoon of Sunday the 9th of May I spent in an attempt to induce Arnold Bennett, at that period the leading English publicist, to come round to our standpoint. I had felt that it might be possible to persuade a man of his origin and wide sympathies—one, moreover, who could regard many things in an unconventional manner—to adopt a more comprehending and less uncompromising view of the position into which, as I saw it, the Trades Union leaders had drifted, or even, to a certain extent, been manœuvred. Moreover it was important that the struggle should be presented in its proper colours in the press of the United States, for which the famous author had just written a most prominently displayed and highly-paid article. His influence across the Atlantic was very considerable, and he was eminent enough there for what he said to be accepted as the truth. As it was, scare-articles were flaring through the American papers every day, and injuring this country; the struggle being painted in simple terms of revolutionary workers versus the chivalrous, true, brave, good, gentle and generous middle-classes. Towards my purpose, I divulged to him a little of what was occurring at Wimborne House, but kind and wise as usually he was, in this instance he had made up his mind, and I think no arguments could have availed to alter it. His grey topknot, his features, a few slightly protruding teeth, the backward tilt of his body as he sat in his chair listening, above all, the expression of his eyes (I have elsewhere in the course of this work drawn attention to the dull look he could infuse into them), all presented that day an appearance of irremediable obstinacy, while his stutter, even in its very beginning, rejected every plea put forward. Like the majority of our countrymen, one way or the other, he was at that instant in embattled mood. In his personal instance, the standards of the bourgeoisie had been challenged, and this rebellion had to be defeated. Moreover I had, if I had only known it, chosen an injudicious, not to say tactless moment to call, for Mrs. Cheston Bennett and their month-old baby had only arrived in the house from the nursing-home an hour before. In his Journals,[1] he records:

Sunday, May 9th. . . . During afternoon Osbert Sitwell rang up to know if he could call. He came a few minutes later, with Richmond Temple, and they had tea. Osbert was wound up in a scheme with Lady Wimborne and Lord Reading for ending the strike. Fruit of a luncheon at which Thomas was present. It appeared that Reading had tried to get at Baldwin but had been stopped by Churchill and F. E. The notion of a man of Reading's eminence being "stopped" on his way to see Baldwin struck me as comic. They then both agreed that the thing sounded very improbable. I said Reading might have reasons for saying he hadn't been able to get at Baldwin personally. I also asked if Thomas could deliver the goods.

The answer to that question was to be seen, of course, four days later when Mr. J. H. Thomas *did* deliver the goods. . . . I have no recollection of the alleged incident concerning Lord Reading. Arnold may have misunderstood something that had been said: his whole technique that afternoon had been to seize on one small point after another, divorce it from the rest of the story, and worry it.

Mr. Beverley Baxter, in a book of reminiscences,[2] devotes a paragraph to a visit he received from "that gallant eccentric" Siegfried, and from me. "One night", he tells us—but no, on reflection I prefer to put the matter for the most part in my own language, less dramatic though that may be. One night, then, returning to his flat in Chelsea at two in the morning, he found two men waiting in the darkness at the top of the stairs. There disclosing their identity, we—for they proved to be Sassoon and myself—were asked into the sitting-room and proceeded at once to explain to him that we wanted to end the General Strike. When he opposed us, stating his belief that the difficulties were due to the temper of the Trades Unions, Siegfried, he says, strode up and down the room, "brandishing his fists at the ceiling", while I remained, apparently, "unnaturally calm". "It was a mad scene." Before we left, the dawn—I am afraid he writes "the first

[1] 1921–28, p. 133.
[2] *Strange Street*, by A. Beverley Baxter. (Hutchinson, 1937).

grisly grey of dawn"—was breaking over the Thames, and he notes, too, with seeming regret, that "Sassoon did not even say good-bye". . . . It is a kindly if picturesque account that he gives, but I do not recall the occasion very clearly—though I certainly went to see him several times, to find out what were the chances of obtaining in the *Daily Express* a modification of the usually bellicose views of the press, and also to ask him to sound Lord Beaverbrook, the proprietor, and find out in what direction his sympathies lay. But this particular call on Baxter, undated in his book, must, I think, have taken place before Sunday the 9th.

The tempo of the negotiations was mounting, and we must now return to enumerate the precise steps by which the parties concerned arrived at the bridge to conciliation and peace. From this point onward, almost until the end of the chapter, I break deliberately the rhythm of my autobiography, for otherwise, were I to deal with the matter in the manner to which the reader is accustomed, these few pages would swell into a volume of history or a long psychological study. No, this is a practical affair in which circumstances and my nature conspired to involve me, and few incidents of the kind possess so detailed a time-table, and therefore the handling must be practical as that of a railway-guide, for we are occupied with the actual means by which something precise was accomplished, with dry facts, with what happened, who saw whom, and why and when. . . . The meeting between Lord Wimborne and Mr. Thomas at Arlington Street on Sunday had lasted until a late hour: but nothing had taken solid shape. Lady Wimborne felt that the tone was hopeful, nevertheless. She had been distressed, in consequence, to realise that Mr. Thomas had left the house without any arrangement having been made for a further conference, since she was sure that the constant interflow of ideas was accomplishing some good. She therefore asked Mr. Davies to telephone to Mr. Thomas and try to make a further appointment with him for the next day. At Lady Wimborne's suggestion also, Mr. Davies rang up Lord Reading, gave him an account of what had taken place, and explained that he was shortly going to speak to Mr. Thomas, and in return Lord Reading offered to come to

Arlington Street the following morning to discuss the whole issue afresh with Mr. Thomas. Mr. Davies then telephoned to the Trades Union leader and asked to see him immediately. Directly afterwards, Mr. Davies motored to Dulwich, where he interviewed personally Mr. Thomas, and persuaded him to agree to meet Lord Wimborne and Lord Reading at Wimborne House at 8.45 the same morning.

Mr. Davies fetched Mr. Thomas to Arlington Street in Lord Wimborne's motor. On their way from Dulwich it was evident that some of the trains which usually carried the men to work had started again. Somehow or other, the Government had begun to get things going once more. It was a straw in the wind, and Mr. Thomas was disturbed by it, and commented on it to his companion.

By 8.30, Mr. Davies was at Lord Reading's house in Curzon Street, and able to inform him that Lord Wimborne and Mr. Thomas were already in conference at Wimborne House, and would be glad if Lord Reading would join them. He did so, and a long discussion ensued. The result of it was drawn up by Lord Reading and Lord Wimborne in the following paragraph:

If some assurance could be given that negotiations would be resumed for the purpose of bringing the recommendations of the Report into operation without delay, it is possible that the T.U.C. might call off the General Strike and indicate that miners accept the Report unconditionally with all its implications, including the question of possible adjustment of wages as the basis of a settlement. This assurance might be accepted if it were made by some person of influence, not a member of the Government.

So important was this summary felt to be, that, so as to save time, it was at once read over the telephone to Mr. Tom Jones, while Lord Wimborne ordered a copy to be sent round immediately by hand, in order to avoid any errors of transmission. Mr. Tom Jones undertook to place it before the Prime Minister at once. A little later, Mr. Davies went to see Mr. Tom Jones, who told him that in the Prime Minister's opinion everything which Mr. Thomas now asked, on Monday, had already been conceded by him in his broadcast on Saturday night, and that Mr. Baldwin therefore did not understand what difficulties could exist to justify the Trades Union Council in persisting with the General Strike. . . . On Monday afternoon Lord Wimborne sent to the Prime Minister's adviser another note, amplifying the previous statement. In it he said he was assured that there would be a possibility of the General Strike being abrogated if Mr. Baldwin, without in any way committing his Ministry and without accepting any conditions from the Trades Union Council, or seeming to make any compromise, could indicate what it was the intention of the Government to do, if and when coal negotiations were resumed. This note was at once placed before Sir Arthur Steel-Maitland,[1] one of the members of the Cabinet concerned with policy at that time.

Tuesday the 11th was the crucial day. I had through my relations kept in touch with Lambeth Palace, and early that morning I suggested that Lord Wimborne should establish contact with the Archbishop of Canterbury, who was on the side of peace and had lately issued a manifesto which the *British Gazette* had not seen fit to publish. (Already, it must be added, the Wimborne House group had received much help from the Industrial Christian Fellowship, and had found the counsel of its General Director, Prebendary Kirk, of the greatest assistance.) The situation looked, if anything, darker, and all those who were working for peace were dismayed and depressed. Rumours of every kind, except any that could bring hope of an early end to the dispute, were more than ever rife. Either on that or on the previous day, Beverley Baxter told me he had talked with Lord Beaverbrook, who, while he had shown at the end a certain sympathy towards our efforts, had remarked to him, as Baxter left the room,

"At any rate, it's too late for that sort of thing now: something is about to occur which will make the country forget all that has gone before."

Certainly a much greater, and still gathering, feeling of suspense prevailed.

Soon, however, a change was to come. At 9.30 A.M., Mr. Clem Edwards, the Counsel for the Trades Unions, called on

[1] Sir Arthur Steel-Maitland, 1st Bt., occupied several ministerial posts. He was Minister of Labour from 1924 to 1929.

Lord Wimborne, to see if they could devise any satisfactory compromise where Mr. J. H. Thomas had failed. Mr. Edwards made the following proposals:

A return to the Status Quo Ante last Friday, except as follows:

1. The principle of National Minimum to remain, but some local adjustment of wages may be made.
2. The principle of closing Uneconomic Mines to be recognised and satisfactory machinery for achieving this purpose to be set up, whether by amalgamation or otherwise.
3. Steps to be taken to secure economic buying of supplies and economic selling of coal to effect savings in other than labour costs.
4. Machinery to be set up to secure economic Railway rates.
5. Royalties to be purchased.
6. Financial help to be rendered to the Coal Trade, such help to be redeemed over a long period of years on security of the royalties.
7. Negotiations to be resumed immediately.
   Then the Strike to be called off.

During the conversation between Lord Wimborne and Mr. Clem Edwards, Lord Reading called, saying he would like to see Mr. J. H. Thomas again. He expressed a new sense of urgency in the matter. He then went in to talk with Mr. Edwards. Lord Reading and Lord Wimborne remained in consultation until Mr. Thomas—to whom a telephone message had been sent directly Lord Reading had expressed his wish to see him—arrived to join them at Arlington Street at 11.30 A.M. While this interview—during the course of which both Lord Reading and Lord Wimborne made sustained and impassioned appeals to Mr. Thomas to call off the General Strike immediately—was in progress, Mr. Selwyn Davies reported privately to Mr. Tom Jones the new developments, and the stage they had reached. Mr. Tom Jones offered to go round immediately to Arlington Street in order that he might obtain fuller information. . . . When, a little later, I arrived at Arlington Street to talk to Lady Wimborne, she remarked, in telling me of the latest developments, that she wondered what could have occurred to make Lord Reading take up this new attitude of extreme urgency, so different from his previous mood, which had been one of patience, and a faith in the method of the most careful discussion; what could have happened to emphasise so greatly his fears, and cause him to be thus eager for the General Strike not to last a single hour longer? He and Lord Wimborne had particularly pressed Mr. Thomas to secure a settlement by a certain time. This request they drove home with every argument at their disposal.

The three men considered the situation in every aspect and in the greatest detail. At first it appeared as if the Trades Union leader would not yield, and could not, even if he wished. He averred that, in so far as he was concerned, the other two were preaching to the converted, but that by the constitution of the body over which he presided, he was bound to obtain at least a majority decision before he could revoke the General Strike. It would be almost impossible for him, he said, to persuade his colleagues to come round to his view. To this Lord Reading and Lord Wimborne answered that they fully understood the difficulties with which Mr. Thomas was faced, but they reiterated that what they most urgently advised in the interest of the whole country, and what in fact they wanted to obtain from him before he returned to Trades Union Headquarters, was a promise that he would call off the General Strike at a late hour that night or early the following morning. They stressed that nothing less would ease their own unbiased anxieties, or satisfy the Government, or meet the situation which they saw arising. The pressure that the two ex-Viceroys put upon Mr. Thomas was tremendous: but the truth is that they were themselves in a difficult position; because they could not divulge to him what had actuated them to adopt a new point of view; something of which they had been informed, a step of the gravest importance to be taken shortly by the Government. It was this knowledge which accounted for the increased and emphatic urgency of their plea. It is possible that, from their tone, Mr. Thomas may have drawn his own conclusions, but apparently he had not deduced the reason of the concern which Lord Wimborne and Lord Reading now displayed, and they were not free to tell him the true cause.

I returned to Carlyle Square, and dined with my brother

and sister-in-law. I knew that it had been settled that at ten o'clock Mr. Selwyn Davies should be at the Trades Union Headquarters. This citadel was an old-fashioned Victorian house in Eccleston Square, and subsequently became—with the occasional irony of chance—the residence of Mr. Winston Churchill. Mr. Davies waited there and between ten and eleven saw Mr. Thomas, who asked him to announce to both the Prime Minister and Lord Wimborne that, though he was encountering the most formidable obstacles, he would, he thought, by 2 A.M., be in a position to say that his colleagues had given him authority to call off the General Strike. Mr. Davies at once passed on the information, as requested, to Mr. Tom Jones and to Lord Wimborne. . . . Lady Wimborne, who was dining that night with her brother Lord Ebury, rang up to tell me what had happened, and promised to let me know the moment there was any further news: which we awaited in a state of profound anxiety and restlessness, not daring to move more than a few yards from the telephone.

At midnight Mr. Selwyn Davies returned to Eccleston Square as he had arranged, and took up a place in the crowd which had gathered outside the building. A few minutes later, he saw the miners' leaders, who had been in consultation with the Trades Union chiefs, emerge. On their faces they bore unmistakable symptoms of the most profound dejection, and they proceeded, without uttering a word to anyone, to climb into a waiting charabanc and drive off. After some moments had passed, the door of the house opened again quietly, and Mr. J. H. Thomas came out. Mr. Davies followed him for a little, and when they had reached a spot where there were no passers-by, Mr. Thomas stopped, and asked Mr. Davies to convey to the Prime Minister, and to Lord Reading and Lord Wimborne, his assurance that he had obtained the majority vote, and that the General Strike would end at noon: by which hour he and his colleagues would be at Downing Street. Mr. Davies at once entered Lord Wimborne's motor, which was waiting in a side-street near by, and drove in it first to Wimborne House and then to Downing Street, where he delivered his message to Mr. Tom Jones at about 2 A.M. . . . As for me, the telephone bell summoned me about 2.15 A.M., and I received the news from Lady Wimborne. So great was my relief and joy that I could not sleep, and my mind dwelt instead on the immense evils the country had so narrowly escaped, and which had drawn so near to us in those few days that their shapes could be clearly distinguished. . . . Even the morning sunlight did not dissipate the sense of suspense that had recently prevailed; until after twelve o'clock, when the news came officially, as Mr. Thomas had said it would, that the Trades Union leaders had arrived at Downing Street, and had called off the General Strike.

So it ended. And, tired but contented, I celebrated the event, and our parts in it, by having luncheon at Wimborne House. I did not, however, know even then what had occurred to make Lord Reading and Ivor so much more anxious in their attitude. It had not been until that very morning, when Mr. Selwyn Davies was fetching Lord Reading from Curzon Street to Arlington Street in the motor, that Lord Reading had revealed to him the nature of the private information which had impelled him and Lord Wimborne to grow so urgent in their appeals to Mr. Thomas: the Government had resolved to arrest the Trades Union leaders the following day. . . . I do not know who had told Lord Reading and Ivor of this decision, or when—though plainly it had come very late in the crisis. A stage had probably been reached on Monday when it had become convenient to lift these negotiations to the highest plane. . . . All this time Sir Herbert Samuel and those who worked with him, it must be remembered, had been equally busy, but of their prolonged and successful efforts I cannot write: I have only concerned myself here with that which passed near me, and with what I heard at the time.

In the early autumn my first novel, *Before the Bombardment*, made its appearance. With the epithets and phrases that thereupon hurtled through the darkling spaces of newspapers and weekly journals, I have already dealt. . . . In November I left for New York, to be present for the publication of my book in America. On the fourth of the month—the day before I sailed—a farewell luncheon was given to me at the Savoy Hotel. It was organised and presided over by my friend

Richmond Temple, and no one else of the age can conjure up such illusions of splendour and occasions of perfection. Seventy people were present, including Augustine Birrell in the Chair, Lord Wimborne, Sir Edmund Gosse, H. G. Wells, Arnold Bennett, Ambrose McEvoy and Siegfried Sassoon. Mr. Birrell rose to speak first. The newspapers of the day, I notice, compared his appearance to that shown in the prints and photographs of Thackeray: yet I hold that in this they did Mr. Birrell an injustice, for in his looks, in his fine head, with the ample white hair curling round the base of the head and top of the neck, in his robust body and its pose, he possessed something monumental which I believe Thackeray lacked. Moreover, for all his air of good-humour, for all the alacrity and allusiveness of his wit, there was nothing playful about him: he was massive and leonine. Certainly, an aura of nineteenth-century perfection shone on his path: but I believe he looked more as if he had stepped out of a great nineteenth-century novel than as if he had written it. In the branch of speaking in which he that day indulged, he was without rival, bold in style, and with a characteristic rough edge to his delightful suavity. Though Mr. Birrell had been Secretary of State for Ireland when Lord Wimborne had been Viceroy, he did not mention politics, but compared the books of his own with those of the contemporary day. Lord Wimborne spoke next, and referred in very generous terms, but without explanation, to the part I had played in the Strike negotiations. Those gathered together in the room, mostly writers and painters, were amazed, being unable to imagine to what the ex-Lord-Lieutenant could be alluding. Some, even, grew angry as men often do at anything they fail to understand; Arnold developed that peculiar dull look in his eye, while Sir Edmund, I remember, already astounded at finding himself in the same room with Wells (whom he very much disliked), grew wasp-like, making fierce darts at me, with questions and comments. "What can the fellow mean, Ossie! How ludicrous!" "What negotiations? What could he have meant?" "What nonsense people talk nowadays! No wonder that impostor Ezra Pound's poems are popular!" "What could he be thinking of?"

In print the share of our little group in striving for, and obtaining, a return to peaceful conditions was never mentioned, except casually, by Arnold Bennett in the excerpt from his Journals already given, and by Beverley Baxter in a passage[1] from which I have quoted. In that same account of how Sassoon and I visited him at two o'clock in the morning in his Chelsea flat, he proceeds to say:

> An hour later Sitwell outlined his formula for peace. It was clear, sane and wise. We agreed he should take it to . . . Lord Wimborne, and try to arrange through him a preliminary conference with Mr. J. H. Thomas representing the strikers. . . . Wimborne and Thomas met and played a considerable part in the ultimate peace settlement. How much of it was coincidence and how much the work of two poets I have never learned. . . .

Lord Wimborne—to whose initiative, far-sightedness and sustained effort in this crisis the nation owed so much—received no recognition of any kind. He continued his mediation, in an attempt to end the Coal Strike, but alas, he was not so successful in this direction; and it dragged on. . . . For the part he played in ending the General Strike there was no sound or breath of gratitude in the press: though I notice in the columns of the *Daily News* for 5th November 1926— which contains an account of the luncheon given to me—an allusion to his share in the Coal Strike negotiations, and the statement that he, perhaps alone of coal-owners, could hear the reference I made in my speech to "giving the men a good living wage" "without feeling awkward or self-conscious".

The events and emotions of those few days in May had so much overshadowed the rest of the year that I remember nothing of the intervening months, until the banquet I have described. Certainly the next morning after the speeches, when I left for America, concluded a stage in my life. In the five null days which followed I enjoyed plenty of time for reflection. The sea was very rough, and it was my first experience of those troughs of despair, the terrible valleys of the Atlantic, which exhale a desolation no less spiritual than

[1] See pp. 202, 226–7 and 229.

physical. Fortunately for myself a good sailor, I sat muffled largely against the winds. Few others ventured on deck. By itself, the force of the elements would have made one ponder on the relative immensities of space and man: but hardly less so did the occasional fair-weather materialisations, in the chair next to me, of my witty, bubble-pricking friend, Mrs. Patrick Campbell, who appeared with a little the air of a luminous-faced seal. What she most enjoyed in conversation was to see how far she could go, like a child playing Tom Tiddler's Ground, without being caught—without being hurt. Sometimes, however, she hurt others in the process. One had to know how to treat her: and the technique to apply was one of surprise, best obtained by agreeing with her in a manner she would not expect. Thus when she said to a friend of mine, looking at her earnestly, "Norah, were your eyes *always* as far apart as that?" she received the reply, "No, Stella: didn't you know?—they had to be *dragged* apart".

I had been acquainted with Mrs. Campbell for a long time, for she had been a friend of my Aunt Blanche's and of my mother's. And I knew her ways: her labels, for instance. Her approach towards the appreciation of good-looks was, naturally, that of her period, the 'eighties; and she had greatly admired my mother's classical beauty. Whenever, therefore, she saw my sister, she always said immediately,

"You'll never have your mother's beauty—poor child! . . . But never mind! You look at one in such a nice way, it doesn't matter."

Finally my sister, when she saw Mrs. Campbell, would get it in first, saying,

"How d'you do, Mrs. Campbell? I know I shall never have my mother's beauty, but I look at you in such a nice way, it doesn't matter."

If, however, Mrs. Campbell hardly ever said a kind thing, she never failed to do one. Once, I remember, when she came to tea with my sister in her flat in Bayswater, Mrs. Campbell made a great disturbance about not being given a silver teaspoon.

"Why haven't I got one?", she kept on enquiring. "Because I'm poor, and can't afford it", my sister said at last.

This quieted Mrs. Campbell. Herself was earning little money at the moment. . . . But when a few months later she scored a great success in a long run—I think in *The Thirteenth Chair* —one of the first things she did in her new affluence was to send my sister a dozen silver teaspoons. And I was much impressed later, in New York, to watch the manner in which she tried to help visiting English painters and writers to establish themselves.

At present then, since the ocean had undoubtedly tamed her inexhaustible mischief, she sat very low in her chair and, turning her lustrous dark eyes upon me, so as to watch every expression on my face, contented herself with narrating to me in considerable detail the plot of a play she was determined I should write for her. It was a very, very long play about a noble-minded scientist, who discovered something or other— I never could quite make out what, nor, I think, could she. . . . In the intervals—long intervals if the sea was sufficiently rough—I sat there, thinking of the past spring, and its strange events—or events, at any rate, of a kind strange to me. Along such paths as those I might have travelled my whole life, arriving at some different, perhaps—who knows? —some more glorious destination. Instead, I had dedicated myself to the isolated and monotonous career of a writer, monotonous, yet to me more exciting than any voyage of exterior discovery or sound of battle.

In the three chapters of this Book—the Eighth—I have given three instances of escape, almost of escapade. Now, in the next chapter, we return to the main themes. The whole long work draws to an end. Only one more volume remains to be written, and that of an order altogether different from that of those preceding. In it my father, my mother and their satellites enter, if at all, with an air of casualness, and since they have been absent almost entirely from the last hundred pages, so, in those which ensue, first I retrace my steps by a year or two, and then follow my parents to the end, beyond the confines of this book, portray them in the final stage of their development, and illustrate it with—because speed is essential at this stage—a shower of anecdotes, tragic or trivial, quick and staccato as the rattle of a machine-gun. These books in their entirety, I once more remind my readers, I planned as a work of art. They concern the family history, childhood, education and self-establishment of a writer, and aim at portraying his likeness directly, as well as (in the next volume, in particular) delineating him through the reflections of him caught as he passes through the lives of others and against the background of his age: and if the early part of my history, as that of any child must be, was largely that of my parents, and if, as and after I grew up, the emphasis shifted, so it is natural in this next chapter for it to swing back; because they, father and mother, are the <u>caryatids</u> who for each one of us support the arch of life and <u>frame</u> the view to be obtained under it.

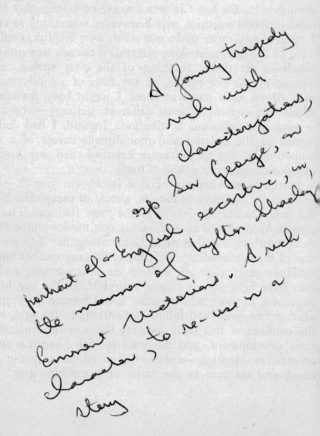

A family tragedy rich with characterizations, esp. Sir George, perhaps of a English secretive, in the manner of Lytton Strachey current Victorian. A rich character to re-use in a story

CHAPTER FOUR

Laughter in the Next Room

IF BY BIRTH mine was a dangerous inheritance, and although I possessed, as I did, most difficult parents, of whom to be the son, alone, without attempting any other labour, would have constituted a profession in itself, at least I was privileged, at times plunged in great misery, at times flooded with the frustrated laughter of both high and low comedy, to watch a unique combination and interplay of forces, an unrivalled disruption of powers and dispersion of assets, and, further, to observe at close—often uncomfortably close—range one of the most singular characters of his epoch, and albeit myself born to these conditions, to have the good fortune to understand what I saw. This, at least, I hope I have established: at a time when people of his kind, of similar derivation, were declining in vigour and in the originality of their character, and becoming lazy in the use of their minds, my father provided a last flash of the old fire, and summed up his own tradition—in rather the same way that, for example, Tiepolo provided the final glory, an ultimate vision, in which all the virtues and faults were emphasised, of Venetian painting. It has been my purpose to portray him—from whom I have inherited certain ranges of interest and veins of thought, but hardly ever of feeling, and against whom I so often made a counter-challenge—with the same solidity with which Boswell has caused Doctor Johnson to stand out from the shadows, with the same recognisability, so that every utterance, even the most unexpected, is immediately identifiable; and, too, with that sense of truth to an epoch that so pre-eminently, so memorably distinguishes several books, not least among them *The Adventures of Sherlock Holmes*. But I have employed a different method, in pursuit of other aims. Because this is the picture of the father of three writers, and part of a no doubt

239

ended getting class structure

ambitious plan to illustrate, through my own career and sensibilities, a family, a background, and an age.

My sister, in the years immediately following the war, had been responsible for drawing attention in England to the work of Miss Gertrude Stein, then greatly neglected here, and in the summer of 1929 Edith and I accompanied Miss Alice Toklas and Miss Stein to Oxford, to hear that gifted writer deliver her celebrated lecture under the auspices of my friend Harold Acton. We had seen in the motor how nervous she was, albeit as I watched her on the platform, while the chairman was introducing her before her speech, I found it hard to credit, for always in her pose as she sat, there was something monumental, as if she were sitting to a painter who was making a record for posterity: the body turned to stone from flesh, but more powerful, in no way dead, and her massive philosopher's head had the eagle-lines of a Red Indian warrior's. When she stood up—and always, because of the latent force to be divined in her, one expected her to be taller than she was—she showed a mastery of her audience, and her address, though couched in her accustomed style, proved a consummate piece of lucidity. I remember, however, a certain commotion arising and some accompanying laughter, when towards the middle of her discourse she remarked, "Everything is the same and everything is different!"

Many undergraduates had come to the hall to amuse themselves after the lecture at the expense of a writer widely and angrily derided, her work dismissed as the "stutterings of a lunatic". But in the presence of this obviously distinguished woman, the wiser of them recognised that there was not much to be done in this line. At the end, two young gentlemen, not so easily discouraged, shot up to heckle her from positions widely apart in the audience: but they asked an identical question.

"Miss Stein, if everything is the same, how can everything be different?"

In a most genial, comforting manner, Miss Stein replied: "Well, just look at you two dear boys!"

Everything, then, in this ultimate chapter is, similarly, the same, and yet different from how it was in the chapter with which the whole work begins. The germ is to be found there, and since the first volume begins with a glimpse of a tall, fair man—young in appearance to all save his small son—, who guarded an inner and personal isolation singular in the modern world, walking in the early morning in the garden he had made, it is fitting that this last chapter should open with a view of him —a rather unusual view, it is true—some thirty years later (for he is still there, though, as the reader will learn, on the point of emigration), on a summer morning, albeit at an hour not quite so early, in the same garden which he had created. In the interval, the pleasances he had made, the landscape he had remodelled, and in some places evolved, had grown up, had become venerable under the glow, and equally the burden, of northern seasons. The stones had weathered, their grain cleared or further obscured by the incidence and rhythm of the months. Not only the long rains of the winter, those dangling strings, but the frantic, unpredictable showers of our summers, tattooing and drumming with the sound of fate on pavement and terrace, all the soft autumn gales of the west wind, whereon race low, earth-coloured clouds, and which, treacherous in their speed, leave the ancient trees in the avenue above the garden as bare of foliage after they have passed as masts of ships are cleared of rigging by the typhoon, the dazzling towers and Siberian plains of the snow, which silences all life under its quilts and cushions, all these have left their own peculiar mark, their branding. That chestnut over there lost its branch in the great wind from the north: when the floods came in 1911, a stream below changed its course, and the lake devoured another piece of land (it was such a summer storm as in England only occurs in this region of hills and chimneys, tall as obelisks, when dams burst, roofs are swept away, courts are flooded, and every lead pipe becomes a fountain), and yonder dent in the yew hedge came from the weight of snow (which should be lifted from it by men with long rods). The huge trunk, hollow as two boats bound together, that lies by the gothic Temple, fell with the crash of a monolith collapsing—a sound that could be heard through the roar of a January night, when the trumpets of the wind bellow in every open space, when the tops of mighty trees bend and flutter, and the whole great house of stone quails beneath the impact, the windows rattle, and there is a moaning and whining at every crevice; (for the aim of wind is to make more room for winds to move in, to unroof and bluster; if only they could enter!). All these local conditions of climate, and the nature of the earth itself here, have given it the character, the accent of a locality. What other garden knows the nightly glory of this—not only the mystery of odorous darkness, and the pale or golden shafts of the moon when the dew glitters on the grass till it seems to lie in dazzling drifts of white flowers, but, in addition, cloudy or fine, the lion-glare of the furnaces, when the sky turns to a sultry gold, and every shape is suddenly revealed within the nimbus of this pillar of fire which lifts the heart of a man on the foulest night, as on the fairest in summer, and makes the stranger gasp at so rich and so unexpected a splendour? . . . But beyond these things, gardens are international as music, to be understood by all, and free of time. The flash of water was the same in Nineveh as here, fountains speak all languages with the same voice, and the light dazzling on a wall from a pool has the same shifting dance and rhythm here as in India or Spain: so, when once its entity has formed, a garden has affiliations infinitely old and cosmopolitan.

What has altered? In these thirty years which have passed, the hedges have grown—perhaps it is that which makes the figure of the man who planted them look smaller. Certainly he complains that he cannot see over them. What else has altered? A whole world has just perished, and the lawns are greener. There have been great and general catastrophes to the nations; and private calamities in the family. The lawns are softer and more smooth.

This is again the month of August, full of green pride. There is a pomp, not only in the full-weighted trees, but in everything, in the clouds, which resemble huge tufts of feathers, or float with the majesty of icebergs in the bursts of sun unloosed by these clouds, in the vanity of the occasional golden weather, when the spangles of the heat dance everywhere above the ground, in the colour of flowers, glossy, coruscating under the light, in the scent of carnation, rose and stock. All is full, over-sweet, over-ripe. . . . At this season, in the decade following the war, we entertained nearly every year a large house-party. Some members of it were invited by my father and mother, others by me, who acted as host. Among my guests was often Constant Lambert, who came on his first visit to us in August 1925, when there were about twenty persons staying in the house. He arrived in time for dinner, at which my father, whose acquaintance he had yet to make, was not present: (for very frequently in these years, my father would go to bed for dinner and come down afterwards, without warning, so as to give us all a jump, and clothed, of course, in full evening dress, tail-coat with white tie and white waistcoat). Constant was only eighteen, and, since this was his first large house-party, was very alert and rather nervous. In consequence, he was punctual to the minute in coming down to breakfast at nine o'clock in the dining-room. He found it empty, though the table was laid and the air was full of the savour of breakfast dishes. A plume of steam hovered in the air from a Viennese coffee machine on a sideboard. An almost electric tension brooded in the emptiness, as if anything might occur at any moment. The young musician, however, concentrated on eggs and bacon and coffee, and sat down, with his back to the chimney, and facing the sash windows. . . . Suddenly, the strange happening for which subconsciously he had been waiting occurred: for, looking towards the window opposite him, he was amazed to see the distinguished, bearded, medieval face of an elderly gentleman, crowned with a large grey felt hat, pass just outside, in a horizontal position,—as if he had fallen prone and was about to raise himself—and holding a malacca walking-stick in the mouth. The vision of this venerable figure proceeding on all fours was startling in its unexpectedness, and strongly recalled to the mind of him who beheld it Blake's picture of Nebuchadnezzar, though it is true that the Babylonish king was notably less spruce in appearance, and that his counterpart was plainly English and lacked those memorable nails shaped like the claws of birds. Constant hurried to the window, looked out—and realised what was happening. It was—it must be—my father, at work, and carrying his cane in this unusual manner in order to observe the views and measure from the new level—for he intended to drop the lawn three or four feet, and so, in his present position, was at the height of a man standing at the altitude he planned. . . . But even though Constant knew in his heart who it must be, he was too bewildered to mention what he had seen to the other guests, who now came into the dining-room, filling it with their chatter.

The atmosphere of the house was gay, this August and in the years immediately preceding and following, for at last we were in full peace, and those of my generation had recovered their spirits and again shed the whole decade that war had added to the age of most of them. But I must emphasise that though I greatly enjoyed the 'twenties, the years of struggle in my career, when it was necessary to fight, and yet, for all the fury, years too of accomplishment, as well as of travel and pleasure, I never, notwithstanding, felt I belonged to them as did those who could only remember adult life after the war: I was conscious of other claims on my loyalty; I belonged by birth, education, nature, outlook and period to the pre-war era, a proud citizen of the great free world of 1914, in which comity prevailed. Nevertheless, with health restored, and energy in consequence renewed, it was easy to relish the days, possible even to be ready for the perpetual traps my father—wishing with his curious, incongruous puritanism to cramp a side of life which seemed to him pleasant—laid for us, and to reply to them, extricate ourselves from them and answer his remonstrances or fresh verbal efforts at entanglement in the manner which, through bitter experience, we had learnt to be the most likely to defeat his plans. Though we saved ourselves by our own exertions, in order to do so we were obliged to introduce into them the same element of farce that now seemed to inhabit his own designs. But, though occasionally amusing —and certainly amusing enough in retrospect, this imposed a great and perpetual strain on the patience. I must confess that my father's fantasies—the System chief among them—and all his individual ways of thought had now attained their fullest range and sweep. During several years, and until as late as 1923, he had seven sitting-rooms in his own occupation as studies, and in three or four of these stood a specimen, straddling a sofa, of the desk he had designed in order to enable him to write more easily when lying down. All his papers he kept on the floor, so that each resembled a drift of dusty snow, or a beauty spot after a public holiday. The majority of documents, some of them folded and done up with red tape, others overflowing from boxes or, again, just loose and ready as an angel's wings to float up to heaven on any casual draught, related to the law-suit he was conducting against the coal-lessees: the rest were concerned with his customary interests, pedigrees, household economies, heraldry, decorative furniture, summaries of his financial transactions with me, or consisted of notes on *Practical Farming*, on the *Use of Ceremony in Byzantine Court Life*, on the *Origin of the Medieval Romances*, the *Buildings of the Emperor Frederick II in South Italy*, or the *Black Death*—of course—, and on his own *Inventions*, possible and impossible.

In these he had recently been taking a renewed interest. Earlier in the summer, when he was staying in London, he had sent for me to see him one afternoon on an urgent matter. When I entered his room, he rose from his bed, in which he had been resting, locked the door so as to be sure we should not be interrupted, and then went back to bed again. In a low voice, he confided in me:

"You know, Osbert, I sometimes have an idea with money in it."

"Yes, Father."

"Well," he gave a long dry laugh like a cackle, "I've just produced an egg."

He waited a little to allow me to look astonished, which certainly I did—sufficiently, even, I think, so satisfy him.

Gratified, he continued, "It's a breakfast egg. . . . The yolk will be made of smoked meat, the white of compressed rice, and the shell of synthetic lime—or a coating of lime. It will be delicious, will last for ever, and be ready at any time. It wouldn't matter where you might be, in the desert or on a polar expedition, all you'd have to do would be to boil it for two or three minutes, as you wished—and there would be your breakfast, ready for you, and very nourishing and sustaining.

You'd feel wonderfully fit after it, ready to do a real hard day's work. It may make the whole difference to explorers!"

"What a good idea! You ought to patent it at once."

"As a matter of fact, that's why I want to consult you. I would like to make a little money for Sachie after I am gone —but how am I to place my egg on the market? . . . I thought perhaps I'd see Selfridge's about it—they seem very go-ahead. But whom shall I ask for, and how shall I announce the reason for my visit? I daren't trust my egg to anyone else —it might be stolen."

"I should ask for Mr. Gordon Selfridge himself. Tell the commissionaire to take you up in the lift, and just step into Mr. Selfridge's sanctum, saying, 'I'm Sir George Sitwell, and I've brought my egg with me!'"

"Capital idea! That is what I will do. Thank you so much, dear boy: I knew you would help me."

Accordingly, he set off for the Oxford Street shop the next morning at eleven: he was dressed in a silk hat and a frock-coat, an article of dress already, even then, nearly extinct, and carried a bundle of papers, with diagrams on them. . . . He was very late for luncheon when he returned, and though his eye seemed to rest on me with a certain coldness, he never explained what had happened during the interview, if it took place. My mother did not like to ask him, nor subsequently did he ever refer to the egg again. Yet it had in no whit discouraged him, for I noticed on the floor of one of his studies that the sheaf entitled *Inventions* had grown much more bulky of recent months.

It was, as he often explained, delightfully convenient to keep everything on the floor. "I know exactly where to find what I want, and can put my hand on it at any moment!" he would say. So that now, when the coal law-suit had just been settled out of court, it was with regret that he began a retreat, and rather ruefully de-requisitioned one sitting-room after another, surrendering them again to the use of the family. But though circumstances obliged him to do this, for he had grown to like many guests to come to the house in August and September, and otherwise there would have been nowhere for them to sit, nevertheless in no least respect did he modify his

CURTAIN DESIGN BY JOHN PIPER FOR THE ENTERTAINMENT
FAÇADE BY DR. EDITH SITWELL AND DR. WILLIAM WALTON

Reproduced by permission of Dr. William Walton

Plate IX

THE AUTHOR'S FATHER " EN VOYAGE "

ideas, moderate his conceptions or abate his flights. Indeed
latterly he had coined several new slogans to express his
individual sentiments, at last developed to their utmost
capacity, and when, having risen from his bed to come down
after dinner, he sat by himself, in full evening dress, white tie
and waistcoat, in the ballroom in the middle of his Regency
sofa, very long, and supported by a carved and painted lion
at either end, so that he resembled a Byzantine Emperor on
his throne, he would often at this hour, and always to the
delight of his children, enunciate his favourite command
disguised as a request:

"*I must ask anyone entering the house never to contradict me or
differ from me in any way, as it interferes with the functioning
of the gastric juices and prevents my sleeping at night.*"

Albeit I tried to persuade him to have this notice printed
on cards, and to cause one of them to be placed on the
chimney-piece of each room in the house, my efforts, though
they came very near success, ended in failure.

Throughout these years of the 'twenties, the life at Renishaw followed the same pattern: so that I may mention here
that later in the decade, in 1928, my friend Evelyn Waugh
formed one of the party, and I would notice how when my
father was present at dinner the young novelist would be
suddenly struck mute in a kind of ecstasy of observation.
Remembering this, fourteen years later, I asked him to make
a short note for me on some personal memory of my father,
and accordingly he wrote the page which by his kindness is
printed at the end of this volume.[1] As typical of these recurrent parties and their atmosphere, I must, however, take
an earlier year, in part composite, but accurate in detail and a
true summary. We will choose that in which Constant Lambert
obtained, as I have already described, that unusual pre-view
of my father. On the particular August in question, it
was a gathering in parts cosmopolitan, in parts provincial,
and mixed in ages and interests. There were the relays
of very young writers, musicians, poets, painters, whom
my sister, my brother or I had asked—and one or two guests
invited for longer periods, such as William Walton,

[1] See Appendix B, p. 341.

I

Constant Lambert and Peter Quennell. Then there were
my parents' importations whom they had contracted abroad;
for example, there were the three ladies to whom my
mother had referred several times in the past few months,
both by letter and in conversation, in such phrases as, "I hope
you won't mind. I've asked the three little Ruritanians I met
last year in Vienna to come to Renishaw this summer. I think
you'll like them. They're funny little things!" or, "They're
unlike anyone else. I wonder what you'll think of them!"
In the minds of the young men gathered together in the house,
these words conjured up the image of a cluster of starry-eyed
exotic Balkan girls, fresh from the plum- and cherry-orchards
of Yugoslavia, the rose-fields of Bulgaria, or the centuries-old
oak-forests of Rumania; squirrel-like, perhaps, impulsive,
attractive, more than regularly beautiful, or, again, with
hands like flowers, and pale, highly-bred and interesting, as
D'Annunzio's Virgins of the Rocks, or, it might be, headstrong,
sacrificing all for love, firebrands from Belgrade, tornadoes
from Bucharest, hurricanes from Bratislava. It was, therefore,
a disappointment to these secret thoughts to find three middle-
aged Ruritanian sisters of unimpeachable decorum, by birth
and self-expression ladies-in-waiting.

Ruritanian ladies-in-waiting have of cruel need to be more
strict than any others in the world, in order to preserve,
as it were, an equilibrium in the court. They may—indeed
they must—be "artistic"; but never enough to give offence.
They are required to know, and to be able to hand out easily,
the names, in painting, of Michelangelo, Leonardo, Greuze,
Winterhalter, Lenbach, Boldini and László; in literature, of
Dante, Shakespeare, Ouida, Carmen Sylva, Paul Bourget and
Emil Ludwig. Music—except for Opera, in which they must
be specialists—they were spared. To lead such a life it would
plainly be necessary to feel a sense of vocation from earliest
years, and this, I am convinced, they had experienced. There
was, too, a call for continual self-sacrifice. Not for them
Russian tiaras, floating veils and audacious conversation on
picnics under the pine trees or on the calmest of lakes. The
style of talk they had to cultivate was a very special one, an
art in itself, that could no doubt be mastered; because there

was need of rigorous training in their small closed profession, as well as of innate inclination. A moment's silence is as the unforgivable sin: the sound of voices must never be allowed to flag—the texture must be peppered with counters of an international ennui, to afford an air of cosmopolitan culture. But the talk must flow at one lukewarm level, except when stirred as it flows round the base of some such granite monolith as, "How small the world is!", "C'est pire qu'un crime, c'est une faute!" or "What a charming writer is your Marie Corelli!" And ladies-in-waiting they proved to be, in more senses than one.

From the earliest morning, they were downstairs, waiting, encased in the clothes considered in the Balkans most correct for the hour and place, too nondescript to remember, though latitude had plainly been allowed them, enough to choose a shade that would bring out the colour of their eyes; there they waited to be entertained, and to entertain others, for the most part by lengthy clambers in the dizzy, now rather mildewed and treacherous, branches of the *Almanach de Gotha*. In Ruritania, they told us, a visit never lasted less than six weeks —it would be impolite—and host and hostess, and the sons and daughters of the house, never quitted their guests for a single instant between 8 A.M. and 3 A.M.: during the whole of those nineteen hours, at meals, or while eating glutinous sweets in the intervals, there sounded a continual and entrancingly cultivated chatter. At threat of a lull it was best to run through the plot, in detail, of *Rigoletto* or *La Bohème*. In appearance, the sisters were shaped like, and had exactly the proportion of, three plump hour-glasses for counting the many minutes of other people's lives which they wasted. Considering their shortness, they held themselves so upright, wringing every inch out of their stature, that the wonder was that they did not fall backwards. This straightness of carriage had been inculcated from earliest to latest years by their mother, also in the previous Ruritanian reign a lady-in-waiting, whose perpetual injunction to them, at the opera, or in almost any public place, had been, "Tenez-vous droites, mes enfants, Royauté vous regarde". . . . For each hour of the day, like the ticking of the clock, or, as for that, the falling sand of an hour-glass, they could proffer the appropriate remark, usually in French. At dinner, for instance, at which my fate was always to sit next one of them, she, whichever it was, would look out on the August eve, and after a melancholy poetic glance at the prospect would remark, "C'est l'heure bleue, c'est l'heure exquise".

There were other guests who approached the three sisters in quality. On my father's side were rivals in a different way. The Silver Bore, for example, paid several visits to Renishaw, coming to revivify the place with a breath of old St. Vitus. He took an interest in plantations, and where they ought to be thinned, and would stand for hours at the end of the garden gibbering and winking at the static tree-trunks in a most equivocal manner. And there came, for a very long stay, old Miss Middelby from the Record Office—known as *The Girl who took the Wrong Turning*, because from whatever direction in the house she started, whether from the Muniment Room on the first floor, where she was working on naming the bones of dead men among dust and cobwebs, or from the ballroom or the garden, she would always, when it was time for luncheon or dinner, have to be rescued in a bewildered and flustered condition from the gentlemen's lavatory on the ground floor. The first night she arrived, she sat next my father, and I was enchanted with a fragment of their conversation which came floating across to me. After a silence, he turned to her, and said, with a forward movement of the head and body, and an indefinable air of gallantry:

"Are you acquainted with the local time-table?"

"No, Sir George, but my young nephew would be deeply interested in it."

My father was intent on making her comfortable, for he believed, quite wrongly, that we did not like her, and in consequence he thought out all sorts of little plans to give her pleasure. As a result, his feelings were hurt later when some one ill-naturedly showed him a letter received from her at this time, which contained the sentence, "This is a very odd house: enormous rents in the sheets, and plates of peaches by my bedside!"

A distinguished archaeologist was also staying in the house for a shorter period, being engaged in excavating for my father the problematic site of the Norman Manor of Eckington, held by the Estoutevilles. The place having been arbitrarily selected, not one stone remained above ground, or was found under it, to suggest that such a building had ever existed. Even Professor Voxall, I apprehend, was surprised when one morning he dug up a bottle of truffles and a tarantula-spider set out on a board; objects which my brother and I, tired of this futile exercise of my father's and of its expense, had, the day before, buried there for the expert to discover. While at Renishaw, this learned man was afflicted with a return of malaria, from which he suffered, having contracted it in the East during the war. When I went to tell my father that his guest was indisposed and would be obliged to stay upstairs for dinner, I found him in bed resting. I ended with the words, "I only hope he's not dangerously ill. It's *malaria*!" The reaction was immediate. Plainly my father was taking no risks. Almost before I had finished speaking, he had whisked out of bed and rung the bell, and when it was answered he said curtly, "Robins, bring me my mosquito-net!" Thereafter for a month he slept under it.

My mother, who had quickly tired of her guests, spent much of her time in her bedroom: for she had now a Swiss maid, and had to her delight learnt that Frieda could yodel. One of the endearing traits in my mother's character was that she could never have enough of a good thing, and so she was continually sending for Edith, Sacheverell and me to help her to persuade her maid to perform. The entertainment delighted her, and she would sit in her chair, her face creased, her whole body shaking with laughter, though her brown eyes were still full of melancholy. The Swiss girl did not notice, for she was very shy, and would only consent to perform for us if hidden by a screen: but once installed behind her Japanese panels of black embroidered with bumpy storks in gold thread, she would tirra-lirra her heart out. My sister was usually successful in inducing Frieda to yodel to us, for she was her pupil, taking yodelling lessons every day. So we would all gather there, in my mother's room with its gay but faded paper of bunches of flowers, and its niche and eighteenth-century cornice; my mother in the armchair, near the wide-open window, where the sun-drenched scent of the sweet green leaves she loved came in at her. My sister would be sitting on the bed. Now a person of the utmost distinction and beauty, with her long slender limbs and long-fingered hands, and the musing but singularly sweet expression which always distinguished her, she belonged to an earlier, less hackneyed age, in which the standards of Woolworth mass production did not exist: (in fact, as an American is said to have remarked in front of her portrait in the Tate Gallery, "Lord, she's gothic, gothic enough to hang bells in!"). My mother, who had so cruelly ill-used her, had come to love her society, her wit and perception, and it was symptomatic of Edith's fineness of character that she responded and, now that my mother was growing old and her spirits flagging, set herself, at a great waste of her own energy and time, to amuse her—and there was little else one could do for her. Edith, then, would be sitting on the bed: while on a very straight Chippendale chair, but thrown backward and supported in front by his own two long legs, Sacheverell would balance his tall frame. His appearance at that age—twenty-five or six—, his very handsome head, with hair curling at the sides, and with its cut and contours so Italian in essence, but so northern in colour, translated perfectly the strange power and intensity that have always been his, the generous warmth of his temperament, so genial and impulsive, the passion of many kinds that burns in him—passion for people, for books, for learning, for works of art, for old lamps that can be lit again at his fire—, the wit, distinguished and apt, which he despises in himself and does nothing to cultivate, instead preferring the jokes of others which he so immensely enjoys: the flash, deep as bright, of his anger, large as the scale of his mind and frame, but never enduring, breaking down eventually into a smile, though by no means an easy smile. Meanwhile, I, with my rather heavy mask and build, would be seated in an armchair opposite. Frieda's shelter was in front of the door, and sometimes, just as her voice had reached to the top of a high mountain, and was preparing to receive answer from another, my father, attracted by the sound, and always liking to know what was going on, would bolt in and find himself enclosed with her behind the Japanese screen. He was tall enough for his bearded face, which recalled more vividly every day the Italian paintings of the Renaissance—he was at no great distance from the portrait of Cesar Borgia or of the Grand Turk by Bellini, and from the heads of effigies of the same, or of an earlier, epoch on tombs—, to show just above the top of the screen with an expression of extreme and dignified distaste. He would say nothing—indeed he could not make himself heard, for the maid had not noticed his entry and continued her song until, a few moments later, she suddenly saw him and stopped. Standing on tiptoe, and blushing, she would then peep over the barrier, and say, "Please, m'lady, I cannot go on with my music". My mother, still laughing, would say, with an effort at control, "I wish you wouldn't always interrupt, George. You're just like an *auguste*—must always be in everything!" He would go out, with that particular lowering of one shoulder that meant that he would not forget and would think out counter-measures for use later on. Meanwhile Frieda's peaceful, innocent mountain-music would soon again drown every other sound—she could not see from behind her screen, and we could laugh to our hearts' content. . . . Exquisitely ridiculous, these intricate vocal exercises summoned up for us vistas of her native peaks: we could hear the cowbells, watch the goats, and pluck the gentians near the melting snow: we could hear the sound of waterfalls and of a thousand waiters placing cups on saucers. She took us, thus, to a far land: we were free of constraint, forgot all but the sounds, and the sight they brought. Frieda took everything calmly and innocently. She spoke English fluently, and wrote it without fear. When she was on holiday one summer in her native mountains, my sister sent her an anthology containing a long poem entitled *Swiss Rhapsody* by my brother. In return, she received the following letter:

Dear Miss Edith,
    Juste I received the lovely poeme from Mr. Sacheveril Sitwell about Switzerland when he was traveling from Italie through Simplon Geneve. Really I am enjoying very much to read this poeme there I am native from this country since like Schiller the great poet from Germany when he was travelling in the wondervoll Lake from Luzerne

and write this work from Wilhelm Tell. I should be very pleased when to have some poem from Mr. Sacheveril Sitwell about Switzerland.—I am remain, Yours sincerely, FRIEDA.

While we were listening to the yodelling downstairs—on our conscience, but by no means on that of my mother, who had invited them—the three Ruritanian ladies-in-waiting were sitting, still petulantly expectant of being entertained.

"England has no *couleur locale*—there is nothing like the Bull Fight, the *Corrida*, in Spain," they would complain, rather rudely, until at last I became angered, and succeeded in revenging myself, as well as obtaining an afternoon off. Observing that there was a fête in the Rectory grounds, and that it featured an Egg-and-Spoon race, I asked them, "Are you not going to the Egg-and-Spoon Race?"

"What is it?" they enquired together.

"An Egg-and-Spoon Race is to England what a Bull Fight is to Spain," I replied.

They eagerly accepted my offer of a motor to take them to the fiesta. But it was not a success.

"It had no picturesqueness, no chic," they maintained with Balkan literalness, when they returned: "we had expected the crowd, too, to be more full of colour!"

It was during one of these summers at Renishaw, so like in tone, that Constant Lambert enjoyed another curious adventure. Very tired after conducting, he had come to spend a few days with us. My father was in the middle of a course of Nauheim baths designed to relieve his heart, which he alleged to be overstrained, and—for the cure has to be done by degrees—he had reached the stage where the treatment becomes the most rigorous, and the whole day has to be given up to it and to resting. There was a nurse in attendance, and she had just prepared his bath, melting the salts in it, and had left the room, to let it cool for a while, when Constant entered, knowing nothing of all this—for he had only arrived the previous evening—, and, seeing a bath ready and steaming for him as he thought, leapt into it. The nurse now returned, and finding the door locked, realised what had happened. She knew my father would be furious if he found out she had allowed someone to have his bath. There was no time to prepare another (since to get the water to the right temperature, with the salts properly dissolved in it, was by no means a short process). Under these circumstances she showed presence of mind. Regarding my father with an expression that plainly said, "Something is wrong with you", she seized his wrist, felt his pulse, and with a note in her voice, both of surprise and gravity, observed that it was far too rapid, and counselled that it would be most unwise for him today to have such drastic treatment as the bath provided. As for Constant, he thoroughly enjoyed the bath, and stayed in a good while. But he developed a curious blue tinge in his complexion for all the remainder of the day, and for at least a week complained of singular palpitations and of a feeling of utter exhaustion.

Though such incidents continued whenever my father paid me a visit at Renishaw, yet, looking back, 1925 appears to me to have been unequalled for excitements of this sort. Perhaps it was because the object for which I had striven so long was near to attainment. I had persuaded my father to emigrate —to Italy. Himself was always far happier there, and I had long realised that he was one of the fortunate few whose energies and wish to control those round them increase and strengthen with age—he was now sixty-five. I had my own work, and so had my sister and my brother theirs. There was no hope of any of his three children being allowed to have a career, unless he could be persuaded to go. The general atmosphere, which was always menacing, the interruptions, the scenes, the surprises, and the ambushes laid, the fussing, the necessity my father felt both for consulting and contradicting me, the economies, the extravagances, all put it beyond possibility to write a line when he was in the house. Though I realised that my parents, of course, would continue to visit me from time to time for long periods in England, and I should have to stay with them in Italy, yet their residence abroad would induce a new feeling of rest and freedom in the air. As an inducement to him, there was Montegufoni, with its enormous house and garden just waiting to be "improved"! He liked the idea; "I shall be known as the Italian Sir George", he remarked—though I never could make out by whom. In addition, he was able to furnish for his own consideration and enjoyment historic precedents and parallels: he thought of the Emperor Charles V and his renunciation of two worlds, and then of his own ancestor, Walter de Boys. . . . But in the interval he would abandon himself to nostalgia and heart-searchings. It was hard, indeed, to be obliged by your care for the future, and by your selfless devotion to your children, to abandon the old home in the autumn of your days: for his inner thoughts on subjects of this kind were now, I fear, always couched in such set phrases—as is nearly always the case with someone who is sentimental without being affec-tionate. Meanwhile there was much to be done. He shut up Wood End and from there moved all the furniture, which he had brought from Italy, to Renishaw—special furniture vans went simply hurtling about on the railway—, sorted the pieces, added to them others he had imported similarly to Renishaw, and then sent the whole lot back to Italy. The same patient frieze of workmen whom we saw in *The Scarlet Tree*—and still without their special felt shoes—plodded by impassively with articles of furniture, backwards and forwards, or placed and extended their ladder, to the same music of my father's perpetual "No, no, no: all wrong!" Sometimes a guest lying in bed would be startled by my father, at the head of his troupe, bursting in and proceeding to remove all the furniture. Neither he nor the workmen would heed protests, and the poor victim, as my father went on remorselessly, inexorably, to dismantle the room, would begin to believe himself in-visible and inaudible, indeed almost to doubt his own exis-tence. At last he might be able to get through some remote hint, as though it were a message in a bottle, to my mother, who would at once stop Frieda yodelling, send for my father, and say, "George, you can't do that!"

"Somebody has to do the work, Ida. I don't know how it would get done without me! It is a great strain on my health."

My mother repeated to herself softly the refrain of a famous clown's song: "A Terrible Lot To Do Today, To Do Today, To Do Today. A Terrible Lot To Do Today, To Do To Do Today."

"You ought to take things more easily," she would urge.

"But how can I? Everybody on the place sometimes has a holiday. But I can never afford to take one!"

"Nonsense, George."

"Well, what would happen to you all if I did?"

(Lodgings again, I supposed!) He went on to explain that he was winding up his interests at Renishaw as fast as he could: but some things he would be obliged to leave unfinished. There was Barber's house (The Folly, as it became known; on the plans for which the reader of *Great Morning* saw him working some ten years previously), the two Golf Club Houses, and the Manor in Warwickshire I had lent to my Aunt Florence for her lifetime, and which my father had been for many years restoring.[1]

"And none of the work is for myself," he pointed out. "It's all for others!"

"Yes, but you know," I interposed, "that in most cases the people you are doing it for have asked you not to do it."

"I'm afraid I can't help that! It's the *right thing* to do— and now most of it will have to wait until I'm able to visit Renishaw—if I'm spared!" . . . And a look of dejection spread over his face, as he thought of how he was setting out to make his way in the world all over again.

On the eve of his departure for a new home, I offer a brief summary, by another hand, of his various activities in the old during the previous decade. The reader, familiar with them already, will find, I trust, that by the addition of this bird's-eye

---

[1] Tudor House, or the Flower de Luce, as it was known in the eighteenth century, is a plaster and timber house, with an overhanging storey and five gables, facing the village green at Long Itchington, some seven miles from Kenilworth. The house, though its style suggests a slightly earlier Tudor period, was built early in the great reign, by Sir Robert Dudley, father of the Earl of Leicester. The village, remote and quiet though it still is, has seen its moments of glory: for here, on the 9th July 1575, Queen Elizabeth, on her way to stay with Leicester at Kenilworth, was received by her host, and the Queen and the royal party dined in a vast tent, erected outside the house, on the green. After the meal was over and dessert had been placed on the table, two prodigies of the neighbouring county were brought in for the Queen's inspection: a gigantic sheep of the Leicestershire breed, and its human counterpart, a boy of six years old, nearly five feet high and monstrously fat and stupid.

The house—after being for a time an inn, and then a farm—was bought by my ancestor, Francis Hurt Sitwell of Renishaw, *circa* 1770. . . . I sold it in 1947.

view to my own he will obtain a solid, almost stereoscopic vision of them. These extracts which, short as they are, disclose, moreover, a glimpse of a fascinating personal, or impersonal, relationship, are taken once again from the Estate Correspondence, and were addressed by the agent to his former chief, Peveril Turnbull, whose pupil he had been.

Jan. 9, 1911. Sir George writes every day. He has taken over Plumbley Railway, and is going ahead with the carriage drive through it.

Jan. 16, 1911. I have just received a letter from Sir G. wanting all sorts of particulars re bringing water from the Eckington Woods to the Lake by piping through the Railway Cutting. I will find out the cost of pipes and that may frighten him.

June 7, 1911. You kindly ask me how I am getting on, but I don't know, for we've just had my pet nuisance (Sir G.) here for a week. I have over 40 men, 11 horses and a traction-engine working, the rent audits begin to-morrow. I am busy getting particulars for this year's land auctions and Merry went to the Auditor to ask when he can come here to go through the accounts. Sir G. wants the rates on woods appealing against etc. etc. etc.

Nov. 21, 1911. We are worrying at a plan for a gardener's cottage. Sir G. alters it every five minutes.

Dec. 21, 1911. We have had Sir G. here all this week (rather a nuisance when one wants to get rent audits squared up). I think I drove him away by developing a bad cold. He is worrying about the gardener's house, alterations to Barber's, and great alterations to the Far Landing.

Jan. 4, 1912. Sir G. is here since Tuesday. We are laying out Barber's garden: and lifting the turf on the lawn at Renishaw, taking out the subsoil and putting in 18 inches of good soil. We are altering the Golf House (at Renishaw), and building greenhouses, etc.

Feb. 19, 1912. I am quite well myself but horribly sick of drawing plans forty times over for Sir G. and continually falling out with him over them.

July 4, 1912. He (Sir George) gets frightfully angry when the slightest thing goes wrong, such as the fact of the loganberries being ripe, and its not being reported to him. He considers everything can be foreseen and arranged. All my time is taken up with going about from one job to another, for we have about 60 to 70 men working all over the estate. . . . My wages are £230 per annum and house.

Jan. 11, 1913. I find it very difficult to get money out of Sir G. to pay for the various works. . . . We are now making a golf-course for Rotherham. We are just about to spend £2000 on the golf house at Renishaw.

Jan. 14, 1913. Sir George sends me a long list this morning of things I have done wrongly through not consulting him. In future, I am to consult him about every thing. I want to build a new earth-closet for Staniforth's cottage, but I suppose Sir G. will tell me to wait until he has had time to consult Lutyens about the best form to build.

March 20, 1913. We have C. E. Mallows, the architect, on with Barber's garden and are delving furiously so that Sir G. may see how it looks before he goes abroad. We are also constructing turrets in plaster to give him the effect of ones in stone. These are for the entrance gates.

Oct. 13, 1913. I've been offered the job of road-surveyor for this district. It's the sort of job I've always wanted, so I'm astonished to find myself not at all anxious to take it on. I don't like leaving Sir G. while he has so many irons in the fire. . . . A good row with Sir G. now would help me to decide. The gardens here looked very wonderful last month but nobody was here to see them.

Feb. 4, 1914. Wages this week £110. We have 80 men, a traction-engine, a steam wagon and 21 horses working. There appears to be no sign of pulling up. . . .

Sept. 8, 1914. Sir G. wants us to take over all the poor pasture on the Estate and plant with wheat. We are to plough up the South Park and no end of a job it is on the top of our work.

March 20, 1915. I had a go at Sir G. this morning, and think I have screwed him up to £300. He sticks at making it permanent, and thinks it should come down again if the cost of living comes down, but I'm hanged if I'll ever do it for less.

May 12, 1916. Sir G. is here, and insists on wasting labour on Barber's garden still.

March 29, 1917. . . . Sir George has given all the Warwickshire tenants notice, and intends to take their farms in hand. This in spite of your warning letter. He would have taken all the Mosbro' and Eckington Woods valley farms, had I not turned very stupid about it.

Feb. 17, 1918. We have over 500 acres of wheat in on the various farms. Thinking of harvest is like a nightmare. Sir G. says I have not enough work to justify a permanent assistant!

Feb. 13, 1920. We are still chucking money away on the old black-and-white house at Long Itchington at the rate of £35 a week.

April 19, 1920. Sir G. came to terms with the Colliery Company on Saturday. I thought it a jolly good thing at the time, but am beginning now to doubt it. All the stored-away plans for gardens, garden-terraces, etc. are being hauled out ready to go on with this summer. I look like having my hands full.

June 17, 1922. (Farming) losses make it very difficult to get any pay out of Sir G. . . . I was a fool for turning down that road-surveying job!

Then there was the Lake Pavilion. My father had not even been able to begin it yet. "Such a misfortune for you two boys", he would often remark.

His ideas on it, however, had taken a more definite shape than when we left him, indulging in airy vistas the day before the war of 1914 broke out, at the end of *Great Morning*. After the war was finished, he formulated the scheme in a page or two which he read aloud to me. The severely practical note he occasionally adopted in this paper helped him, I think, to come to regard the structure as something quite simple, neither extravagant nor illusory, and further, as a duty he owed the world.

It is strange that, since writing the end of *Great Morning*, when I visited Montegufoni in May 1946 to see what damage it had suffered from the Second World War, I should have found these notes which I had not seen for twenty and more years. My father's study was not one of the rooms which had been used for housing the great pictures from the Uffizi and elsewhere, but had, together with other apartments, been occupied in turn by German, English, American, Indian and New Zealand troops. The dusty tiled floor was a litter of papers, the majority of them manorial records from Derbyshire and family papers of the seventeenth century. My father's notebooks and extensive collection of miscellaneous jottings had, for the most part, disappeared: but one paper caught on a draught from under a door suddenly fluttered towards me. It was the Lake Pavilion Memorandum!

LAKE PAVILION

Purpose. For visitors to be able to bathe and breakfast there, and if desired spend the whole day on the lake. As a place for afternoon tea. Occasionally for entertaining a large number at tea or for small luncheon parties. For the owner when the house is empty to be able to be there alone for study or business.

Site. The site demands shade. It catches the last rays of the evening sun almost an hour after the Hall and gardens have lost it. The prevailing wind is also from the west. There should be some planting near the pavilion on this side.

Materials. Brick and stucco, for the pillars iron and stucco or cast concrete. The side walls will be plain brick with arcade motive in stucco and should rise from a base. The floors may be of rubber, to avoid injury from boots and from skates. The foundations of concrete in mass formed with flank facings.

Plan. A bathing-pool in a pillared rectangle like the old bath at Bath, but open to the sky. A balcony shaded by an arched pergola will surround it above the pillars. There will be 16 pillars, namely four at each end and six at each side. They should have bases, in order to give interest to the reflections in the pool, and might have capitals with water lilies at the corners, as with the quadrangle at Lecce. There will be a semicircular apse at the further end, which may be combined with a double staircase. It should be possible to floor over the pool, as it might be wanted some day to have music or dance there. The pool should be lined with blue tiles. There should be a velarium of red, and another of yellow to draw over it from above. The pillars must of course be white, in order to reflect well. The back walls might be sea-green.

I would have preferred to put in front of the building a pillared vestibule with a parlour on one side of it and a kitchen on the other. But on account of cost this should be omitted: it can be added later if desired. The entrance will then be by three arches straight into the passage which runs round the pool, off an hexagonal landing platform. The place to lunch will be in the north-west corner of the said passage, by a window giving the lake view. There are advantages in being less overlooked, and in the pool opening more directly upon the lake and being better lighted.

The balconies above will be shaded by an arched pergola covered with flowering creepers, and will have small pavilions at each corner. It will be possible to set tables here for a large number of people to have tea.

Dimensions. These will settle themselves. The floor of the balconies should be not less than 18 nor more than 22–24 feet above the water. The spaces under the pergola must be 8 (?) feet broad to enable people to sit at tea at a two-foot table, and there must be an inner passage for service. Remember the master-passage round the inside of the court at Castel del Monte.

The building will in any case be too big for the lake, and therefore every device must be used to break it up and give it scale, in order to prevent it making the lake look small.

Floor level. Two steps above the high-water level. Above flood level.

Other buildings. A caretaker's cottage and a tower, both on the west. The lower story of the tower will open into the passage round the pool and may be used for dining in on cooler days when a fire is required. The first-floor will open on the balcony, under the pergola. The floor above will be a study-bedroom, with *bifora* windows.

The caretaker's rooms will also be on the west side. The lower windows will open to the pool, those above to the balcony. The approach to the pavilion will be across a drawbridge close to the tower, and up to the balconies by a wooden stairway covered by a wooden canopy.

Well, he was afraid, he remarked after reading his scheme to me, that he could not get it all done before he left, "But I certainly ought to try to make a start with it". . . . And before emigrating, there remained several other, smaller, more immediate matters to be attended to, the details arranged.

For example, there was the matter of costume. As the day of departure drew near, he worried about what clothes to wear at the Castle—for, just before the restoration of public order by the Fascists, there had been much lawlessness, and not long ago, in the very neighbourhood, a case or two had occurred of bandits equipped with fire-arms, who had stopped motor-cars on the more deserted portions of the mountain roads and had demanded money. Walking in the park at Renishaw, with Sacheverell on one side and with me on the other, he discussed with us the form of dress most suitable to the circumstances and to the coming winter. "I shall stick to my grey wide-awake," he said, "though I think I had better now have leggings and boots, rather than trousers and shoes: certainly I must have a belt, with a revolver: and over my coat one of those new transparent blue raincoats." To this costume in his mind's eye, we persuaded him to add a dagger in his belt. The picture of a swashbuckler which gradually emerged from the discussion amused both Sacheverell and me; but my father remarked severely, "For *me*, it's a serious matter!"

There was also much business to be transacted, much writing to be done. He composed and sent letters, identical in terms, to the Chancellor of the Exchequer and the Archbishop of Canterbury. In them he pointed out that it was a hard thing for an old man to be driven out of his own home by the burden of taxation: but there it was, in future his dear son would pay, and he was setting out, with the capital sum he had acquired in his lifetime, to make a new career for himself and his descendants in Italy. (He did not add that he intended to come to stay with me when it was possible.) The manner in which he viewed the sacrifice he was making, and the self-identification he indulged in in his own mind, is visible in his "literary work", as he used to phrase it, of the time. He was writing the first chapter of the family history.[1] I quote the following passage to illustrate the parallel which to his own contentment he was able to furnish. First I must explain that the ancestor to whom he alludes was starting on a pilgrimage to the Holy Land.

It was in mid-May of the year 1299 that Walter de Boys set out upon his journey; in mid-May, when the long northern winter was over at last and a spell of fine weather had made the Derbyshire roads fit for wayfaring. On that morning the house stood empty; for the first time since it was built there was no one, not even a dog, within the walls. At the head of the village, just where the road begins to rise towards the ridgeway, a small crowd had gathered round a tall, grey-bearded man clad in a red-brown sclavine, or hooded robe of wool, with a cross of white cloth sewn upon the shoulder, a purple-grey tunic, dark hose, and broad-rimmed, low-crowned hat of felt lying upon his shoulders and fastened under the chin with tasselled strings. By him was the old horse which had borne him eight years before as a mounted archer in the Scottish expedition, and was now to carry him on his last campaign. . . .

Standing at a little distance were some of the bond-tenants of the manor, poor cottars and bordars, who had their holdings at Ridgeway; a shorter, sallower, shifty, cringing folk; some of the men fresh from the plough, others, and even a few women, bearing hoes for weeding, or the green wooden mallets with which they had been breaking clods in the common field. . . .

Walter bade farewell to his friends, embraced his grandson John, who was but a little lad, and turned weeping to his mother, spoke to the farm-servants and to the old shepherd in his long robe of russet wool, acknowledged the salutations of the rest, and mounting his horse turned to the road above him. His two sons walked with him across the moor, which near the village was scattered with ancient yews and overgrown with an extraordinary number of wild, stunted hollies. . . .

Walter moved on slowly with his sons, speaking but little, for the English were ever a silent folk, and all that ought to be said had been said already. He had parted his lands between them, keeping only for himself the little house and garden at Barlborough, which was to be the refuge of his old age if he returned alive. He had gathered in all that was owing him for rent and wool and corn, to provide for his

[1] *The Story of the Sitwells*. Though most of it was already set up in proof by the Oxford University Press, this long book still remained unfinished at the time of my father's death. Copies of the proofs were struck off and I presented them for the use of students to various museums in England and America.

journey. He had stood again by the green hillock in the churchyard under which his wife lay sleeping, had ridden over to bid farewell to his married daughters, had given what counsel he could to his sons, summing up for them the lessons of a stormy life; and now for the first time free from all earthly care, he saw the world he was leaving as he had never seen it before, drinking in its beauty with the heightened perception, the enhanced senses of a dying man. . . .

So much for his prototype. By now, he had fallen badly into the mock-gothic idiom, and later, when he had reached the Castello, he made the following entry: "In mid-September, 1925, the Lady Ida and I set out, with fair wind, for France, and thence to Italy, to make a new home for ourselves. Before leaving, I had divided my lands and goods between my two sons, and collected the rents and debts due to me: those which I could not collect, I forgave: we propose to settle in the ancient Castle of Montegufoni, which I purchased in Osbert's name in 1906."

It was a pity, he reflected, that Walter had found so many difficulties to contend with, and had not been able, when he divested himself of his land, to tie up the income for a few decades so that no-one at all could receive it—a much better plan! But in some ways people had been singularly thoughtless in the Middle Ages. . . . There were other differences, he reflected. He had left the family home in mid-September, not mid-May, and the old horse, the Arab charger[1] which had carried him through the Volunteer exercises at Scarborough, had not, he was obliged to admit, supported him as a mounted archer in the Scottish campaign. His two sons, again, would, he feared, prefer to accompany him by motor or rail rather than on foot—recklessly extravagant, though it was true that

[1] A letter from Maynard Hollingworth to Peveril Turnbull, in the Estate Correspondence, dated 16th July 1909, says: " Sir George has sent his old *Arab Charger* to Renishaw. He was captured at the battle of Tel-el-Kebir in 1882. We shall soon have a menagerie. . . ." This Arab stallion, Abdul, which my father had bought from the Colonel of Volunteers whom he succeeded, lived to a great age, and was an unusual animal. His tongue had been cruelly cut, rather in the shape of a fern, with incisions each side, a trick the Arabs were said to employ to make the mouth more gentle. He was so old that he had to be fed on cooked food, as his teeth were ground down to the extent that he could not manage to eat anything else. He was probably about forty when he died, just before the First German War, and was buried in the north park at Renishaw.

they would have to pay for it themselves! And perhaps, too, he had left a rather bigger margin for himself than Walter de Boys had—but it was in the family interest. The children, he was afraid, had no idea what an advantage it was to them to have been granted a father so capable and versed in affairs, and who had spent fifty years in forming his taste. They did not seem much interested, either, in "the lesson of a stormy life". . . . To revert to Walter, the villeins, he was sorry to notice, were rather in control at present both at home and abroad. . . . On the other hand, the place looked lovely still. It had been sad, leaving it.

My mother took the change philosophically, except for her fear that she would not get the English newspapers punctually.

"The Government muddle everything," she would remark.

Certainly it was a new life for my father and mother. . . . The first night was to be spent at Boulogne, because a long journey, he averred, tired his back, and probably too because, an ancient town, it had lain on the old pilgrim route—a fact which always now greatly influenced the direction of his travelling. Unlike Walter de Boys, my father took his two sons with him. Our adventures, which ranged in tone from tragedy to farce and back again, started on the cross-Channel steamer, where my mother sat on deck, near a couple of parents who were on their way to visit the grave of their son, who had been killed at the Battle of the Somme in 1916. On the boat the poor father had a heart attack; his first one. My mother, with a kindly impulse to help, said, "I've the very thing! The doctor has given me some stuff for the heart. Call Frieda, and tell her to get it out of my bag!" Unfortunately, the action of my mother's heart was fast, that of the traveller slow: the medicine at once further retarded it, and he grew rapidly worse. At Boulogne, an ambulance had to be called to meet him at the quay. My father sat near by, watching, and remarking from time to time, "One day your mother will be the death of someone!" or "Poor man, you'd have thought having to go to see his son's grave was enough!" . . . I never heard whether he recovered.

Meanwhile it was found that my father had told his servant to register all the luggage through to Paris, where we were not going: there was no way of obtaining it until the next day, and we were doomed to pass a miserable night without our belongings at Boulogne, in a large seaside hotel with interior walls of a paper-like thinness. By the time we arrived at the hotel my father, unprepared for the brand of gothic discomfort with which he was thus faced—the System had been put out of action by the loss of equipment—was in a far from good humour. My brother and I went upstairs to see our bedrooms, and as we came down the double staircase, mean in its Louis XV hotel pretensions, we could hear my father indulging in the curious buzzing-like humming we knew so well, for he always made this noise when irritable or angry. He was walking up and down the hall with a rapid, impatient gait, just outside the dining-room.

"It sounds exactly like a bluebottle," I remarked to my brother.

At that moment my father approached, and looking in the direction of the dining-room, said at once, and in character: "I was just wondering which table to settle on!" That we laughed—and it was difficult not to do so—made the atmosphere still more uneasy.

Baveno, on Lake Maggiore, was always my father's first Italian stopping-place, and we set out for it the next day, going straight through on the train-de-luxe,—for here my father's Walter de Boys parallel broke down—while Robins and Frieda came on by a cheaper train. Directly Robins arrived he went up to my father's room. It was about two in the afternoon, and he found the old gentleman resting. He was in bed, as usual with the head of it turned against the light, so that he lay facing the door, and he was wearing a coat over his pyjamas. As Robins came in, his master looked at him severely, and remarked:

"You've again forgotten my keys, Robins! I've told you repeatedly not to let me travel without them."

Robins crossed behind him, and taking up the keys, which were lying on the dressing-table beside a heavy gold watch and chain, as they had been taken out of his pocket by my father when he had undressed, said, "I knew I hadn't forgotten them. Here they are, Sir George, with your watch!"

Without looking round, my father said, "No they're not! And by forgetting them, you've put me to a great deal of trouble and expense. I've had to force the locks of all the luggage."

As he finished speaking, pandemonium broke loose in the passage outside. There were sounds of sobbing and shouting, even screams. Robins rushed from the room and found two ladies, the manager, valets and porters and maids in furious altercation. He remarked, too, what he had not observed when he came in, all my mother's and father's luggage lying there, and at once noticed that there seemed more of it than usual. . . . At this moment the quarrellers united and attacked him in a body. What did he mean by it? Had other people's property no value for him? They would call in the Carabinieri: he would soon be shut up in a cell. It was a scandal! Other phrases of the same kind poured out. . . . The explanation of all this disturbance was that my father had not only broken open his own luggage and that of my mother, but also two large trunks which had been lying near it, outside neighbouring doors. These had been placed there, packed and locked, ready to be taken to Baveno station, in order to be registered to Paris by the train-de-luxe, in which the owners of the two boxes were travelling. The train was due to start in an hour's time. Indeed, the two ladies had just been leaving in the omnibus, when they looked for their luggage and discovered what had occurred. The locks were destroyed beyond repair, the contents in disorder, turned upside-down as if a Customs-House officer had been running wild through them.

Robins escaped back into my father's room, and told him what had happened. My father calmly bolted the door, and said: "I'm afraid I really can't help other people's troubles!"

Eventually the manager found two other trunks (my father refused to contribute a centime to the cost), and the two poor ladies hurriedly re-packed and, still in a woebegone condition, just caught the ordinary passenger train, on which, no doubt, they were compelled to sit up all night.

Even after this, the new life did not move at once into an easier rhythm. . . . The weather was unexpectedly bad. It rained without ceasing: and we sat silent at luncheon, in a bay window overlooking the lake. It was like being in an aquarium—sky, lake, land, were all water. And we had to drink water, too—for thus embarking on a new career had increased my father's attention to economy, and we were not allowed wine, though it was the beverage of the country. At least, however, my father's decorative sense never deserted him and one particularly cold, wet day, after sweeping aside the waiter's suggestion of a bottle of red wine, he remarked with the familiar flutter of his hand, as water was brought in a light-blue jug:

"That's always been my theory: water should be served in a glass jug, with just a touch of blue in it."

To which my mother added, in a melancholy but rather angry tone:

"Yes, George—and a gold fish!"

All these superficially humorous incidents were, of course, only the minor episodes of a life in many directions tragic, and certainly unsuited to its times: they gained their humour from the often grave and always resourceful character of the man, and the dignity of person against which they were displayed. Such was the strength of will my father exercised that argument on any point with him was outside the bounds of possibility. One could only protest, make a gesture, or ridicule; he would never listen to reason now, and, as ever, that he could be in the wrong was inconceivable to him. Thus even such occurrences as I have just narrated produced an extra sense of frustration in those who shared in them.

Sacheverell and I had soon been able to stand it no longer. We had been with our parents without a break for many weeks, and decided to leave them and proceed to Milan, where they were to join us five days later. To our surprise, my father welcomed the plan. He remarked, "A capital idea of yours. I like Milan. We'll stay in a hotel near the railway station, and then if it rains and your mother is bored, she can always go for a walk in it. She'll love it."

To me, it seemed an unattractive prospect for her, and I said so, but he replied, "No, no, no! Nothing more delightful. Always something going on."

After the five days had elapsed, we waited in vain. Not until two more days had passed did my mother and father arrive. It transpired that the rain had continued (never, the manager had assured them, had such a thing been known before in the early autumn), the ground floor of the hotel had been flooded, and they had eventually been obliged to leave by punt from a first-floor window—an adventure which, I am sure, had never occurred to Walter de Boys. The new life was proving to be a strange experience.

The shack in which a fresh start in life was to be made looked more imposing, immense, dilapidated yet splendid, than ever, as we approached it that September day. We were driving in my father's motor-car, the first he had owned, and the body of which, as the reader may remember, had been specially built for him. Even my father's place, however, was far from comfortable, because its antique lorry engine, if it allowed progress of any kind—since often it would go on strike altogether—would indulge in a startling series of thumps, bumps and explosions for which, throughout the long life of this commodious instrument of torture, no adequate explanation was ever forthcoming: and this again, since he judged even motors in terms of his own, furnished him with a very poor opinion of this whole form of locomotion. Nevertheless, today the machine conducted us decorously enough, to what was to be for their remaining years my mother's and father's home.

Montegufoni was now a very different place from what it had been when my father bought it. The courts had been cleared of their accretions of buildings, so that vistas of other rooms or of courtyards could be obtained from every room in the house. The vegetables, lettuces and Indian corn and tomatoes, had been removed from the terraces, and Tuscan roses bloomed month by month in their place. The oleander, in size a tree, which had been moved, flowered now in the middle of a small box parterre my father had made in the Cardinal's Garden: but in spite of alterations, the main changes were still to come. This vast labyrinth of a building, in which for the past thirteen years, since he had bought it, there had been perpetual discoveries and openings-up, and renovating and repainting, was in the next fifteen years never to know an hour's rest from structural repairs and decoration: it was being continually carried back, pinned down to a past that—like the present—only existed in my father's mind. During this period, both my mother and father were to find a comparative contentment, even happiness, they had never yet known, for my mother liked the climate, and the life in Florence, and my father enjoyed the absence of life in the house. Another rhythm and tempo had been substituted for the Renishaw comedy, those of the *Commedia dell' Arte*. The old play of my father's aloofness, and lack of interest in people, the largeness and smallness of his mind, with its contradictory layers of intense nonconformity and yet of respect for the conventions, against my mother's unthinking, easy, unfailing sociability, and complete want of intellect or esthetic understanding, was acted once again in this new setting, still more grandiose, romantic, and yet in a sense derelict (for it was without life and belonged only to the theatre), so that the action had now the fullest sweep and scope. My mother, for example, would ask twenty people to luncheon, and forget to tell either my father or the butler or chef; indeed it would pass from her mind altogether. Suddenly, just as my father was having a quiet early luncheon, the guests would arrive, tired and hungry after their long mountain run—that was the sort of incident which would occur regularly, affording, as it were, a theme for variation. . . . As for my father, nobody, when he was out of his study, would know where to find him, though he would be in the house or on the terrace: one moment he would be inspecting the well in the cellars; the next, peasants, wandering below, would be astonished to see Il Barone at the top of the tower, with his glasses to his eyes. Sometimes they would think they descried him there after dusk, high up under the sky, outlined against it in the lily-like opening, until they began to believe that he was an astrologer practising his craft, telling the course of the future. Actually, he was more concerned with the earth than formerly. He began, too, almost to *like* people in the excitement he derived from showing them the Castello, and what he had done to it.

As yet, it was hardly a comfortable dwelling, for heating and electric light had not so far been installed, and as usual in my father's houses, the largest rooms, such as the Gallery, were badly arranged and had no chairs in which it was possible to sit with ease: he would take at least two years, sometimes ten, to think out how to dispose the furniture in one room alone. My mother slept in an ancient gilded iron bed, in a room like a cave, divided into two halves, the outer being painted with fantastic landscapes, gardens and villas, while the sky was full of swarms of cupids, some rosy, others negroid and equipped with bats'-wings. This had not yet been furnished in character: but much else had been done. In especial, my father had collected beds, the finest in Italy, great constructions supported by twisted and gilded pillars and carrying carvings of vine and rose, but, further, galleries and painted halls were all full of fine furniture and rather mediocre pictures. He would lead the party round—the tour would take at least an hour—until at last he came to the chamber on the first floor painted by Gino Severini (for the idea of which, as the reader knows, my brother and I shared the responsibility). The vitality and breathing life of this administered, amid the encircling deadness, a shock to him every time he entered it. He invariably forgot its existence, opened the door—for it is a passage room—, rushed in at the head of his rout, and was brought up sharp by the sight of the frescoed walls on which was depicted, more true in its purity and essence than the real landscape outside, of which it had been born, a landscape in which his contemporaries and companions of the *Commedia* moved, or sat drinking wine under the shade of the vines. He would gaze at them for a moment, rather sadly, until, summoning his point of view, he would give a patronising laugh, and remark, with a strong note of disapproval in his voice, and always in Italian,

"Non è mio gusto!"

Then he would gallop out again, followed by his motley pack. . . . Occasionally he would administer shock-treatment to one of the band. I recollect, for instance, a rebuke, rather reminiscent of *Alice in Wonderland*, which he delivered to a very nervous young Englishman, anxious to please.

"Do you see the beam up there?" my father asked him.

"Yes, Sir George," he replied.

"Well, that's very clever of you," my father said, "because there isn't one!"

Many of the visitors were distinguished in the arts, but my father and mother never knew who they were. Sometimes, therefore, when I was in England, my mother would, if she remembered the names, write to me, to make enquiries concerning the identity of her guests, or to give me a description of them. And I found that my mother's pen-pictures were always more vibrant and full of point than my father's. "A Mr. D. H. Lawrence came over the other day," she wrote, "a funny little petit-maître of a man with flat features and a beard. He says he is a writer, and seems to know all of you. His wife is a large German. She went round the house with your father, and when he showed her anything, would look at him, lean against one of the gilded beds, and breathe heavily."

Time had supplied my father with a new foil for his comedy; another, that is to say, in addition to Henry. This was Signor Bracciaforte, a charming, amiable, child-like, elderly antique-dealer, who had begun life as a painter. My father's only friend in Italy, he played an enthusiastic Bouvard to his Pécuchet and excelled in the pricking of the bubbles which in conjunction they had blown. Together they would search for antique copper wash-basins of the fifteenth century, and hat-racks and coat-hangers of the seventeenth. Sometimes, embarking on even more abstract antiquarian wild-goose chases, they would motor for whole days at a time in each other's company. On one occasion, for example—and it always remains in my mind as the best instance of the kind of episode which at this period of his life was so usual—, my father decided to motor to Spezzia along the old Pilgrims' Route, in order to identify to his own satisfaction the places mentioned in a medieval romance. Bracciaforte had, of course, to go too; but worse, my father insisted that Sach-everell and I, who were staying with him at the time on one of our short visits, should also accompany him. It was plain that he was set on it, would be offended if we refused, and so the only thing was to accept the position and make the best of it. As we bumped drearily along the ancient road, in our almost equally ancient motor—already, even in those early days, known in Florence as the Ark—, my brother kept on saying to me, "Don't be irritable or interfere! Leave them alone, and something funny is sure to happen!" This he said since I was inclined to be annoyed because my father had already, by his continual changing of plans, contrived to lose for me the whole of the manuscript of *Before the Bombardment*.[1] Now, however, that my father had already found much that he had wanted to see, he began to be pleased with life, and in consequence to alter less his programme for each day. It only remained for him to trace the site of the Castle of Ogier or Ogher the Dane, a celebrated character of the Romances, a Paladin of Charlemagne and a ward of the fairy Morgan le Fay. It was difficult, he admitted, to obtain the clue to the exact whereabouts of this stronghold, but certainly it had existed—he was sure of it—somewhere in the precise neighbourhood where we now found ourselves. Happily, while he talked, the motor gave a sudden leap like a bucking horse and broke down in the piazza of a very small hill town: which, with its three converging streets of stone houses and its shop windows hung with Bologna sausages, afforded a perfect background for old-fashioned pantomime action and humour. Bracciaforte immediately got out and wandered off, down one of the crow's-foot alleys, first framing in his broken baby-English his invariable cue or theme-song on such an excursion. "We go look old t'ing: maybe we find somet'ing: 'oo know?" But my father's mind at the moment was too much occupied with thoughts of the Paladin to let him join in the hunt. His eyes were carefully searching the piazza, scanning the façades. After some moments, he noticed the name over a shop, and suddenly blazed up into an excitement unusual for him. "But look over there! This must be the very place! That shop is called *OGHERI*! Probably its owners are actually descended from the Great Dane himself!! Fetch me my notebook at once—it's in my hat-box—and I'll make a note of it!" At this moment, Bracciaforte, who had drifted back, and had heard what my father had said, remarked,

[1] It was found a few weeks subsequently.

"But that not *OGHERI*, Sir George! that *DROGHERIA*! The first two letters and the last, they 'ave fallen themselves off: these little shop, they no money to repair."

After that, things went rather flat for a while.

During the journey, however, my father and Signor Bracciaforte were still engaged, as they had been for a long time, in buying breastplates and cuirasses and other odds and ends of ironmongery, in order to invest the Castle Armoury with an impression of authenticity. Sacheverell and I considered the money would have been better expended on the purchase of modern pictures, or upon objects of beauty in general. We became so bored with this, to us, emasculate worship of objects utterly dead, that had never possessed any esthetic appeal, while at the same time they had long ago lost any usefulness they had formerly possessed, and so chagrined, too, at the large sum spent on their pursuit and capture that, soon after we returned to the Castle, we placed in the Armoury among the other pieces an old stove-pipe we had found in a corner of the cellar at Montegufoni. This grooved and tubular shape in iron so greatly resembled the armour in design and surface, that for about ten days my father accepted it; that is to say he did not notice it as alien and obtrusive but displayed, as it was, among his other rusty acquisitions. But one afternoon Mr. and Mrs. Bernhard Berenson came over to pay us a visit, and my father showed them round the Castle. When he entered the Armoury, he took up the stove-pipe in an absent-minded way, and observed,

"Rather an interesting braslet which my artist friend Signor Bracciaforte and I found a week or two ago at Castel Tedesco!"

Then, as he took hold of it and lifted it up to show to them, he examined it himself more carefully, and a new expression came into his pale eyes. In a tone of disgust he remarked,

"*Purely Puerile!* . . . Another joke of the Boys!"

He had, of course, no notion of Berenson's celebrity, distinction or even identity. Indeed, as my father grew older, he plainly lost his bearings and ceased to know any longer who was alive and who dead. I have already described how he invented a novelist who did not exist: now, in somewhat similar but more macabre fashion, he planned to give a party.

"I thought next May, I'd give an Artists' Party, Osbert," he announced to me; for artists were still a tribe, like the Levites, set apart. "May is always the best month here. And it would be nice if you two boys could come out to join me. We'd get some really interesting people together, who could be relied upon to entertain one another—far less tiring for the host!"

"Who would you ask?" I enquired cautiously, well knowing already that he would not, of course, ask any of our own friends among painters, and was, indeed, quite unaware of their names or profession when they arrived to stay at Renishaw: nor would he be likely to ask the older masters we admired, of whom Picasso was the chief. But I was startled when, as he reeled off for me the list, I comprehended both how thoroughly he had thought it out, and that all of his proposed guests, Whistler, Degas, Renoir, Rodin, Lalique, Sargent, at least possessed one thing in common: they were all dead! Some had died recently, their corpses still surrounded by candles in the press, the bones of others had been immured for years in their tombs. It would have been a party only to be thought of *after* the Judgment Day, when the dead rise up and shake on their flesh again; a party of ghosts, which would have added known names to those anonymous spirits whose presence could surely at times be detected in the sensitive, dry, Italian air of chamber and corridor.

Meanwhile, a flicker of daily life was afforded by the constant coming and going to Florence of my mother, who seemed always either just on the point of leaving for the city, or to have just returned, and to be walking slowly through the courtyard with a motor-load of friends she had imported. . . . My father usually preferred to stay behind at Montegufoni. He occupied as his study a room in a good strategical position for comedy, for it was situated right in the middle of the Castle. Moreover its three doors faced the vistas of rooms leading north, east and west: while, in addition, a person entering any of the courtyards had to pass near by, and the two windows to the south—the only ones except those in his bedroom wired against mosquitoes—afforded a detailed view of the

The consummate dilatante

terraces below. In fact, it was impossible to go from any one part of the house or garden to another without walking by, or through, his room. It smelt of strong Turkish cigarettes. Two high painted beams obscured a ceiling frescoed with one of the several triumphs of Cardinal Acciaiuoli. Under this was a design in grisaille, and at one side of the door there hung a picture without a frame, representing the Fair at Impruneta, on the other, a frame without a picture, showing, like a mirror, a blank space of brown wall: and never, it seemed, the twain could meet. The room was crowded with furniture, a large octagonal centre table, a sideboard in *noce*, two console-tables in brown and gold, with marble tops, all littered with miscellaneous objects. Its air was somewhat that of a superior—or, at times, inferior—antique-dealer's private apartment, full both of valueless possessions that he liked and of others that, because he could not get rid of them, he had taken to himself; somewhat that, too, of a medieval alchemist's laboratory, so that one expected to see a skull and retorts on the table. Instead, there were several early charters, documents belonging to the Manor of Eckington, and many books on pedigrees, modern scientific thought, nineteenth-century philosophy, the Black Death (to which he still remained faithful), pamphlets on the correct methods of making coffee, volumes of photographs of Italian gardens, and innumerable fragments of which it was difficult to tell the purpose: half a cupid in carved wood, a bit of a reliquary devoured by death-watch beetles, a broken, rusty cuirass, part of an early piano-front, a silver two-pronged fork, very rickety in the prongs, a coat of arms from a smashed terracotta vase, with a portion of a wreath of fruit attached to it, and countless scraps of brocade, tiles and *petit-point*, as well as the lids of Venetian boxes and enamelled watch-cases and a few pieces of rough glass bowls and cylinders. There was a sofa for him to lie down on; but all the chairs were covered with books and boxes of papers. Between the windows stood a cupboard, full of neatly docketed cardboard boxes in a murrey colour, containing his manuscript notes, all, as usual, assembled under the wrong labels. With the sight and names of many of them the reader is familiar: others are new to him.

Reresby and Sacheverell Pedigrees.
Osbert's Debts.
The History of the Acciaiuoli.
The Black Death at Rotherham.
Walter de Boys Sets Sail.
Sachie's Mistakes.
English Pilgrims in Tuscany in the Fourteenth Century.
The Use of the Bed.
Chaucer's Presumed Visit to Boccaccio.
Boccaccio as Guest.
The Sitwell Investments.
Acorns as an Article of Medieval Diet.
My Inventions.
Ogher The Dane.
My Advice on Poetry.
Byzantine Herbals.
The Best Methods of Making Wine.
The Errors of Modern Parents.
Pig-keeping in the Thirteenth Century.
A Castle of Romance.
The Character of the Villeins.
Arthurian Romances,
   and
The Art of the Loggia.

From this room, my father led the comedy, and directed the alterations, usually in company with Bracciaforte and a character whose name nobody ever found out. He was known as *Il Professore*, and it was his duty to superintend the scraping and restoring and faking that was everywhere in progress. It was difficult sometimes to tell what were the improvements on which the workmen were engaged. Once, for example, I remember my father taking me into a room where six plasterers had been employed for a fortnight, from early morning till dusk, scratching the walls like a mischief of monkeys.

"Do you notice any change here?" he asked.

And when I replied, "No, none," he said with an air of intense gratification, "Good, that's just what I've been aiming at!"

Robins had married early in 1924, and had left my father's service, entering mine once more at Renishaw. In his place, Henry Moat had gone back to look after my father. . . . Henry took to life at the Castello with joy. Now he presided with a still more immense dignity over my mother's luncheon parties, and the sound of his tread as he came to announce a guest was equivalent in stateliness to a procession. He still retained his observant eye, and I remember his telling me of an incident that had occurred when the three Ruritanian ladies-in-waiting, who were paying a visit to Florence, had come over to luncheon at Montegufoni. They had sat stiff as back-boards at the table, images of decorum and etiquette: but, according to Henry, at sight of the large old lemon trees on the terrace, the principles of the youngest sister had at last given way. Balkan peasant ancestry had begun to assert itself, and he had seen her snatch some of the fruit while she thought no-one was looking. My mother was taking the three ladies back to Florence in the motor, but just as the fair plunderer was going to step in, a shower of lemons began to fall from her stocking, bouncing on the ground. My mother had kindly pretended not to notice. . . . Henry liked the red wine, the peasant girls, the sunshine, the sleepiness. Apart from occasional attacks of the gout from which he now suffered, this period formed a long Indian Summer for him, as it did for my parents. While my mother was in Florence, and my father resting, Henry would retire to read in his small room upstairs, which rather resembled a cabin. Its chief feature was a string which hung across from above the door to above the one small window. From this aerial line were suspended by wooden clips several immense pairs of trousers. His favourite book at this time was Herman Melville's *Moby Dick*, which he had borrowed from me. When next he visited England with my father, spending some months there, he lent the novel to the various retired sea-captains who were his friends and neighbours in the fishermen's quarter of Whitby, and who also so greatly enjoyed it that the volume was only returned to me after some two years, its pages dog-eared and covered with their powerful thumb-marks. "By Gum," Henry would remark, "It's a grand book! You can fair smell them Whales!" After reading it, he associated the Great White Whale with my father, and would often refer to him under that name. Thus once at Montegufoni, as he was going to my father's room, he met Constant Lambert in the passage, and confided in him, "Moby Dick's up to his usual tricks today! . . . I don't think

Plate X

THE COURT OF THE DUKES OF ATHENS, MONTEGUFONI
By John Piper

Plate XI

THE GROTTO, MONTEGUFONI; THE PEASANTS STONING JUNO
By John Piper

I can stand this job for another moment more than seven and a half years!"

The trials were, indeed, numerous. Henry would have to call my father at five and bring him breakfast not long afterwards. My father would then read *The Times* of two days before, and other journals and letters, till seven, when he would get up. At eight he would go round the Castle in detail, telling all the workmen to stop what they were doing, and do something else instead. Then he would consider the garden, interfere with the gardeners, and go back to write in his room, probably various severe letters. If he intended a letter to be really disagreeable, he would pen it many times, at each correction infusing into it a fresh but icy venom. After this fashion he would both perfect it, and also be able to keep a copy. Now, while we watch, for example, he must pen one so as to give his English lawyers "a rap over the knuckles", he must dispute the item 4s. 8d. in a London chemist's bill, write to the tailor on the subject of turn-up trousers, forward hints on Florentine medieval banking to Messrs. Coutts (who would be sure to be interested), tell Hollingworth how to plant beech-trees, and he must instruct the firm from which he obtained cigarettes on divers points, such as that they used the wrong kind of paper for rolling. He must also remember to enter notes in his note-book. He would have luncheon, usually by himself, at 11.30; then a siesta till three, when he would get up again, and go the rounds of the Castle once more, this time informing the men that they were gravely at fault, had misunderstood what he had said earlier, must undo everything they had done since, and go back to what he had stopped them doing in the morning. The Italian plasterers and painters, in their round caps made of newspaper and their light overalls, with their faces covered with fine dust from the walls, seemed thoroughly to enjoy all this. But Bracciaforte and *Il Professore* became sunk in melancholy. "You fader, Sir George, 'e no understand", Signor Bracciaforte would say. And my mother would sometimes confide to me, "It's not very amusing for me here alone. The three of them never speak after dinner. Your father sits in one corner, looks up and says 'Ba!', Bracciaforte says 'Ma!', and the Professore, 'Pa!'"

K

In other directions, life had not attained to this dadaist simplification. What, for example, rendered Henry's day a little difficult, was that nearly all the Italians working at the Castle were called *Guido*, including the acting chauffeur, the son of the *contadino*, and the plasterer, known as Guido il Muratore.

"Any orders for the motor today, Sir George?"

"Yes, Henry; tell Guido to drive into Florence, fetch Guido back here, to help Guido with the painting. Guido can wait while Guido has luncheon, and then Guido will take Guido back to Florence and fetch Guido here."

"Sir George, if you are going on like that, I had better give notice before my mind gives way!"

My father and Henry, it will be observed, still had differences of opinion. Thus one winter night when my father was travelling in Sicily, Henry entered his master's bedroom, to tidy it and to take his clothes away, rather later than usual—very late, according to my father's standards, it being about 8 P.M. My father was already in bed, with the light out, and a sharp altercation followed. In the course of it Henry remarked that he did not like having his "head bit off". He then left the room, slamming the door behind him; only to find himself in complete darkness, for in the passage the lights had been turned out by an economically-minded porter. Too proud to go back and open the door, or to ask my father's help, he proceeded on his way, blundered with all his immense weight into a piece of furniture with sharp corners, and for a full week subsequently carried about with him the mark of this misadventure in the shape of two black eyes.

My father was greatly delighted at the turn things had taken, and told me all about it when next I saw him.

"Henry burst into my room late one night in Taormina," he related, "and was very insolent. . . . I suppose the charitable thing would be to think that he'd been indulging in those heavy Sicilian wines (Such a mistake! He's getting on, and should be more careful!). But I'm glad to say, when he left the room, the great man forgot to turn the light on outside, fell against a cupboard, and completely knocked himself out. You never saw such black eyes! Like Turner sunsets. He's been much more civil since. . . . Of course, I haven't mentioned it to him!''

Henry, for his part, complained that during his own long absence my father's manners had deteriorated. He had, his servant averred, abandoned his former dignified choice of language. Previously he had never even been known to use a single colloquialism: but whether owing to my influence—to that knowledge of modern slang which he sometimes alleged I possessed—, I do not know, Henry asserted that now, when he approached his master one morning and politely asked for the settlement of an account, long overdue, my father sidled towards him, and slowly bringing his face very close to that of his servant, pronounced clearly, in quiet but menacing tones, the words,

"SHUT YOUR UGLY MUG, CAN'T YOU!"

"Believe me, Mr. Osbert, you could 'ave knocked me down with a feather, when I 'eard 'im demean 'imself like that,'' Henry added.

On learning this, I decided to make use of the reputation with which my father had endowed me, of being a master of modern slang. The worst of it was, I knew so little of it. Almost less than my father, of whose customary innocence in this respect, I produce, as prelude to what followed now, an example from a year or two earlier.

One afternoon in London, I had gone to see him and found him lying on his bed, with a pleased and meditative expression. He at once remarked to me:

"Dr. Borenius called on me this morning. It appears he wishes to give me a present. Very kind of him, I'm sure. But I don't like putting him to the expense.''

"What sort of a present, Father?''

"A ring—one of those Merovingian rings, I presume. He knows I'm interested in such things, and has lately written on them in the *Burlington* or some other paper.''

"I'd like to see it some time.''

"Well, he said he'd send it to me on Thursday. . . . So any day after that . . .''

There seemed to me something odd about the matter, but it was not until I related to William Walton in the evening what my father had said, that the explanation struck him, and he elucidated it for me; as our friend Borenius himself later confirmed to us.

"Of course what Borenius said was that he'd telephone! 'I'll give you a ring, Sir George, on Thursday!'"

I think that my father, though in general, as we have seen, he disliked receiving presents, was in this instance disappointed. At any rate, he remarked to me a few days later, but without any indication to whom or what the remark applied,

"Such a pity to promise people things, and then forget about them. It is most inconsiderate—really, inexcusable."

So, at Montegufoni that autumn, I decided to experiment. Having first taught my father to substitute for "If I should pass away this month", a favourite phrase of his, the less formal, more intimate, "If I should pop off", which, pronounced with great dignity and pathos, was most effective, I was encouraged to more spectacular flights. He did not always notice things at once if you wanted him to, and so, to make sure, I pronounced in very clear tones to him, for several evenings running, the word *Blotto*, saying, "I don't know why, but I feel completely *BLOTTO* tonight". Finally he remarked it, and asked me what it meant. I replied, it meant tired—very tired.

"A term of military origin, I presume, Osbert?"

"Indian, I should say, Father, like tiffin and mufti, and perhaps muffin."

"Very interesting."

After that he adopted the new expression, and, a few days later, when two ancient American men came over to luncheon, remarked at the end of the meal with genial condescension, "I've had rooms prepared for you for a siesta after lunch, in case you feel *blotto*. I'm completely *blotto* myself!" The two Americans looked astonished, and on their return to Florence complained to their friends that it was not the sort of thing they expected a dignified English gentleman like Sir George to say to them.[1] . . .

---

[1] A few years subsequently the late W. J. Turner heard the story, incorporated it in a not very good play he had written, and made me in some way the victim of it.

Life at Montegufoni, and in Florence, was full of such small incidents. If the winter were severe, the family would usually move to a hotel in the city. From there, Henry would sometimes write to me, and relate the occurrences of the preceding weeks. I give two of these letters in a moment, but first I must explain that he liked sometimes to parody my father's rather arch mock-gothic: hence the form of address: since my father had in recent years taken to sending me startling communications about the Black Death without any preliminary explanation of the fact that the episodes described had happened seven centuries before, and that he had found the references to them in chronicles and other documents in local records or at the British Museum. Of course I preferred these letters from my father, when I had grown accustomed to them and understood their origin, to the sort I more usually received from him, which were for the most part concerned with my financial affairs: but nevertheless, when they were new to me, they used for a moment, when I opened them, greatly to astonish and perturb me. Here is a specimen taken from memory and therefore no doubt imperfect, as well as shorter than in reality, but absolutely true in spirit.

July 21, 1921

DEAREST OSBERT,

Ye Rector and his attendants were travelling along an antient ridgeway from Rotherham to Chesterfield, when, hearing cries for assistance, Ye Rector was alarmed, and he hurried to the ditch (beneath an hedge of hawthorn, now blooming in palest pink and white over the lace of cow parsley, ragged robin, old man's beard and eglantine) and found ye olde fosse full of groaning villeins, dead and dying. By the side of the road was a yeoman, his stout staff beside him, with his dog lying dead at his feet. Both had passed away of ye Black Death. Even ye swine had caught ye infection! It seemed to the Rector that the dread spectre was hidden on every hand. Voices from the sky called *Beware!*—Ever, dear boy, Your affectionate father, GEORGE R. SITWELL.

The letter from Henry, which I believe to be the first of this period, though it is undated, and merely headed Anglo-American Hotel, Firenze, runs:[1]

---

[1] As in other volumes, the original spelling and punctuation have been retained.

LE GALOP FINAL

My dear young Maister,

There has been terrific excitement here, for a time all hands manned ye rigging. A young Spanish gentleman staying in the hotel went to dance at Royola's[1] one afternoon—while he was dancing with a young lady, also from the hotel, he suddenly fell down, stone dead.

Well, when the news reached ye hotel, all ye olde guests sat in the hall, never speaking, holding their pulses in one hand and their watches in the other. But Sir George beat the lot of them, so he retired to bed between tea and dinner on a milk diet. By dinner time he was better and came down and he ate a real good dinner. Here is the menu—

> Minestrone
> Spigola Bollita.   Salsa Mayonnaise
> Pollo Cacciatore
> Suppa Inglese
> Frutta e Caffè!

—though coffee keeps Sir George awake all night, as you know, till he falls asleep.

I am glad to say my rheumatic gout is nearly better now. Fortunately, when it came on, we were here in Florence, with women, wine and tobacco thrown overboard, I feel real proud of myself—I do hope it will last. Sir George changes his plans like the wind. First he talks of Sicilia then the French Riviera. We don't know whats coming next so we are never dull. Yours obedient servant,

Henry Moat.

A word of explanation is perhaps needed concerning Henry's reference above to coffee. My father had a great liking for coffee, and always drank it after meals, though it bears the reputation of being a stimulant to the brain and he complained continually of sleeplessness. I recall that, one summer evening when we had been dining in the garden at Renishaw, Mrs. Nevinson—Richard's mother—who was sitting next my father, looked at his cup and said, "I'm surprised, Sir George, to see you drinking coffee at night," and I remember in particular the melancholy emphasis with which he replied, "Awake anyhow!".

Another letter from Henry, headed Agenzia Egidi, Via Vigna Nuova, gives me news of my father's progress after an operation, for which he had gone into the Hospital of the Blue Nuns at Fiesole.

[1] A night club in Florence.

My DEAR YOUNG MAISTER,

Re Sir G. the Barone is going on first class, but very nervous of himself.

The doctors and nurses reports are that during the operation his (G.R.S's) pulse never varied ever since he sleeps well and eats well the nurse told me quietly for a man of his age he eats too much and must have a good constitution to stand it.

Sir George reports to H.L.[1] "Ah (long drawn) there is no one knows how severe this operation his but me if I had only known it was a quarter as sever I would never have had it," and last week he asked H.L. to ask the nurse "if she thought he (G.R.S.) would recover." Of course he knows perfectly well now he will he did not dare ask a fortnight ago for fear it was a little doubtful. Of course he says he needs building up but the nurse says if he wants more to eat he will have to do with less sleep has he is eating all the time he is awake. He is receiving all letters and answering them himself do write him by return.

Please accept my kindest regards and best wishes. Yours obedient servant, HENRY MOAT.

A further letter, dated May 1931 from the Castle, gives something of the atmosphere of Montegufoni.

DEAR MASTER OSBERT

Some weeks ago Sir Geo and I came to stay at the Castle, and enjoyed ourselves grand though the weather was rather hot, the wine cellar always cool, But then H.L. came and our peaceful days were o'er. Mr and Mrs Sachie were coming with Master Reresby but they have cried off, just as well for the house is full. Sir George keeps very well in health but sometimes very touchy and unreasonable in temper and very awkward to do with the poor workmen must have an uneasy time often nothing done right and their heads bit right off—Sir George has had central heating put in the Castello they are just finishing and the real hot weather is just beginning. He has also had all the W.C's pulled down and they are all down so no-one has anywhere to perch and the language is fearful.

Obviously G.R.S. has forgot his great loss of income because he is carrying on full sail all alterations, a sure sign.

I trust this will find you well in mind body and estate and that you may live a teetotal (not forgetting boiled water cold[2]) and righteous life to the glory of your father who is in Castello di Montegufoni. Amen. Your obedient servant HENRY MOAT.

[1] Abbreviation for Her Ladyship.
[2] Cold Boiled Water was always provided by my father when in economical mood, for his guests to drink. Henry did not approve of it.

Henry's tongue, like his pen, retained its quality. An incident of roughly this period, when my nephew Reresby was four or five, returns to my memory. He went to stay at Montegufoni, accompanied by his nurse, the blackest of negresses from Jamaica, and a woman of great charm, simple cleverness and devotion. Nurse Cole—for such was her name—never proved popular with white servants, who resented waiting on someone of so much darker a hue. Even Henry, broadminded though he was, felt it to be a slight on his dignity; besides, he maintained that she was inquisitive and apt to domineer or, more colloquially, to be 'bossy'. Accordingly, he resolved when she came to Montegufoni to administer a snub if the occasion should offer. . . . The meals had to be carried to her and my nephew up a spiral flight of stone stairs, and one morning, hearing Henry moving about below, she called down to him in her rich voice:

"Mr. Moat, what's on for lunch today? I can't remember."

"Let me see," came the answer in tones kind but firm; then after a pause—"Slices of cold boiled Missionary it is today."

After this, poor Nurse Cole became notably more subdued in manner.

To others he was more genial, and when Constant Lambert and William Walton were staying at Montegufoni in 1928, for the performance of *Façade* at the International Music Festival at Siena, Henry several times entertained them to supper, with plenty of red wine, after the rest of the party had gone to bed. And they needed it, to steel them against the extraordinary events that occurred. William, I remember, took the design Severini had made for *Façade* to Florence: but he could never afterwards remember the address of the scene-painter to whom it had been entrusted for reproduction on the curtain or anything about him except that his name was Barone, that he was about thirty-five and the son of a man who had formerly worked for my father at Montegufoni. As the day grew nearer and the curtain, promised for a certain date, failed to arrive, anxiety grew. A day or two before the performance, my mother said to Edith, "You leave it to me. I'll find the curtain. But I'd like you to come with me in the motor." She then drove to Florence, to the hotel where she and my father often stayed in the winter, and sent the driver in to inform the concierge that she required the names and addresses of all the Barones in Florence: this message the porter misunderstood, taking it to mean that she wanted a catalogue of all those of the rank of Baron, and accordingly he returned with the list; a large list, albeit fortunately the fact that Baron was a comparatively new title in Italy curtailed it. My mother did not look at it, but said, "Guido, drive to every address in turn". On arrival at each, she told the chauffeur to ring the bell, and ask if the owner was in, and inform him in the Italian style that two Noble Ladies awaited him outside. Barones, of one sort or another, would appear, startled, wondering what could be amiss. My mother, who spoke no Italian, fixed each poor nobleman with her dark gaze, and after examining him closely, if he were old, imperturbably announced, "It's not you we want", or, if it seemed likely that he might have a son of the right age and sort, would pronounce the esoteric message:

"*Your* son has *my* daughter's curtain!"

"But, Madam, I 'ave not got 'im!" some of them would reply.

Finally, the day before the performance, the curtain was discovered in Florence by Lady Aberconway, who was staying with us. It had required all her detective instinct to find it: but so anxious was my father to return to the Castle without it, in order that it should not reach us in time to be used, that she was obliged to stamp her foot at him, and personally to watch it being rolled up and then tied to the top of the motor.

The Indian Summer lasted long. My mother, though she could not talk the language, made many friends among Florentines and our Tuscan neighbours. They appreciated her simplicity and impulsive kindness, and could sympathise with, or at any rate understand, her rages. The large rooms, the flowers, the warmth, suited her. She would join in the Comedy both consciously and unconsciously, by continually providing situations in which my father's contradictory qualities—the mainspring of character comedy—were given full play. Through the many autumn hours of sunshine, he would recline on a long wicker chair, aloft in the Cardinal's

Garden, planning and scheming as though death did not exist: and my mother, if she were not in Florence, would sit in a low comfortable arm-chair just inside, by the central window—which was also a door—of the Gallery. As I entered, she would look up from her rattling cloud of dis-membered English newspapers, and would remark—it was one of her favourite labels for him—"Your father's pretty preposterous today!" She habitually ran the alliterative syllables into one word, and added an extra "r"; *pretty-preprostrous*. Then she would gaze, with her large melancholy brown eyes, at the hedge of verbena, the golden mounds of sweet geranium, the scent of which filled the house, just as the bumping and buzzing of large winged beetles and bees outside filled it with the lazy sound of their droning. Occasionally, too, a huge butterfly or some immense droning insect would enter the long room, and flutter or rise and fall under the coved and painted ceiling. Outside the oleander flowered now, its branches and green-grey leaves sprinkled with rosettes of pink blossom, and the few surviving song-birds that the Italian sportsmen had so far failed to shoot found their voices again. The entire parade of light, sound and scent conjured up a vista of endless and immortal summer, fuller perhaps than summer itself, a different season with a rind of gold, and ripe as the ripest fruit. But though she enjoyed all these things, she regarded them as a peasant regards them; and she disliked the conscious display of semi-esthetic pleasures, such as when my father would call, "I'm just going to the lower terrace, to observe the sunset".

"Don't, George! I advise you not to," she would reply, in a voice of discouragement. "I know a lunatic who used always to do that!"

But my father, at this moment, is still sitting in the Car-dinal's Garden, at about four o'clock. The sun has turned the colour of the stucco of the Castle to a rich yellow, and the supports of the Cardinal's coat of arms over the door seem almost to swim in the light, for they are full of baroque action. For a time, he pondered deeply on the details of a new lay-out, placing them in his mind against the principles of garden design which he had formulated and rediscovered. He looked at the parterre he had recently created. People were very stupid over such things. Only the other day a visitor had suggested that it would improve the borders to it if there were more flowers in them; they could not understand that the brown of the earth was an important element, forming a background for the colours of the stocks and ranunculus! . . . Now he changed the line of his thought, stroked his beard, and gave his mind to his descendants—ideally different, in his imagination, from his children—, and the financial edifice he was devising for their advantage increased in intricacy. With age, his will-power had hardened, and his plans became more and more involved. Nor did he ever detect the evident error in his calculations: that when he died, and his death set in motion the involved and secret machine he had created, the one person who understood it and could work it would automatically have ceased to exist. . . . After half an hour or so spent in reading the chart of the future—which he saw always more clearly than the present, and with a delusive perspective that rendered it almost as vivid for him as the past —he began to wonder what the workmen were doing. He looked at the face of his large gold watch. It was almost time for him to go up and give them the benefit of his advice based on a lifetime of experience—or if it were the spring or autumn, my brother and Georgia, and Edith and I, would often be visiting him for a few weeks, and he would feel it his duty to advise and guide "the children": for such we remained to him. Edith's technical experiments, especially, fretted him. He was afraid, he said, she would "do herself no good" by them. For example, in 1928, when we all four of us went to stay at Montegufoni for the International Festival of Modern Music at Siena,[1] my sister had just published *Gold Coast Customs*, and was at the zenith of her first period of poetic achievement—and famous everywhere except in her own home —my father told me he was afraid her satire would "offend people". In reality, she had broken through, as Gosse—the friend of many poets and a man who knew their ways and the possibilities latent in them—had prophesied a few years

---

[1] *Façade* was given twice on the 14th of September 1928, at Siena; on the same day as the *Palco*.

previously that she would, into a new kind of perfection and beauty.

"I think our noble Edith", he had written to a friend, "enjoyed her visit. . . . We both like her very much, and I admire her sincerely. I feel that she is a sort of chrysalis, in a silken web of imperfection, with great talents to display, if only she can break out into a clear music of her own. There is no one I watch with more interest, and her personal beauty and dignity, which are even pathetic, attract me very much."[1]

Alas, after 1929 began the long and mortal illness of our old friend Helen Rootham. And in the next decade, until Helen's death in 1938, the concern my sister felt for her, and the necessity she found herself under to earn money, compelled her to turn away from the natural expression of her being, towards prose: for some ten years she was obliged to abandon poetry. Also her close attendance upon the invalid often prevented her from going with us to Italy.

We liked, I think even more than the spring, the brief, hot days of September and early October, when flowers are blossoming for the second time, and when figs and grapes are carried into the Castle on enormous flat rushwork trays, of a rough oval shape. Then the peasants move slowly everywhere among the leafage of the vines, picking the fruit, the air is full of the odour of must from the vats, great purple stains show on the stone floors by the entrance to the cellars, where the grape juice has run. Everyone is at work, and the Great Court is empty of all movement, of all sound, except for the occasional explosion of a flight of grey, white and tawny pigeons, who leave their perch on the cornice to whirr down to the pavement. On the south side the walls of the Castle have been baked through for months by the Italian sun, and the glitter of the almost olive-green stone makes it seem to be dissolving in the light. Often at such times in the day the vast building seems empty of everything but of the heat pouring in through open windows, or of the equally intense solace of the cool of the inner vaulted and shuttered halls. But though

[1] In a letter dated 31st December 1926 to Siegfried Sassoon: quoted in *The Life and Letters of Sir Edmund Gosse*, by Evan Charteris, K.C. (William Heinemann, Ltd., 1931).

there are these moments of silence and vacancy, the life of the countryside is part of the Castle; it belongs to the soil, and much of its space is still given over to the drying of fruit and making of wine and oil. Forty peasants then still lived in the corner of it. All these practical uses, however, only add to its air, at once ripe, sleepy, dream-like, until age and history seem to invest its walls with a bloom perceptible to the senses, delicate and all-enveloping as the bloom of a grape. The very hamlet under the walls of the Cardinal's Garden exhales the same feeling. Even today, after war has passed over the countryside, the Cardinal's hat in stone, surmounting his marble coat of arms, still hangs over the door of the church: not to be confounded with the chapel in the Castello; though both, at the time of which I write, were presided over by my friend *Il Priore*, who cherished a delightful but incongruous passion for amateur theatricals.

In the day-time, looking from the Cardinal's Garden, the village of one street of farms would be deserted save for, here and there, an old woman sitting in her doorway placidly plaiting a straw hat, the colour of April sunlight: but every evening, before the Angelus sounded with, here, a syncopated and slightly sour jangle, you could watch the harvest being brought home by the peasants and their milk-white, vermilion-wreathed bullocks. Then the air would grow a little darker, though the earth glowed under the gigantic, shifting, scarlet panorama of the skies, where the sun was going down in gore like a bull in the arena. As the autumn night came on, it was easy to tell how different it was from a spring night: it lacked the throb and vitality of the earlier season, and there were no constellations of fireflies to observe, no singing of nightingales to hear, though the cicadas rattled of their jingling, mechanical love from every bush and cornfield: but there was now, also, a sleepy warmth in the air, and on Saturday nights, when Tuscan peasants are apt to relax after their week's labour, the over-cheerful voice of a *contadino*, who had sampled the new wine, would sound lagging after a tune from some Italian opera, as he tried to find his way home through the empty night. The skies flowered more prolifically too, in these months, showing the glittering stars of the Milky

Way; but few lights were to be seen below. My father and
mother retired to their rooms early, my father at nine, my
mother at ten, and after that there would only be a great flood
of spluttering illumination coming through a door from an
acetylene flare in a room on the lower terrace, where Henry
was still treating a few friends to some of the Castle wine. In
this vast sector, spreading out into the darkness like a search-
light, you could see huge russet moths for a moment assume
an imperishable glory of gold, amid the dances of the lesser,
wire-like insects. Everything was very quiet.

We were, therefore, all the more puzzled one week at the
end of September by a strange and unaccountable sound of
enormous volume; apparently an animal hullabaloo, and yet
for all its ferocity with something of broad human good-nature
lying under it. It persisted, and was repetitive: regularly, as
if by clockwork, it started at midnight and ended at one-thirty.
We wondered whether some strange beast, supposedly
extinct, could be raiding the countryside from a forgotten lair
in the mountains: but no, it could not be that! There must
exist some more probable explanation. Eventually, after a
week, my father sent down to the Prior, to enquire if he could
help us solve the mystery. . . . And, indeed, he could: his
letter elucidated the matter. The enterprising priestly impresario was planning to give a performance of *Quo Vadis* the
following Easter, and, since midnight turned out to be the
best time for the peasants who were to act it to rehearse, he
had convened those of them who were to play the lions at that
hour every night, in order to teach them how to roar! . . .
There was something very appropriate in that this rustic
incident, so reminiscent of Bottom and his band in *A Mid-
summer Night's Dream*, occurred just below the very walls of
the Castle of the Dukes of Athens. . . .

In short, it exhaled an air of remote and true rusticity, as
well as wafting across the centuries the breath of a grandeur
belonging to a legendary past. And the incidents of the life
that hence radiated partook of the same quality. Occasionally,
for instance, we would go to dinner with friends in their villas,
and nearly always my father's celebrated motor would break
down on some secluded stretch of road—it could never stay

even its own moderate, if pounding, pace for more than a few miles. When thus once again brought to a standstill in the aromatic darkness of a wood of stone-pine trees, I would get out and wait, in order to breathe their sweetness more easily and to observe the slight difference between our own and this alien but classic night; (here the stars, in their millions, seemed to lift the canopy of the sky higher than it hangs in England, and the bright stains of the Milky Way smeared more emphatically the more transparent blue). If it were autumn, the cicadas would everywhere be rattling their dry limbs in a rhythmic shuffle, while in the spring an amazing volume of song poured forth from the throats of nightingales, revealing their hearts in dark turret or leafy bower, while whole squadrons and flights of fireflies signalled and twinkled in the darkness round me. But, whatever might be the correct sound for the season and for the night, invariably I would hear the chauffeur—a peasant from the Castello and quite ignorant of mechanics—addressing the engine as if it were one of his white oxen, which had obstinately decided, as is their way, to go no further with its load of grapes or olives. So he would reproach or coax it in his harsh Tuscan voice, pitched low, urging it to resume its labour. It was fascinating to hear him thus invoking the spirit of a machine.

Sometimes, too, when we stayed at home, our band—La Società Filarmonica di Montegufoni—would come to serenade us in the evening. When this happened, the rustic orchestra, caught in the grips of their brazen serpents, would always play as chief piece special variations on "God Save the King" written by the conductor: these lasted a full half-hour, during the whole of which time we would, to return the compliment, have to remain on the terrace, illuminated by an acetylene flare and standing stiffly in full view of the public, eager to note every tremor or shifting of weight.

Each year, with the opening-up of courts and rooms, Montegufoni seemed to become more enormous; an infinite amount of thought and labour had been expended upon its reparation: yet my father had been singularly successful in retaining the air of forlorn grandeur, of pomp and riches in decline, which had impressed him as one of its beauties when first he saw this

great building. Though he had always and consciously
determined to preserve this atmosphere, it now also had become emphasised as the result of an incident that had taken
place a year or two before. . . . One afternoon, when I was
in England, and when my father was at Montegufoni without
my mother, a motor drove up to the Castle door and a smartly
dressed chauffeur got down from the box, and explained to
Henry that his master was the Fascist Minister of Finance,
who happened to be motoring past, with some friends, and
would like to see over the Castello. My father, overjoyed at
the prospect of explaining to an altogether new audience
how much he had already achieved and what he hoped to
accomplish in the future, took the famous man and his party
into every room, the while pointing out for their benefit all his
chief treasures: the pictures, furniture, silver, and old jewelry
he had collected. After the Minister and his friends had gone,
my father remarked sadly to Henry, "I'm afraid His Ex-
cellency seems more interested in financial values than in
beauty!" . . . And this time he was proved to be right:
for early in the dark of next morning all the objects he had
specially singled out for admiration were removed by a gang
of robbers, equipped with the same motor. . . . After this,
for many months my father continued in a state of dejection:
Henry said he had never known him so visibly a victim of
melancholy. However, he had always possessed a firm faith in
happy endings; and sure enough, he was recompensed finally
in full measure, pressed down and overflowing. For when, some
months later, joining him at the Castello, I remarked, "You
seem to have recovered your spirits, I'm glad to see", he
explained, "Well, I've had good news. The police have found
the burglars' hoard, and returned me all my things." And
then, smiling to himself in a complacent way, he added, in a
lower tone, "And, between ourselves, a good many, as well,
that never belonged to me—including two quite good Primi-
tives, and a bag of gold coins!" In effect, therefore, my father
had used the burglars as the Chinese use cormorants to do
their fishing for them.

The consequences of this burglary were several and evident.
After it, for example, my father always slept with an eighteenth-

century rapier ready to hand. And decoratively, too, the results were singular. In the state rooms, by the side of two or three of the most pompous beds, gilded, hung with brocades, and garnished with plumes, were placed thin slumb-bedsteads of 1880, made of metal with the enamel peeling off, so that peasants could sleep therein to guard the approaches: but looking through the windows from the courtyard, it was as though James Pryde and Walter Sickert had collaborated in painting a picture on the same canvas. Similarly a tin basin with a scrap-metal tripod would accompany a grand marble washing-stand.

The rather painful fun that my parents in combination so continually evolved against this new background became more rapid in action every year: though the stage grew to be less crowded. Gradually my father's contemporaries, and those others who had made part of his life, were receding. The Silver Bore died early in the 'thirties. Poor Pare was dead. My Aunt Florence was dead. Henry retired in the spring of 1936, and took lodgings in Scarborough. From beside the northern waters, he kept an eye turned towards his old master at Montegufoni; the same sort of life, from the appended letter, still evidently continued there, as late as the spring of 1937.

1 BEULAH TERRACE, FALSGRAVE, SCARBORO'
March 17, 1937

DEAR MASTER OSBERT,

The sight of your handwriting on an envelope addressed to me fills me with great joy, for which I am very grateful and proud, and I send you great thanks for the cheque, with which I will buy a pair of Sunday boots, and wear them in remembrance of you. Not that I ever forget you.

I had a letter from Miss Dawkins[1] this morning, telling me Sir G. had called in another professor which makes three in all and he found nothing wrong so now Sir G. likes the new professor very much, and the undertakers have had to take the box back. I bet the verdict of the Professor makes G.R.S. change all his plans now the lire has gone down I wonder what he will do about the reduction of hotel charges. I had a letter from H.L. saying Dawkins had accused her of listening at doors, and a letter by the same post from Miss Dawkins saying H.L. had accused her of it. So everything goes on in the same old way at the Castello.

[1] My mother's maid.

The weather is wintry indeed and many people popping off sudden about here, but it is very nice being in a warm bed. . . . The life-boat has been called lately to escort vessels into the harbour, strong gales from the N.E. and S.E. with heavy falls of snow, the gun fired last week for the life-boat I went down to the beach and was coated about two inches thick with snow. The craft got in alright. The boatmen all now beginning to overhaul their craft for the coming summer, we hope we shall soon have fine weather.

Well, Sir, this is all I can remember to write down but when I am out walking I often think of things to write to you and then forget them. I must take a notebook and a pencil with me.[1]

Now with all my heart's best love and best wishes. I remain Your obedient servant HENRY MOAT.

In July of this year, the decline in Henry's health, which had caused him to retire, became more emphatic, and he wrote to Maynard Hollingworth:

I have to undergo an operation which I fear will prevent me coming to Renishaw this August. Captain Osbert asked me and I had been looking forward to that treat The hospital are waiting a special instrument I have been X-rayed four times and nothing showed. Then they put search lights inside me in fact I was floodlit I told the doctor who is a jolly chap if he found any anchors or scrap to fetch them up as scrap is a good price.

However, with his great strength, he made temporarily a good recovery.

In the summer of 1937 my mother died in London after a short illness at the age of sixty-eight. To her last days, she remained in part child, with a child's impetuosity and humour, and in part older than her years, though she did not look more than fifty-five, and was as straight as though she had been a young woman, retaining her particular carriage of the head, so distinctive to her. She always told me that she entertained a great horror of old age. Indeed, as I drove round in a taxi-cab at six o'clock on a July morning to break to my father in his hotel—she had been removed to a nursing home—the news of her death, there came back to me, unbidden, but perhaps with a certain cruel relevance typical of the way the human mind works on very mournful occasions such as this, a frag-ment of conversation from many years before. It had taken

[1] My father's invariable advice.

place in the dining-room at Renishaw, at luncheon, on a fine August day. Only my mother, my father and myself had been present. My mother, who had been silent, suddenly observed:

"How much I should hate to live to be old!"

This remark, harmless as it seemed, pierced my father's armour, and he replied, but addressing his words to me, and in that unnaturally placid voice which in his case sometimes heralded a storm:

"I think all *intelligent* people would like to live to be old, wouldn't they, Osbert?"

My mother then interposed, "But I should hate to feel I was being a trouble to anyone."

And I, answering her, said, "But *really intelligent* people don't mind that, Mother!"

My father had glowered at me, and had fallen back on one of his favourite rebukes:

"Rude without being funny!"

That had been fifteen years ago, and now I was on my way to tell him she was dead.

In the autumn, my father returned to Italy. He seemed happiest at Montegufoni, which he seldom left: happier I think than he had ever been, though he still, I know, greatly enjoyed his rare visits to me at Renishaw. Ernest de Taeye had, alas, died in 1934, and a new but able chief reigned in his stead over the flowers. I recall that my father, one morning during his last stay, entered the hall in an obvious state of exhaustion.

"What have you been doing?" I enquired.

"Just been showing the gardener round the garden," he replied, bestowing on this task of supererogation an air of indefinable patronage.

To a certain extent his advancing years had compelled him to cease from continual active interference in the plans of his children, for he grew tired more easily. He now relied more on a sole weapon: *will-rattling*, as Samuel Butler has described it. He continually altered or threatened to alter this document, and made a different one with several firms of solicitors. He liked from time to time, too, to stage a death-bed scene, when

he would summon out for the occasion from England the
ancestors of his descendants—that is to say his children.
When thus sent for, I would always ask if I might see his
doctor, and I remember the despairing voice of the celebrated
Florentine doctor he consulted, as he said to me:

"Such an illness as Sir George lays claim to is a matter of
X-ray plates, and not of faith. Sir George has *not* got it.
I am twenty years younger, and he may outlive me[1] by many
years. He is an old man, but if he does not get pneumonia,
he may live for twenty years."

When I returned from Florence to Montegufoni, I found
my father in bed, awaiting the end, and looking extremely
melancholy.

"How long does he give me?" he gasped out.

"Another ten to twenty years," I was able to reply. This
cheered him up. And usually his fears—or at any rate the
same fears—did not last long. He had too much to do, and
he could not combine a perpetual death-bed scene with giving
orders to the workmen and countermanding them. Besides,
in some ways he liked change (indeed one of his favourite
maxims was "one ought to ring the changes more often")
and before very long he would believe himself to be—or with
part of his brain would believe himself to be—in the grip of
another mortal illness. (It must be noted that, when genuinely
ill, he always showed courage and stoicism.)

At railway-stations he would now be carried in a chair. And
a letter from Henry to my father, who was aged seventy-
eight at the time, contains a reference to this method of con-
veyance, and in fact constitutes plainly a mischievous attempt,
born of his sense of humour and knowledge of psychology, to
persuade his former master to insist instead on being carried
pick-a-back. By this time, the following year, Henry had been
on his promised visit to Renishaw, and in this same letter he
gives his impression of it, and courageously extols several old
friends, as well as delivering a few hard raps. I print it as it
stands, including the over-flattering references to myself,
which should perhaps be omitted, yet cannot be removed
without spoiling the character of the letter.

[1] He did.

1 BEULAH TERRACE, FALSGRAVE, SCARBOROUGH
Sept. 20, 1938

To Sir George R. Sitwell Bart.

SIR GEORGE,

I write to thank you for the letter I received from you this morning. I am sorry to hear of your illness. Naturally you will feel tired, you are at a great age. I think you are wonderful and much to be proud of, but you must go slower now. You still have a young mind which must be controlled when active exercise is demanded or desired. I hope you eat slower and eat a minimum of salt, has salt hardens the arteries. . . . It will save you much strain being carried at the stations. I once lived with a gentleman who had heart trouble, he was nervous of chairs, so I always carried him upstairs on my back and I have often seen men on stations being carried on the back of another.

I thoroughly enjoyed my stay at Renishaw I was tired of tinned soup, tinned salmon, tinned meat, tinned peas, tinned fruit and the good wholesome food soon put me right. Captain Osbert looks real well, a big fine handsome gentleman, and I should say his body is too small for his big kind heart. He has made the rooms look as if he had let perpetual sunshine into them. I was pleased to see Miss Edith there too. I think she gets more aristocratic-looking every year, and her beautiful manner, so different from these painted hussies who are filling up all over. The gardens are just beautiful, I never saw more beautiful flowers anywhere nor finer grapes and peaches. I thought the gardener very efficient. Mr. Hollingworth looked well, I admire him and marvel at his clever brain, and yet always meek, works hard but does not look at work as drudgery, but like eating food, a necessity and pleasure.

It will be very pleasant for you to have Signor Bracciaforte join you at Bologna he is always so kind-hearted and considerate except being a little unpunctual at times. Please Sir George give him my kindest regards and to the Masti family, Also Dino and Otello. I hope the Hon. Mrs. Keppel is well, it was always nice and pleasant when she came over to the Castle. I often think of the old days, and can truthfully say I have not had a single happy day since I left your service. I have become a member of the Constitutional Club here and Mr. Follis often talks to me loudly so that all roundabout can hear, about Budapest, Italia, Austria etc and I am often spoke about as travelling all countries in the world with Sir George Sitwell for many years, of course those voyages with you get me much respect, but I modestly pretend not to hear, and that saves me from having to correct it of course if I took a glass or two I could enlarge upon it but I only drink boiled water now for I go to a herbalist and am giving these herbs a fair chance and feel grand.

Please Sir George you said your feet get tired well its fortunate letters are not read by the feet or yours would be very tired before you got as far as this, for which I apologize. Kindest and best wishes to you Sir George from your obedient servant HENRY MOAT.

On the visit he mentions above, Henry enjoyed more leisure than ever before at Renishaw. I do not think he looked old for his age, though his hair was now almost white. He had lost weight owing to illness and to the change of food he suffered after his retirement, but he still gave the impression of great physical strength. His immense and imposing frame, even without, to crown it, the dome of his bowler hat—which he still always wore when out, since this was all that now remained to him of his former butler's pomp—, made him a notable figure in the landscape on the long walks he took, swinging his arms with a ceremonious air. Each of these promenades, more than a walk, seemed to be a one-man procession, reminding us of the old days when he entered the drawing-room after dinner, followed by a footman with a tray. Usually he took the route round the lake, for if the sea was far away—and to it he still belonged in spite of his career on land—, fresh water, provided you were not obliged to drink it, was the next best thing, he said. Twice each Sunday he marched in state to church, clasping a large prayer-book. I thought at first that his thus attending both matins and evensong was merely because he liked to join in the hymns in his rich and pious bass: but now I believe he had become genuinely religious. Certainly he gave us fewer profane songs during the week. And I noticed other changes in him. He had, for example, toward the end of his life, grown strangely economical, saving every penny, and altogether forgetful of the ways of his spendthrift youth.

In the winter of 1937 I went out to Montegufoni to warn my father that in my opinion Italy would before long be involved in war with Great Britain. For my trouble, however, I was dismissed with an outsize flea in my ear. "There won't be a war!" he maintained with an air of omniscient finality. I countered this, for I was worried about what might happen to him, by saying:

"All right, there won't be one, then—but if one *was* to occur what would you do?"

In the manner of Robin Hood, he replied, "I should take refuge in the mountains!"

When I could not help adding, "I suppose to look for the mountain-ash berries", he was annoyed, but I do not think he knew what I meant, or remembered that fragment of conversation of long ago to which I was alluding.

The same kind of life he had always led was continuing at the Castle. He was still at work, entering notes, writing long books, tracing pedigrees. He had just completed a new garden lay-out beneath the old rampart ("Between ourselves," he observed to me, "I believe I'm the only person living who could manage that double axis properly!"), and had recently disclosed a new vista of small, high rooms, painted and furnished in elaborate, but very individual pseudo-gothic. He had been delighted at the surprise people who knew the Castle well displayed when these apartments were shown them, for no one hitherto had been aware that they existed. His views on life had not much changed: though in one respect he had modified them. He attached more importance than formerly to the effect of the mother's heredity upon the children. In talking to our friend Francis Bamford, who stayed at Montegufoni for a considerable time at this period, he expatiated on the fact that it might be the blood of his Irish mother and Scottish grandmother mingling with that of the English Sitwells which had been responsible for producing so remarkable a character as himself. He added, "Sacheverell probably acted wisely in choosing to marry a Canadian: it may be Nature's attempt to reproduce *me*!" I do not think he was lonely, his time was more than fully occupied, and as Henry once remarked, "Sir George always liked to know where people *were*!, and now he knows they're all in the cemetery". None of them now could contradict him, or interfere with his plans. He was undisputed lord of his own territory in space, time and imagination. He thought what he wished to think: and as a small instance of this I remember his remarking to me suddenly, "Edith made a great mistake by not going in for lawn-tennis". As for myself, I had my uses, from his point of view. Thus, conveniently remembering that I was an author, he proceeded to restore and decorate a room for me, in which I could work, between the courts. It is true that I never used it, but he enjoyed preparing it, and when in the spring of 1938 he was showing Somerset Maugham round the Castle, he looked into the room, and remarked, "I made this room for my son Osbert; he is a writer, you know" . . . He had grown more than formerly to *like* seeing people; though he still seldom knew who they were. Sometimes he gave large luncheon parties (I always wondered on what principle he gathered the guests, and how it was arranged), and when I was staying with him he would preside at a table in the vaulted dining-room, while I would be in charge of a smaller table in the hall beyond. And I recollect being struck by the pathos and symbolism of a remark he made to me one afternoon, after the guests had gone: "I don't know how it is, but always it seems to me that I hear more laughter in the next room!"

In August 1939 my father came on a visit to England, but towards the end of the month hurried back to the Continent. From Spiez in Switzerland, where he stayed for a while, to break the journey to Italy, he wrote to me on 29th August 1939:[1]

MY DEAREST OSBERT,

I find it difficult to settle to anything, because of the crisis, so take the opportunity of sending you some brief notes about Renishaw.

On a separate piece of paper was written:

Renishaw. Several things still need doing. A beginning at least should be made with the Lake Pavilion, the building of which has been delayed for too long.

A bridge of fine cut stone should span the ravine at the end of the garden vista; beyond it should rise a replica of the Temple of Vesta. This need not be expensive.

G.R.S.

As soon as he arrived in Italy he set to, and began to renovate the stucco statues of gods and goddesses and peasants in the seventeenth-century grotto, the finest in Tuscany.[2]

---

[1] Great Britain declared war on the 3rd September 1939.

[2] Plainly, I think, by the hand of an architect from Rome. These figures had been smashed, fifty years previously, by village children throwing stones at them: but before five more years had elapsed they had again suffered almost precisely the same injuries, this time from the hands of German soldiers.

The domed and painted ceiling had become so fouled by weather and so obscured by dirt that the mythological personages and symbolic emblems portrayed upon it were unrecognisable: now, however, with washing and a little judicious aid from an expert in this line of work, they had become plainly identifiable. In his enthusiasm at these results my father wrote me a letter of, in a sense so abrupt, and certainly to prying eyes so mysterious a kind, that it was not delivered for a full two months: during which period, no doubt, the officials of the English Censorship, their gaze then directed towards the Mediterranean nations, were busily trying to interpret the cryptic message they were sure it must contain.

DEAREST OSBERT,

The figure of Athens, under the Crown, is now clearly visible rising from sea, at the moment when Aurora's chariot is topping the horizon. She gazes in the direction of Rome, behind whom are to be distinguished the figures of Mars, the God of War, and Neptune, who governs shipping. Egypt, in the guise of a priest, looks on in dismay, wondering what her fate may be. And, in the right corner is an owl, the attribute of both Athene and Minerva. Ever, dear boy, Yr affectionate father, GEORGE R. SITWELL.

After this, for many months, the letters which arrived for me from my father were stained with acid, and had obviously been subjected to a thousand tests of one sort and another. It looked to me, further, as if the Italian authorities were also on the track, for out of one letter fell a scrap of paper with *niente* scrawled on it in pencil.

For my father's eightieth birthday, on the 27th January 1940, I sent him a telegram of congratulation, adding Henry's name to that of others still living who had been in his employment on the Renishaw estate. I wrote to inform Henry that this had been done.

I received one morning some weeks later a letter from him in reply. It was headed 7 Cliff St., Whitby,[1] and dated 23rd February 1940.

---

[1] Henry's old family home in Whitby, formerly known as The Cragg. It, and the street in which it stood, had been condemned by the local council, but eventually reprieved on the grounds of picturesqueness and local historic interest. See *Left Hand, Right Hand!* p. 96.

DEAR CAPTAIN OSBERT,

It did me good to see your fist again, and really you write a good hand now. Thank you for adding my name to the telegram that proves you think of me and I must ask you to forgive me for not writing before to answer your letter but I have had ten days in bed with pleuresy, but it has left me weak but getting better slowly.

There was an anxious time here on Feb. 3rd a German bomber was chased right over the town and land by three Spitfires they brought him down just above Ruswarp. 1½ miles from here he was riddled with bullets and one of the German crew had his head, chest and arm perforated at about 9 p.m. a Belgian ship came on the rocks 6 of her crew being drownded and two of our lifeboatmen fine fellows. It was the blackest night I ever saw and (as) there is no navigation light along the coast it is most difficult and dangerous. The two dead german airmen were to be buried at the cemetery here but rumour got about that the fishermen had been bombed and machine-gunned there looked like being trouble so they were taken to Catterick near Richmond in the middle watch and buried there. I had a nice letter from Sir Geo which I will send you on by reading between the lines he has every hope of living a good many years yet if he is going to see the perfection of his new gardening scheme at the Castle he often told me he would like to see 80 I now think he is heading for 100. I was rather tickled about him going into the Blue Nuns Home for fear of hurting their feelings I don't think it is habitual of him considering others feelings.

Now dear Sir, with all my very best wishes for you and Miss Edith from your obedient servant HENRY MOAT

P.S. I often think Mr Hollingworth ought to have been a gunner on a Spitfire. He would have brought them down like ninepins.

The night before my receiving this letter, I had been startled several times by the sounds of a heavy tread down below, and by bumpings in the pantry, which for nearly forty years, on and off, had been the principal scene of Henry's professional activities. In the morning, my sister, who slept in a distant part of the house, had complained similarly and independently of having been woken up on three or four occasions in the night by ponderous footsteps moving about. Later in the day, I received the letter reproduced above, and an hour after that a telegram came informing me that Henry had died the previous afternoon. He had written his letter to me on the morning of his death.

When I think of Henry now, it is not so much to the early

days of his association with my father that my mind goes back, nor even to the innumerable jokes and romps of my childhood, or to the occasions when he would bring down tea for us to the boathouse, as we sat with Davis in the flat-bottomed, blue-painted boat, floating on the lake, while, as he unpacked the hamper, he shouted conversation to us across the level waters, nor to the time when I was nine or ten and we were already old friends, and he told me many stories as I sat swinging my legs on the table in the pantry—tales, some of them true, no doubt, but others specially invented in order to answer or prevent the continual questions with which I plied him—, nor to the fabulous period of his membership of the Camorra, when I was seventeen, but to one Christmas I spent in Venice with my father, shortly before Henry left his service. During the short days, I was engaged partly in sight-seeing, and partly in composing and putting together for William Walton the words of our Oratorio, *Belshazzar's Feast*. In the evenings, however, after my father had retired at his usual early hour to bed, Henry and I would go out, through the narrow streets and dark alleys, to drink a glass of red wine or two together, or a hot *poncino*, in a tavern. We had already begun to dread rather the next few days, for Christmas was almost upon us, we were staying in a large, ornate hotel deserted save for a pack of hungry waiters and our three selves, and my father had already announced his determination, in view of the particular crisis of the day (we had already entered the Age of Crises), to bestow no tips. In fact, he said he felt that voluntary abstention in this respect was now a moral as well as a patriotic duty. It was plain, then, that any young waiter who ingratiatingly lisped to him on the morning of the festival the few words of English he had so painfully learnt, "'Appy Christmas, sir, and 'appy New Year!", would come in for a surprise! . . . However, Henry and I felt that there was nothing we could do to save him, and so, as we sat there, in the hot, smoky, indoor atmosphere that Venetians so greatly love, we talked, instead, about old times at Renishaw. I asked Henry, I remember, what traditions lingered in the neighbourhood concerning the ghost, for in the course of his forty years' employment, I felt sure that some must have reached his ears: and he told me that Henry Sacheverell[1] (who, the reader may recall, had been drowned and was supposed to haunt the house) walked through the rooms, when he thus returned, with his body still dripping with water, and his face hung with river weeds. And this tale interested me, because though I had never heard these two details before, yet only the previous year a friend of mine, who had been staying alone with me at Renishaw, had undergone a singular and, as I realised now, apparently related experience. At about midnight, against my advice, he had gone into one of the dark, large bedrooms in a wing seldom used, to find out whether he felt any presence or influence in it. When, half an hour or so later, he returned, obviously in a much shaken condition, I first gave him some brandy and then asked him to explain what had occurred. At first he replied that it was too difficult to attempt to convey, but, on being pressed, said, "I know that it sounds ridiculous: but I felt that I was drowning, that I was wretched beyond words, and that my face was covered with hanging wet stuff; it might have been weed. I could feel it with my hands." . . . And this, though he was ignorant of the fact that the alleged ghost had been drowned, and I had known nothing then of the manner in which he was said to materialise—so that it looked as if for those moments my friend had been invested with, or had assumed, the sensations of the ghost as he had died. . . . It is not of spectres, however, that I wish to write, but of Henry Moat as he was in the flesh—very much in the flesh—and as he sat talking to me of many things and people, but especially of fishermen, and of the turbulent life in the old quarter of Whitby and in the usually peaceful surrounding villages, where life as a rule continued to its old ancient beat, when the fishing fleet returned. . . . But above all, more than to this memory of him sitting opposite me at the table topped with red Verona marble almost the shade of his face, my thoughts revert to him as he was on one particular day at this time.

My friend Bertie Landsberg had invited me to have luncheon with him at his celebrated villa, the Malcontenta, on the mainland. Having first obtained my father's permission to

[1] See *The Scarlet Tree*, p. 37 and note, of this edition.

take Henry out for the day, I then telephoned to my host to explain, as shortly and graphically as I could, the unique character of the guest I was proposing to bring, and he welcomed the suggestion. Henry could have dinner, he said, with the other servants. . . . Accordingly we set out together early one fine Sunday morning in mid-December, when the palaces of marble and Istrian stone had taken on a singularly rich but subdued glitter, and the sun was spinning its vast aqueous cocoons of mist over the wide and dazzling surfaces. By the hour that the steamer, painted like a swallow, reached Fusina, the atmosphere had cleared and the Venetian sun now defined every object with an unequalled and sparkling precision. It illumined for us, as we stood waiting on the road—built, in case of floods, a little higher than the level of the land—every object within view very distinctly: but it did not show the motor-car we had been told to expect. Henry, however, observed that it was "a grand day for a walk" and, since this was plainly the truth, we adopted his proposal, and soon started to accomplish on foot the four miles along the side of that famous canal, the Brenta, to the villa.

As I watched Henry walking, I recognised that this was just the sort of off-maritime landscape he needed, to be seen in his perfection. The skin of his face, now generally copper-coloured from the effects of wine and sun, glowed a lusty red, and he swung his arms as he went with the jolly swagger of a fat man out for a day's enjoyment, the gaiety of the animal-paragon, who, being contented in himself, can, though no longer young, still take pleasure in scent, sound and the feel of the air. Clad in a favourite blue suit and wearing black boots, square-toed, which he had only obtained as a bargain after much hard argument, he had crowned his head with the formidable dome of the bowler hat we have several times noted, and which did invariable duty as a cap of ceremony or maintenance. If he had been alone, I judged, he would have now broken into one of the more familiar and unctuous hymn-tunes that he so loved, as a chant to creation. Isolated after this fashion, in a globe of crystal above the canal on one side, and on the other a flat land intersected by gleaming lines of water, there still emanated from him and remained about him something unmistakably nautical; nature seemed to supply an immutable background of threshing whales, an analogy of porpoises that none could fail to perceive. In the mind's eye seagulls bumped and squealed in arcs round his head, the herring, their scales twinkling with light, weighed down the nets. His epidermis itself appeared to present an hereditary effect of exposure to wind, sun, sea spray, salt air and tar, and his gait, too, I observed, retained in its motion the memory of an early response to the waves. . . . So we proceeded on our way, while the driver of our host's motor-car searched everywhere for us, since in Italy no one could be found to believe that two persons would of their own accord set out to walk so great a distance: we must, it was presumed, have been lost or gone mad.

We arrived, it is true, a little late at Malcontenta, that legendary palace, but my host found time to show me before luncheon the splendid series of painted rooms, the frescoes of which he had recently uncovered, so that the giant figures of gods and goddesses still glowed through the last coat of whitewash, as the lordly figures of a vanished age might for a moment shine through the mists of popular memory.[1] Greatly I enjoyed, when it came, the meal—but not so much as Henry relished his dinner downstairs, or so it seemed as we listened to the gusts and roars of laughter that rolled upstairs to us. My host told me that his servants could speak no word of English, so that all the exchanges must have been in Henry's fluent Italian, richly spiced with Yorkshire. Still the vast gales of merriment—and not, I should say, so innocent merriment—continued, until the whole delicate shell of the huge villa echoed and shook. . . . And so it is that most I like to think of him, in his Indian Summer, not, after all, so many years ago, sitting drinking red wine with friends—for though he had never seen them before, these Italian men and women quickly became his friends—on a fine winter's afternoon, and irresistibly sweeping his robust and idiosyncratic humour, full of an imagery governed by the comic eye (the same that is visible in his letters), into another and an alien tongue. Surely

[1] For a fuller description of Malcontenta, see *Winters of Content* (Duckworth, 1932).

that mature laughter, triumphant over circumstances, over middle age and darkening days, should, as it rolled under the vaulted ceilings, have rid the famous building for ever of any shadow of the unhappy lady who gave it a name.

This was already nearly ten years ago. We were now in 1940, Henry was dead, and the world had entered Sneak's Alley, the land of rags and bones. Soon, in the middle of May, I was going to visit my father. The opportunity offered itself in this fashion: the British Council asked me to lecture in Milan, Florence, Rome, Naples, Palermo and other cities. I could take the opportunity of spending a few days with him on my way from Florence to Rome. . . . I arrived in Milan, and the following evening delivered the first lecture—and the last: for as a consequence of the anti-English feeling being so carefully organised and exploited, the war which Italy was planning against us had drawn so near that one could almost feel the ferine breath of the God Mars, as, his armour covered with the verdigris of centuries, he rose from the ruined Roman temples and tombs, and strode towards us. . . . Already strange news filtered in, news that had not broken in France or England. Sedan had fallen, its very name bringing a reverberation of disaster, and the large, dark, Neo-Classic or Renaissance hotels of Fascist Italy were full of groups of smartly dressed men and women, poring delightedly over maps of France, in between drinking cups of black coffee strong as only Italy could provide. Outside the station, that vast monument to Fascist power, large and heartless and cosmopolitan as the buildings of ancient Rome, an edifice made for triumphal banners more than for men (and now rain drips through its roof, and the only flags are the ancient rags of poverty), crowds of students sang vivacious anti-English songs, and any shop with an English name had to be guarded. Every day tension increased, and the morning after my lecture I was advised to abandon my tour and to return home. I therefore never reached Florence or Montegufoni.

The trains to the frontier were crowded with English invalids, retired governesses, and old people living on small pensions, who had spent whole decades in Italy and were now obliged to abandon the homes they loved, and the people they liked. To reach French soil seemed like stepping on dry land: everything appeared still secure, unthreatened; but another sound from the armoured footsteps in Italy was nevertheless to be detected here, that of a faint but terrifying creak, the preliminary, almost imperceptible shifting of a mass about to fall. In a day or two the Germans would reach Dieppe, and the thrasonic discourses on the radio, by democratic politicians almost already in flight, were due to begin. Every day the trains from Italy arrived at a later hour, and were more crowded; few English remained in that country, few even in Florence, for centuries their chosen city. But my father stayed on, in his Castle that was at the same time objective and subjective, a very solid structure, floating on its little hill, its towers surrounded by the pennons of the Italian skies, and a delicate edifice created out of long and often painful dreams; a fortress that was simultaneously physical, emotional and mental. Surely this triple stronghold would prove impregnable?

He never listened to the radio, and I was told that when in the morning he heard the news that Italy had declared war on England, he climbed the tower of the Castle—with some difficulty, for he was over eighty and had been ill for a long time—and remained up there for an hour or more. It was still early on a June morning of delusive trembling shadows, and already the air was dancing, spangling with motes the enormous expanse of tiled roof patterned with circular lichen, shaped like the patches of water-lilies on a pool, in silver, almond green and gold, that lay below him. Under these again were the areas of stone, the paved courtyards, dark green, with a sparkle of glass in their darkness, and the organisation of terraces and buttresses by which the great building was held up. Round and outside that, for miles the landscape was visible, lying as it were in folds and mounds of crinkled, wrinkled silk and sweeping up to a horizon pricked by the battlemented towers of other castles. Here and there in the sheen of gold and green was a patch almost black, where a cypress wood lay: within the cloistered, aromatic peace of which the nightingales still sang all the day long, as well as all the night: sang, they say, even when, three years later, the tanks came pounding through these same odorous groves.

Aloft, then, at the top of his tower, at the summit of his eighty years, my father was contemplating the view: but in spite of the clearness of the day, the view was indistinct. He wondered where best to place the belvedere: but, he realised, with the war in progress, it would be difficult and very expensive to build now. A war always unfortunately sent up the cost of materials and labour. (Thank goodness, the Grotto was finished! Signor Bracciaforte had been most kind in helping.) Yes, very difficult: (he knew, though he would not admit it to himself, that not only would building be difficult, but his own independence of action and liberty were threatened).[1] Usually he found it easy to concentrate; but today the prospect before him kept dissolving into other scenes; the sheen of sun and shadow, the cups and hollows, the extreme width and undulation of the Tuscan landscape would merge into another, that was, though distant from him in time and space, still more familiar. The hollow of the stream below turned into a lake, the terraces into other terraces, the fountain into other fountains, the clumps of cypress into tall, antlered deciduous trees. Then these gardens, now themselves ancient, with the stout green walls that he had with such virtuosity contrived, melted into still earlier shapes. The vast bulk of a battlemented house, looming against its background of trees and of tangled vapours from sky and earth, was muffled in darkness, just as the winter skies were obscured by smoke from the giant furnaces recently established: everything seemed muffled in grief and darkness; and his mother, similarly, was swathed in black Victorian weeds, a young widow. She was struggling with the accounts for a large part of the day, trying to understand the losses that had fallen on the family; the echoing rooms, through which he ran by himself, seemed all the more immense for the emptiness. Somehow the exterior seemed more real, more bound to existence, than the inside of the house; he ran outside. There were the formless lawns, that yet had exercised a fascination by their glossiness; beds, carefully regulated and planted out with flowers in geometric patterns,

[1] See Appendix C for subsequent developments at the Castello.

vases, trees, the Gothic Temple, and the view; the great view
as one day he would present it. Women in dark vast crino-
lines, in little bodices and bonnets, swayed over the green
lawns with a curious sailing motion. . . . He returned to the
present, and wondered what had made him think of that; the
clouds that hung over Montelupo, he supposed. . . . Then
the present collapsed again: he was playing croquet with Ida
on the new lawn, and the dull clatter of the wooden balls and
mallets mingled with the cooing of doves in the summer air;
they were playing, four of them, the men in tight coats and
trousers, and with boaters on their heads, the women with leg-
of-mutton sleeves and straw hats. The laughter floated up
among the flutter of leaves. He hadn't played croquet—in
Italy they never seemed to play it!—for years, he reflected: not
since Sargent had come down that time. . . . He was afraid
the surface of the group showed signs of deterioration: but
there it was, artists were all alike, and refused to consult him
as to the correct methods of making the pigments they used.
He could have given them several valuable hints. Fortunately
he had insisted on having his own way with the grouping of the
picture, and on choosing the clothes for it. Ida, standing
beside him, but a little distant, in a sequined white evening
dress, with a hat with a transparent brim (a clever idea), and a
scarlet feather (it needed just a touch of red): the two boys on
the Aubusson carpet, playing with their toys. And Edith,
with his arm round her shoulders. (Fathers should always
stand in portraits, with their arms round their daughters'
shoulders.) A pity that her nose was the wrong shape. But it
seemed to him, looking back, that in life things often turned
out like that. The whole group, he thought, showed English
family life at its best: but much had changed since then: he
had forsaken politics for literature—and by the way, Edith and
the boys had taken to writing, too (such a mistake!). The
children were not round him now, as they had been in the
group, and he wondered where they were—missing his advice
and guidance in these difficult times, he had no doubt,
wherever they might be! It was singular: a man called
Lawrence had been over to call, two years before, who had
heard of all three of them as writers. That poem of Edith's

about the half-witted girl waiting for her lover by the stream was quite interesting: but he wished she would consult him about rhythm. When he had spoken to her about it, she had merely denied that she had ever written the poem: but he remembered it well. Literature and painting had gone downhill, he was afraid. There was no-one equal to Sargent nowadays, though there had been an improvement in popular taste, in furniture and clothes. But the decline elsewhere was evident.

Though it was better not to think of it, yet, as he looked northwards, he could not help wondering what was happening behind the barrier of mountains. . . . *La Grande Nation* was tottering to collapse. He was not surprised. Democracies were essentially selfish: now he feared they would sink into the ground drenched with their own blood. The papers said the roads were crowded with motors, all going in the same direction towards the sea: all the vehicles moving at the same pace —that was democracy all over!—slow as a man walking. Modern progress ended there, in great cities burned and whole races enslaved. At least the chivalry of medieval times would have prevented that! The innocent would have found sanctuary in the cathedrals, and the ladies of the castle and their children would have been safe within their massive walls of stone (as for the villeins, with whom he felt little sympathy, *serfs* they enjoyed watching other people—especially their masters —go to war and not return). He thought of the splendid cathedrals in Normandy, of his long visit there a few summers ago, when he had stayed at Valmont to study the ancient holdings in land and the fortresses of the Estoutevilles and of the Sacheverells; castles which had already, centuries ago, dwindled to broken mounds of stone.

It was difficult to know how to divide up the day: for the poor workmen had most of them been mobilised (amazing, when he thought how much more valuable was the work they had been doing for him than that on which they were now employed!). He must have been up here quite a long time. He looked at his heavy gold watch, which he had presented as a boy of thirteen to his grandfather, the Waterloo veteran, who had at his death kindly left it back to him. He remembered, again, how the old gentleman had told him, as a boy of four or five, that he was to be a poet when he grew up. (Singular that all the children should be writers!) Ten o'clock, just after. (The second hand was slightly crooked, and it was difficult now to get anything mended.) He looked over the edge towards the court—already you could feel the intense heat coming up from the pavement, the tiles, and the terraces. Everything was very quiet, except for two hens that had escaped into the court from outside, and a pigeon that flapped and cooed out of the cote (he thought of Ida's pigeons at Renishaw, which the white owl had dispossessed). Somewhere below a man was whistling *Giovanezza*, the Fascist Anthem, as he watered the lemon-trees, and there was a sound of raking going on among them. Certainly it was peaceful up here. A tower made a great addition to a residence; one ought always to insist on breakfasting up it, but now, with the labour shortage, servants jibbed at a hundred steps even. Twenty people could easily breakfast here; it would be delightful. One's friends would enjoy it. Sometimes he wished he had always lived in a tower—indeed, almost felt as if he had done so. (No doubt, if he had, poor Henry would once again have given notice. . . . Still, looking back, there was something to be said for him. He was always cheerful. . . . If only he'd taken the advice given him, he'd have been healthy—most probably still here—and sometimes it was difficult not to wish he were!) Every country house should have at least one tower: better still, two. It had been a mistake not to build those two square towers at Renishaw, on the north front. They would have been most useful to Osbert, and Hollingworth could have a really modern office in one of them. In war-time, the roofs would have been invaluable, too, for watching—or spotting: and how much the sentinel —what did they call him—roof-spotter?—would *enjoy* being up there on a nice, fresh, frosty night!

He must go downstairs now, and begin work: he had got on well with the last chapter of the family history, and must really try to finish it. He began slowly to turn towards the steps: but now he noticed that in spite of the purity of the air a white cloud of dust hung over the road far below. Troops, he supposed. Well, he must be going down—as he descended into the darkness, he wished, all the same, that he could fore-see what would happen. He'd like to know what his English acquaintances in Florence thought of the position—but he'd forgotten; they'd all gone! He was alone at last.

Meanwhile, I had left Italy and returned home, without being able to visit him.

I never saw him again.

Envoy

IT IS difficult to know the end of the world when you reach it, as difficult as to sound the depths of Hell's all-consuming fires, illimitable and unconfined. There are no signposts to tell you where you are. The sky is still there, the light shines down, from heights canopied or azure. In the shapes of the clouds, in their groupings and shiftings, you can still read visions of fortune as easily as of disaster. You think in the same way. Moreover there is the cruel physical, or animal, persistence. You sleep and eat—eat with the same movements of jaws and hands. Nothing comparable to the collapse of the West, which we are witnessing, has happened since the fall of Constantinople to the Turks: and even then the shock was not so violent, because the inhabitants of the great maritime city, though for so long masters of the world, had not called in Science to give them an assurance of infallibility; they too, however, those of them who survived to see the next day, were by habit and necessity compelled to eat and sleep, and in time to work.

Since I began to write this autobiography, in 1940, the world has again changed out of recognition. Some dangers have disappeared, and others, if possible more stupendous, have tumbled into their places. To disregard for a moment—before returning to it—the future, in the last few years tens of millions of human beings have perished in circumstances of execrable torture, by the ragings of war, the wastings of peace, the malice of man. For this the actions of no person or group of persons are solely to be impugned. No-one can read the chart of the future, even if it exists. However, it is permissible to blame the selfishness of those who lived in upholstered towers constructed to last only until their death. To these my father, of whose tower I have so often written, had never belonged: the materials he had used were of fine quality, and its design was individual, fantastic but complete. Moreover the future

—as he saw it—was ever in his mind, and the edifice was dedicated to it, to house countless impersonal generations, armies of descendants. No: I refer to those who mouthed in first-class railway carriages the comfortable Edwardian slogan, "It will last my time!" or the equivalent, in trams and buses, "Why worry?" For myself, I had never expected the world I knew to endure, and this, perhaps, gave a sharper edge to my vision, to my living. From my earliest youth, I had, I believe, an unusual sense of time, of the recession of the present into the past, and its emergence into the future. Even as a child, I had tried to fix in my mind scenes that I wished to stay with me, so that I could enact them again in memory. And so it was that later I set myself to record them, and to fuse with them into a work of art the story of the development of three artists—for, whatever the future may bring, the temperament of poet and painter, volatile though it may be, will remain true to type and, in such manner, stable.

We cannot peer across at the future, though its people can gaze at us with a cool and detached curiosity from across the chasm. But it is well that we are thus curbed, since it is unlikely that we either should see much that would please us or hear much good of ourselves. (Indeed the living, even the most trivial and unworthy, always extend a patronage to the dead, however famous.) Even if we could foresee the events of a few years, we should not, I believe, add to our contentment. It was happy for my father that when, as I have just described, he climbed the tower at Montegufoni, and remained there for a while, looking out, he did not understand then the present state of affairs, for June 1940 was already a time of calamity. My father often in years past had pointed out the error in my literary outlook. I was pessimistic, he said. A book should always have a happy ending. Tragic things, he was glad to say, seldom happened in real life. Yet, had he now been gifted with the power of prognostication, what a vista of miseries, individual no less than terrestrial, would have been disclosed to him! A man of eighty must know that Death is not far away in the wings, is already hovering for his cue: but my father would have seen, as well as his own end in Switzerland, some three years ahead, in utter isolation, in a house in which

1943

he could see no-one, and send and receive no letters, the ruin of all he planned for, through the vicious cupidity and deceit of those who pretended to serve him; a result that had come to pass because of his own continually increasing blindness to character.

An omniscient being, again, posed high in a refuge on the mountains and looking out from it, would, if well disposed towards humanity, have perceived little that could gratify him. The second instalment of the atrocious cataclysms of the twentieth century, which no statesman, and only one writer of genius, Flaubert, had foreseen, were on the point of being realised, and would soon reach a new culmination. Gifted with an eagle's vision, he would, on the same day of June, have perceived the prostrate body of Europe crawling with grey German armies like lice. Just over the border of the morrow, he would have seen France, for centuries the light of Europe, vanish for the space of four years, to emerge in a new guise, and beyond that, Italy, Mother of the West, crawl out from the wreckage with a broken spine. As a child, I used to be depressed by the Jewish doctrine of vengeance, of an eye for an eye, and a tooth for a tooth: but now Christian nations recognised it as insufficient and out of keeping with the age. When I wrote the introduction to the first of these books, *Left Hand, Right Hand!*, the bombing had already begun, but who could have guessed the ultimate harvest of fire? The Germans attacked London, and reaped their reward in cliffs of desolation, in angular mountains of rubble, taller and more obsolete than the Aztec pyramids, which had been their great cities, and which now choke and encumber the survivors. The Japanese bombed Pearl Harbour and paid for it with a gigantic totempole of smoke, surely fated, in the same fashion as the story of the Flood, to become a legend for savage men in the future. That monstrous shape rose over Hiroshima, a city which for an infinitesimal fraction of time glowed with such a light as man on earth had never seen; a light which, though in itself it was Western Man's final tribute to Darkness, seemed more potent than the radiance which had once attracted the Three Kings to the Manger, and, indeed, its shadow still lies over the future of the world. But what the price may be that will one day be exacted from the whole of humanity for that devil's picnic in the flower-sprinkled isles, we can still as yet only comprehend at times in the dumb and sable corners of consciousness, where a knowledge of the future and a terrible awareness of justice abide.

At last, then, total peace came with the stridency of a scream in the night. It possessed the violence of a nightmare. Europe turned turtle, and half of it was submerged, cut off from view, but the democratic statesmen continued to play their games. They chose this solemn moment of death and exhaustion for a frivolous strutting among the ruins. The enemy was perforce utterly silent, but our masters of the East and West shouted at one another across the champagne, through the fumes of vodka and cigar-smoke, their impious threats or partial acceptance of abominable bargains. Each in turn, with faces sly or swollen, fitted the clown's cap to his head and grimaced at the spectres marching towards them, in mobs and armies and hordes, from past and future. At this hour, in every western country, national character, though in process of dissolution, became for the instant emphasised. The English celebrated the world's end with neither a bang nor a whimper, but with their old traditional booby-trap, a general election. Nevertheless, a change in them was evident. Their former vigour and robustness had succumbed before a cult of timid, pallid suffering, alternating with paltry rewards. Issuing victorious from a long war waged with stubborn heroism by the whole people, they now dingily begged—out of an Empire which their buccaneering forefathers had smashed entire nations to build, salvaging it from the ensuing chaos—only to retain a few dehydrated or reconstituted eggs, a once-a-week dusting of tea, and a banana for the children. ("*More sweeties for the kiddies next month*", the papers proclaimed to a world of unparalleled suffering, as if it were a major triumph over Siva the Destroyer.) Clear or prophetic sight became, in the new code, a treachery to patriotism. A novel democratic folly possessed the educated, making them praise virtues that did not exist: the very faces of the former rulers had altered, softened, lost force, while a creeping wave of envy about small things seeped into the homes of the people ("She has a quarter of an ounce of marge more than I have; I don't mind how little I have, but no one must have more!"). The Americans, who had first emerged as a people out of the fight against tradition, were thus now left, together with the Republic of Switzerland, and the Principality of Monaco, as the sole defenders of it. . . . Meanwhile, the world's engines turn, and the greatest of cataclysms, which we can all foresee, and none seems able to prevent, prepares itself. Beyond that, who knows, who sees—I had almost written "who cares"? . . . I care, most certainly. But it may be there is little immediate future for mankind, and that only many centuries hence the ruins will be uncovered, and our distant successors in some form of civilisation will, as they contemplate the various buildings of which the very use is forgotten, wonder, as I have wondered before the Bayon and the Vats of Angkor, about the life of a people, already forgotten, though so few hundreds of years have passed: a life of which, in the case of the Khmers, only the writings of a Chinese traveller to Cambodia provide for us any information. And how much we wish his account of it had been composed more precisely with a view to our enlightenment, as well as for that of the head mandarins and the Emperor of his own epoch.

So, gentle and contemporary reader, as well as to you, I have talked over your shoulder to those strangers of the future. This is, as you know, the fourth volume of my reminiscences, and we are, in a sense, at the end, for the fifth volume, though essential to the rest, is to be of a different kind from the others, more in the nature of salvos fired in honour of our epoch, a bouquet of rockets, timed to explode in future skies as well as in our own. It is concerned not mainly with my brother, my sister and myself, and not in the least with the story of our careers, but with other artists seen through my eyes. Other volumes of memories I design to write, if there is time: but they will be part of another work, governed by a separate master-plan. One or two, again, I leave behind me to await publication for a century after my death: until their indiscretions become historical, and thus discreet. They may have, however, to remain unseen for much longer than that: for what may not have happened in the interval! . . . If there

Osbert himself
sees himself as the author
of an historical
document.

ENVOY   321

is time, I write—and only the reader over your shoulder can
tell me that. He will want, I think, to know more how we
lived than how we died, more of the sort of existence that was
pleasant, more of its joys than of its miseries. The emphasis,
so unfair in itself, which makes the idle good-for-nothing
always more interesting than the blameless Secretary of a
Co-operative Stores, and the rakish Pepys more alluring than
many of the virtuous and heroic, will again assert itself: for
though Blake be right and

> The prince's robes and beggar's rags
> Are toadstools on the miser's bags,

all three, prince, beggar and miser, will claim future attention
more easily than will the Little Man. And, just as it has been
with us, so that we read with pleasure of a lost and, indeed,
unenviable world of folly and presumption in the pages of
Petronius, so it will be in a new and different culture. For that
reason I have recorded many little incidents, as well as great,
for they are illustrative.

I, a Citizen of the Sunset Age, an Englishman, who saw
the world's great darkness gathering, salute you, Stranger,
across the Chasm. I strain toward the dawn of a new age, and
offer you the story of events and persons in a day when the
light flared up before it failed. I have tried, by such art as I
could capture in my sum of days, to transmit to you almost the
physical sensations, the feeling of our hours of warmth and
cold, I have summoned to my aid every power I possess of
evocation, to paint for you the life of which I was part, the
places I saw, the people, the absurdities, cruelties, immensities,
virtues and comic lapses of man's character, the incomparable
capacity for joy and sorrow of that paragon of animals. I have
tried to prove how a child is the centre of experience and light,
from which the limbs and souls of men and women grow,
radiate like the petals of a sunflower, and into which, like
flowers, they die back. To achieve this, I have called into
service not only hand and head, but the heart and the nerves of
my whole body. I have endeavoured to make you feel what it
was like to be alive before the world fell into the pit. I have not

wanted to justify or explain, but to make a statement, to record; this is how it was for one of my origin, experience and temperament. Those of my generation obtained an end to our world in 1914. We scarcely expected the second and more fatal. Be warned, Stranger, that the fool returns to his folly, and that kindness and good feeling, and the sense of a kinship to nature which is their fount, should be cultivated as well as intelligence and the ability to make, or take, or distribute money. Above all, my message is that the world could only have been saved—perhaps still can be—through the spirit of man, especially through art, its noblest and most important manifestation. Alone of men—though with the farmer, the gardener, and the sailor following him at a distance—the artist exercises a profession that is entirely beneficial, and creative in itself. He unlocks for others the gates of the mind, the senses and the soul.

This I can tell you, Stranger, from things observed in my world: but what of yours? . . . I cannot see your face, neither its colour nor shape, nor hear what tongue you speak. It may be—who knows?—some dog-English, learnt from old scripts and used as a general language, variously pronounced as dog-Latin in the Middle Ages (for the English language, whatever else is in decay or collapse, remains, as I have essayed, too, to show, magnificently alive, its possibilities unexhausted). I must content myself, then, with such facts as are clear, and build on them my own edifices. The sky and earth will be the same, though the planets are conquered, and men's loves and jealousies and follies. The vast panorama of the heavens, offered to me now, will be what you will behold also. I stare out of window, trying to conjure up the metropolises of the future, when men have again crept out of the ground into which they will have been forced. Once out of their burrows, they will build with renewed vigour and aspiration. As the reader knows, who has had the patience to accompany me so far, I have indulged in sciomancy and the magic of clouds all my life, and I see vast cities, palaces and domes, spires and arches, rise up, reform, as the clouds tumble like children upon the hills. Towards the apex of the sky are whole clusters now of gigantic towers, crowned with the sun, and through the vast thoroughfare of the firmament run rivers and torrents and cascades of light. On walls huge as hills, and undulating like the Great Wall of China (which once I saw) are set giant images, gods or demigods, drenched in light, the reflections of the times in which the states and cities were born. Among the golden rush and swerving of the clouds, maned like horses, from the vaulted halls where sit in conclave the ancient philosophers, with their grave eyes, wide-open as those of statues, and with their white beards flowing in the spectral, polar winds, while they listen to music or ask questions of the past, I hear voices, reaching to me faintly. What was the world like before it fell, they ask: was there deep sorrow? . . . No, there was a peculiar sadness in the air, a feeling of hundreds of days leading up to this particular day, and every now and then the breath of a change to come as when the great airs of summer move under August trees: only that, and a surge of vanity in man. It is difficult to know the end of the world when you reach it.

RENISHAW,
22nd February, 1948

(I was
9 months
old)

on the end of
his world as
he is growing into
old age; He is in
his late 50's here I
think, about my
age now

APPENDIX A

THE EXHIBITION OF MODERN FRENCH ART, 1919

A NOTICE AND CORRESPONDENCE IN *THE NATION*

A Notice by Clive Bell

August 16, 1919

The French Pictures at Heal's

ANYONE who cares for art and happens to have been left out of the British Peace delegation will be thankful to those enterprising poets, the two Mr. Sitwells, and to M. Zborowski for bringing over from Paris just what he wanted to see. We stay-at-homes have long been asking what the French painters have been about since the summer of 1914, and, above all, whether any new ones have appeared. We are answered. Here is, not exactly a third Post-Impressionist exhibition, but one so rich and representative that any professed amateur who fails to return from the country and visit it may safely be reckoned a fraud.

The grand and thrilling fact that emerges from this exhibition is that French art is vital still. The war has not killed the movement. Still it goes forward along the course set by Cézanne. There is stir and effort and experiment: within the movement there is a lively reaction: there is a *jeunesse*.

Of the four young, or youngish, masters of modern painting—Renoir I reckon an old one—three are here represented. Four pictures by Matisse are about the first things to catch the eye as one enters the gallery; and two of these (the *Nude* and the *Lady with Rings*) are exquisite examples of his subtle, yet vigorous art. They are as surely and economically planned as Romanesque churches, and as delicate as flowers. His very latest work—the girl with a parasol—is, it must be confessed, less satisfactory. Frankly, it is too pretty, a bit too clever, and something empty. Still, if one swallow does not make a summer, neither does one thistle-down make a fall. Matisse cannot be much above fifty, and as yet I see no reason for refusing to hope that, going steadily forward, he will in ten or fifteen years be to another generation what Renoir is to ours. Meanwhile, here we have the last word in his art, so the spectator can form his own opinion. Neither of the two Picassos, as anyone who saw his curtain at the Alhambra will remark, are in his latest manner. They are first-rate examples of an earlier style; and it is a joy to see them. Only, it would have been even more interesting to have seen a few of those drawings that he has been making during the last six months. Unless I mistake, it is towards this new Picasso—the superficially realistic Picasso who has been influenced by Ingres—that the youngest painters are now turning for leadership.

Though since the end of 1914 Derain has been almost incessantly at the wars no painter has since then advanced farther in public esteem. What is more, judged by his curtain and scenery for *La Boutique Fantasque*, his artistic progress has been equally great. Five years ago everyone who knew anything knew that he was a fine painter: he is now a chief. His two little Watteauesque pictures are likely to surprise some who admired his curtain: of his drawings three, at least, are superb, while one—the head of a negress—is, to my taste, shocking. It is probable that Derain will continue as long as he lives to make a certain number of bad drawings. Making bad drawings is part of his system. Apparently there is nothing he fears so much as falling into a habit of making good ones. He keeps a ferocious watch over his facility. To counteract it he sets himself the most unpromising problems and makes the most unlikely experiments. He has the courage of his conviction, and seems to mind not at all if the results are preposterous. The thing for him is to preserve an open mind and a free hand.

There is nothing here by Bonnard. Perhaps the organizers of the exhibition hold that because he derives more from Renoir than from Cézanne he is not of the movement. If so, I think they mistake. In any case, it would have been a treat for us to have seen something by this charming and intensely modern painter. Matisse, Picasso, Derain, Bonnard—these are the four names that 1919 sets against those of 1880—Cézanne, Renoir, Degas, and Manet. The comparison is formidable; but 1919 will not easily be daunted.

Behind the chiefs come a group of first-rate painters, several of whom are well represented in this exhibition. The collection of Modiglianis is the best that I have seen. Modigliani will never be a great painter, but he is a very good one. To begin with, he is not a painter at all; he is a draughtsman who colours his drawings. Indeed, it is in his pencil drawings that he is seen to the greatest advantage. Evidently Modigliani is admirably aware of his own limitations. Never does he set himself a task beyond his powers. Unfortunately, that means that he never sets himself the sort of problem from which comes the greatest art. He exploits his slightly literary sensibility with infinite tact, and, as his sensibility is great, there is not much risk of his becoming a bore. But, when one notices how much he has been influenced by Picasso and Derain one notices, too, how impossible it is that he should ever be a match for either of them.

Vlaminck is an artist more to my taste and, perhaps, a better one: albeit he is not of the great. The end wall which has been devoted to his pictures presents a flash of joyous colour that is, as the saying goes, a sight for sore eyes. These rapid, tremulous statements are as lovely as jewels: and it is amusing to observe how, when he chooses to construct a work of art out of vulgar, melodramatic materials, his sensibility, skimming round and about them, runs no more risk of a collision with the subject than does a swallow with the wall whereon it hangs its nest. If many of these Vlamincks go back to Paris I shall think the worse of my compatriots.

Friesz is not dull though he looks it. Examine this work closely—especially the military procession or the tiny picture of a pear—and you will find what one always expects to find in a Friesz—admirable painting. Lhote is disconcerting. His water-colours are as seductive as ever, but it is not his water-colours that interest me most. He seems to have forsaken his old masters, the popular colour-printers of the last century, and to have plunged into that new realism towards which *la jeune peinture* is visibly moving. Unlike his water-colours, his portraits and his family group are anything but seductive. I suspect, however, they are the best things he has yet done. And if Lhote goes on at this rate he will soon be one of the best painters alive. Utrillo will be a new name to a good many English amateurs. What a misfortune that this remarkable painter, the discoverer of a new significance in the bricks and stones and iron, and even in the pseudo-marble of Paris, is now so ill that he will perhaps never paint again! And he is only a little over thirty. Marchand is not represented. Also, there is nothing by Braque or Gris. So, unless they prefer the great, dreary machine of Léger, or the pretty affectations of Archipenko, the young cubists must be represented by Marcoussis. For Marcoussis much could be said: for Donas, another young cubist, little; and for Van Rees nothing. But the future—the immediate future at any rate—is not with these. There is a reaction against cubism, and this reaction, naturally enough, is being led by the inventor of cubism—Picasso.

It is not to be supposed that the reaction from cubism implies any break with the tradition of Cézanne or any leaning towards literature. Those who adore anecdote and sentiment, and have no liking for art should be warned, at once, that they will find nothing to please them here—unless it be the work of Russell and Krog. There is a tendency towards realism, but none towards illustration. The younger painters seem to feel that the problem of creating significant design out of real forms is more inspiring than the problem of creating it out of imagined. Without suggesting that geometrical forms are in themselves less aesthetically significant than the forms of Nature, they feel that the latter are to them more useful. But, it must be understood, they use the forms of Nature precisely as the cubists use their geometrical forms—they use them, that is to say, as mere shapes and colours out of which an aesthetically satisfying whole is to be built. With Nature they play what tricks they please. They never hesitate to distort.

Of the young artists who here represent the divergence rather than the reaction from cubism I remember, particularly, six—Durey,

Mondsain, Féder, Favory, Gabriel-Fournier, and Halicka. Gabriel-Fournier, to be sure, is not young, but he is new to me. He seems to be a sort of sophisticated *douanier* Rousseau who has looked, for perhaps a moment too long, at Vlaminck and Marchand. All his three pictures pleased me extremely. Féder is probably the best of the bunch, the most gifted and the most accomplished. I cannot think how so good an artist came to do anything so tiresome as his portrait of an old woman (No. 87). Durey interests me because he appears to be so young and so very much in earnest. Look at his picture of a bridge over a cutting, which, though it shows some trace of Marchand's influence, is admirably personal and sincere. One can see that he has had his vision and has set himself to express what he felt without pretension and without trickery, without trying to make himself appear in any way better than he is. He allows us to see just what his personal reaction amounts to; and it amounts to something well worth stating. Mondsain I like a good deal; but I don't believe in Soutine with his catch-penny prettiness of paint, nor much in the amusing and gay, but rather trivial Survage. Dufy is an extremely able and slightly vulgar illustrator.

Perhaps the most charming, though certainly not the best, of the artists who are making their début in London is Halicka. Halicka is impressionable; but, unlike most of the younger painters, Halicka has not been influenced by Picasso, but by Matisse and Derain. Any sharp student can learn something profitable from Picasso; from Matisse, theorist though he be in words, few painters can get more than this not very helpful injunction—exploit your sensibility. Halicka is lucky in having so much to exploit. I should not be surprised if one of the most generally liked pictures in the gallery were the self-portrait of this artist in her studio. *Her* studio—for Halicka turns out to be a woman. So, amongst other things, this exhibition adds a name to our tiny list of distinguished female painters.

CLIVE BELL

THE NATION

August 23, 1919

LETTERS TO THE EDITOR

The French Pictures

SIR,—After all it is the patient, not the College of Physicians, who best knows the doctor's worth; none but a specialist believes that a thief is the best thief-catcher. There is sufficient mother-sense left in us to know if the treatment of our sickness is efficacious; the remnant of predatory instinct in the average man gives him enough understanding of the law-breaker's tricks to lay him by the heels.

Indeed the specialist's outlook is notoriously lacking in breadth of vision; and I claim that an average person like myself may be a better judge of modern art than the artist, or even the highly-specialised art-critic himself.

For the average person is such only because he possesses the common instincts—native gifts, as distinguished from educational—of his kind. He judges a doctor by his instinct of suffering, a thief by his own grim needs, an artist by the fact that all humanity is comprehended in the instinct of art. The evolution of man is the evolution of his means of expression, and nothing more signally proves the infinity of his nature. His real growth is to be found not in the vicious circle of competitive thieving, but in the ascending spiral of personal and social expression; not in commerce or Empire, but in art and service.

I was yesterday impelled by Mr. Clive Bell's article in your latest issue to visit the French Pictures. I confess that, as one not emancipated from his mother-instincts, I had no right to look at those pictures. They were bad for me. I tried to see them as I hoped it was intended that I should see them; tried to find where I was wrong in missing the beauty of the forms portrayed, the genius of the painters. I will not say that the indecent distortions, the obscene colourings, the immodest subjects, were deliberate intentions to shock us out of our conventional ideas of beauty, truth, sweetness and law, for I suspect *intention* of any sort, like purpose in art, is repudiated by these reformers. I admit in some of these pictures a wonderful cleverness—is it perhaps "genius that does what it must, or talent no more than it can"?—a cleverness especially in portraiture which, while rendering its subjects technically uglier than any human beings have any right to be, yet gives them undeniable portraiture. Indeed this seems to be the aim of the new genius—to deny the use of accurate drawing, to earthquake all perspective; to combine colours so that they shall in the practice of falsehood become decorative; to whip beauty, truth, morality, imagination for worn-out jades; and yet still to suggest something that might have been worth painting. But obscenity pervades the simplest subjects: is not one guilty of this, Sir, when he strips everything he touches of its clothing in beauty? At one moment I felt the whole show to be a glorying in prostitution; for it is a spiritual law that the higher the exaltation the more terrible the fall. At another I felt it must be an attempt to prove that all revolution, however necessary for the redemption of society or morality or art, has only one ending—that of sans-culottism: and that, meaning less the exchange of court-breeches for plebeian trousers, than the discarding of every convention of decency.

Sir, I dare claim to be an ardent disciple of William Blake, he beyond all others being the Apostle of Revolution. But just as surely as he indicates the fossilizing influence of all systems—the "mundane shells", as he calls them, of our liberty, our truth, our imagination—whether intellectualism that destroys art, or religion that builds brothels, or law that erects prisons, so and as surely he will not let us forget the sickening horror of prostitution, of denying the law, the tradition, that has governed whatsoever of nobility there may be in our art, our literature, our music.

The critic will find in my ignorance of art, or my prejudices, or my astigmatism, easy explanation of this outburst. I plead and speak not personally, but as an average educated man who believes in art, beauty, imagination as the highest of his universal gifts. Our speech itself, our dancing, our music, our games, are all art—the outward and visible signs of those spiritual things which, without such means of expression, could never be told, never discovered. Our art is everything to us. Blake and Tolstoy, Ruskin and Morris are its apostles, as surely as Darwin, Huxley, Mendel are the exponents of our more tangible evolution. But these young painters in Tottenham Court Road are no more artists than certain religionists are scientific. If I am wrong, will Mr. Clive Bell inform me and in untechnical words that the simple-minded can understand?—Yours, etc., GREVILLE MacDONALD, M.D.

REFORM CLUB. August 19th, 1919.

SIR,—To see Messrs. Heal & Son's model flat one has to pass through the Exhibition of Modern French Art being held by the same firm.

It was my fate, therefore, to see this collection of grotesques just a few hours before reading your article on them. I am a Philistine, I admit, and an engineer by trade, with a strong dislike of having my leg pulled. Is Mr. Clive Bell pulling our legs or is he not? If not, what in the name of goodness does he mean by saying that a picture of a bridge over a railway cutting is personal and real? Is the object of a picture to show us the artist's psychology or to show us something in the thing depicted that the untrained eye cannot see? If the artist had managed subtly to show to us, and to future generations, all that a modern bridge means, the difficulties of design and construction, the contract and labour troubles, etc., if that were possible, then it might be a work of art, as revealing something to every man that without the artist's vision would be concealed. But I cannot conceive that an individual's distorted view of a normal feature of a landscape can be of any interest except to an alienist if it shows us nothing but the picture on his retina. Then, again, Mr. Bell talks of Vlaminck's flash of joyous colour on the end wall. If Mr. Bell really enjoys the pink of the centre picture I can give him an address in Margate where he can feast his eyes on it, if he will stay in the drawing-room of the address I give him! In the side room of the exhibition there is a great space of wall covered by rectangular slabs of glaring colours. Is that aesthetically satisfying, and, if so, what effect on the person so satisfied do the following have:—Praxiteles' *Flora* in the Vatican and the Taj Mahal? I am honestly eager to learn, and I quite understand that the trained eye sees more in a picture than I do, just as I see more in a wall or a canal, say, than the ordinary layman. But then I can explain in clear terms what it is I see, whereas the artist and his critic can only, it seems to me, cloud the landscape with a sepia-flow of generalities and abstractions incapable of definition. Can we not have this thing stated clearly? What is it about this new art, cubism, post-impressionism, etc., that leaves the normal educated man gasping? What is it I do not understand about it? If somebody will only state the mystery the first steps will have been taken in the artistic education of myself and brother Philistines. I am tired of being told I don't understand. I know I don't; but what *is* there to understand?—Yours, etc., PHILISTINE.

August 18th, 1919.

THE NATION

August 30, 1919

LETTERS TO THE EDITOR

The French Pictures

SIR,—Without wishing to trespass in the province, or within the sound of Beau Bell, may I venture to draw attention to a few of the psychological problems raised in your last issue by the letters of Dr. Greville MacDonald and " Philistine " with regard to the French pictures at Messrs. Heal's?

The curious feature of the display is that both these gentlemen claim to be the " average " sheep. Now, sir, would an average sheep have heard of Blake or William Morris? Would even a normal wolf, perhaps a little unbalanced by a desire for food, see in our games, including, one may suppose, croquet, football, and auction bridge, a manifestation of the art of our times? But Dr. Greville MacDonald is, in reality, no wolf; he is a Romulus reared on the milk of Rossetti and on the wild treacle of Burne-Jones. He comes before these pictures, not as an " average educated man ", but as one with definite preconceived notions. Before he can enter into the spirit of Modern Art Dr. Greville MacDonald must be " born again ".

" Philistine " is different. This unfortunate stray sheep has dressed himself up for the part, and seeks to play the " wolf grandmother " to Mr. Clive Bell's " Red Riding Hood ", which one fears may lead to a considerable period of toothache and mental indigestion.

But Grannie is colour blind! Where among the Vlamincks is to be found that " pink ", which for better or worse reminds our " Philistine " of Margate? I cannot argue about *Flora*, which I have not seen, nor can I undertake the journey to Ind to see the Taj-Mahal which has far too long been rendered a byword as the club topic of Anglo-Indian colonels, and engineers-by-trade-with-a-strong-dislike-of-having-their-legs-pulled, but surely to suggest that to like these pictures you cannot appreciate the Taj-Mahal is to argue that a fondness for roast chicken prevents a due appreciation of strawberries and cream!

Finally, let me express a pious hope that " Philistine " before adding his presence to the collection of grotesques which he mentions paid the entrance fee of 1s. 3d. By his phrase " To see Messrs. Heal & Son's model flat one has to pass through the Exhibition of Modern French Art ", I am rather inclined to doubt this, but *Qu'il retourne à ses moutons*, which is to say—engineering.—Yours, etc., OSBERT SITWELL.

SIR,—Mr. Bell is probably extremely bored by demand for the explanation that always arises after an article by him on modern painting. He will, then, perhaps forgive me for stepping in and trying to explain to " Philistine " at least something of why he does not understand. The reason is, briefly, that he is a normal, educated man; which implies, I think, that he is a normally educated man, and as a consequence, that he has been taught nothing about art, its evolution, and its traditions, and that he has had no opportunity of learning. Our galleries hardly contain any pictures of value painted during the last century—Glasgow, for instance, possesses one beautiful Daumier [sic] and nothing else better than a Corot in his finer moments. The National Gallery has little more, apart from the small collection left by Sir Hugh Lane. The result of this is that normally educated men are totally ignorant of the traditions, and so unaware of their ignorance, that they accuse the modern artist of an assault upon tradition. The galleries encourage this ignorance not only by boycotting all the masters of the nineteenth century, but also by placing poor school works under the name of a famous painter. The ordinary man looks at a Raphael and then at a pseudo-Raphael; he notices that the only quality they have in common is their portrayal of sweetly charming faces; logically he deduces that Raphael was a great artist because of his capacity to reproduce charm. Actually Raphael's charm is as irrelevant to the value of his work as Russell and Whitehead's " Prolegomena to Cardinal Arithmetic " is irrelevant to bookkeeping.

Modern artists have been doing two things—stripping their work of irrelevancies and trying to use colour as something more than a decoration, or than a filling-up of the drawing. This is not a new and sudden revolution, for Delacroix, Turner, Daumier and Courbet began the two movements early in the last century. They were hardly noticed in England, for Turner and Constable were isolated phenomena. Courbet and Millet both painted peasant life, Millet added sentimentality and religion to an extraordinary incapacity for producing anything but the simplest design, and reproductions of his work flooded the country, while Courbet's *Les Casseurs de Pierres*, with the rhythmic quality of a masterpiece, is almost unknown.

It is not surprising that the normally educated man, brought up from childhood on Watts and Millet, does not understand the pictures at Heal's.—Yours, etc., E. R. BROWN.

GLASGOW, August 25th, 1919.

SIR,—Your correspondent, Dr. Greville MacDonald, wrote in your last issue: " At one moment I felt the *whole show* (the Exhibition at the Mansard Gallery) to be a glorying in prostitution "—the italics are mine.

Now the Exhibition contains 157 pictures, roughly distributed as follows:

Nudes	12
Genre	15
Portraits and Portrait Studies	31
Still Life and Interiors	46
Landscapes	53
Total.	157

As regards the nudes, let us assume that all nudes shock the Doctor; there still remain 143 glorifications of prostitution to be accounted for. Among these 53 are landscapes, 46 are paintings of still life. Possibly Dr. MacDonald can find immorality in fruits and flowers as Serjeant Buzfuz did in chops and tomato sauce. But, however that may be, may I, sir, on behalf of several ladies and gentlemen who are my companions, venture to protest against our inclusion in the Doctor's charge? I assure you we do not glory in anything of the kind.—Yours, etc., ONE OF THE PORTRAITS.

August 25th, 1919.

THE NATION
September 6, 1919

LETTERS TO THE EDITOR

The French Pictures

SIR,—Captain Sitwell, Mr. Brown, and the justly indignant portrait are all delightfully witty and intelligent and crushing. They have answered my excited and not very thoughtful critics finely. But, as none of them has said just what I hoped he would say, I suppose I must say it myself. If the chaste Dr. MacDonald and his pathetic engineer really want to understand; if, in truth, all they ask for is a simple, straightforward account of the modern movement, let them harden their hearts and bung down five shillings for a copy of *Art* by Clive Bell (Chatto & Windus).

Thanking you, Sir, in advance for the honour of their esteemed orders.—Yours, etc., THE AUTHOR.

P.S. Captain Sitwell is not likely to have seen the *Flora* of Praxiteles. The Philistine must have discovered it, along with the pink Vlaminck, and kept it to himself—sly dog!

SIR,—Clearly Mr. Osbert Sitwell does not understand the position of " Philistine " and myself. When we speak of Art it is of a different subject and in different tongues: *we* mean something come to us rich through an eternity of inheritance; *he*, some " jazz " degeneration of that same gift. Art to us is our means of understanding Beauty, and through it certain Truths not otherwise getting utterance. And, I suppose this Art of ours is as mawkish to him as these French painters are repulsive to our sense of what is lovely.

For my part, I claimed to be an " average man " not in any admission of inferiority, as it appears to Mr. Sitwell, but because I delight in the possession of those common attributes which sum up our *humanity*. At the very foundation of this humanity lies the recognition of *Beauty* as a virtue utterly desirable and wholly unselfish. The baby clutches at, dances with joy at sight of, a peacock's feather: as soon as he can toddle and pluck a daisy for himself he must run with it to his mother—the best beloved—for instant sharing. This is the common sense which I, matured in experience, delight in as the basis of all art and all spiritual evolution. But this sense is shamed and nauseated when the human form is presented to my eyes—and worse, to young-eyed students—not only robbed of its native modesty, but gross in attitude; or, as in a certain sculptured torso, with the buttocks and belly four times the girth of chest and shoulders; or, again, in colours found only in the post-mortem theatre or dissecting-room.

In the letter signed " One of the Portraits " my point is curiously missed: I had allowed these portraits, in spite of being grotesques, quicker wits! In using the word *prostitution* I intended to imply that all falling from a high ideal is just that, and that these artists, almost without exception, are prostituting their native traditional genius. I bow to the suggestion that I discover among these pictures a real immorality in the treatment of some innocent and lovely subjects—which, here and there, one discovers them to be, in spite of their protectors dragging them in the mud.

With a great deal of Mr. E. R. Brown's I am in sympathy. But he must remember that the normally educated man has not been brought up solely on Watts and Burne-Jones, and that many of us have even found in Constable and Turner divinely revolutionary spirits. And in spite of Mr. Brown I dare add to these revolutionaries his despised Millet; for it was he who revealed to us in the peasant, notwithstanding grinding poverty and ignorance, the ineradicable divinity of man. But these new painters, and apparently their apologists, are as lacking in humour as in reverence: to them, I more than suspect, religion, however expressed, is either an artistic offence or a sentimental absurdity. Let me say once more that the good effected by the French Revolution was not a political upheaval of the proletariat so much as a discovery of the traditional worth in the individual, traditional man. As far as Art is concerned, the foundation of it all lies in peasant-art—whether we speak of painting or music or dancing or play. It took a Tolstoy to make this plain, though a child may understand it.

Mr. Sitwell says that we Philistines must be born again; and, for my part, I do most reverently desire this, whether by revolution or the Grace of God. But such new birth will be worth having only through the exaltation and purification of that *average* sense of Beauty and Truth in Art, which, poor as is my technical knowledge, makes nearly all these pictures in the Mansard Gallery repulsive to my sense of moral and spiritual well-being.—Yours, etc., GREVILLE MACDONALD.

BUDE, CORNWALL, September 1st, 1919.

THE NATION

September 13, 1919

LETTERS TO THE EDITOR

The French Pictures

SIR,—" The Author " invites us to buy and read his book. I am not tempted to do so by the quality of his letter. Its levity is the characteristic of the serious art of to-day, and the less said or read about it or its authors the nearer we shall be to its extinction. This accomplished, Art may again occupy the attention of mankind. At present the artist has no vocation. He is an idler on the earth, lost in admiration of his own inventions.—Yours, etc., T. J. COBDEN-SANDERSON.

THE DOVES PRESS, 15 UPPER MALL,
HAMMERSMITH, W.6.

SIR,—I am much obliged to Mr. Clive Bell for the reference to his book on *Art*, in which I hope to find the answer to my question, " What is there to understand? " which your correspondents have hitherto not answered.

I am quite prepared to accept Mr. Brown's explanation, that because I have been brought up on Watts, Burne-Jones, etc., I do not appreciate the French pictures as a whole—but I do appreciate some of them, and would suggest they can be divided roughly into three classes.

1. The Impressionist school, who produce fine landscapes by a new technique or an extension of an existing one. I should say the pictures

on the end wall (on the left as you enter) belong to this class, and anyone who is prepared to clear his mind of formulae can accept them as *bona fide* pictures by real artists.

2. The Pavement school, who produce the distorted ladies with flesh the colour of underburnt brick. There seems to be no particular object in producing these pictures: they are neither beautiful nor interesting, and should be classed with the efforts in coloured chalk by the artists of our streets who label themselves " entirely self-taught ".

3. The Cubist school. These are the gentlemen I suspect of pulling my leg. Do they really see things like that, or are they trying it on to see how much the critics and the public will stand?

I have tried the pictures from every angle short of standing on my head, and to me they are absolutely meaningless. Granted it is a new convention, cannot the base of the convention be stated? I should like to be able to appreciate the pictures, but that I despair of—is it impossible to understand the convention they use?

Shapes in three dimensions and colours cannot be represented on a canvas by the aid of pigments without the use of a convention that is understood both by the artist and his public. If this is not done, the artist is like a poet declaiming in Choctaw to an English audience.

The ordinary conventional representation we learn to understand from babyhood, and those who are fortunate enough to understand art can appreciate great works carried out in this convention, while those less fortunate can at least see something they recognise on the canvas. Even if I cannot appreciate *La Gioconda*, I can at least see that it is a painting of a woman whereas with the Cubist pictures I am in the position of the unfortunate savage who is as likely to hold a photo of himself upside down as right side up. It conveys nothing to him, and the Cubist pictures convey nothing to me.

The artist is using a convention that has not been explained to his public, and seems to me to be defeating his own object, which I take it is the expression of himself to a public. Does he say the convention he uses is too high for a mere Philistine to understand, must I believe in him as an act of faith?

Will you allow me to point out that Captain Sitwell begs the question by his analogy of roast chicken and strawberries-and-cream? The point I fail to understand is how a palate that appreciates *pêche Melba* can also appreciate *fesikh* (decayed fish dried in the sun, and salted—a great delicacy in some parts of the world).

If the pink thing in the centre of the end wall at the Mansard exhibition is not by Vlaminck, I apologise to him, but my remarks about it stand, as far as I am concerned. No catalogue was obtainable, so I cannot say who really is responsible for it.

As to the *Flora*, by Praxiteles, which Mr. Bell appears to consider a myth, I should have said " attributed to Praxiteles ", but, again, the name of the artist is not important. The comparison is between the school that produces the pink things and the distorted females on the one hand and the school that produced the *Flora*, the *Laocoon*, etc., on the other.

If you love the Elgin marbles, how can you stand the Mansard Gallery? If you like strawberries-and-cream, how can you stand tripe-and-onions?—Yours, etc., PHILISTINE.

September 8th, 1919.

SIR,—Dr. Greville MacDonald has dragged a peacock's feather across the trail; but his opening remarks, about the difference between his ideas of art and my own, rather recall the typical beginning of a well-known comic variety turn:—

> Of course, *I* don't know the sort of people you know—
> And I don't expect they would like me if I did!

May I point out that the fact that Dr. Greville MacDonald's baby clutches a peacock's feather, and crows delightfully, is merely a sign that it *is* a baby (of the aesthetic period, I judge)—not an educated individual with a cultured appreciation of art?

Delightful as the action may be in its simplicity, it does not amount to a very serious criticism. However, I hope Dr. Greville MacDonald has, by this time, bought *Art*, as recommended by its author, and studied Mr. Clive Bell's theory of significant form. It will help him, I think.

I am rather puzzled by Dr. Greville MacDonald's theories of distortion and immorality. If he saw a painting of a peacock with its head ten times the usual size, would it make an immoral picture or an immoral peacock?

Finally, let me express the hope that when the Doctor is born again—and I feel convinced he will be—he will clutch, not at a peacock's feather, but at a Vlaminck or Modigliani. Yours, etc. OSBERT SITWELL.

WOOD END, SCARBOROUGH.

SIR,—I fear I am one of those despised people who, without being in the least puritanical, would not be persuaded even by a sounding Bell (at five shillings) or a tinkling Symbol (at half-a-crown) to regard productions like those described by Dr. Greville MacDonald as falling under the category of art.

But it may be of interest to recall that a combination of ugliness and indecency, so far from being *le dernier cri*, is really rather *vieux jeu*, and that a similar perverse cult flourished in Paris rather more than a generation ago.

For proof I would refer to Zola's forgotten, but extremely well-documented novel, *L'Œuvre* (1886). Here is a descripton of Claude

Lantier's crazy " masterpiece ", in front of which he finally hangs himself:

" C'était à la femme nue qu'il travaillait. . . . Il peignait le ventre et les cuisses en visionnaire affolé, que le tourment du vrai jetait à l'exaltation de l'irréel; et ces cuisses se doraient en colonnes de tabernacle, ce ventre devenait un astre, éclatant de jaune et de rouge purs, splendide et hors de la vie. Une si étrange nudité d'ostensoir, où des pierreries semblaient luire pour quelque adoration religieuse. . . ."

A normal person, utterly revolted on inspecting an earlier work of Lantier's, delivers his verdict in the simple phrase: " C'est cochon ". And so, when face to face with like exhibitions, say all of us.— Yours, etc., JACQUES BONHOMME.

THE NATION

September 27, 1919

LETTERS TO THE EDITOR

The French Pictures

SIR,—Ten years ago I should have felt inclined to argue with some of your correspondents. To-day it would be absurd. Even *The Times* now admits officially that the battle is won and, in its special French supplement (September 6th), recognizes Cézanne, Renoir, Van Gogh, Gauguin, and *le douanier* Rousseau as the old, and Matisse, Picasso, Derain, Lhote, Vlaminck, etc., as the young masters of modern painting. The same truths were, of course, recognized long ago by *The Times* art critic; but, for my purpose, the judgment of a highly trained and sensitive expert counts as nothing in comparison with the pompous pronouncements of a special supplement. It must now be obvious to all that the battle is over, and that Dr. Greville MacDonald and his friends are the gallant defenders of a lost cause. As such they are entitled to our affectionate esteem, for which, however, they are not likely to thank us.

Nevertheless, I should be glad, in all friendliness, to offer some of them a word of advice. For instance, who has been telling Dr. MacDonald that when a baby picks a flower it takes it to its mother? Don't you believe it, doctor. It was this fellow, not the cubists, who was pulling your leg. When a baby picks a flower it puts it into its mouth, and, if given time, swallows it. There was a bit in the papers the other day about a child's dying from having thus swallowed a scrap of lettuce. What might not have happened had it been a dandelion or a peacock's feather? I call it a shame to put such jokes on "a family man", which is what I take the doctor to be.

The Philistine seems anxious to learn, so I will do my best to help him. In the first place, it is a mistake to attack an artist by name until you have taken the trouble to make sure that the picture complained of is really his doing. And, then, about that *Flora* of Praxiteles, the title of which, by the way, should have put my critic on his guard. We have but one authentic statue by Praxiteles, the *Hermes* at Olympia. Lord Leconfield's *Head of Aphrodite* is supposed to be not very far from the original; and the following copies are reckoned by experts to have about them some reminiscences of the real thing: the *Silenus*, the *Satyr*, two figures of Eros, the *Artemis*, the *Zeus*, two figures of Dionysos, and the *Apollo*. All existing copies of the *Aphrodite of Cnidos* are generally considered too feeble to give any idea of the original. It is to be presumed, therefore, that our Philistine has either dubbed one of these copies *Flora*, or—and this seems more probable—wandering through the Vatican, has been enchanted by some bit of Roman rubbish which, in a gallery from which the rude breath of scholarship is appropriately enough excluded, still bears the thrilling label *Praxiteles*. May I hope that this little controversy will suggest to Philistine, who seems to be a good, modest sort of man, the extreme impropriety, not to say folly, of meddling in matters about which one knows nothing?

I cannot tell whether the gentleman who prefers to conceal his name will be glad or sorry to learn that "Claude Lantier" is Zola's conception of Cézanne. In any case, this scrap of information should help to tidy up his mind by showing him that the movement of whose beginnings Zola wrote in *L'Œuvre*, is the one that to-day triumphs throughout Europe and America.

Finally, may I say how happy it made me to see a letter from Mr. Cobden-Sanderson. I had made sure that he was dead. It is a pity that he will not read my book, which might have put him in the way of new aesthetic pleasures. But Mr. Sanderson I suspect would regard it as an act of disloyalty to care much for anything for which Morris had not cared; and loyalty is a virtue that excuses worse things than obstinacy and ill-temper.—Yours, etc., CLIVE BELL.

SIR,—My only excuse for a further trespass is that having taken Mr. Clive Bell's advice and bought his book I see clearly I must always differ from these French artists. We hold different concepts of Beauty. Mr. Bell claims that aesthetics concern only Art, and that it alone can give us Beauty's peculiar emotion—one, in fact, altogether separate from the common human emotions. But most of us decline to dissociate Beauty from Art—at any rate, as soon as we are emancipated from Royal Academy standards. Many, moreover, will agree with me in claiming that a passionate sense of Beauty is an intimate belonging of Man, and is quintessential in every emotion and ideal he is capable of experiencing. Some may even venture to define the relation of

Beauty to Art and declare that the sublimity of Beauty is found wherever the Divine Spirit has moved over the Waters of the formless and void; and that Art is achieved when Man, inspired by some vision of magical Beauty—as the Matterhorn piercing the heavenly blue, a primrose glade, or a woman's face—must perforce worship, and then, because of the spiritual joy awakened, comes down to earth again and does what he can to let his brother see also some of the light that should light every man. Such a one, if he be any sort of craftsman, will decorate some bowl he has made, paint some picture, imagine some cathedral in such wise that he is taking part, great or small, in the everlasting mission of Beauty.

Judging from Mr. Clive Bell's teaching, one has no more right to trust his instinctive love of Beauty without first graduating in the school of post-impressionism than a child his instinct for food until he has qualified himself in experimental physiology! It is because of an increasing sense of our instinct's authenticity that so many have revolted from Burlington House and South Kensington, and do now again revolt from the preciousness of Mr. Clive Bell's acid test, "Significant Form". But not even violence in destructive criticism invokes power to teach or create. Though these French painters do not inspire me, they would be dangerous were they not very sick men: their malady is incurable, because, believing in nothing else, they overeat *themselves*. So we need take no thought for the morrow: *Ars longa, vita brevis*; or, in freer English: A long rope and a quick drop!—Yours, etc., Greville MacDonald.

Bude. September 16th, 1919.

APPENDIX B

SIR GEORGE SITWELL

By Evelyn Waugh

I MET your father once only, on my first visit here thirteen or fourteen years ago this summer, and I remember him most particularly as I saw him one evening just before dinner.

We had all come out on the terrace to enjoy the beauty of the sunset which was breaking through the mist and was lighting up the opposing hills.

Your father was wearing a long-tailed evening coat with a black waistcoat as though he had gone into mourning with the Court many years before, had taken a liking to the style and retained it in deference to some august and secret bereavement of his own. He seemed slightly estranged from the large party you and Sachie had invited and edged away to the extreme fringe of the group, where I was standing, and stood silently, gazing out across the valley.

I had noted with fascination during my stay how his beard would assume new shapes with his change of mood, like the supple felt hat on an impersonator. Sometimes he would appear as King Lear on Dover cliffs, sometimes as Edward Lear on Athos, sometimes as Mr. Pooter at Margate. Tonight he was Robinson Crusoe. I think it was in his mind, then, that rather than being, as he was, a rare visitor at Renishaw, he lived there uninterruptedly all the year round and had in consequence lost touch with the life of fashion which was his birthright.

In the valley at our feet, still half hidden in mist, lay farms, cottages, villas, the railway, the colliery and the densely teeming streets of the men who worked there. They lay in shadow; the heights beyond were golden.

Your father had seldom addressed me directly during my visit. Now, since I was next to him, he turned and spoke in the wistful, nostalgic tones of a castaway, yet of a castaway who was reconciled to his solitude. "You see," he said, "there is *no one* between us and the Locker-Lampsons."

Renishaw, 20th June 1942.

APPENDIX C

PRIMAVERA AND FELLOW-GUESTS

IN the autumn or winter of 1940 the Italian Government seques-
trated Montegufoni, and in 1942 it became the chief storehouse cf
Italian pictures in North Italy, being filled not only with the chief
works of the Uffizi and Pitti Galleries, but with others from churches
and museums throughout Tuscany. The Castello was chosen for this
purpose, I understand, because it is situated in a remote district, but,
still more, because the doors and windows of the chief rooms were big
enough to allow the largest pictures to be carried in and out without
risk of damage. These treasures were consigned personally to the
contadino in charge of the Castle, Guido Masti, the representative of a
family who had occupied the same position of trust under various
owners for well over a century. He has been kind enough to lend me
the papers of consignment, and though the lists are long, I reproduce
them here, for they constitute a remarkable document in the history
of Art, and bear testimony to one of its most extraordinary episodes.
For here, very near what was to become for some days one of the most
fiercely contested portions of the front line, was gathered together the
rarest of all house-parties; (of which, for some time, I had the honour
to be the absent and unknowing host). As these papers show, the
guests assembled, in companies large or small, during the last weeks of
November 1942, except for one straggler whose coming was delayed
until June 1943; and among the very first arrivals, on the 18th of
November, were Uccello's *Battle of San Romano*, the Cimabue *Virgin
Enthroned*, the great *Madonna* of Giotto, and Botticelli's *Primavera*.
Even my father had never foreseen or thought of a house-party of this
fantastic order. For guarding the paintings, valued, as I have stated,[1]
at three hundred and twenty million dollars, Guido Masti received
the sum of seventeen lire a day!

When the war swirled up suddenly in the direction of Siena and
Florence, this development seems to have taken the authorities completely by surprise. Professor Fasola, who had been appointed
curator, is said to have walked out to Montegufoni through the lines,
from Florence. At the Castle, refugees, estimated by some to exceed
two thousand persons, had swarmed into the cellars and dungeons
from towns as far away as Empoli and Castel Fiorentino: for the old
reputation of Montegufoni as a stronghold had revived in the popular
mind. There were, then, for some ten or fourteen days, these two
populations: the huddled crowds of homeless and terrified souls in

[1] See *Great Morning*, p. 179 n. of this edition.

the darkness below, where, at any rate, it was comparatively safe, and on the ground floor above, in grave danger, hundreds of world-famous pictures, piled against the sides of the walls, in the lofty painted rooms and halls. . . . Next, the Germans arrived, occupied the Castello, and turned out the refugees. They lived in the rooms above, and often threatened to destroy the pictures, but Professor Fasola and Guido Masti continued somehow to preserve them. When the German General, on entering the Castle, uttered menacing words about these great canvases being in his way and that they should be burnt, Guido said to him, as only an Italian, with the natural imaginative rhetoric of his race, could say:

"These pictures belong not to one nation, but are the possession of the world."

By sheer persistence and integrity, he won the day. Similarly Signor Fasola never relaxed his efforts, even when the battle surged round the Castle in several directions. In the end, as the reader knows, the great building, and its treasure, came through unhurt in the main. Few pictures were damaged, though the celebrated circular Ghirlandaio from the Uffizi was rather badly injured—and cannot, I understand at the time of writing in 1947, yet be shown—because the Germans used it, face upwards, as a table-top (though the table beneath had a top of its own), and it was stained in consequence with wine, food and coffee, and with the marks which the soldiers made on it with their knives.

Subsequently, the Castle sheltered in turn New Zealand, English and Indian troops.

The discovery of the pictures by a party has been fascinatingly described by Eric Linklater, in his recent book *The Art of Adventure*.

The pictures continued to be housed at Montegufoni for several years, and I reproduce, at the end of the lists, the letter written to me in 1946, when all the paintings had been restored to their homes, by Signor Poggi, the Superintendent of the Galleries of Florence, Arezzo and Pistoia.

R. SOPRAINTENDENZA ALLE GALLERIE
PER LE PROVINCIE DI FIRENZE
AREZZO E PISTOIA

FIRENZE

I/a consegna a Montegufoni

Firenze li 18 Novembre Millenovecentoquarantadue   XXI

Verbale di consegna di dipinto della R. Galleria degli Uffizi

---

Dal presente verbale risulti che il R. Sopraintendente alle Gallerie consegna al Signor Guido Masti il seguente dipinto da conservare per il periodo bellico nella Villa di Montegufoni:

Inv. 1890 N.479 — PAOLO UCCELLO — La Battaglia di San Romano

Il R. Sopraintendente
(Consegnante)

F.to Filippo Rossi

Il Consegnatario
F.to Guido Masti.

R. SOPRAINTENDENZA ALLE GALLERIE
PER LE PROVINCIE DI FIRENZE
AREZZO E PISTOIA

FIRENZE

1.a Consegna a Montegufoni

Diciotto Novembre Millenovecentoquarantadue   XXI

Verbale di consegna di dipinti della R. Galleria degli Uffizi

---

Dal presente verbale risulti che il R. Sopraintendente alle Gallerie consegna al Signor Guido Masti i seguenti dipinti da conservare per il periodo bellico nella Villa di Montegufoni:

Inv. 1890 N.8343—Cimabue — La Vergine in trono angeli e profeti.

Inv. 1890 N.8344—Giotto   — La Madonna in trono Santi e Angeli.

IL SOPRAINTENDENTE
(Consegnante)
F.to Filippo Rossi

Il Consegnatario
F.to Masti Guido.

1.*a Consegna Montegufoni*

Diciotto novembre Millenovecentoquarantadue XXI

<hr>

Verbale di consegna di dipinti delle R. Gallerie degli Uffizi

<hr>

Dal presente verbale risulti che il R. Sopraintendente alle Gallerie consegna al Signor Guido Masti i seguenti dipinti da conservare per il periodo bellico nella Villa di Montegufoni:

Inv. 1890 N.751 —Baroccio Federico di Urbino—Madonna del Popolo.

Inv. 1890 N.8360—Botticelli—La Primavera.

Inv. 1890 N.916 —Sebastiano del Piombo—La Morte di Adone.

Inv. 1890 N.8361—Botticelli—La Vergine in trono con SS. Barbara, Agostino, Caterina, Giovanni Battista, Ignazio, Michele Arcangelo.

Il R. Sopraintendente
(consegnante)
F.to Filippo Rossi

Il Consegnatario
F.to Masti Guido.

REGIO MUSEO NAZIONALE
F I R E N Z E
Palazzo del Bargello

<hr>

Firenze, 18 novembre
1942 XXI

VERBALE di consegna di oggetti d' Arte del
R. Museo Nazionale di Firenze

<hr>

Dal presente verbale risulti che il Direttore del R. Museo Nazionale di Firenze consegna al Sig. Guido Masti gli oggetti contenuti nelle casse sotto indicate, da conservarsi per il periodo bellico nella Villa di Montegufoni.

CASSA N. 212 — Cartapesta colorita—La Madonna col Figlio. Inv. N.471 Opera del Sansovino.

CASSA N. 972 — Dipinto—Collezione Carrand. Inv. N.2058: il Cambiavalute.

CASSA N. 971 — ARAZZINO—Collezione Carrand. Inv. 2198.
 — Dipinto—La Pace—Collezione Carrand. Inv. 2064.
 — Dipinto—L' Annunciazione—Collezione Carrand. Inv. N.2050.
 — Dipinto—La Presentazione al Tempio—Collezione Carrand. Inv. N.2051.
 — Dittico in legno (scuola bolognese) Collezione Museo n.11.
 — N.12 Bass. in legno. S.G. Battista.

CASSA N. 970 — Trittico di scuola senese. Collezione Carrand Inv. N.2025.

CASSA N. 1027 — Collezione Carrand. No. 9 catalogo: La Vergine in trono col Figlio, a quattro Santi.
 „ „ No. 26 catalogo: Tre angeli a Banchetto.
 „ „ No. 27 catalogo: La Vergine col Figlio.
 „ „ No. 28 catalogo: La Decollazione di S. Giovanni.
 „ „ No. 34 catalogo: La Vergine col Bambino.
 „ „ No. 36 catalogo: La resurrezione.

Collezione Carrand. n.37 Catalogo : La Discesa di Cristo
 „ „ n.41 „ : Santa Crocifissione e conversione
 „ „ Inv. N.2082 : La Crocifissione.

IL DIRETTORE:
(Consegnante)
F.to Filippo Rossi

IL CONSEGNATARIO
F.to Masti Guido

R. SOPRINTENDENZA ALLE GALLERIE
PER LE PROVINCIE DI FIRENZE
AREZZO E PISTOIA

FIRENZE

2 Consegna Montegufoni

Firenze 19 Novembre Millenovecentoquarantadue XXI

Verbale di consegna di dipinti della R. Galleria dell' Accademia

Dal presente verbale risulti che il R. Soprintendente alle Gallerie consegna al Signor Guido Masti i seguenti dipinti da conservare per il periodo bellico nella Villa di Montegufoni:

8606 — Polittico di Giovanni del Biondo
463 — Annunciazione Mariotto di Nardo
3152 — Trittico della maniera di Nicolo Gerini
475 — Trittico: Madonna Rossello di I. Franchi
8461 — Trittico di Spinello Aretino
8464 — Trittico arcagnesco
8605 — San Caio
8690–92—Storia di S. Apollonio—Gravacci
471 — San Lorenzo—Zanobi Strozzi
1562 — La Vergine in Trono—Cosimo Rosselli
456 — L'Incoronazione della Vergine—Jacopo di Cione
6146 — La Vergine col Figlio—Firenze sec. XIV.
8575–76—Crocifissione del Berlinghieri
441 — Madonna Toscana sec. XIV.
8571–8572–8573—Trittico di Jacopo del Casentino
8611 — Vergine e putto—Bicci di Lorenzo
5381 — Storia di Santi—P. Uccello
435 — Madonna di Guido da Siena
3493 — San Luca—Secolo XIII.
9313 — Madonna duecentesca
8463 — Apparizione della Vergine a S. Bernardo—Maestro della Cappella Rinuccini
458 — Incoronazione della Vergine—Giovanni dal Ponte
4632 — Annunciazione—Firenze sec. XV.
5069 — Deposizione—Jacopo del Sellaio
455 — Annunciazione—Agnolo Gaddi

3460 — Madonna Mariotto di Nardo
8459 — Albero della croce—Pacino di Bonaguida
8661 — Natività—Lorenzo di Credi
8466 — Maddalena—Maestro della Maddalena
438 — Orazione nell' orto—Lorenzo Monaco
8651 — Maddalena—Lippi

8648-49—Angioli—Ridolfo del Ghirlandaio
8653 — Battista—Lippi
8568 — Polittico—Pacino di Bonaguida
433 — Madonna italo-bizantina
8610 — Polittico di Lorenzo di Niccolo

IL CONSEGNATARIO

f°. Masti Guido

IL SOPRINTENDENTE
CONSEGNANTE

f°. Giovanni Poggi

R. SOPRINTENDENZA ALLE GALLERIE
PER LE PROVINCIE DI FIRENZE
AREZZO E PISTOIA

FIRENZE

Firenze, 20 Novembre 1942 XXI   3ª Consegna—Montegufoni

Consegna dei quadri della R. Galleria dell' Accademia

Num. Invent.
8550 — Maria Assunta—Francesco Granacci
8645 — Madonna col Bambino e 4 Santi—Mariotto Albertinelli
8462 — Trittico—Presentazione al Tempio—Andrea
3450 — La Vergine col figlio Sec. XIV.
1621 — S. Giacomo—Bastiano Mainardi
8635 — S. Barbara—Cosimo Rosselli
3146 — Annunciazione—Mariera di Angiolo Gaddi
436 — Gesù Crocifisso—Ignoto toscano sec. XIV.
3153 — Crocifisso—Lorenzo Monaco
432 — Gesù Crocifisso e Misteri—Sec. XIII.
434 — „   „   con 8 storie „   „

Num.   Invent.

432 — Gesù Crocifisso—Ignoto toscano—Sec. XIV.

s.n. — Incoronazione—Bandini (Museo Fiesole)

467 — Il Redentore—Lorenzo Monaco

3236 — La Vergine seduta—Andrea di Giusto

122 — Frammento di Antependium—Scuola toscana sec. XII.

6115 — Madonna col Bambino sec. XIV.

431 — La Vergine col Figlio—Bizantino sec. X.

8579 — L'Incoronazione della Vergine—Scuola Fiorent. sec. XIV.

8566 — Crocifisso—Bartolommeo de Giovanni

8627 — S. Girolamo   ,,   ,,

8628 — La Deposizione ,,   ,,

8567 — La Vergine in trono—Bernardo Daddi

8654 — Visita di Maria a S. Elisabetta—Iacopo del Sellaio

3151 — La Vergine col Bambino—Scuola toscana sec. XV.

8655 — Gesù deposto—Iacopo del Sellaio

8639 — Annunciazione—Fine sec. XV.

8701 — Un Santo Vescovo—Sec. XIV.

8702 — S. Lorenzo Martire—Sec. XIV.

3145 — Dittico S. Agnese—Scuola Senese

3164 — La Resurrezione—Sec. XIV.

IL SOPRINTENDENTE   IL RICEVENTE

f°. Giovanni Poggi   f°. Masti Guido

1° *Carico*

R. SOPRINTENDENZA ALLE GALLERIE
PER LE PROVINCIE DI FIRENZE
AREZZO E PISTOIA

FIRENZE

Firenze, 20 Novembre 1942 XXI

3ª *Consegna*
Montegufoni

Consegna dei quadri della R. Galleria dell' Accademia.

Dal presente verbale risulti che il R. Soprintendente alle Gallerie
ha consegnato al Sig. Masti i seguenti quadri da conservarsi nella
Villa di Montegufoni per il periodo bellico:

Num.   Inv.

8636 — S. Trinità—Scuola fiorentina sec. XV.

470 — La Vergine col Figlio—Sec. XIV.

Num.   Inv.

3449 — Incoronazione della Vergine—Bernardo Daddi (Ancona)

461 — La Vergine seduta—Ignoto Toscano XV Sec.

3247 — La Madonna in piedi—Francesco Granacci

8660 — La SS. Trinità—Mariotto Albertinelli

448 — Parte supl. di un tabernacolo—Taddeo Gaddi

8626 — S. Monica—Giovanni Botticini

8694 — Storia di una Santa—Francesco Granacci

8693 — Storia di una Santa—   ,,   ,,

8625 — S. Agostino—Bartolommeo di Giovanni

3162 — La Vergine seduta col Bambino—Toscano sec. XV.

8615 — Storie di S. Onofrio—Lorenzo Monaco

8616 — La Natività   ,,   ,,

8617 — S. Niccolò Vescovo   ,,   ,,

478 — La Vergine col Bambino—Ignoto Toscano sec. XV.

4634 — Antependium 5 scomparti—Scuola di Giotto

3470 — Cinque Santi—Paolo Schiavo

3449 — Incoronazione della Vergine—Bernardo Daddi (gradino)

8609 — Polittico l' Ascensione—Paolo Schiavo

961⎫
961⎭ due quadri—con Angeli e Padreterno

4653 — Madonna col Bambino—Rossello Jacopo Franchi

437 — Le Stimmate di S. Francesco—Berlinghieri

8465 — Tabernacolo—Giovanni da Milano

8580 — Incoronazione della Vergine—Giovanni da Milano

2141 — Gesù Crocifisso—Lorenzo Monaco

3156 — Vergine col Figlio—Scuola Fiorentina Sec. XV.

9202 — La Sacra Famiglia—Lorenzo di Credi

8563 — Retto—Crocifissione con Angeli—Bernardo Gaddi

8562 — La Vergine della Misericordia—Agnolo Gaddi

8032 — Santa Caterina di Alessandria—Antemisia Lonni

5614 — Maddalena—tela—Scuola francese

8020 — Bozzetto in chiaro—Cigoli

IL RICEVENTE
F.to Masti Guido

IL SOPRINTENDENTE
F.to Giovanni Poggi

R. SOPRINTENDENZA ALLE GALLERIE
PER LE PROVINCIE DI FIRENZE
AREZZO E PISTOIA

FIRENZE

4ª Consegna Montegufoni

Firenze, 23 Novembre 1942 XXI

Consegna dei quadri della R. Galleria dell' Accademia

Dal presente verbale risulti che il Soprintendente alle Gallerie di Firenze ha consegnato al Sig. Masti i seguenti quadri della R. Galleria dell' Accademia da conservarsi nella Villa di Montegufoni per il periodo bellico:

Num.   Inv.

2140 — San Giovanni—Lorenzo Monaco

2169 — La Vergine Addolorata—Lorenzo Monaco

8618 — L' Incoronazione della Vergine—Neri di Bicci

8577 — Vergine in Trono—Scuola Fiorentina sec. XIV. Agnolo Gaddi

8578 — Vergine seduta col putto—Nicolo Gerini

8622 — L' Annunciazione—Neri di Bicci

8460 — La Vergine in trono—Rosello di Jacopo Franchi (3 pezzi e 2 verticali)

8508 — Vita della Vergine—Scuola Fra G. Angelico

3462 — S. Bernardo—Ignoto sec. XV.

3461 — S. Vincenzo Ferreri—Ignoto sec. XV.

 450 — Parte di tabernacolo—Ignoto toscano sec. XIV.

8570 — Crocifissione—4 angioli—Giottino

8581 — Lunetta in due parti—Taddeo Gaddi

6004 — Madonna e Bambino—Andrea di Giusto

 121 — Frammento di Antependium—Scuola Toscana sec. XV.

8623 — La Pietà—Andrea del Castagno

8699 — Un Santo Dottore—Scuola Fiorentina sec. XIV.

8698 — Un Santo Vescovo   ,,   ,,   ,,   ,,

8700 — S. Agostino   ,,   ,,   ,,   ,,

1953 — Il Redentore a la Madonna—Migliore—Toscano sec. XIII.

8457 — Fronte di cassone con una festa di nozze (cassone Adimari) Scuola Fiorentina XV. sec.

8565 — Gradino con tre pannelli—Agnolo Gaddi

Inv. Dep. N. 18.

4655 — Predella

4655 — Trittico

Inv. Dep/ N. 61—Crocifissione e Santi—Prov. Chiesa di Carmignano

Inv. 1890 *N.* 480—Annunciazione di Neri di Bicci

8624 — Tre Angeli e Tobiolo—Giusto di Andrea

3160 — Madonna col Figlio e 2 Angeli—Fiorentina XV.

3333 — S. Francesco—Lorenzo Monaco

8656 — S. Andrea—Scuola Botticelli

8614 — Vergine in Trono—Scuola Fiorentina sec. XIV.

8632 — David e Mose—Maniera di Cosimo Rosselli

8634 — La Vergine che adora il Figlio—Maniera di C. Rosselli

484 — S. Pietro in Pulpito—Ignoto Toscano XV.

485 — Epifania

IL RICEVENTE

F.to Masti Guido

IL SOPRINTENDENTE

F.to Giovanni Poggi

5ª Consegna

R. SOPRINTENDENZA ALLE GALLERIE
PER LE PROVINCIE DI FIRENZE
AREZZO E PISTOIA

FIRENZE

Firenze, 23 Novembre
1942 XXI

Verbale di ritiro di dipinti delle RR.
Gallerie dalla R. Villa di Poggia a Caiano.

Dal presente verbale risulti che il R. Soprintendente alle Gallerie ritira dalla R. Villa di Poggio a Caiano i seguenti dipinti delle R. Gallerie degli Uffizi e della R. Galleria Palatine:

Inv. n. 1568 — Filippino Lippi—Adorazione dei Magi

,, ,, 8397 — Fra Bartolommeo—Madonna

,, ,, 8370 — Filippino Lippi e Perugino—Deposizione

,, ,, P.124— Andrea del Sarto—Annunciazione

Il Consegnatario della R. Villa di Poggio a Caiano rimane discaricato di ogni e qualsiasi responsabilità dei quadri sopra descritti.

I predetti quattro dipinti sono stati trasportati nella Villa di Montegufoni e consegnati al Sig. Masti nella data suindicata.

IL CONSEGNANTE
F.to Giovanni Poggi

IL RICEVENTE
F.to Masti Guido

R. SOPRINTENDENZA ALLE GALLERIE
PER LE PROVINCIE DI FIRENZE
AREZZO E PISTOIA

FIRENZE

6a Consegna
2 Verbale

Firenze 24 Novembre 1942   XXI
Consegna di quadri del R. Museo di S. Marco.

Dal presente verbale risulti che il Soprintendente alle Gallerie ha consegnato al Sig. Masti i seguenti quadri da consegnarsi nella Villa di Montegufoni per il periodo bellico:

Inventario		Numero		
1918	—	477	—	Il supplizio di Savonarola—sec. XVI.
,,	—	,,	—	La Deposizione con Santi senna angeli
1890	—	8496	—	Vergine in trono col putto—Fra. G. Angelico
1812	—	373	—	Vergine col bambino e Santi—Scuola Angelica
1890	—	8493	—	Vergine col putto e sei santi—G. Angelico
,,	—	3204	—	Vergine col bambino e 4 angeli—Scuola Angelica
1910	—	39	—	Cristo e sei santi—(Prov. Accademica)
1890	—	8494	—	Sepoltura dei santi Cosimo e Damiano—Angelico
,,	—	8495	—	Storia dei santi Cosimo e Damiano—La sostituzione di una gamba di un negro —Angelico
1890	—	8499	—	Pietà—Adorazione dei Magi—Angelico
,,	—	8689	—	Ritratto dell' Angelico—Carlo Dolci (Dall'-Accad.)
1918	—	499	—	Ritratto del Beato Lorenzo da Ripafratta
,,	—	494	—	Stendaretto di seta del Crocifisso
,,	—	497	—	Albero dei religiosi Domenicani
,,	—	498	—	Albero genealogico della famiglia di S. Antonio
,,	—	465	—	Ritratto di Savonarola

Inventario   Numero

1890	—	5325 —	Ritratto di Cosimo il Vecchio
1910	—	8486 —	Predella con storie dei Santi Cosimo e Damiano—Beato Angelico
1910	—	209 —	Ritratto di S. Pietro Martire
,,	—	8488 —	Scuola Beato Alberto Magno
,,	—	8504 —	Scuola S. Tommaso d' Aquino

IL SOPRINTENDENTE
Fᵒ. Giovanni Poggi

Il Ricevente
fᵒ. Masti Guido

In pari data si consegna al Sig. Guido Masti il dipinto di Tullio da Boninsegni, Madonna col Bambino e angioli, della Chiesa di S. Maria Novella di Firenze.

Il Soprintendente   Il Ricevente
fᵒ. Giovanni Poggi

R. SOPRINTENDENZA ALLE GALLERIE
PER LE PROVINCIE DI FIRENZE
AREZZO E PISTOIA

───────────

FIRENZE

7ᵃ Consegna Montegufoni
1º Verb.

Firenze li 25 Novembre Millenovecentoquarantadue   XXI

───────────

Verbale di consegna di dipinti delle RR. Gallerie di Firenze

───────────

Dal presente verbale risulti che il R. Soprintendente alle RR. Gallerie di Firenze consegna al Signor Guido Masti i seguenti dipinti delle RR. Gallerie di Firenze da conservare per il periodo bellico nella Villa di Montegufoni:

Inv. 1890	N.1575 —	Bronzino—Ritratto di uomo
,, ,,	N.3469 —	Bottega dell' Orcagna—Polittico in cinque pezzi
,, ,,	N.1619 —	Ghirlandaio—Adorazione dei Magi (tondo)
,, ,,	N.4344 —	Botticelli—Madonna e Santi
,, ,,	N.3515 —	Nardo di Cione—Crocifissione (già al Museo Bardini)
,, ,,	—	Nardo di Cione—Polittico (in sei pezzi, già a S. Croce)

Inv. 1890 N.8386 — Masaccio—S. Anna, la Vergine e il Bambino

,,   ,,   N.5374 — Attribuito al Baroccio—Salomè

,,   ,,   N.8740 — Pontorno—L' ultima cena

,,   ,,   N.6165 — Scuola di Bernardo Daddi—La Vergine detta
                     la Ninna

Inv. Castello   — Maestro   della   Natività   di   Castello—La
                     Natività

                   — Scuola di Cimabue—Madonna e Santi (già
                     nell' Oratorio di Pian del Mugnone)

D.S. Apollonia

Inv. 1890 N.4666 — Scuola di Filippino Lippi—La Madonna
                     della Cintola

                   — Neri di Bicci—Madonna e Santi

Dal Bargello

Inv. 1890 N.8362 — Botticelli—Incoronazione della Vergine

IL SOPRINTENDENTE
(Consegnante)
F.to Giovanni Poggi

Il Consegnatario
F.to Masti Guido

R. SOPRINTENDENZA ALLE GALLERIE
PER LE PROVINCIE DI FIRENZE
AREZZO E PISTOIA

FIRENZE

7 Consegna
2 Verbale

25 nov. 1942 XXI

Consegna dei quadri delle R. Gallerie Palatine

Dal presente verbale risulti che il Soprintendente ha consegnato
al Sig. Masti i seguenti quadri delle R. Gallerie Palatine da conservarsi alla Villa di Montegufoni per il periodo bellico:

Inv. N.191 — Assunzione—Andrea del Sarto

,,   N.225 — Assunzione—Andrea del Sarto

,,   N.165 — Madonna del Baldacchino—Raffaello

,,   N.141 — Ninfe e Satiri—Rubens

,,   N.125 — S. Marco—Fra Bartolommeo

Inv. N.123 — Madonna—Andrea del Sarto
,, N.166 — Rebecca al Pozzo—Guido Ricci
,, N.159 — Gesù Risorto—Fra Bartolommeo
,, N.587 — Ratto Sabine (Prov. Uffizi)
,, N.792 — Filippo IV di Spagna—Scuola Rubens
,, N. 4 — Marina—Salvator Rosa

IL RICEVENTE
F. to Masti Guido

IL SOPRINTENDENTE
F.to Giovanni Poggi

R. SOPRINTENDENZA ALLE GALLERIE
PER LE PROVINCIE DI FIRENZE
AREZZO E PISTOIA

FIRENZE

8 *Consegna Montegufoni*
Firenze li 8 Giugno 1943   XXI

Verbale di consegna di dipinti alla Villa di Montegufoni

Dal presente verbale risulti che la R. Soprintendenza alle Gallerie per le provincie di Firenze, Arezzo e Pistoia ha consegnato oggi al Signor Guido Masti il seguente dipinto della R. Galleria dell' Accademia per conservarlo durante il periodo bellico nella Villa di Montegufoni.

Rossello di Iacopo Franchi—Tre parti della predella dell' Incoronazione della Vergine n.8460.

Il R. Soprintendente
(Consegnante)
F.to Giovanni Poggi.

Il Consegnatario
F.to Masti Guido

R. SOPRINTENDENZA ALLE GALLERIE
PER LE PROVINCIE DI FIRENZE
AREZZO E PISTOIA

FIRENZE

Florence, July 8th, 1946.

Sir Osbert Sitwell
2 Carlyle Sq.
London, S.W.3.
Sir:

As you undoubtedly know, this Superintendency has duly provided for the removal from your villa at Monte Gufoni of all the art treasures that you so kindly authorized us to store there.

I feel it my duty to express to you the most profound gratitude for what you did in behalf of the preservation of such treasures, and it is through me that the City of Florence, which is the legal owner of said works of art, sends you its cordial thanks.

To have been able to put in security such works as the Madonnas of Cimabue, Duccio and Giotto; the Botticelli, the Paolo Uccello, the Raphaels and all the other leading masterpieces of the Schools of Tuscany and Italy, was surely a great opportunity.

Now that all these wonders of art are safely back in the deposits of the Uffizi whence they will eventually go back to their places of exhibition for the enjoyment and delight of the world, I am sure you will consider that your kindness in allowing us to store them at Monte Gufoni will have been duly compensated by your great joy of having contributed to the salvation of such an inestimable artistic patrimony from the destructive fury of the war and the even more barbaric pillage of the Germans.

Renewing my feelings of deep gratitude, I beg to remain, Sir Sittwell, yours very faithfully,

the Superintendent of Galleries and Museums.

GIOVANNI POGGI.

INDEX